INDIVIDUAL DUTY WITHIN A HUMAN RIGHTS DISCOURSE

This book is dedicated to my children, Kent and Kim

Individual Duty within a Human Rights Discourse

DOUGLAS HODGSON
Faculty of Law
The University of Western Australia

ASHGATE

Published by
Ashgate Publishing Limited
Gower House
Croft Road
Aldershot
Hants GU11 3HR
England

Ashgate Publishing Company
Suite 420
101 Cherry Street
Burlington, VT 05401-4405
USA

Ashgate website: http://www.ashgate.com

British Library Cataloguing in Publication Data
Hodgson, Douglas
Individual duty within a human rights discourse. - (Applied legal philosophy)
1. Duty 2. Human rights
I. Title
172 . 1

Library of Congress Cataloging-in-Publication Data
Hodgson, Douglas.
Individual duty within a human rights discourse / Douglas Hodgson.
p. cm. -- (Applied legal philosophy)
Includes bibliographical references and index.
ISBN 0-7546-2361-0
1. Human rights. 2. Human rights--Moral and ethical aspects. 3. Duty. I. Title. II. Series.

K3240.H63 2004
340'.112--dc22

2003054482

ISBN 0 7546 2361 0

Printed and bound in Great Britain by MPG Books Ltd, Bodmin, Cornwall

Contents

Acknowledgements

I wish to express my gratitude to my research assistant, Robin Perry, for his useful insights and diligent efforts in accumulating materials and information in support of this undertaking. I am also grateful to Cheryl Marshall for her assistance with correcting and formatting the manuscript. Finally, I wish to acknowledge the efforts of my father, Charles Hodgson, in helping me to compile the various index entries.

Douglas Hodgson
Perth, Western Australia
September 2003

Foreword

The Honourable Justice Michael Kirby AC CMG[*]

Why do many lawyers of the Western liberal tradition respond adversely to the idea of human duties? Why would many of them answer Anne-Marie Devereux's question 'Should duties play a larger role in human rights?'[1] with a resounding 'no'?

These are the puzzles, with others, that are explored in this book. The answers emerge from a consideration of the nature of the problem and the identity of some of the people who are often in the forefront of advocacy for greater attention to duties.

It is not as if the notion of duty is alien either to modern liberal legal traditions or even to the international law of human rights. The common law spends a lot of its time considering whether duties exist or do not. By treating particular conduct as a crime or a tort at common law, duties are cast on the subject of the law to conform or otherwise to pay the penalty expressed in terms of loss of personal liberty or an obligation to make recompense. Similarly, statutes are full of duties imposed on us as taxpayers, electors, company directors, employers, pet owners or mere human beings. Even the Australian Constitution, largely bereft of human rights provisions, contains a few such duties. Some of these may be formulated in terms of the obligations owed by governments.[2] Sometimes, although not expressly stated in the text, rights or privileges have been found to be implied. And with those rights may come judicial duties of protection of the beneficiaries.[3]

We can therefore approach a book on duties in the context of human rights, with a clear-sighted appreciation that there is a lot of law that imposes duties on all of us. Some such laws have the result, and perhaps the purpose, of protecting the rights of others. The crime and the tort of trespass, for example, represents one way by which the common law, even in its earliest days, imposed duties supported by sanctions with consequences that sometimes protected individual privacy. To this extent, rights and duties, Janus-like, reflect the alternative images of the same legal mechanism. It is sometimes said that for every human right there is a competing right of others that may present a conflict to be resolved. But it can also be said that for every human right that has legal protection, in the manner in which the law is usually expressed in common law systems, there is usually a duty that the machinery of the State can be set in train to enforce.

---

[*] Justice of the High Court of Australia.
[1] (1995) 1 UNSWLJ 464.
[2] See e.g. Australian Constitution, ss 51 (xxxi), 80, 92, 116 and 117.
[3] e.g. *Lange v Australian Broadcasting Corporation* (1997) 189 CLR 520; *Roberts v Bass* (2003) 76 ALJR 292.

Nor is the notion of human duties alien to the modern expression of human rights. In the *Universal Declaration of Human Rights* of 1948, it is stated in Article 29(1):[4]

> Everyone has duties to the community in which alone the free and full development of his personality is possible.

So if human rights and correlative duties are so commonly interrelated, why the resistance to, and suspicion about, the discourse on duties among many human rights organisations and defenders and their organisations?

Douglas Hodgson vividly illustrates in this book that notions of human duties have a very long history in virtually every culture and legal system. Indeed, the idea stretches back millennia to the earliest recorded times. One cannot study the many instances of early expressions of individual duties in societies on different continents and with utterly different cultural and ethical traditions, without realising how strong are the forces of family, neighbourhood and state and how insistent are the demands concerning duties to each of them.

A clue to the cause of the suspicion about the duty discourse emerges from a reflection on the sources of the modern advocacy for putting that subject on the agenda of international human rights and insisting that duties have equal prominence and respect with dialogue about rights. In recent years, it has often been countries and leaders accused of the worst human rights abuses who have been foremost in proclaiming the correlative obligations of human duties. Thus, the Constitution of the Soviet Union contained many statements about the duties of Soviet citizens. These ranged from the performance of public duties and respect for the rules of socialist society to compliance with the standards of socialist conduct and the maintenance of the honour and dignity of Soviet citizenship.[5] The Soviet Union is no more. But as the author points out, there are many similar provisions in the constitutional texts of countries that copied the Soviet model: the People's Republic of China, Cuba, North Korea and Vietnam.

In the case of the Soviet Union, the constitutionally-imposed duties often became instruments for the oppression of individuals, subjected to autocratic and often arbitrary and unaccountable interpretations of what such broadly-stated duties involved. Commonly, the notion of civic duties became debased so as to be equivalent to little more than doing what the Party or the leader or the current power élite dictated.

If one reads these pages, and looks at the societies whose constitutions or governmental proclamations embrace the notion of human duties, as a check on the excessive Western talk of human rights, all too often one is driven to a conclusion that the 'duty advocates' are not reaching back to the noble ideas of family, neighbourhood and state described by the author. All too commonly, they are insisting on the duty to themselves and the impermissibility of holding, expressing or acting on views of individual freedom that conflict with their own.

---

4   See *infra*, 238.
5   See *infra*, 201.

Somewhere between this kind of cynicism and the ancient sense of personal duty to others lies a healthy corrective to the extremes of indifferent selfishness common in the impersonal world of modern technology and in assertions of individual rights at all costs. In that space the doctrine of human duties emerges as a good idea. It is the idea explored in this book. It reaches deeply into the evolution of the notion of duties that accompanied the necessities even of the most primitive human societies. It draws on the philosophical and legal traditions of every continent. It recognises the misuse of some of the advocacy of duties to qualify rights. But it suggests that a truly global approach to human rights will find a space for such deep-seated notions as duties to family, neighbourhood and state alongside the flowering of individual human rights. Clearly, if we are serious about deriving a global consensus on such matters, we will listen to the voices of other societies when they proclaim that rights and duties go inextricably together.

Although it is true, as the author says, that the ancient religions, including those of the Book (Judaism, Christianity and Islam) are commonly expressed in terms of duties – to God, community and family – there is one sense in which the great religions have also underpinned the global movement for human rights. Most, if not all, of them posit an idea of the human being as a reflection of God – someone unique who lives in a spiritual communion with God and is individually loved by God. In the private relationship of the individual to God lies the reflection of divine love. For believers, this idea reinforces the importance of each precious individual that non-believers also accept on humanist, utilitarian or other grounds.

Increasingly, respect for human dignity is seen as the driving force of individual human rights.[6] The United Nations may sometimes fail. The State may occasionally be an oppressor. The community may turn its back. Neighbours may be unkind. Even the family may sometimes prove selfish and oppressive. But the reason for the flowering of individual human rights has been the idea that, in the midst of all these wrongs and despite all the wrong-doers, the human being necessarily retains an irremovable dignity that cannot be taken away by anyone or anything.

Because virtually every human being now lives in society, increasingly the global world of cyberspace, robotics, jets, AIDS and SARS, it is inevitable that we should see the individual's rights increasingly in relation to the rights of others. That imports the notion of human duty. It is an idea with ancient roots that will not go away simply because some of its proponents, including recently, have been unlovely autocrats who use duty as a code word for the oppression of human rights.

Douglas Hodgson has written a clear and scholarly analysis of a very important issue. As he demonstrates, it is an issue over which continents, nations and individuals divide. As we enter a new millennium and search for the fault-lines in our world, the rights versus duty debate is clearly one of them.[7] That is why this is a timely and significant book.

---

6 D. Kretzmer and E. Klein (eds) *The Concept of Human Dignity in Human Rights Discourse* (Kluwer, 2002).

7 cf. S. Huntington *The Clash of Civilisations and the Remaking of World Order* (Simon and Schuster, 1996); cf. R. Inglehart and P. Norris "The True Clash of Civilisations" in *Foreign Policy*, March/April 2003, 63.

Series Preface

The objective of the Applied Legal Philosophy series is to publish work which adopts a theoretical approach to the study of particular areas or aspects of law or deals with general theories of law in a way which focuses on issues of practical moral and political concern in specific legal contexts.

In recent years there has been an encouraging tendency for legal philosophers to utilize detailed knowledge of the substance and practicalities of law and a noteworthy development in the theoretical sophistication of much legal research. The series seeks to encourage these trends and to make available studies in law which are both genuinely philosophical in approach and at the same time based on appropriate legal knowledge and directed towards issues in the criticism and reform of actual laws and legal systems.

The series will include studies of all the main areas of law, presented in a manner which relates to the concerns of specialist legal academics and practitioners. Each book makes an original contribution to an area of legal study while being comprehensible to those engaged in a wide variety of disciplines. Their legal content is principally Anglo-American, but a wide-ranging comparative approach is encouraged and authors are drawn from a variety of jurisdictions.

Tom D. Campbell
Series Editor
Centre for Applied Philosophy and Public Ethics
Charles Sturt University, Canberra

Chapter 1

Introduction

> The fulfillment of duty by each individual is a prerequisite to the rights
> of all. Rights and duties are interrelated in every social and political
> activity of man. While rights exalt individual liberty, duties express the
> dignity of that liberty.[1]

The main purpose of this book will be to examine the principle of individual duty
from a number of different perspectives, including history, the law (both
international and national), philosophy, jurisprudence, religion, ethics, socialism
and cultural relativism. For a long time national legal systems have recognised and
enforced in their constitutions and ordinary legislation various duties which
citizens owe to their own families, the communities in which they reside and their
country. Such duties include the duty to pay taxes, the duty to provide
maintenance and a basic education for one's children, the duty to undertake
military service for a specified period and the duty to obey the constitution and
other laws.

A central focus of discussion will be the controversial and emerging trend,
particularly since the end of World War II, to recognise individuals as the bearers
of duties under international law. This development was foreshadowed by an
American judge in 1793 in the following passage:

> When men have formed themselves into a political society, ... they cannot, by this
> union, discharge themselves from any duties which they previously owed to those
> who form a part of the political association. Under all the obligations due to the
> universal society of the human race, the citizens of the state will continue ...On
> states as well as individuals the duties of humanity are strictly incumbent ...[2]

The term 'duty' may broadly implicate any act or abstention from action which is
considered morally or legally incumbent upon the duty-holder. The source of a
duty may be obedience to the dictates of one's conscience, custom, a particular
religious or ethical tenet (such as the duty not to harm others or unjustifiably enrich

---

1   Second preambular paragraph of the *American Declaration of the Rights and
     Duties of Man* Resolution XXX. Final Act, Ninth International Conference of
     American States, Bogota, Colombia, 30 March - 2 May 1948 (Pan American
     Union, 1948), p. 38.
2   *Henfield's Case* 11 F. Cas. 3099, 1107 (C.C.D.Pa. 1793) (No. 6, 360) *per* Wilson
     J.

oneself at their expense), the secular law itself or it might be based upon personal relations (such as the mutual duties of parents and their children). A useful explication of the meaning of the term 'duty' follows:

> In its use in jurisprudence, [duty] is the correlative of *right*. Thus, wherever there exists a right in any person, there also rests a corresponding duty upon some other person or upon all persons generally. But it is also used, in a wider sense, to designate that class of moral obligations which lie outside the jural sphere; such, namely, as rest upon an imperative ethical basis, but have not been recognized by the law as within its proper province for purposes of enforcement or redress. . . In this meaning 'duty' is the equivalent of 'moral obligation', as distinguished from a 'legal obligation'.[3]

This book will identify and analyse mainly legal duties arising for individuals under international and national (constitutional) law, although references will be made from time to time to moral duties.[4] As will become apparent in Chapter 6, the meaning of the concept of duty, the manner in which duties are performed and the degree of emphasis and importance attached to them will vary across different cultures, belief systems and historical traditions as well as political, socio-economic and legal systems.

As the above-quoted third preambular paragraph of the *American Declaration of the Rights and Duties of Man* emphasises, human rights and duties form a basic unity or organic whole. The linkage between rights and duties is very tight in the sense that virtually every right implicates a corresponding or correlative duty.[5] The discharge of a duty is the guarantee and precondition of the realisation and enjoyment of human rights. Nonetheless, one commentator has recently referred to the principle of duty as 'that great neglected rule'.[6] The observation that human or individual duties do not today enjoy the same exalted status as human rights, at least in Western liberal democracies, has also been made by a Special Rapporteur of the United Nations Sub-Commission on Prevention of Discrimination and Protection of Minorities:

> [I]n the systems of the Eastern countries the principle of equal rights and equal duties prevails. This could be said for a number of less developed countries, in particular in Africa, Asia and Latin America. In the systems of most of the Western European countries and others, on the other hand, the emphasis is put on the effective protection of individuals' rights. An overwhelming majority of statesmen, legislators, jurists and sociologists of the West consider that the primary

---

3   *Black's Law Dictionary* (Revised Fourth Edition, 1968) p. 595.
4   The term 'duty' will be used interchangeably with the terms 'obligation' and 'responsibility' since their meanings are largely synonymous.
5   The correlative nature of rights and duties will be examined in more detail in Chapter 3.
6   David Selbourne *The Principle of Duty* (1994) p. 148.

role of the law is to protect individual rights, even if logically, duties should in certain cases have priority.[7]

As will be discussed in Chapter 9, 'it is rights which are the dominating subject of discourse'.[8] David Selbourne has complained:

> The principle of duty, ... as the obligation of the individual to ... fellow-members of the civic order, now sounds strange to many ears, and no longer possesses real moral status. The idea of the enforcement of such obligation suggests the very spirit of reaction, not of progress.[9]

Yet why is this so? The principle of duty, as will be demonstrated in Chapter 2, has venerable and ancient roots in Judaism, Confucianism and Greco-Roman philosophy and jurisprudence. The principle of duty, moreover, is the historical antecedent of the concept of human rights. The contemporary decline of the principle of duty can be traced back to the mid-nineteenth century, if not earlier, coinciding with the emergence of liberal democratic theory under the influence of *laissez-faire* and the writings of John Stuart Mill. The notion that the State should interfere as little as possible in the private lives of individuals, coupled with the call for citizens to be protected from arbitrary exercises of authority by the State itself through a system of civil liberties, eventually displaced the principle of duty from its pre-eminent historical position. Today, most liberal theorists support 'rights' over 'duties' as a preferable system for attaining individual freedom and dignity.[10] This preference is based upon a variety of factors. It is argued that duties are insufficiently precise in their content or lacking in foundation to be considered enforceable.[11] By contrast, 'rights' are considered superior because of their greater ability to be enforced, their empowerment capacity and their rhetorical strength. Furthermore, the emphasis placed upon 'individual freedom' creates an environment inimical to notions of extensive obligations to one's neighbour.[12] Rights tend to enjoy more popular appeal than duties (which can require significant personal sacrifices for the common good). While we like to be fully cognisant of our rights, we may not always enjoy being reminded of our duties which can prove to be an annoyance or intrusion into our individual realms. Furthermore, as the force of divine prescription has gradually diminished within the Western secular State, much of the spiritual basis of duties has disappeared.

7	Erica-Irene A. Daes *Freedom of the Individual under Law: A Study on the Individual's Duties to the Community and the Limitations on Human Rights and Freedoms under Article 29 of the Universal Declaration of Human Rights* (United Nations, New York, 1990) 40.41 (footnote excluded).
8	Selbourne, *op. cit.*, p. 2.
9	*Id.* p. 5.
10	A. Devereux 'Should "Duties" Play a Larger Role in Human Rights? A Critique of Western Liberal and African Human Rights Jurisprudence' (1995) 18 *University of New South Wales Law Journal* p. 464, p. 467.
11	The enforcement of legal and moral duties will be canvassed in Chapter 10.
12	Devereux, *op. cit.*, p. 467.

It is the author's intention to demonstrate in the succeeding chapters that the contemporary emphasis upon rights over duties is incompatible with the following:

- a cultural relativist critique inasmuch as some cultures (principally those in Africa and Asia) place much greater emphasis upon the recognition and fulfillment of individual duties;

- mainstream religious and ethical systems which consider duties to occupy a more central position in human affairs;

- early natural law theory and Greco-Roman political and social philosophy;

- the experience of national legal systems (both civil and common law) which have traditionally prescribed legally enforceable individual duties in civil codes, constitutional and statutory provisions and judge-made common law;

- regional human rights systems (particularly those in Latin America and Africa) which explicitly mention duties in their constituent documents;[13]

- certain socio-political philosophies (notably socialism and communitarianism);

- the dictates of good public policy;

- certain conventional sociological postulates concerning the nature of human existence (regarding humans as essentially and innately a group-dependent social species).

Chapter 2 will provide an overview of the historical development of the principle of duty and discuss the contributions of certain political philosophers to that process. Chapter 3 will examine the correlative nature of rights and duties and the various ways rights theorists have sought to classify duties. Chapter 4 investigates the dominant position the principle of duty occupies in a number of mainstream religious and ethical systems. The emergence of the concept of individual responsibility and accompanying individual duties within the framework of international humanitarian law (particularly in relation to war crimes and crimes against humanity) will be covered in Chapter 5. Chapter 6 catalogues the extent to which the principle of individual duty has been explicitly addressed by the international and regional human rights systems. Chapter 7 compiles a representative sampling of provisions contained in constitutional documents and ordinary legislation which impose duties upon individuals. Chapter 8 analyses the sources and content of the principle of duty from a socialist perspective. Chapter 9 discusses the perception that rights are overemphasised at the expense of duties and the alleged deleterious consequences of such a disequilibrium, which has given birth to the communitarian movement (particularly within the United States of

---

13   The regional human rights systems and their constituent documents will be examined in Chapter 6.

America).   The penultimate chapter identifies the extent to which duties are capable of being enforced as well as the main impediments to such enforcement. The concluding chapter calls for the assignment of a greater, indeed revived, role for the principle of individual duty in order to achieve a more salutary balance in the relationship between rights and duties and in the relationship between individual freedom and the welfare of the general community.

Chapter 2

The Historical Development of the Principle of Duty and Its Contemporary Philosophical Sources

> As all the virtue and credit of our lives proceed from the due discharge of our duties, so all the baseness and turpitude of our lives result from their non-observance. (Cicero)[1]

Introduction

The purpose of this chapter will be to trace the evolution of the principle of individual duty from the Greco-Roman era to the present. The contributions of those political philosophers who made the greatest impact on this process will be examined in particular. As will be seen, the principle of duty occupied a pre-eminent position in political and social philosophy and thinking until its relatively recent supersession by the principle of individual right. The latter portion of this chapter will propose a number of contemporary sources or justifications for the principle of duty.

Historical Origins of the Principle of Individual Duty

History is richly endowed with conceptions of duties and the important role they play in securing a better life for the individual and the community. The ancient Greeks and Romans understood well that a person who is completely private and autonomous is lost to civic life.[2] On the basis of a morality common to all humanity, boundless in terms of time and place, the Greek philosopher Aristotle declared that '[it] is not right ... that any of the citizens should think that he belongs just to himself.'[3] The Greco-Roman republican ethic and the Aristotelian tradition of virtue ethics, as one commentator has observed, '[sought] to cultivate

---

1   Cicero *Offices, Essays and Letters* translated T. Cockman (1690), London, 1909, I, ii.

2   A. Etzioni *The Spirit of Community* (1995) p. 259.

3   Aristotle *Politics* translated T. Sinclair, Harmondsworth, 1962, VIII, i, 1337a; D. Selbourne *The Principle of Duty* (1994) p. 162.

civic virtue, and to orient citizens to a common good beyond the sum of individual interests'.[4]

Aristotle

Aristotle (384-322 B.C.) lived most of his adult life in Athens, initially as a member of Plato's Academy and then as a founder and director of a research institute called the *Lyceum*. In his treatise entitled *Politics*, Aristotle maintains that human beings are by nature and from birth sociable and gregarious rather than solitary creatures, suited to live together in social groups.   Indeed, Aristotle considered the human being to be a political animal (*politikon zoon*).   Aristotle also emphasised the fundamental importance of the phenomenon of *koinonia* or community. *Koinonia* is what is shared or held in common as opposed to what is enjoyed in the private realm. Families and households are forms of *koinonia* which together comprise the highest form of community - the *polis* or city-state.[5] According to Aristotle, the city-state, being virtually self-sufficient, exists not only for the sake of life but for the 'good life' as well.[6] The city-state 'is a partnership of families and of clans in living well, and its object is a full and independent life'.[7] Unlike social contracterians such as Hobbes, Locke and Rousseau, Aristotle believed the city-state 'is ... prior by nature to the individual'.[8] A city-state, for Aristotle, is concerned with public standards of virtue and promoting the common welfare and a shared conception of a happy, flourishing and noble life (*eudaimonia*).[9] The city-state 'must therefore be deemed to exist for the sake of noble actions, not merely for living in common'.[10] For Aristotle, then, human beings are by nature so made as to flourish best within a city-state, since it alone can provide the environment within which they can realise their natural potential for practical reason, by actively engaging in public affairs.[11] Reminiscent of Aristotelian thinking, Article 29(1) of the *Universal Declaration of Human Rights* of 1948 recognises that '[e]veryone has duties to the community in which alone the free and full development of his personality is possible'.

A central tenet of Aristotle's *Politics* is the notion that citizenship within the city-state demands participation in the running of its affairs. For Aristotle, '[t]he best life, whether separately for an individual or collectively for states, is the life conjoined with virtue furnished with sufficient means for taking part in

---

4   M. Sandel 'The State and the Soul' *The New Republic* (10 June 1985) p. 39.
5   T. O'Hagan 'Aristotle and Aquinas on Community and Natural Law' in R. Bellamy and A. Ross (eds) *A Factual Introduction to Social and Political Theory* (1996) pp. 35, 36.
6   Aristotle *Politics* Book I, pp. 1252-3.
7   Aristotle *Politics* Book III, pp. 1279-80.
8   Aristotle *Politics* Book I, p. 1253.
9   T. O'Hagan, *op. cit.*, p. 37.
10   Aristotle *Politics* Book III, pp. 1279-80.
11   T. O'Hagan, *op. cit.*, p. 36.

virtuous actions'.[12]   Aristotle opined that '[i]f happiness is to be defined as well-doing, the active life is the best life both for the whole state collectively and for each man individually'.[13]   To be a free citizen of a city-state is to be active in fulfilling civic duties. This entailed participation in the administration of justice and in debates and votes on political issues. In Athens, citizens were in direct daily control of the legal system through jury service. All citizens were available to serve on large juries, whose members were picked by lot. These juries handed down verdicts in both civil and criminal cases. The misuse of judicial power by the citizens in this extreme form of direct democracy was circumvented by educating citizens in the virtues of responsible citizenship.[14]

Another legacy of Aristotle's writings is his development of the concept of natural justice or natural law.   From approximately 500 B.C., Greek philosophers formulated the idea of a form of higher law conceived of as the unwritten law of the gods or as that basic moral knowledge or intuition derived from the nature of human existence itself. This higher law, it was believed, could be ascertained by a study of nature (and hence the term 'natural law'). Aristotle considered political justice to be of two kinds - natural and conventional. 'A rule of justice', for Aristotle, 'is natural that has the same validity everywhere, and does not depend on our accepting it or not'.[15]   Aristotle considered that there exist universally valid rules of natural law or natural justice which transcend local laws and customs. These rules arise from the shared or common features of human nature. Natural laws were immutable (in terms of locality and time), rational and capable of being discerned and understood by human reason. Although these rules were not always followed by states, Aristotle and his successors believed that states should be governed by, and held accountable to, them. Each secular law and constitution had to be measured against this external, objective and critical standard to assess the extent to which it contributed to the flourishing (*eudaimonia*) of the community. Natural law theory was later endorsed and developed by the so-called Stoic school of Greek philosophers (*circa* 300 B.C. to 200 B.C.) who held to the universality of natural law for all people because of their common human nature.

The concept of natural law, or *jus naturale*, acquired significant prominence in the philosophical speculations of the Roman jurists of the Antonine age.[16]   For Roman jurists, natural law was intended to denote a system of rules and principles for the guidance of human conduct which, independently of enacted law or local custom, might be discerned by the rational intelligence of human beings. Cicero (104-34 B.C.) declared:

> There is in fact a true law namely right reason, which is in accordance with nature, applies to all men and is unchangeable and eternal . . . It will not lay down one rule

---

12   Aristotle *Politics* Book VII, pp. 1323-5.
13   *Ibid.*
14   T. O'Hagan, *op. cit.*, p. 37-8.
15   Aristotle *Nicomachean Ethics* Book V.
16   *Black's Law Dictionary* (Revised Fourth Edition, 1968) p. 1177.

at Rome and another at Athens, nor will it be one rule today and another tomorrow. But there will be one law eternal and unchangeable binding at all times and upon all peoples.[17]

Such rules and principles originated from, and conformed to, the nature of human beings (comprising the whole mental, moral and physical constitution).[18] For some Roman jurists, natural law also imposed certain duties of humanity upon individuals. Thus, natural law requires human beings not only to strive for their own preservation and perfection, but also to aid their fellow human beings in these efforts. Only in this way can a person strive to perfect himself or herself.[19] So, for Cicero, '[w]hatsoever is created on earth was merely designed ... for the service of man; and men themselves for the service, good and assistance of one another'.[20]

Thomas Aquinas

Thomas Aquinas (1225-74) was born into the impoverished feudal nobility of southern Italy. After joining the Dominican Order, he furthered his studies in Naples, Cologne and Paris. Aquinas spent two terms in Paris as a professor of theology (1256-59; 1268-72). His master work is considered to be the *Summa Theologiae* which embodied the most advanced philosophy of the day and whose thesis proclaimed the compatibility of Christian doctrine with Aristotelianism. *Summa Theologiae II* (written in 1268-72), which addresses human morality and society, particularly exhibits the influence of Aristotle.[21]

Like Aristotle, Aquinas believed that human beings are endowed, unlike other animals, with reason which allows them to identify principles of natural law and to embody them within positive, enforceable legal codes. The concept of natural law had been incorporated into Christian theology much earlier, in the form of a belief in a universal divine law or law of God which was superior to human laws. 'The true eternal law by which all human behaviour is judged', declared St Augustine (354-430 A.D.), 'leaves no aspect of man's life out of its purview; it is the same everywhere and at all times'.[22] But for Aquinas, however, human beings, as creations of God and possessors of immortal souls, have a more divine destiny than they had in Aristotle's secular *polis* or city-state.[23] Aquinas therefore

---

17   Cicero *De Officiis* Vol. I, c vii.
18   *Black's Law Dictionary, op. cit.*, 1177. See also Sir Henry Maine *Ancient Law* (1905) (section on '*Jus Naturale*').
19   Erica-Irene A. Daes *Freedom of the Individual under Law: A Study on the Individual's Duties to the Community and the Limitations on Human Rights and Freedoms under Article 29 of the Universal Declaration of Human Rights* (United Nations, New York, 1990) 54 (para. 239). See also P. Remec *The Position of the Individual in International Law, According to Grotius and Vattel* (1960) pp. 191-2.
20   Cicero, *op. cit.*, I, vii.
21   T. O'Hagan, *op. cit.*, 41.
22   *The Encyclopaedia of Philosophy* (London, Collier-MacMillan, 1967) Vol. I, 203.
23   O'Hagan, *op. cit.*, pp. 42-3.

supplements natural law with divine law as an external standard by which to judge the legitimacy and justice of the secular law. For Aquinas, natural law is a 'rational participation in the eternal law of God'.[24]

Once again, like Aristotle, Aquinas considers human beings to be essentially social beings. The following passage from the writings of Aquinas illustrates the Aristotelian influence upon his thinking:

> The fact that man is by nature a social animal - being compelled to live in society because of the many needs he cannot satisfy out of his own resources - has as a consequence the fact that man is destined by nature to form part of a community which makes a full and complete life possible for him. The help of such a communal life is necessary to him for two reasons. In the first place it is necessary to provide him with those things without which life itself would be impossible. For this purpose there is the domestic community of which man forms a part. We all get life and food and education from our parents, and it is thus that the various individuals of a family assist one another with what is necessary to existence. But life in a community further enables man to achieve a plenitude of life; not merely to exist, but to live fully, with all that is necessary to well-being.[25]

For Aquinas, as for Aristotle, the phenomenon of 'community' is central to their view of how human beings should conduct themselves. Aquinas provides numerous examples of when individuals should restrain themselves for the sake of the interests of the community. Apart from constituting a contravention of divine law, theft is regarded as a breach of natural law, since it conflicts with one of the main goals of community of living together peaceably. For the same reason, human beings have an obligation to obey the general laws of the community. In terms of suicide, apart from contravening the natural law principle which enjoins self-preservation and the notion that human life is a gift from God, Aquinas alludes to the damaging effects the act entails for the community (including the family and wider community). And, reminiscent of Augustine's conception of human beings as charitable beings,[26] Aquinas emphasised the importance of a person acting through a sense of obligation, based upon love of God and love of one's neighbour.

Niccolo Machiavelli

Niccolo Machiavelli (1469-1527) was a citizen of Florence at a time when Italy comprised a series of small and unstable states. Machiavelli rose to prominence in 1498 with the emergence of a republican form of government in Florence. He served as second chancellor and secretary to the chief foreign relations committee until his dismissal in 1512 when the republic was overthrown and the Medici

---

24   *The Encyclopaedia of Philosophy*, op. cit., Vol. I, 112.
25   T. Aquinas *Summa Theologiae* as extracted in T. O'Hagan, *op. cit.*, p. 55.
26   A. Devereux 'Should "Duties" Play a Larger Role in Human Rights? A Critique of Western Liberal and African Human Rights Jurisprudence' (1995) 18 *University of New South Wales Law Journal* pp. 464, 466.

family returned to power.[27] As one writer has remarked, Machiavelli remains some five centuries on so notorious for his observations on the nature of politics that no politician cares to be labelled 'Machiavellian'.[28]

According to Machiavelli, there are only two viable forms of government - the principality and the republic. He wrote a book about each. Written in 1513, *The Prince* is a handbook of statecraft for rulers of principalities containing counsel on how to acquire and maintain power by whatever means is necessary. Machiavelli's second book entitled *The Discourses* is a commentary on the first ten books of Livy's history of the ancient Roman republic. Machiavelli's basic thesis is that no republic can remain independent of its neighbours and free within its borders unless citizens accept civic obligations as an integral component of their individual liberty.[29] As is evident in the following passage, he strongly endorses the republican form of government and recognises the importance of community well-being:

> It is easy to see how this affection of peoples for self-government (*del vivere libero*) comes about, for experience shows that cities have never increased either in dominion or wealth, unless they have been independent ... most marvellous of all is to observe the greatness which Rome attained after freeing itself from its kings. The reason is easy to understand; for it is not the well-being of individuals that makes cities great, but the well-being of the community; and it is beyond question that it is only in republics that the common good is looked to properly ... [30]

The critical theme which is common to both of Machiavelli's treatises is the concept of *virtu* which is most accurately translated as 'public spiritedness', embodying an ancient rather than a contemporary moral injunction. The key elements of *virtu* are proper conduct and the requisite qualities for realising one's full potential. These notions originated in Aristotle's definition of a human being as a political animal (*politikon zoon*) whose flourishing depends on participation in the public life of the *polis*. For Machiavelli, public-spiritedness or civic-mindedness is what secures independence, prevents corruption and keeps the people free.

John Milton

Apart from his poetic works like *Paradise Lost*, John Milton (1608-74) was a prolific author of treatises on political, social and religious matters. Having denounced monarchy in all its forms, Milton, like Machiavelli, argues that the key to liberty lies in civic-mindedness within a constitutional framework wherein citizens are educated to practise a responsible individualism. In his *The Readie*

---

27   M. Hollis 'Machiavelli, Milton and Hobbes on Liberty' in R. Bellamy and A. Ross (eds) *A Factual Introduction to Social and Political Theory* (1996) p. 63.

28   *Idem*. p. 64.

29   *Idem*. p. 63.

30   Machiavelli *The Discourses* (Book II, Chapter 2).

and Easie Way to Establish a Free Commonwealth (1660), Milton describes a free commonwealth as one:

> wherein they who are greatest are perpetual servants and drudges to the public at their own cost and charges, neglect their own affairs; yet are not elevated above their brethren; live soberly in their families, walk the streets as other men, may be spoken to freely, familiarly, friendly, without adoration.[31]

The Aristotelian civic virtue ethic is clearly an underlying premise of this passage.

The Social Contracterians

For most of the sixteenth and seventeenth centuries, Europe was shaken by political instability as Reformation ideas such as freedom and the separation of Church and State took hold and spread political dissension across the continent. As democratic ideals began to emerge, European monarchies began to slowly erode. This led to a rethinking of the nature of political institutions and of the relationship between the individual and the State. Various political and social philosophers attempted to produce answers which would accommodate these momentous changes occurring within Europe. As commentators have observed, social and legal thought within Europe until the seventeenth century emphasised, on the one hand, privileges and duties rather than general human rights and, on the other, rights and obligations flowing from status, law and religious prescriptions. Then, with the early social contracterians such as Hobbes and Locke, attention shifted from the social dimension of human existence to the notion of the private and autonomous individual.[32]

Thomas Hobbes

The most influential of these philosophers was the Englishman Thomas Hobbes (1588-1679) who originated the concept of the 'social contract'. As has been pointed out previously, Aristotle, Machiavelli and Milton held that a free state requires citizens to be virtuous in contributing to the common good by duly fulfilling their civic duties. Hobbes, however, had a radically different conception of what liberty entails, a conception that is more contemporary in its implications. In 1651, Hobbes's most famous book, *Leviathan*, was published. Human beings, argued Hobbes, are driven by two basic impulses: fear of death and the desire for power. They are driven by their passions, guided by reason and bent on 'felicity' (intense happiness) or 'continuall successe in obtaining those things which a man

---

31   J. Milton *The Readie and Easie Way to Establish a Free Commonwealth* as quoted in M. Hollis, *op. cit.*, p. 66.

32   E. Kamenka and A. E.-S. Tay 'The Philosophical Bases of Human Rights' *Human Rights for Australia* (Human Rights Commission Monograph Series No. 1, Canberra, Australian Government Publishing Service, 1986) p. 77.

from time to time desireth'.[33] If left unchecked, human beings would act on these impulses and passions and live violent, brutish, inhumane and solitary lives. In order to keep these impulses in check, human beings entered into a social contract among themselves. According to Hobbes, the root problem of social order is that human beings by nature seek their own preservation and gratification and become enemies whenever any two of them 'desire the same thing, which neverthelesse they cannot both enjoy'. On becoming enemies, they 'endeavour to destroy, or subdue one another'. In a state of nature, they quarrel so frequently that no one is safe and the happiness which all desire is unattainable. That requires domestic peace but 'during the time men live without a common Power to keep them all in awe, they are in that condition which is called warre ... [34] The only recourse for these warring individuals is to create a common power to keep them all in awe, which is 'that great LEVIATHAN called a COMMONWEALTH, or STATE, (in Latin CIVITAS) which is but an Artificiall Man'.[35] Leviathan, or the State, is created by the social contract and is composed of all those party to it. The ruled originally united themselves into a body politic and subjected themselves to rule, contractually exchanging their natural autonomy and insecurity for their ruler's protection.[36] The social contract concept itself, however, remains a fictitious and *ex post facto* intellectual construct.[37]

In ceding all authority and sovereignty to a single person in exchange for security from each other and from foreign invaders, the people enabled the ruler to control their violent and selfish impulses through the imposition of force. The people would lose some of their individual liberty but would gain domestic security and community. The State or Leviathan would also arbitrate disputes between citizens and ensure the performance of contractual undertakings. Hobbes did not have a preference as to what form this single rule might take - whether that of a dictator or a monarch - as long as absolute power was brought to bear to hold society together. Hobbes did not envision the revision of this social contract; if the people attempted to wrest back from the ruler some measure of authority, society would, Hobbes feared, regress into violent chaos.

Unlike Machiavelli and Milton, Hobbes is sceptical in *Leviathan* of republican forms of government and calibrates liberty by whether individuals can pursue their own personal ends without state interference.[38] Echoing the sentiments articulated two centuries later by the father of English liberalism, John Stuart Mill, the State, according to Hobbes, cannot legitimately cross the line by telling people how to live or by concerning itself with their misfortunes. Once again, in contrast to Aristotle, Machiavelli and Milton, Hobbes does not strive to

---

33   T. Hobbes *Leviathan* (1651) Chapter VI.
34   Hobbes, *op. cit.*, Chapter XIII.
35   Hobbes, *op. cit.*, Introduction.
36   Selbourne, *op. cit.*, 167.
37   *Ibid.*
38   In Hobbes's view, republics can be as tyrannous as monarchies and dictatorships, the test being whether they impose duties on their citizens which go beyond the original purpose of the social contract: M. Hollis, *op. cit.*, p. 69.

link individual liberty or freedom with civic duty or public participation. For Hobbes, no moral obligations existed in the 'state of nature'. In leaving individuals to their own ends, Hobbes's thesis is open to the criticism that the common good and the community will inevitably suffer at the hands of self-interested citizens, each contributing as little as possible to anything or anybody outside of their own private realms. Yet Hobbes did not close the door to individual duty. One of the main purposes of the law, declared Hobbes, is to create and maintain conditions for the individual citizen's well-being and to adequately secure the exercise of his or her rights and liberties. To these ends, the law must 'limit the natural liberty of particular men, in such manner as they might not hurt but assist one another'[39] and 'encourage men to serve the commonwealth or deter them from doing disservice to the same'.[40] Therefore, for Hobbes, the State, as a 'commonwealth', was not merely a source of individual rights, liberties and privileges; it was also a source of individual civic duty, not only to the State itself but to fellow citizens.

John Locke

The seventeenth-century English philosopher John Locke (1632-1704) is arguably the most important natural law theorist of the modern era. Locke lived at a time when Europe was undergoing fundamental economic and social changes - the decline of its monarchies, the separation of Church and State, the gradual erosion of feudalism and the emergence of a new industrial/capitalist class and the rise of the modern European nation-state. The need was felt to protect the individual from the coercive and potentially arbitrary, abusive and invasive exercise by the State of its powers. The concept of natural rights was put forward as a possible counterbalance. The possession of individual rights would act as a barrier between the individual and the State as well as a control upon the exercise of governmental power.

Like Hobbes, Locke portrayed the State as the product of a social contract between free and equal individuals living in a state of nature. Central to Locke's thinking was his theory of consent. Consent theory posits that human beings are under an obligation to obey the law only if they have first agreed to do so. Several important assumptions underlie this notion: individuals are by nature free and equal and are capable of governing themselves and of discovering, through reason, the laws of nature (that is to say, the general rules of morality prescribing our rights and obligations towards other human beings). Locke believed that natural rights are derived from the law of nature:

> The state of nature has a law of nature to govern it, which obliges everyone; and reason, which is that law, teaches all mankind who will but consult it, that, all

---

39   Hobbes, *op. cit.*, Chapter XXVI.
40   Hobbes, *op. cit.*, Chapter XVIII.

being equal and independent, no one ought to harm another in his life, health, liberty or possessions.[41]

In contrast to the ancient Greeks who believed that some people were born to be citizens and others to be slaves, Locke argued that no one is by nature the subordinate of another. Hence, the creation of a system of government is an artificial human construct. Locke's argument was aimed at monarchical theories which contended that societies were naturally hierarchical and akin to families, with the monarch fulfilling a parental role.[42]

Locke's natural rights of life, liberty and property were derived from natural law, based on reason and sustained by a belief in the existence and providence of God. Locke's social contract theory required the people to surrender certain natural rights to a civil government created jointly by them, which in turn would protect the citizen's person and property. In contrast to Hobbes, however, Locke believed that the natural rights surrendered to government are only those rights which can be exercised better collectively for the welfare of the community (such as defence and the administration of justice). All other natural rights were retained or reserved by the individual. These reserved natural rights constituted the individual's basic liberties. They pertained to human beings by nature and could not therefore be surrendered to, controlled or denied by, the State. Locke insisted that upon entering the social contract, the people only entrust government with the right to adjudicate on and enforce these natural rights. The people do not, as Hobbes had maintained, surrender those natural rights irrevocably to the State. Were that to be the case, government would remain beyond the realm of political accountability, with the people unable to judge or punish it for violations of their natural rights. Failure by the State to fulfill its contractual undertaking to protect those reserved natural rights would render the government illegitimate, justifying civil disobedience and even a popular uprising in extreme cases.

John Locke's *Two Treatises of Government* remain the classical statement of natural rights theory. But, as Michael Freeman points out:

> The critique of Lockean liberalism and its theory of rights finds the source of its errors in its *individualism*, precisely the idea that is commonly said to distinguish Western from non-Western cultures. According to this critique, Locke and most liberals after him ground their moral and political theory in an 'abstract' individual, who is non-social and anti-social. The Lockean-liberal individual is said to have rights independently of and in opposition to society. It is supposed to follow that these rights-holders are self-centred beings indifferent to the good of society. This conception of individual rights is commonly contrasted with non-Western conceptions of the collective good to show not only that the Western

---

41   J. Locke *Two Treatises of Government* (1690) II.2.6.
42   R. Bellamy 'Socrates and Locke on Political Obligation' in R. Bellamy and A. Ross (eds) *A Factual Introduction to Social and Political Theory* (1996) p. 8.

conception of rights is culturally peculiar to the West but also that it is morally inferior in privileging individual self-interest over the common good.[43]

There is a strong tradition in Western political theory that feels uncomfortable with the concept of individual natural rights in so far as they are said to originate from the anti-social nature of human beings.[44] Freeman contends that the foregoing critique of Locke's liberal individualism is based on a misunderstanding of his theory. As was indicated previously, Locke's writings were influenced by Christian doctrine. For Locke, morality was based on the relations among human beings ordained by God. This morality consisted not only of the rights each individual possessed but of the duties each individual had to respect the rights of others. Locke's theory of individual natural rights comprised a moral theory of human social relations, based on a theory of religious obligation.[45] By requiring respect for the rights of each individual, such theory also required a social system of 'mutually sustaining rights and duties'.[46] The Lockean theory of rights neither accords pre-eminence to the individual *vis-à-vis* the community or the State nor does it deny the existence of individual duties thereto. What the Lockean theory does entail is a shift in emphasis from the social to the individual; from the public and community realms to the private. Locke's consent theory, however, offers a questionable explanation of how human beings incur duties to the community and the State. As Richard Bellamy has observed, some duties arise less out of choice than from the human condition of dependence on an existing social framework. Human beings are not born autonomous and self-sufficient but rather ultimately attain such status through a matrix of human social relations.[47]

Jean-Jacques Rousseau

History has confirmed French philosopher Jean-Jacques Rousseau (1712-78) as one of the most influential thinkers of the eighteenth century. In his two famous works *The Social Contract* and *Discourse on Inequality*, Rousseau argued that eighteenth-century society was founded on an imperfect social contract since it fostered inequality and servitude. Rousseau called for a rebuilding of the social contract to secure equality and freedom. Like Hobbes and Locke, Rousseau based his thinking on the notion that the people agreed to surrender certain of their natural freedoms to a body politic in order to gain the benefits of security and community. In stark contrast to Hobbes, however, (but in agreement with Locke) Rousseau believed that if the government was unwilling or unable to guarantee

---

43   M. Freeman 'Human Rights: Asia and the West' in J. Tang (ed.) *Human Rights and International Relations in the Asia-Pacific* (1995) p. 18.
44   *Ibid.* See also Jeremy Waldron (ed.) *Nonsense upon Stilts: Bentham, Burke and Marx on the Rights of Man* (1987) and later portions of this chapter dealing with various nineteenth-century philosophers.
45   Freeman, *op. cit.*, p. 18.
46   *Idem.* p. 19.
47   Bellamy, *op. cit.*, p. 13.

those benefits, the people were free to disobey and establish a new political contract.

There are commonly considered to be two traditions or schools of democracy - 'classical' democracy and 'liberal' democracy. Rousseau's theory is regarded as an exemplar of the first school. For the liberal school of democracy, the people are defined by their differences and by their individual private interests, and the aim of democracy is to safeguard this pluralism through a system of representative and accountable authority. For the classical school of democracy, however, the people are defined as a collectivity or community with a shared or common interest, which is realised, in the Aristotelian tradition, through active participation in the business of ruling.[48]

Rousseau sought to adapt ancient collectivism to eighteenth-century society.[49] The fundamental problem which Rousseau attempted to solve in *The Social Contract* he stated as follows:

> Find a form of association that defends and protects the person and goods of each associate with all the common force, and by means of which each one, uniting with all, nevertheless obeys only himself and remains as free as before.[50]

In other words, Rousseau is seeking to find a political association which combines pursuit of the common good and stability with individual freedom. 'What man loses by the social contract', according to Rousseau, 'is his *natural* freedom and an unlimited right to everything that tempts him and that he can get; what he gains is *civil* freedom and the proprietorship of everything he possesses'.[51] Rousseau then argues that individual freedom emerges through a particular kind of collective order which he terms the 'General Will':

> Each of us puts his person and all his power in common under the supreme direction of the general will; and in a body we receive each member as an indivisible part of the whole. Instantly . . . this act of association produces a moral and collective body . . . This public person, formed by the union of all the others, formerly took the name City, and now takes that of *Republic* or *body politic* ... As for the associates, they collectively take the name people; and individually are called *Citizens* ... [52]. As soon as this multitude is thus united in a body, one cannot harm one of the members without attacking the body, and it is even less possible to harm the body without the members feeling the effects. Thus duty and interest equally obligate the two contracting parties [that is to say, the body politic and the people] to mutual assistance ... [53]

---

48   See J. Street 'Rousseau and James Mill on Democracy' in R. Bellamy and A. Ross (eds) *A Factual Introduction to Social and Political Theory* (1996) p. 205.
49   This is an ambition which is still pursued today by the communitarian movement. See Chapter 9 for an examination of communitarianism.
50   J.-J. Rousseau *The Social Contract* Book I, Chapter VI ('On the Social Compact').
51   Rousseau, *op. cit.*, Book I, Chapter VIII ('On the Civil State') (emphasis supplied by author).
52   Rousseau, *op. cit.*, Book I, Chapter VI.
53   Rousseau, *op. cit.*, Book I, Chapter VII ('On the Sovereign').

For Rousseau, true freedom consists of obeying rules which people collectively impose on themselves. The people accept these constraints not only because they are self-imposed but because they represent the best possible mutually agreed option. In voting on political decisions, the citizens do not consider their own individual, private preferences but instead consider what the people want in pursuing the collective good. Although this may entail some personal cost, obedience to the General Will is predicated on an awareness that personal freedom is dependent upon co-operation with other social beings.

What of the recalcitrant citizen? Rousseau has this to say:

> [E]ach individual can ... have a private will contrary to or differing from the general will he has as a Citizen. His private interest can speak to him quite differently from the common interest ... he might wish to enjoy the rights of the citizen without wanting to fulfill the duties of a subject, an injustice whose spread would cause the ruin of the body politic.[54]

If citizens fail to obey the General Will, the body politic can legitimately force them to obey, since it is by their own previous decision that they have undertaken such obedience.

Thus, Rousseau has attempted to combine the concepts of freedom and collective good. Citizens recognise, through reason, their common interests and they embody within their laws their civil freedoms. Rousseau's is not a liberal democracy since the people are a collective entity rather than an aggregation of many diverse, individual interests. Nevertheless, Rousseau's classical democracy is a form of democracy which would be readily recognisable in ancient Athens and to contemporary communitarians.[55] For Rousseau, individual civil rights and freedoms are important, but they must be interpreted and enforced in the context of, and even sometimes subordinated to, the General Will or collective good.

The Legacy of the Social Contracterians

The social contracterians wrote their treatises at a time of growing opposition to despotic government which originated in France, England and America during the seventeenth and eighteenth centuries. Ultimately, citizens' rights (the 'Rights of Man') were secured by the French, English and American revolutions. These rights were embodied in such instruments as the American *Declaration of Independence* of 4 July 1776, the *Virginia Declaration of Rights* of 12 June 1776 and the French *Declaration of the Rights of Man and of the Citizen* of 26 August 1789, all of which reflect the philosophy of John Locke and Jean-Jacques Rousseau. In terms of the balance of emphasis between individual rights and

---

54   *Ibid.*
55   Street, *op. cit.*, p. 209.

duties, while these instruments marked a discernible shift towards rights, they did not altogether ignore, as we shall see, the notion that citizens were indeed bound by certain duties to fellow citizens and to the body politic. The primary concern of liberal political theorists of the time was to restrict the power of governments because of their significant concentrations of power and their corresponding capacity to harm citizens through its arbitrary use. To protect citizens, philosophers like Locke urged the embodiment of natural rights within the secular law in the form of civil rights, and called for governments to be subject to the rule of law rather than be above it. Nevertheless, as Rousseau and the French *Declaration of the Rights of Man and of the Citizen* recognised, governments may legitimately restrict individual rights and impose duties upon citizens if the collective good so warrants.

The influence of natural rights theory is clearly evidenced in Thomas Jefferson's famous Preamble to the American *Declaration of Independence*, adopted by the 13 American Colonies, which proclaims: 'We hold these truths to be self-evident, that all men are created equal, that they are endowed by their Creator with certain unalienable Rights, that among these are Life, Liberty, and the Pursuit of Happiness'. The same influence is apparent in the *Virginia Declaration of Rights* adopted by the representatives of the people of the then Colony of Virginia. The various rights enumerated in the *Declaration*, such as the right to the free exercise of religion and certain due process guarantees in civil and criminal trials, are stated to appertain to the people of Virginia 'as the basis and foundation of government' (Preamble). In language echoing the writings of Locke, Article I of the *Virginia Declaration* proclaims:

> That all men are by nature equally free and independent, and have certain inherent rights, of which, when they enter into a state of society, they cannot by any compact deprive or divest their posterity; namely, the enjoyment of life and liberty, with the means of aquiring and possessing property, and pursuing and obtaining happiness and safety.

Article III also recognises the right of the community to abolish any government which fails to govern for the common benefit, protection and security of the people. While most of the articles of the *Virginia Declaration* enshrine citizens' rights and liberties, the final Article XVI alludes to 'the duty which we owe to our Creator' and 'the duty of all to practise Christian forbearance, love and charity towards each other'.

The first two articles of the French *Declaration of the Rights of Man and of the Citizen* bear the hallmark of Locke and Rousseau. Article 1 affirms that human beings 'are born and remain free and equal in respect of rights' while Article 2 states:

> The purpose of all civil associations is the preservation of the natural and imprescriptible rights of man. These rights are liberty, property, security, and resistance to oppression.

Four of the remaining articles of the French *Declaration*, however, purport to set limits on the exercise of individual rights, thereby impliedly imposing individual duties on citizens. Article 4 provides:

> Liberty consists in the power of doing whatever does not injure another. Accordingly, the exercise of the natural rights of every man has not other limits than those which are necessary to secure to every other man the free exercise of the same rights; and these limits are determinable only by the law.

Article 5 recites that '[t]he law ought to prohibit only actions hurtful to society'. Articles 10 and 11 respectively require citizens to exercise their rights to freedom of religious and other opinion and freedom of expression in such a manner as not to disturb public order or to injure other citizens. Read together, these four articles prescribe for citizens an individual duty to exercise their rights and to otherwise act so as not to undermine the common welfare or to interfere with the exercise of the same rights by other citizens. Finally, Article 13 establishes a progressive taxation system, requiring citizens to contribute to public expenses according to their abilities.

The Nineteenth-Century Philosophers

Two of the greatest nineteenth-century Western philosophers, Jeremy Bentham and John Stuart Mill, respectively rejected natural rights theory and the classical school of democratic theory. As we shall see, however, both accomodated the principle of individual duty within their respective theories.

Jeremy Bentham

Jeremy Bentham (1748-1832) was a leading and strident critic of natural rights and natural law theory. In his *Anarchical Fantasies* (first published in 1816), Bentham wrote:

> Right is the child of law; from real laws come real rights, but from imaginary laws, from the 'laws of nature', come imaginary rights ... Natural rights is simple nonsense: natural and imprescriptible rights, nonsense upon stilts ... They know not of what they are talking under the name of natural rights, and yet they would have them imprescriptible.[56]

For Bentham, then, natural law and natural rights were unreal metaphysical phenomena. The real test for the existence of an individual right was whether that right was legally enforceable, that is to say a 'positive' right existing in legislation of judge-made common law. Legal positivists distinguished natural rights as a

---

56 J. Bentham 'Anarchical Fantasies' in A. Melden (ed.) *Human Rights* (1970) pp. 28, 30-34.

class of mere moral rights. They argued that only legal rules vest rights in, and impose obligations on, citizens. For Bentham, the happiness of society should be the primary concern of government. As one of the founders of utilitarianism, he developed the 'principle of utility' - 'the greatest happiness of the greatest number' - as the goal to which society should aspire. But, as Selbourne has lamented, this 'nineteenth-century pleasure principle . . . rained down further blows, those of an amoral hedonism, upon the principle of [individual] duty'[57] to fellow citizens, the community and the State. Although Bentham did examine the concept of individual duty, it was mainly in the context of the correlative nature of the relationship between rights and duties.[58] This contributed to the shift in emphasis from duties to rights, as duties gradually lost their former central role in the body politic and non-correlative duties came to be perceived as a matter of mere charity or of moral obligation.[59]

John Stuart Mill

John Stuart Mill (1806-1873) is commonly regarded as the philosopher of modern English liberalism, the significant contributions of which include the values of political and economic liberty, equality, the rule of law, pluralist democracy and respect for diversity. Although a Benthamite in early life, J. S. Mill's philosophy later diverged from strict utilitarianism. He believed that government should strive to achieve not happiness as such, but what society ought to desire.[60] The concepts of individual liberty, dignity and autonomy were central to his philosophy. Mill postulated a social welfare function of government with the aim of achieving greater equality of opportunity for individuals to pursue their own private interests and ends, unhindered as far as practicable by governmental regulation. Mill maintained that it is 'indispensable to a good condition of human affairs' to 'find the limit' to the 'legitimate interference of collective opinion with individual independence'.[61] And, in the 'Introduction' to *On Liberty* (1859), Mill remarked that '[t]he only liberty which deserves the name, is that of pursuing our own good in our own way, so long as we do not attempt to deprive others of theirs or impede their efforts to obtain it'. Thus, for Mill, individual freedom translated into freedom from interference by government and by others in one's private realm. Another key liberal democratic principle that that which is not specifically forbidden by the law is lawful for the citizen to do, echoes Article 5 of the French *Declaration of the Rights of Man and of the Citizen* which directs that '[w]hat is not prohibited by the law should not be hindered'.

　　The foregoing brief overview of Mill's philosophy contains no suggestion of any civic ethic or sense of individual duty at all. Some commentators who have attempted to critique Mill's philosophy have suggested that there must be a limit in

---

57   Selbourne, *op. cit.*, p. 32.
58   This relationship will be examined in more detail in Chapter 3.
59   Devereux, *op. cit.*, p. 467.
60   J. S. Mill *On Liberty* (1859) p. 6.
61   *Idem.* pp. 13-14.

any self-respecting civic order to what may be permitted in terms of the indulgence of individual desires. In other words, individual liberty must transcend the mere absence of external impediments to an individual's will. Yet Mill himself appeared to recognise that the principle of individual duty is not antithetical to, nor even incompatible with, liberal ideals. In *On Liberty*, Mill equated the fulfillment of duty to others with 'social morality'.[62] Although individual liberty was, for Mill, the ultimate value, an 'inner feeling of humanity' was accepted as a sound basis for a utilitarian morality.[63] Thus, declares Mill, '[t]here are many positive acts for the benefit of others which [anyone] may rightfully be compelled to perform'.[64] These positive, beneficial acts include not only the bearing of a 'fair share in the common defence' but also 'in any other joint work necessary to the interest of the society of which he enjoys the protection'.[65] The citizen can even be 'compelled to perform certain acts of individual beneficence, such as saving a fellow creature's life, or interposing to protect the defenceless against ill-usage, things which wherever it is obviously a man's duty to do, he may rightfully be made responsible to society for not doing'.[66]

Nonetheless, the decline of the principle of individual duty was accelerated in the mid-nineteenth century in the face of the overriding orthodox liberal democratic principle that the State should interfere as little as possible in the private life of the individual citizen, while simultaneously guaranteeing the latter's rights and freedoms.[67] Not all eighteenth and nineteenth-century philosophers, however, agreed with the concept of rights, or at least the degree of emphasis placed upon them. For them, it is only within the community, with its matrix of supportive human relationships, that the concept and content of rights can be recognised and formulated. One of Bentham's mentors, David Hume (1711-1776), had declared that '[t]he general obligation, which binds us to government, is the interest and necessities of society; and this obligation is very strong'.[68] Similarly, Hegel (1770-1831) believed that '[t]he reality and significance of the human individual are subordinated to the greater reality and significance of human society'.[69] 'In duty', considered Hegel, 'the individual finds his liberation'.[70] And, although a departure from the 'duties to God' tradition, the Prussian philosopher Immanuel Kant (1724-1804) enunciated certain 'moral duties' which were to be the unconditional directive for human conduct.[71] 'The degree of [man's] freedom

---

62   *Idem.* p. 150.

63   J.S. Mill *Utilitarianism* (8th ed., 1882) Chapter III, p. 40-43.

64   J. S. Mill *On Liberty* (1859) p. 24.

65   *Ibid.*

66   *Ibid.*

67   Selbourne, *op. cit.*, p. 30.

68   D. Hume 'Of the Original Contract' in A. Macintyre (ed.) *Hume's Ethical Writings* (1748) p. 272.

69   J. Burns 'The Rights of Man Since the Reformation: An Historical Survey' in Sir Francis Vallat (ed.) *Human Rights* (1971) pp. 16, 27.

70   F. Hegel *Philosophy of Right* (translated by T. Knox) (1942) Third Part, para. 149.

71   Devereux, *op. cit.*, pp. 466-7.

grows with the degree of his morality', Kant declared in his *Lectures on Ethics*.[72] In addressing the laws of duty in his *The Metaphysics of Morals*, Kant formulates a duty to respect others and a duty of benevolence or beneficence (that is to say, a duty of practical love for one's neighbour or the duty of making others' ends one's own).[73] Kant explains the underlying reasoning for his duty of beneficience in the following passage:

> It is every man's duty to be beneficient - that is, to promote, according to his means, the happiness of others who are in need, and this without hope of gaining anything by it. For every man who finds himself in need wishes to be helped by other men. But if he lets his maxim of not willing to help others in turn when they are in need become public, i. e. makes this a universal permissive law, then everyone would likewise deny him assistance when he needs it, or at least would be entitled to. Hence the maxim of self-interest contradicts itself when it is made universal law - that is, it is contrary to duty. Consequently the maxim of common interest - of beneficence toward the needy - is a universal duty of men . . .[74]

Thus, Kant's duty of beneficience is principally founded upon the notion of reciprocity. As we shall see in the next chapter, such duty is essentially a positive, freestanding or non-correlative, welfare duty.

The 'Liberty of the Ancients' Versus the 'Liberty of the Moderns'

The crucial difference between the philosophers examined in the foregoing sections is the manner in which they sought to define the concept of liberty. Philosophers like Aristotle, Aquinas, Machiavelli and Milton spoke for the liberty of the ancients while those like Hobbes and Mill spoke for the liberty of the moderns. This contrast was observed by Benjamin Constant (1767-1830) in a speech on 'The Liberty of the Ancients Compared with that of the Moderns' made in 1819:

> The aim of the ancients was the sharing of social power among the citizens . . . this is what they called liberty. The aim of the moderns is the enjoyment of security in private pleasures; and they call liberty the guarantees accorded by institutions to these pleasures.[75]

This fundamental tension between these two polar opposites is as real today as it was in 1819. The ancient republican tradition links freedom with self-government and assigns citizens a solemn duty to participate therein. They are citizens first and private persons second, after their public or civic duties have been discharged.

---

72   I. Kant *Lectures on Ethics* (translated by L. Infield) (1963) p. 29.
73   I. Kant 'The Doctrine of Virtue' in *The Metaphysics of Morals* (translated by M. Gregor) (1964) p. 116, paragraphs 24-5.
74   *Idem.* para. p. 25.
75   As quoted in Hollis, *op. cit.*, p. 70.

Although these citizens do have rights as well as duties, these rights are to afford them opportunities to lead a more complete life, which includes public participation. By contrast, contemporary thinkers generally regard citizens as private individuals who form the body politic for mutual advantage.[76] Having warned that the liberty of the ancients could deprive citizens of all private life (especially in the versions reinvented by the French Revolution), Constant also cautioned that the liberty of the moderns threatens the public life of society. Constant urged a combination of the two whereby individual rights of citizens would be respected by the body politic while their moral and civic education would be secured. This indeed is the contemporary communitarian thesis which will be examined in greater depth in Chapter 9.

The Historical and Logical Primacy of Duty Over Right

It is evident from the foregoing discussion that the principle of individual duty is not new; indeed, it is as old as natural rights theory itself. Duties were the staple of ethics for many centuries prior to the emergence of discussion of the modern concept of rights during the period of the Enlightenment.[77] It is also arguable that the principle of duty is the historically prior constituent of human association.[78] As has been observed, 'in pre-colonial Africa, as in most non-Western and preindustrial societies, forms of social and political organization rendered the means to attain human dignity primarily through duties and obligations, often expressed in a communally oriented social idiom and realized within a redistributive economy'.[79]

On one level, it is possible to conceive of the modern concept of rights as subordinate and relative to the concept of individual duty. A right *per se* is not efficacious; it draws its effectiveness only from the duty to which it corresponds.[80] The effective exercise of a right stems rather from the recognition and performance by persons other than the right-holder of the corresponding or correlative duty which attaches to the right. Thus, while the exercise of the individual's rights as a member of the civic order enables that individual to attain dignity and self-fulfillment, such individual is a prior bearer of duties to that order.[81] This analysis may partially explain the tendency of some cultures (particularly African and Asian),[82] religions and political philosophies to view what some consider 'rights'

---

76   *Ibid.*
77   Devereux, *op. cit.*, p. 467.
78   Selbourne, *op. cit.*, p. 3.
79   T. Fernyhough 'Human Rights and Precolonial Africa' in R. Cohen *et al.* (eds) *Human Rights and Governance in Africa* (1993) p. 39.
80   S. Weil *The Need for Roots: Prelude to a Declaration of Duties toward Mankind* (1952) 3. The correspondence or correlativity of rights and duties will be examined in detail in the next chapter.
81   Selbourne, *op. cit.*, p. 20.
82   See Chapters 4 and 6 for more detail.

as mere 'privileges' contingent upon one's fulfillment of one's duties. This notion of the 'contingency of rights' has received contemporary recognition in the second preambular paragraph of the *American Declaration of the Rights and Duties of Man* of 1948 which states that '[t]he fulfillment of duty by each individual is a prerequisite to the rights of all'. In the Islamic *Shariah*, human rights are considered a consequence of human obligations rather than their antecedent. As a result of fulfilling obligations to God, nature and other human beings, individuals acquire certain divinely-ordained rights and freedoms. Those who do not fulfill such duties have no legitimate rights.[83] Similarly, for many communist states, the fulfillment by citizens of their constitutional duties is an important precondition for the enjoyment of their rights and for guaranteeing the conditions necessary for such enjoyment.[84]

The Contemporary Sources of the Principle of Duty

The identification and detailed discussion of the juristic and philosophical contemporary sources of the principle of individual duty have never been systematically addressed and none will be attempted here. What follows is a brief overview in the form of a non-exhaustive list of the primary sources of such duty which have been suggested from time to time by various commentators and theorists. While some sources are conventional and widely accepted, others are more controversial and nascent.

Status and Contract

Anglo-American legal systems have recognised and enforced for a long time positive duties to assist others that are based on either a contractual relationship (such as the duty of a paid nurse or lifeguard) or a special status relationship (usually by birth, such as the duty of a parent to provide the necessities of life to his or her child).[85] In the civil law realm, Anglo-American statute and common law has more recently extended duty of care obligations to, for example, employers and teachers to take positive steps to ensure that workers and students enjoy a safe working and teaching environment.

Religion

As we shall see in Chapter 4, religion has historically been one of the most important sources of individual duty. As one Hebrew proverb aptly puts it, '[t]he

---

83   S. Nasr 'The Concept and Reality of Freedom in Islam and Islamic Civilisation' in
        A. Rosenbaum (ed.) *The Philosophy of Human Rights: Contribution in Philosophy
        No. 15* (1980) pp. 95, 97.
84   Daes, *op. cit.*, p. 30.
85   A. John Simmons *The Lockean Theory of Rights* (1992) 348. See also Sir Henry
        Maine *Ancient Law* (1905) pp. 169-70.

path of duty in this world is the road to salvation in the next'.[86] Although religion's influence in this context may be waning in relative importance, divine injunction or 'God's will' still continues to provide for many a sufficient basis for the performance of their basic moral/ethical duties to other human beings.

Social Solidarity or the Common Good

As the English philosopher David Hume observed centuries ago, '[t]he general obligation, which binds us to government, is the interest and necessities of society; and this obligation is very strong'.[87] Some modern constitutions explicitly stipulate that certain duties towards society are imposed on individual citizens on the basis of 'social solidarity' and that citizens are expected to perform those duties in order that they may live peacefully and securely in a civilised community.[88] Similarly, Article 1 of the *Charter of the Spanish People* [89] recognises Spanish citizens to be the holders of duties, the performance of which the Spanish State 'guarantees for the common good'. And, as we shall see in Chapter 8, the notion of social solidarity or the common good is a central foundation in many socialist and communist constitutions upon which to impose individual duties on their citizens.

Membership of the Civic Order or Body Politic

Membership of the civic order or the fact of citizenship has also been put forward as a sufficent foundation for the imposition of individual duties.[90] Indeed, in some cultures (for example, in pre-colonial Africa), the imposition of individual duties and their required fulfillment are perceived simultaneously as the consequence of one's membership of the community and the precondition to one's possession of membership therein.[91]

The Basic and Shared Needs of Humanity

It has been argued that it may be possible to found the imposition of individual duties upon the same rationale as human rights. Just as natural law theory posits that each human being possesses certain inalienable rights because of his or her humanity, similarly duties should be imposed on humans because they are human. Each human being shares a common existence with other human beings, all of whom possess basic needs and require dignity. As Devereux suggests, '[r]ather than having to resort to religious justifications which are far from universally

---

86   As quoted in Selbourne, *op. cit.*, p. 158.
87   Macintyre, *op. cit.*, p. 272.
88   See the discussions of the Iraqi and Venezuelan Constitutions on this point in Daes, *op. cit.*, p. 25 and 31 respectively.
89   16 July 1945, amended 15 December 1966.
90   Selbourne, *op. cit.*, pp. 167-9.
91   Devereux, *op. cit.*, p. 474.

accepted, it is possible that humans could be regarded as bearing a certain level of responsibility for each other, simply because of their shared humanity'.[92]

Ethics, Reason and Utility

The doctrine of utilitarianism or practical necessity has been invoked to provide yet another foundation of the principle of individual duty. It is argued that it is necessary in the interests of all to safeguard the necessities of life and to preserve the very existence of the body politic itself. Each person has a vested interest in his or her personal safety and security of property, giving rise, for example, to a voluntary or conscripted duty to defend the body politic of which he or she is a member.[93]

Reason, or the intellectual faculty by which conclusions are drawn from premises, may also sustain the principle of individual duty if we recall[94] the reasoning underlying Kant's reciprocal duty of beneficence. But perhaps, as Selbourne maintains,[95] as an ethical principle, the principle of individual duty rests upon firmer ground for being so than as a principle founded on reason alone. For Selbourne, the principle of duty is a positive ethical principle through whose observance the citizen is educated in morality and proper human conduct.[96]

---

92   *Idem.* p. 479.
93   Duties of military service and defence of country will be examined in detail in Chapter 7.
94   See the quotation relating to n. 74 *supra.*
95   Selbourne, *op. cit.*, pp. 160-161.
96   *Ibid.*

Chapter 3

The Taxonomy of Duties

> [T]he enjoyment of rights and freedoms also implies the performance
> of duties on the part of everyone.[1]

Introduction

The purpose of this chapter will be to examine the extent to which rights and duties correlate with each other and to classify duties according to these main conceptual frameworks - perfect/imperfect, positive/negative and moral/legal. All of these types of duties will be examined in later portions of this book, although with varying degrees of emphasis. Various instruments (both international and national/constitutional) which acknowledge the correlative nature of the rights/duties relationship will be cited. Questions concerning to whom are individual duties owed and a possible hierarchy of duties will also be addressed.

Correlativity Theory

Rights and duties do not contain the same conceptual elements but rather perform different (but arguably complementary) tasks. As Stoljar observes:

> A right refers to an individual's interests, while the duty indicates the requisite
> commissions or omissions protecting those interests. A right reveals a person's
> complaint or grievance, the duty specifies actions a duty-bearer must avoid. A
> right defines an area of freedom, the duty specifies conduct for which one is
> answerable or responsible. Rights, in short, relate to benefits, duties to the burdens
> responding to these benefits.[2]

It remains a matter of controversy between philosophers whether every right which an individual possesses can be translated into a duty that others have towards that person and *vice versa*. While some maintain that all rights are translatable into duties, the majority of Western theorists reject such complete correspondence.

---

1 Seventh preambular paragraph of the *African Charter on Human and Peoples' Rights* adopted by the Organization of African Unity at the 18th Conference of Heads of State and Government on 27 June 1981, Nairobi, Kenya (entry into force 21 October 1986).

2 S. Stoljar *An Analysis of Rights* (1984) p. 46.

Most accept a significant degree of correlation but acknowledge that rights and duties may have areas of independent operation.[3] In particular, some duties are perceived as not possessing corresponding rights.[4]

Generally speaking, individual rights cannot make sense operating in a social vacuum, devoid of duties incumbent upon other individuals. Rights must be contextualised in relation to other human beings and cannot be perceived as rights for an individual living entirely alone.[5] Living alone on his tropical island, Robinson Crusoe owed no duties because there was no person to whom he owed any duty. The moment other persons are present, duties *ipso facto* arise in the form of their duties to us or our duties to them. To effectuate Friday's right to life, Crusoe had a correlative duty to attempt to save it. Thus, duty is a relation or a normative rule.[6] It is a distinctive feature of such rules that they operate through pairs of rights and duties. The right-holder claims an appropriate response: that the duty-holder should make reparation for an injury sustained, or return money or a chattel belonging to the right-holder or, as in the Crusoe example, take positive steps to effect a rescue. Normative rules or relations are therefore dually constituted in the sense that two-party relations must include a right on the one hand with a corresponding duty on the other.[7]

Another example relied upon by Bailey[8] illustrates that in the usual context, in any meaningful discussion of rights, the concept of duty inevitably emerges and is equally as important. Both right and duty are inextricably linked in logic and operation:

> Objections to the rights-emphasis are familiar. They are raised when individuals claim, for example, that their right to the privacy of their suburban home and family has been infringed by the way in which a neighbouring religious community conducts its religious observances. What is implied is that the members of the religious community have an obligation to respect the family's privacy. However, the right/obligation relationship can be reversed if the religious group sees its right to worship as threatened by the family's protest. What needs to be noted is that two rights - to privacy and to manifest one's religion - are in conflict, and that the other side of each right is an obligation ... [I]f the family has a right to privacy (Article 17 of the [*International Covenant on Civil and Political Rights*]), then others have an obligation to respect that privacy. Equally, however, the householder will have an obligation to respect the right of members of the religious group to manifest their religion (Article 19). The discussion almost

---

3   A. Devereux 'Should "Duties" Play a Larger Role in Human Rights? A Critique of Western Liberal and African Human Rights Jurisprudence' (1995) 18 *University of New South Wales Law Journal* pp. 464, 469.

4   These duties, often referred to as 'imperfect duties', will be examined in the next section.

5   M. Flekkoy and N. Kaufman *The Participation Rights of the Child: Rights and Responsibilities in Family and Society* (1997) p. 10.

6   M. Radin 'Natural Law and Natural Rights' (1950) 59 *Yale Law Journal* pp. 214, 217.

7   Stoljar, *op. cit.*, p. 36.

8   P. Bailey *Human Rights: Australia in an International Context* (1990).

immediately becomes one of how the rightholder can expect the person with the duty to discharge that duty. Thus in the context of analysing the simple right, the question of duty inevitably arises.[9]

This example aptly illustrates what Stoljar labels 'functional complementarity'[10] or what Radin metaphorically describes as the concave and convex sides of the same shield. Right and duty are the converses of one another; they are the same relation looked at first from one end and then from the other.[11]

Perfect and Imperfect Duties

A starting point for a conceptual framework of individual duty is the simple but important distinction between perfect (correlative) and imperfect (non-correlative or freestanding) duties. Perfect duties give someone a correlative right against us. They require a strict, uniform adherence because they directly reciprocate or correlate with others' rights. Perfect duties tend to be negative in nature inasmuch as they require the duty-holder to refrain from harming others. So, for example, the right to life entails a correlative or perfect duty not to kill. The right to the secure possession of one's property implicates a correlative duty not to steal. Perfect duties may also entail positive conduct, particularly in the civil law realm. In a debt situation, for instance, the debtor's duty to pay correlates precisely with the creditor's right to receive. In these examples, a correlative duty is imposed either upon the world at large or on a particular person. Thus, for each person who possesses a right, there is another person (or persons in general) who possesses a duty to respect that right. As a matter of logical necessity, the express recognition of a specific right impliedly acknowledges the existence of a duty correlative to that right.

Correlative duties constitute the primary type of duties. A right would be devoid of meaning and effect if it failed to seek recognition or protection, or did not entail a claim against, and a response from, another individual.[12] To the extent that a right is a call for protection, the correlative duty circumscribes the responsive protective measures. As Stoljar observes, the interests seeking protection would go without it in the absence of correlativity, for there would be no other person whose responsibility would be engaged.[13]

Correlativity theory has been acknowledged in a number of international human rights instruments and national constitutions. The second preambular paragraph of the *American Declaration of the Rights and Duties of Man* provides:

---

9   *Idem.* pp. 25-6.
10   Stoljar, *op. cit.*, p. 46.
11   Radin, *op. cit.*, p. 218.
12   Stoljar, *op. cit.*, pp. 40-2.
13   *Id.* p. 44.

The fulfillment of duty by each individual is a prerequisite to the rights of all. Rights and duties are interrelated in every social and political activity of man.

Similarly, the seventh preambular paragraph of the *African Charter on Human and Peoples' Rights* declares that 'the enjoyment of rights and freedoms also implies the performance of duties on the part of everyone'. In the Asian context, the fourth preambular paragraph of the *Kuala Lumpur Declaration on Human Rights* recites that '[w]hereas, the peoples of ASEAN recognise that human rights have two mutually balancing aspects; those with respect to rights and freedoms of the individual, and those which stipulate obligations of the individuals to society and State'.[14]

In numerous socialist/communist constitutions, a direct and inseparable linkage exists between the enjoyment of rights by citizens and their performance of duties to their communities. This unity of rights and duties stems from a belief that the enjoyment of the former and the discharge of the latter constitute an organic whole. So, for example, Article 59 of the *Constitution (Fundamental Law) of the Union of Soviet Socialist Republics* [15] proclaims that '[c]itizens' exercise of their rights and freedoms is inseparable from the performance of their duties and obligations'. Again, Article 32 of the 1982 *Constitution of the People's Republic of China* states in part that '[t]he rights of citizens are inseparable from their duties'. As the Head of the Chinese Delegation explained in an address to the 1993 Vienna World Conference on Human Rights:

> The rights and obligations of a citizen are indivisible. While enjoying his [or her] legitimate rights and freedom, a citizen must fulfil his [or her] social responsibilities and obligations.[16]

But such recognition of correlativity theory is not confined to socialist/communist constitutions. The fourth preambular paragraph of the October 1987 *Constitution of the Republic of Korea*, for example, refers to each person discharging 'those duties and responsibilities concomitant to freedoms and rights'.

By contrast, imperfect (or non-correlative or freestanding) duties do not correlate with others' rights. Imperfect duties are not individualised and therefore

---

14   The *Kuala Lumpur Declaration on Human Rights* was approved by the Second Plenary Session of the 14th General Assembly of the A.S.E.A.N. Inter-Parliamentary Organisation (20-23 September 1993) in Kuala Lumpur, Malaysia. The full text of the *Declaration* may be located in F. de Varennes *Asia-Pacific Human Rights Documents and Resources* (1998) p. 107.

15   Adopted at the seventh (special) session of the Supreme Soviet of the Union of Soviet Socialist Republics, Ninth Convocation, on 7 October 1977.

16   Statement by Liu Huaqui, Head of the Chinese Delegation, Vienna, 17 June 1993 as quoted in J. Tang (ed.) *Human Rights and International Relations in the Asia-Pacific* (1995) p. 215.

give no particular person a determinate right against us.[17] Such duties allow a considerable measure of discretion by duty-holders in how, when and where they perform the required actions.[18] Imperfect duties tend to be positive duties to assist others or to prevent harm from befalling them. Also, the beneficiaries of some imperfect positive duties lack legal power to enforce them.[19]

Because the imposition of perfect duties only arises if there is a corresponding right in place, imperfect duties are potentially of significant importance to society in so far as individuals may possess a moral or ethical duty to do a certain act even if no one has a correlative right to expect its performance. It is arguable that in the long-term interests of the community, individuals should be subject to duties to other individuals without the need to identify correlative rights to secure their performance.

Two oft-cited examples of such imperfect duties are the duty to rescue and the duty to provide charity. Concerning the former, when another person is in peril, an individual who is in a position to rescue that person has a non-enforceable moral duty (at least in most Western legal systems) to effect such rescue, notwithstanding the endangered person has no right to expect it. In terms of the latter, we have a moral duty to assist and care for those much worse off than ourselves, notwithstanding the absence of a correlative right of a particular person to expect it. Since a duty-bearer cannot possibly benefit all those in need of charity, he or she must select from amongst many possible candidates. The nomination of the recipient of the beneficial effects of the duty remains the exclusive and unfettered choice of the benefactor. The duty-bearer can change his or her mind without being held accountable to anyone, since others have no grounds to complain that the duty-bearer is not charitable to them in particular.[20]

By their nature, imperfect duties are broader and more indeterminate than perfect duties. Apart from the duties of rescue and charity, it is difficult to compile an exhaustive list of imperfect duties. Some commentators have suggested the utility, indeed the necessity, of devising a multi-factored formula to apply in order to determine whether an imperfect duty should be owed in a particular set of circumstances. Reminiscent of the 'calculus of negligence' factors[21] applied by

---

17	E. Kamenka and A. E.-S. Tay 'The Philosophical Bases of Human Rights' in *Human Rights for Australia* (Human Rights Commission Monograph Series No. 1, Canberra, Australian Government Publishing Service, 1986) pp. 77, 82.
18	A. John Simmons *The Lockean Theory of Rights* (1992) p. 338, n. 77.
19	The legal and non-legal enforcement of duties will be addressed in Chapter 10. As will be discussed therein, imperfect positive duties are generally not legally enforceable in legal systems founded upon the English common law. The situation is different, however, in some European continental law or code systems where positive duties of rescue are prescribed in certain situations.
20	Stoljar, *op. cit.* pp. 38-9.
21	In *United States v Carroll Towing Co.* (1947) 159 F. 2d 169, 173, Learned Hand J. described the standard of care to be expected of the owner of a moored barge as 'a function of three variables: (1) The probability that she will break away; (2) the gravity of the resulting injury, if she does; (3) the burden of adequate precautions …'

common law judges in civil suits to determine the standard of care required in the particular circumstances of a case, a 'calculus of duty' formula comprising the following factors has been proposed so as to provide a flexible framework to determine whether a person owes an imperfect duty in a given situation:

Special Placement

A person may owe an imperfect duty to another person where he or she is specially placed in a particular situation *vis-a-vis* the latter. This may occur either on the basis of their geographical propinquity or the possession of a special skill by the former. So, for example, if A sees B drowning in a nearby swimming pool, A is specially placed, in terms of physical closeness, to rescue B. Or, if C, a motor vehicle mechanic, passes by D, a motorist stranded on a secluded country road, C is specially placed to assist D, not only in terms of physical proximity but in terms of his special skill. These factors involving physical closeness and special skill should be relevant in determining whether an imperfect duty is owed in the particular case. However, 'special placement' in itself will not suffice to found such a duty. Other factors or variables are significant in this regard.

Cost

According to Simmons, it is difficult to imagine a better way of failing to show respect for others and their dignity than by refusing to provide them with critical assistance, the provision of which would entail only minimal or acceptable risks, costs or inconvenience.[22] By contrast, it could be argued that a significant or harmful cost could negate an imperfect positive duty to act. In some situations, assistance may simply be beyond the call of duty. The cost factor would then have to be balanced against the special placement factor to determine whether the imposition of such a duty is warranted in that situation. In terms of the previous example, although A is specially placed in a physical sense to rescue B from drowning in the pool, the fact that A cannot swim (and so risks possible death in any rescue attempt) may suffice to negate the duty.

Proximity of Relationship

A third factor comprising the 'calculus of duty' is the proximity or closeness of relationship between the potential duty-bearer and beneficiary. In general (and also in the particular context of the existence of a duty of care in the tort of negligence), the strength of a person's duty to another person will diminish as the distance in the relationship between the two increases. Thus, to borrow once again from a previous example, if A is the father of B who is drowning in the pool, a stronger case can be made for imposing a positive duty of action on A (than if B were a total stranger).

---

22   Simmons, *op. cit.*, p. 351.

Need

A fourth factor to be balanced in the 'calculus of duty' scales is the degree of the victim's need in the particular case. The stronger that need and the more dire the consequences for the victim of not receiving assistance, the easier it will be to impose a duty of positive action.

A Hierarchy of Duties?

Two of the 'calculus of duty' factors - special placement and proximity of relationship - suggest the possibility of the existence of a hierarchy of duties. Indeed, such a notion is not new. Cicero declared that '[w]e should pay the first regard to our country and parents'.[23] In setting out a hierarchy of individual duties to others, Epictetus spoke in descending order of 'my duty to God, to my parents, to my relations, to my community and to strangers'.[24] Closer to our time, Lockean theory impliedly endorsed a descending scale of moral priority that was a strict function of proximity to oneself: self, family, local poor, others.[25] Despite the inherent equality of all humanity recognised in the *Universal Declaration of Human Rights*, the old addage 'charity begins at home' has a special place here. We tend to feel a stronger duty towards the poor we see and those who live around us than towards needy persons abroad. As Simmons observes:

> [D]uties to those 'closer' to us are often stronger than duties to others, because we often have additional special obligations or duties to those close to us (and they have special rights against us). While we have general duties to all other persons (e.g., to help the distressed), we enter into additional special relations with spouses, partners, children, and friends, which ground further duties and thus make our duties to them more imperative ....[26]

Assistance to others is likely to be more efficient where the beneficiaries have special relationships with the benefactors or where the latter are specially placed to provide the assistance (since the benefactors are more informed and concerned in these cases). As the physical and emotional distance between the benefactors and beneficiaries increases, so does the likelihood that the assistance efforts will be inefficent.[27]

---

23   *Offices*, I, xvii.
24   Epictetus *Moral Discourses* (translated by E. Carter) (1910) II, xvii, 2.
25   Simmons, *op. cit.* p. 336.
26   *Idem.* p. 341.
27   *Idem.* p. 350.

Negative and Positive Duties

Negative and positive duties refer to the distinction between duties of forbearance and duties to perform positive actions respectively. Negative duties essentially require the duty-holder (be it government, groups or individuals) to refrain from obstructing the right-holder in his or her exercise of the correlative rights. Negative correlative duties derive from the classical liberal rights or civil liberties which delimit an area of freedom into which others are not permitted to intrude. So, while I enjoy the rights to freedom of movement, of thought, conscience and religion, of speech, of assembly[28] and so forth, others have a specific negative correlative duty not to interfere with my exercise of those rights.

Positive or affirmative duties, on the other hand, impose obligations on persons or agencies to take positive steps to fulfill the needs of the right-holders recognised by the correlative rights. In the words of Mazzini:

> Your most important duties are positive. It is not enough *not to do*; you must *do* ... It is not enough *not to harm*; you must *do good* to your brothers.[29]

Under international human rights law today, numerous positive human rights have been incorporated into the *International Covenant on Economic, Social and Cultural Rights* of 1966.[30] These are essentially welfare rights in the economic and social fields and impose positive, correlative duties primarily upon governments and their agencies to progressively secure these rights. Leading examples of positive rights to be found in the *International Covenant on Economic, Social and Cultural Rights* include the rights to health, education and work.[31]

Generally speaking, positive duties are more onerous on the duty-holder in terms of their fulfillment than negative duties. The 'Ten Commandments'[32] are framed in terms of negative duties and it is arguably easier, for example, for one to 'not kill' than to protect or preserve life. Similarly, it is much more arduous for governments to fulfill their positive duties under the *International Covenant on Economic, Social and Cultural Rights* than it is to fulfill their duties of forbearance under the *International Covenant on Civil and Political Rights* of 1966.[33] Kenneth Minogue writes:

---

28   For the corresponding provisions in the *International Covenant on Civil and Political Rights* guaranteeing these rights, see respectively Articles 12, 18, 19 and 21.
29   G. Mazzini *The Duties of Man and Other Essays* (translated by E. Noyes) (1907) 35 (emphasis in original).
30   Adopted by United Nations General Assembly Resolution 2200 A (XXI) of 16 December 1966.
31   To be found respectively in Articles 12, 13 and 6 of the *International Covenant on Economic, Social and Cultural Rights.*
32   *The Old Testament, Book of Exodus* Chapter 20, Verses 1-17.
33   Adopted by United Nations General Assembly Resolution 2200 A (XXI) of 16 December 1966.

[Positive human rights] require much more positive action on the part of whoever is charged with the running of society. The natural rights to life, liberty, and property require little more of government and other citizens than forbearance, but the right to be provided with an actual job requires that governments shall manage the economy, and it may also require that governments shall manage the lives of their citizens in very considerable detail.[34]

This may explain in part why negative duties of forbearance tend to be stricter and more legally enforceable than positive duties of aid. At any given moment, we are fulfilling our negative duties by not harming or interfering with others without any conscious effort. It is easy for most not to murder or steal. Indeed, as one commentator has wryly remarked, '99 per cent of the time I can fully respect your first generation civil and political rights simply by ignoring you'.[35] Some positive duties are already recognised and enforced under domestic law, including duties based on contractual undertakings, status or relations (for example, parental duties relating to child maintenance) and duties associated with holding public office. Nonetheless, if ease of fulfillment remains one of the main criteria for recognising and enforcing duties, then some duties of assistance should also be included. Duties of charity can be as basic and important as negative duties of forbearance inasmuch as failure to give assistance in certain cases can result in irreparable harm to others and prejudice their rights.[36] It is no insuperable burden on a person, for example, to have to contact the police, shout a warning or throw a lifeline to a drowning person. Nor is it difficult for most of us to render assistance to the poor. These acts hardly interfere with our autonomous pursuit of individual self-fulfillment any more seriously than refraining from harming others.[37] These issues will be more fully canvassed in Chapter 10.

Moral and Legal Duties

The distinction between law and morality continues to fascinate philosophers. Law and morality often coincide. Moral prohibitions on murder and theft have been incorporated into the law from time immemorial. Cases often arise, however, where a person may legally do what he or she ought not to do (for example, foreclosing on a mortgage debt where the reason for default was beyond the control of the debtor), and where a person may legally refrain from doing that which he or she ought to do as a matter of basic morals or ethics (for example, effecting a simple rescue). Moral duties lie outside the jural sphere. They are based upon an imperative ethical or religious basis or the dictates of one's conscience and have not (or not yet) been recognised by the law for purposes of enforcement or

---

34   K. Minogue 'The History of the Idea of Human Rights' in W. Laqueur and B. Rubin (eds) *The Human Rights Reader* (1979) pp. 14-15.

35   H. Rosemont Jr 'Human Rights: A Bill of Worries' in W. Theodore De Bary and T. Weiming (eds) *Confucianism and Human Rights* (1998) pp. 54, 59.

36   Simmons, *op. cit.* p. 345.

37   *Idem.* p. 348.

redress.[38] Value judgments therefore abound in the realm of moral duty.[39] By contrast, legal duties are those which arise from contract of the parties or by operation of law.[40] They include those duties which the law requires to be done or forborne to a determinate person or the public at large, correlative to a vested and coextensive right in such person or the public.[41]

Those moral duties which have been recognised by law become legal duties, and failure to perform them is generally attended by the imposition of legal sanctions. For example, some moral duties owed to family members, community members and the State have been transformed into legal duties through their recognition by the law. Thus, a person owes a legal duty to support his or her spouse and children, not to harm other persons or their property, and not to attempt to overthrow the State. Breaches of these duties will engage the imposition of sanctions under family law, tort law and criminal law respectively. As far as moral duties are concerned, however, a person is entirely free to perform them or not. If a person neglects his or her duty to render assistance to the destitute or the sick, there will be no legal implications, although that person may be subjected to social comment and ostracism.

To Whom Are Individual Duties Owed?

As will become apparent in the chapters which follow, the primary objects or beneficiaries of the duties which individuals owe under national and international law are: to self, family, society, the State and the international community. Article 32(1) of the *American Convention on Human Rights* [42] states that '[e]very person has responsibilities to his family, his community, and mankind'. Article 27(1) of the *African Charter on Human and Peoples' Rights* goes beyond the *American Convention* by adding two additional objects of duty: the State and 'other legally recognized communities'. Article 27(1) provides that '[e]very individual shall have duties towards his family and society, the State and other legally recognized communities and the international community'. The phrase 'other legally recognized communities' is probably referable to the Organization of African Unity in the context of the promotion of African unity. And, as we shall see in Chapter 5, individuals are now regarded under international law as bearing a duty not to commit war crimes, genocide, crimes against humanity and crimes against peace.

---

38   *Black's Law Dictionary* (Revised Fourth Edition, 1968) p. 595.

39   Radin, *op. cit.* p. 217.

40   The term 'operation of law' expresses the manner in which rights and liabilities devolve upon a person by the mere application to the particular transaction of the established rules of law, without the act or co-operation of the party himself or herself: *Black's Law Dictionary, op. cit.*, p. 1243.

41   *Black's Law Dictionary, op. cit.*, p. 1039.

42   Adopted by the Organization of American States in San Jose, Costa Rica, 22 November 1969.

Although the above-cited instruments do not refer to the individual possessing a duty to himself or herself, it is possible to argue at the philosophical level for a duty of self-development. Of the 'several duties man owes to himself', the first, according to Kant, is that of 'so ordering his life as to be fit for the performance of all moral duties'.[43] And, for Mill, the notion of a duty to oneself included 'self-development'.[44] A leading example of a 'self-regarding duty' would be education and training, affording benefits not only to the individual but to his or her immediate family, and making that individual a more knowledgeable and useful member of his or her community and body politic.

In terms of the incidence of individual duties, excluded from their fulfillment on a functional basis are those persons not able, or not yet able, to fully enjoy the rights and perform the role of citizens in society. Children, the sick, the aged and the mentally infirm are not so much subject to duties as the beneficiaries of duties owed by other individuals and governmental agencies.[45]

---

43   I. Kant *Lectures on Ethics* (translated by L. Infield) (1963) p. 125.
44   J. S. Mill *On Liberty* (1859) p. 141.
45   D. Selbourne *The Principle of Duty* (1994) p. 189.

Chapter 4

Religion, Ethics and the Principle of Individual Duty

The path of duty in this world is the road to salvation in the next. (Hebrew proverb)[1]

Introduction

This chapter will examine the central position which the principle of individual duty occupies in the realm of religion and ethics. For this purpose, 'religion' will refer to a system of belief in, or worship of, a god or other supernatural being while 'ethics' is referable to non-theologically-based moral principles or rules of conduct. In terms of the former, Judaism, Christianity, Islam and Hinduism will be briefly considered. As a system of ethics or philosophy, Confucianism will also be analysed in this regard. These religious and ethical systems all share the following features: they uphold and promote the dignity and worth of the human person through their precepts concerning proper conduct; they affirm a moral responsibility for the welfare of others and they perceive human beings as potential members of a community comprised of those who share certain ideas or explanations about humanity and its destiny.

Judaism

Generally speaking, contemporary international human rights law expressly proclaims the rights of human beings but is silent on their assumption of individual duties. However, it is the converse with the world's mainstream religions. The concept of rights sits uncomfortably with Judaism (and, indeed, Christianity, Islam and Hinduism). On the contrary, the principle of individual duty or obligation is deeply rooted in Judaism (the religious, cultural and legal traditions of the Jewish people). That is not to say that Judaism has not elaborated systems to uphold the worth and dignity of the human person. Rather, it has approached that task from the duty end of the rights-duty correlative relation.

---

1   As quoted in D. Selbourne *The Principle of Duty* (1994) p. 158.

The source of human dignity in the Judaic tradition is to be found in the divine origin and nature of human beings. They were created in the image of God and thus embody intrinsic and supreme worth. According to the Book of Genesis (Chapter 1, Verse 27):

> God created man in his image; in the divine image he created him; male and female he created them.[2]

Human beings, therefore, are to be treated with love and respect. Judaism has been described as a religion of duties.[3] To be a Jew is considered to be a significant privilege, carrying with it commensurately significant duties.[4] The imposition of these duties upon Jews is to both acknowledge and secure the dignity and worth of human beings. The Decalogue[5] lays down the Ten Commandments which impose primarily negative duties of forbearance. These injunctions are, *inter alia*, designed to protect the person and property of the objects or beneficiaries of the duties. As Robert Cover points out in the following passage, the basic word of Judaism is obligation or '*mitzvah*':

> [B]ecause it is a legal tradition Judaism has its own categories for expressing through law the worth and dignity of each human being. And the categories are not closely analagous to 'human rights.' The principal word in Jewish law, which occupies a place equivalent in evocative force to the American legal system's 'rights', is the word 'mitzvah' which literally means commandment but has a general meaning closer to 'incumbent obligation.'[6]

An alternative interpretation of the Hebrew term '*mitzvah*' is a virtuous action or good deed.[7] Cover continues:

> [T]o be one who acts out of obligation is the closest thing there is to a Jewish definition of completion as a person within the community. A child does not become emancipated or 'free' when he or she reaches maturity ... the child becomes bar or bat mitzvah, literally one who is of the obligations.[8]

This belief that the giving of oneself is the process by which the self comes to be reflects the philosophy underpinning Article 29(1) of the *Universal Declaration of*

---

2   *New American Bible* (1970) p. 4.
3   A. Kaplan 'Human Relations and Human Rights in Judaism' in A. Rosenbaum (ed.) *The Philosophy of Human Rights, Contribution in Philosophy No. 15* (1980) pp. 53, 70.
4   *Ibid.*
5   The *Book of Deuteronomy*, Chapter 5, Verses 6-21. See also the *Book of Exodus*, Chapter 20, Verses 1-17.
6   R. Cover 'Obligation: A Jewish Jurisprudence of the Social Order' (1987) 5 *Journal of Law and Religion* p 65.
7   Kaplan, *op. cit.*, p. 70.
8   Cover, *op. cit.*, p. 65.

Human Rights which states '[e]veryone has duties to the community in which alone the free and full development of his personality is possible'.

Apart from the centrality of individual duty in Judaic tradition, two other of its aspects are worth mentioning: the Judaic association of justice and righteousness with concern for the poor and the powerless, and the importance of the community over the individual. To a certain extent, Judaism is in fact individualistic as far as the morality of conduct is concerned. Both the prophets Jeremiah (Chapter 31, Verses 29-30) and Ezekiel (Chapter 18, Verses 1-4) insist on personal rather than familial responsibility. Each person will be brought to account only for his or her own sins.[9] Judaism attaches religious significance to the discharge of moral duties by each Jew, failure of which will incur individual moral responsibility. Individualism as a social doctrine, as distinct from individual moral responsibility, is generally foreign to Judaism.[10] Whereas Western liberalism tends only to be concerned with the welfare of each individual competing against other individuals, Judaism looks more to securing the common good through co-operative action.[11] The notion that human beings need one another is not only sociologically sound; for Judaism it is scriptural wisdom:

> Two are better than one ... If the one falls, the other will lift up his companion. Woe to the solitary man! For if he should fall, he has no one to lift him up. So also, if two sleep together, they keep each other warm. How can one alone keep warm?[12]

Group or community identity is more important than individual identity. To the question 'Who are you?' the traditional reply among Jews is 'A Jew.' '*Kol Yisrael chaverim*' - all Jews are comrades - is the folk expression of group loyalty and solidarity.[13] One of the fundamental aims of the *Torah* is to engender a sense of community in which I and they are one. In terms of religious practice, the *kehilla* (the congregation or community) takes priority over the individual. If at all possible, prayers are to be recited communally. Individual, personal prayers are the exception.[14] Also, as Kaplan observes, the Judaic sense of community is not merely a matter of reciprocity - letting you do for me what I do for you - but of mutuality: doing together what we cannot do separately.[15]

This same sense of community also implies the caring of one individual community member for, and by, another. The Judaic social justice ideal of giving to each according to his or her need remains a basic component of rabbinic Judaism.[16] Job describes in the following passage what has been the operative ideal from the time of the prophets:

---

9   Kaplan, *op. cit.,* pp. 57-8.
10   *Idem.* p. 59.
11   *Ibid.*
12   *Ecclesiastes*, Chapter 4, Verses 9-11.
13   Kaplan, *op. cit.,* 60.
14   *Idem.* pp. 59-60.
15   *Idem.* p. 61.
16   *Idem.* p. 75.

> For I rescued the poor who cried out for help, the orphans, and the unassisted; The blessing of those in extremity came upon me, and the heart of the widow I made joyful . . . I was eyes to the blind, and feet to the lame ... [17]

The Judaic social justice ideal comprises both negative and positive moral obligations. Not only must an individual be diligent in avoiding committing injustice against the weak and helpless; he or she must also be diligent in alleviating their distress. In the words of the prophet Isaiah, '[m]ake justice your aim: redress the wronged'.[18] Positive individual duties are also prescribed in the *Torah*:

> You shall love your neighbour as yourself.[19]

> If your brother has become poor and his hand fails, you shall uphold him, even if he be a stranger.[20]

Although the Judaic duty of charity subsumes the qualities of benevolence and goodwill, it is something more. In the words of Kaplan:

> For Judaism charity is not something to be bestowed if and when we feel charitable. Giving is a duty; the recipient is taking possession of what is his by right. The Hebrew word for charity is *tsedakah*, from the same root as the words for righteousness and for justice.[21]

From this brief overview of Judaism, then, it is apparent that it is a way of life heavily influenced by community-oriented positive duties of assistance as well as negative duties of forbearance. Although the concept of 'rights' is not recognised *per se*, human dignity and worth are still protected through the recognition and performance of these duties.

Christianity

Contrary to the Judaic conception that 'the Lord thy God is one', Christianity revolves around the belief that there is one God but that He is triune: partaking of the forms of God the Father, God the Son (Jesus Christ) and the Holy Ghost (Spirit). However, the Christian faith is thoroughly grounded in Judaism through its inclusion of the previously-mentioned Ten Commandments as one of its most important prescriptions of moral conduct. Judaism and Christianity are also at one in their respective concern for the poor and powerless, for 'the least of these my

---

17   *Book of Job*, Chapter 29, Verses 12-13, 15.
18   *Book of Isaiah*, Chapter 1, Verse 17.
19   *Book of Leviticus*, Chapter 19, Verse 18.
20   *Book of Leviticus*, Chapter 25, Verse 35.
21   Kaplan, *op. cit.*, p. 76.

brethren'.[22] Reminiscent of the Judaic injunction in *Leviticus* Chapter 19, Verse 18, Jesus Christ exhorted his followers:

> You shall love the Lord your God with all your heart, with all your soul, with all your strength, and with all your mind; and your neighbour as yourself.[23]

Apart from a duty to love and serve God and one's neighbour (loosely meaning all persons with whom an individual has contact), Jesus also alluded to a duty to obey the secular law and authorities in order to preserve the peace and stability of the civic order: 'Give to Caesar what is Caesar's, but give to God what is God's'.[24] The concept of religious duty or obligation has remained a cornerstone of Christianity throughout the Christian era. The great Catholic theologian and philosopher Saint Thomas Aquinas emphasised the importance of a person acting through a sense of obligation, based upon love of God and one's neighbour, and an appreciation that individual self-interest must sometimes yield to the interests of the community.[25] The Catholic, Protestant and Orthodox Churches of today continue to emphasise the importance of discharging social obligations in a Christian's acting out his or her faith.[26]

As for 'rights', an important distinction must be drawn between the Western liberal tradition and Christian theological approaches. As we have seen in Chapter 2, philosophers like Hobbes, Locke and Rousseau perceived the possession of individual rights to be an innate attribute of a human being, involving freedom from oppression by the State. By contrast, any rights which a Christian enjoys are derived from the Creator God. They are 'consequential' in the sense that they are enjoyed as a matter of grace (that is, by a gift of God) and dependent upon the faithful performance of one's spiritual and social duties as a Christian. The Christian tends to be more conscious of the rights-duties correlation discussed in Chapter 3 and critical of the contemporary human rights movement 'as emphasising unduly the concept of rights without the correlate of responsibility'.[27]

Hinduism

The Hindu faith is one of the world's oldest religions, having evolved some 3,500 years ago. Although there are many strands in the Hindu tradition, none of them naturally gives rise to a rights-based philosophy *per se*,[28] although as we shall see shortly the five social freedoms and the five individual virtues were premised upon the dignity and worth of the human being. Social structures and the underlying

---

22   *The Gospel According to Matthew*, Chapter 25, Verse 40.
23   *The Gospel According to Luke*, Chapter 10, Verse 27.
24   *The Gospel According to Mark*, Chapter 12, Verse 17.
25   See Chapter 2 for more detail on the writings of Thomas Aquinas.
26   P. Bailey *Human Rights: Australia in an International Context* (1990) p. 39.
27   *Idem*. p. 40.
28   *Idem*. p. 42.

social visions of human dignity in traditional India, as in other traditional societies, rested not on rights but rather on the primacy of social duties and status hierarchies.[29] This is associated with a group orientation which India shares with other traditional societies, in contrast to the Western liberal tradition's emphasis upon individualism and the belief that each person is the possessor of natural and inalienable rights.[30]

From about the beginning of the Christian era, the caste system had emerged as the fundamental institution of traditional Indian society. A caste is a named group of persons within the community which is characterised by endogamy (marriage within the same group), hereditary membership and a specific lifestyle which sometimes includes the pursuit of a particular occupation by tradition. The caste system was characterised by separation (not only in matters of marriage but in terms of personal contact), division of labour (each group had different duties and roles to perform within society), and hierarchy (the ranking of groups as relatively superior or inferior to one another). There were four traditional castes or *varnas*: *Brahman* (priests), *Kshatriya* (warriors/rulers), *Vaishya* (landed and mercantile classes) and *Shudra* (servile classes). Beneath these four *varnas* were *Chandalas* (or the so-called 'untouchables'). The caste system developed such a rigid hierarchy that one's duties were virtually defined by birth.[31] Unlike the Western liberal tradition, one's rights (to the limited extent that these were enjoyed) and duties were specified in traditional Hindu society not in terms of one's humanity but in terms of one's specific caste, age and sex.[32] Based on the proposition that there are fundamental and unchangeable differences in both the status and nature of human beings, the caste system was designed to assist people to find their place within society and to live truly within their allotted caste.[33] Donnelly describes the central position individual duties occupy in the caste system:

> One's station [caste] has its duties (*dharma*) and the discharge of those duties, whatever they may be, gives one a place and a certain dignity. Both the *Bhagavadgita* (3:35) and *The Laws of Manu* (X.97) emphasize that it is better to perform one's own duties poorly, even to die doing so, than to perform another's well. And the proper discharge of the duties of one's station will be rewarded in the next life. The idea of a station in life thus has a special force in the Hindu worldview: this life is only a way station on the route to ultimate purity, self-

29   J. Donnelly *Universal Human Rights in Theory and Practice* (1989) p. 126.
30   J. Donnelly 'Traditional Values and Universal Human Rights: Caste in India' in V. Leary and C. Welch Jr (eds) *Asian Perspectives on Human Rights* (1990) 55, 67.
31   *Ibid.*
32   K. Mitra 'Human Rights in Hinduism' (1982) 19 *Journal of Ecumenical Studies* pp. 77, 79.
33   Bailey, *op. cit.,* 42. See also Pannikar 'Is the Notion of Human Rights a Western Concept?' (1982) 120 *Diogenes* p. 75.

awareness, and reunion with the divine, and each soul passes through a very large number of these separate stations.[34]

Although traditional Hinduism did not evolve a rights-based philosophy *per se*, it did consider the immortal spirit of humanity to be the source of human dignity. This is expressed in the so-called 'five social freedoms' and the 'five individual virtues'. The five social freedoms identified within the Hindu historical tradition are:

- freedom from violence (*Ahimsa*)
- freedom from exploitation (*Aparigraha*)
- freedom from violation or dishonour (*Avyabhichara*)
- freedom from want (*Asteya*), and
- freedom from early death and disease (*Armitava and Aregya*)

The first three social freedoms entail negative correlative individual duties (of forbearance) on the part of others while the remaining two social freedoms imply positive correlative duties (of assistance).[35] The five individual virtues included in the same tradition are:

- absence of intolerance (*Akrodha*)
- compassion of fellow feeling (*Bhutadaya, Adreha*)
- knowledge (*Inana, Vidya*)
- freedom of thought and conscience (*Satya, Sunrta*), and
- freedom from fear and frustration or despair (*Pravrtti, Abhaya, Dhrti*)

The Hindu tradition is to regard these five social freedoms as requiring virtues or controls by way of counterparts. Although there is no definite concept of rights in the Western tradition, there is a sense of obligations which arises from the combined effect of the freedoms and virtues.[36]

Although in the secular sphere, the Indian Government acceded in 1979 to the *International Covenant on Civil and Political Rights* of 1966 and the *International Covenant on Economic, Social and Cultural Rights* of 1966, two of the best-known articles on Hinduism and human rights deny that the concept of human rights exists in Hindu India.[37] As Saksena observes, 'Indians ... base their

---

34   J. Donnelly 'Traditional Values and Universal Human Rights: Caste in India' in V. Leary and C. Welch Jr (eds) *Asian Perspectives on Human Rights* (1990) pp. 55, 66.
35   See Chapter 3 for an explanation of the meaning of these terms.
36   Bailey, *op. cit.,* 43. See also Y. Khushalani 'Human Rights in Asia and Africa' (1983) 4 *Human Rights Law Journal* pp. 403, 407.
37   K. Mitra 'Human Rights in Hinduism' (1982) 19 *Journal of Ecumenical Studies* 77; R. Thapar 'The Hindu and Buddhist Traditions' (1966) 18 *International Social Science Journal* p. 31.

social structure on duties and obligations rather than on rights'.[38]   Hindu Indians are seen first and by nature as bearers of duties and whatever rights they do possess rest on the discharge of duties assigned to one's status.[39]

Islam

Islam, with Judaism and Christianity, proclaims a belief in One God. The primary sources of the Islamic faith are the *Qur'an*, *Sunna* and *Shari'a*. For Muslims, the *Qur'an* is the literal and final word of God and Muhammad is the final Prophet. During his mission from 610 A.D. until his death in 632 A.D., Muhammad elaborated on the meaning of the *Qur'an* and supplemented its rulings through his own statements and actions. This came to be known as *Sunna*. The Prophet also established the first Islamic state in Medina around 622 A.D. *Shari'a* is derived from both the *Qur'an* and *Sunna*. According to one Muslim writer:

> *Shari'a* is not a formally enacted legal code. It consists of a vast body of jurisprudence in which individual jurists express their views on the meaning of the *Qur'an* and *Sunna* and the legal implications of those views. Although most Muslims believe *Shari'a* to be a single logical whole, there is significant diversity of opinion not only among the various schools of thought, but also among the different jurists of a particular school ...

> Furthermore, Muslim jurists were primarily concerned with the formulation of principles of *Shari'a* in terms of moral duties sanctioned by religious consequences rather than with legal obligations and rights and specific temporal remedies. They categorized all fields of human activity as permissible or impermissible and recommended or reprehensible. In other words, *Shari'a* addresses the conscience of the individual Muslim ... [40]

Although the status of *Shari'a* has declined somewhat since the middle of the nineteenth century, it still exerts supreme influence over family law, including marriage and divorce.

As with Judaism, the concept of individual 'rights' is quite foreign and unnatural to the Islamic faith. The emphasis is rather upon the acknowledgement and discharge of individual 'duties' and 'obligations'. A. K. Brohi, a former Pakistani Minister of Law and Religious Affairs, has written a number of articles on human rights in Islam. In the following passage, he contrasts the Western and Islamic perspectives:

---

38   S. Saksena 'The Individual in Social Thought and Practice' in C. Moore (ed.) *The Indian Mind: Essentials of Indian Philosophy and Culture* (1967) p. 372.

39   J. Donnelly *Universal Human Rights in Theory and Practice* (1989) p. 126.

40   Abdullah Ahmed An-na'im 'Human Rights in the Muslim World' (1990) p 3 *Harvard Human Rights Journal* p. 13, as quoted in H. Steiner and P. Alston *International Human Rights in Context: Law, Politics, Morals* (1996) pp. 211-2.

The Western man's perspective may by and large be called anthropocentric in the sense that there man is regarded as constituting the measure of everything since he is to be regarded as the starting point of all thinking and action. The perspective of Islam, on the other hand, is theocentric, that is, God-consciousness, the Absolute here is paramount; man is here only to serve His Maker ... [In the West] rights of man are seen in a setting which has no reference to his relationship with God - they are somehow supposed to be his inalienable birthrights.[41]

The notions of 'collectivity' and 'the greater good' enjoy a special sanctity in Islam. If necessary, the individual may have to be sacrificed in order that the life of the social organism be saved.[42] Writing from an Islamic perspective, Ahmad Yamani has complained that '... the West is so over-zealous in its defence of the individual's freedom, rights and dignity, that it overlooks the act of some individuals in exercising such rights in a way that jeopardizes the community'.[43] By contrast, in his book entitled *The Islamic Law and Constitution*, Mawdudi states that '[i]t is ... obligatory on the citizens of the Islamic State to co-operate wholeheartedly with the government and to make sacrifices of life and property for it ...'[44]

Historically, Islam has been a very decentralised religion hosting a wide range of dissimilar opinions and competing schools of thought. An appreciation of this diversity of thought within Islam is necessary when addressing the extent to which Islam is compatible with human rights. No definitive Islamic model of human rights exists: opinions range from those more conservative schools of thought which completely reject the Western concept of human rights to other more liberal schools which endorse it.[45] The primary Islamic sources - particularly the *Qur'an* and *Sunna* - provide little in the way of express guidance on possible scriptural bases for human rights (as opposed to duties).[46] As Donnelly states:

'Human rights' cannot be translated into the language of the Islamic holy works. Alleged human rights prove to be only duties of rulers and individuals, not rights held by anyone. The scriptural passages cited as establishing a right to protection of life are in fact divine injunctions not to kill and to consider life as inviolable. The right to justice proves to be a duty of rulers to establish justice. The right to freedom is merely a duty not to enslave unjustly. Economic rights turn out to be duties to earn a living and to help provide for the needy. Muslims are regularly and forcefully enjoined to treat their fellow men with respect and dignity, but the

---

41   A. K. Brohi 'Islam and Human Rights' (1976) 28 P.L.D. Lahore pp. 148, 150.

42   A. K. Brohi 'The Nature of Islamic Law and the Concept of Human Rights' in International Commission of Jurists, Kuwait University, and Union of Arab Lawyers, *Human Rights in Islam: Report of a Seminar Held in Kuwait, December 1980* (International Commission of Jurists, 1982) pp. 43, 48.

43   A. Yamani *Islamic Law and Contemporary Issues* (1968) 15.

44   Abu'l A'la Mawdudi *The Islamic Law and Constitution* (1980) p. 252.

45   Ann E. Mayer *Islam and Human Rights: Tradition and Politics* (2nd ed., 1995) p. 48.

46   *Ibid.*

bases for these injunctions are divine commands that establish only duties, not human rights.[47]

In a similar vein, Brohi adds:

> [In Islam] there are no 'human rights' or 'freedoms' admissible to man in the sense in which modern man's thought, belief, and practice understand them: in essence, the believer owes obligations or duties to God if only because he is called upon to obey Divine Law, and such Human Rights as he is made to acknowledge seem to stem from his primary duty to obey God.[48]

Thus, in Islam what is important is duties rather than rights. Whatever rights are acknowledged to exist are a consequence of one's status and actions in fulfilling one's duties, not the simple fact that one is a human being. As Abdul Aziz Said observes:

> The essential characteristic of human rights in Islam is that they constitute obligations connected with the Divine and derive their force from this connection. Human rights exist only in relation to obligations. Individuals possess certain obligations towards God, fellow humans and nature, all of which are defined by *Shari'a*. When individuals meet these obligations they acquire certain rights and freedoms which are again prescribed by the *Shari'a*.[49]

Said's observations are confirmed by those of Seyyed Hossein Nasr in the following passage:

> Human rights are, according to the *Shari'a*, a consequence of human obligations and not their antecedent. We possess certain obligations toward God, nature and other humans, all of which are delineated by the *Shari'a*. As a result of fulfilling these obligations, we gain certain rights and freedoms that are again outlined by the Divine Law. Those who do not fulfill these obligations have no legitimate rights ... [50]

The primacy of God over human beings, of divine revelation over reason, of God-given rights over humanistic inalienable rights, of duty over right, of collectivism or communitarianism over individualism in Islamic traditional orthodoxy has shaped the content of Islamic human rights instruments and constitutions of Islamic states. Three such instruments will be examined in this connection: the *Universal Islamic Declaration of Human Rights* of 1981 (UIDHR), the *Cairo Declaration on*

---

47   J. Donnelly *Universal Human Rights in Theory and Practice* (1989) p. 51.

48   A. K. Brohi 'Islam and Human Rights' (1976) 28 *P.L.D. Lahore* pp. 148, 151.

49   Abdul Aziz Said 'Precept and Practice of Human Rights in Islam' (1979) *Universal Human Rights* I (April) pp. 63, 73-4.

50   Seyyed Hossein Nasr 'The Concept and Reality of Freedom in Islam and Islamic Civilisation' in A. Rosenbaum (ed.) *The Philosophy of Human Rights, Contribution in Philosophy No. 15* (1980) pp. 95, 97.

Human Rights in Islam of 1990 and the *Constitution of the Islamic Republic of Iran* of 24 October 1979 (As Amended to 28 July 1989).

The *UIDHR* was prepared by representatives from Egypt, Pakistan, Saudi Arabia and other countries under the auspices of the Islamic Council.[51]   It was adopted at Paris on 19 September 1981. An examination of the Preamble to the English version of the *UIDHR* reveals that divine revelation has given the 'legal and moral framework within which to establish and regulate human institutions and relationships'. Throughout the text of the Arabic version, texts of the *Qur'an* and *Sunna* of the Prophet Muhammad are extensively quoted. It is evident that, for the authors of the *UIDHR*, these divinely-inspired texts enjoy primacy over human reason (*al-'aql al-bashari*) which is considered insufficient by itself to provide the best plan for human life.[52]   In the corresponding part of the English version, after stating that 'rationality by itself' cannot be 'a sure guide in the affairs of mankind', the authors of the *UIDHR* express their conviction that 'the teachings of Islam represent the quintessence of Divine guidance in its final and perfect form'. Apart from according divine revelation a central role in the *UIDHR*, its authors refuse to accept the recent shift from an emphasis on human or individual duties to an emphasis on human rights. In a passage in the English version of the Preamble to the *UIDHR*, its authors proclaim 'that by the terms of our primeval covenant with God our duties and obligations have priority over our rights'. This reaffirms the traditional orthodox position that Islam provides a scheme of individual duties as opposed to individual rights.

The *Cairo Declaration on Human Rights in Islam* was endorsed by the member states of the Organization of the Islamic Conference on 5 August 1990. Once again, divine revelation - as opposed to human reason - is the operative principle. Reference is made in the Preamble to 'the Revealed Books of God' while Article 1(a) declares in part that '[t]rue faith is the guarantee for enhancing [basic human] dignity ...' The operative text of the *Cairo Declaration* variously refers to duties, obligations and responsibilities. For example, Article 1(a) proclaims that '[a]ll ... are equal in terms of basic human dignity and basic obligations and responsibilities ...' Article 2 considers life to be 'a God-given gift' concerning which it is the 'duty of individuals . . . to protect' through forbearance and positive measures. Article 6 alludes to the duties of women and the responsibilities of men within the family context, while Article 9 regards '[t]he quest for knowledge [as] an obligation'. Compared with non-Islamic human rights instruments,[53] the provisions of the *Cairo Declaration* place considerably more conscious emphasis upon the identification of individual duties and the importance of fulfilling them.

---

51   The Islamic Council is a private, London-based organisation affiliated with the Muslim World League which is an international, non-governmental organisation headquartered in Saudi Arabia. The Muslim World League tends to represent the interests and views of conservative Muslims.

52   Mayer, *op. cit.*, pp. 49-50.

53   These non-Islamic instruments will be discussed in Chapter 6 from the duty perspective.

The fundamental role played by divine revelation in Islamic law and justice is also evidenced in the constitutions of Islamic republics. The *Constitution of the Islamic Republic of Iran* of 24 October 1979 (As Amended to 28 July 1989) is a leading illustrative example. Article 1 states that '[t]he form of government of Iran is that of an Islamic Republic, endorsed by the people of Iran on the basis of their longstanding belief in the sovereignty of truth and Qur'anic justice ...' Article 2 recites in part that:

> The Islamic Republic is a system based on belief in:
>
> 1. The One God (as stated in the phrase 'There in no god except Allah'), His exclusive sovereignty and the right to legislate, and the necessity of submission to His commands;
>
> 2. Divine revelation and its fundamental role in setting forth the laws;
>
> ...
>
> 6. The exalted dignity and value of man, and his freedom coupled with responsibility before God ...

The Iranian *Constitution* is also replete with explicit references to individual duties. Article 14, for example, imposes a duty of tolerance in prescribing that 'all Muslims are duty-bound to treat non-Muslims in conformity with ethical norms and the principles of Islamic justice and equity, and to respect their human rights'. Article 8 recognises for Iranian residents a mutual duty to respect others and a mutual duty of care and beneficence. Article 8 reads in part:

> In the Islamic Republic of Iran, *al-'amr bilma'ruf wa al-nahy 'an al-munkar* is a universal and reciprocal duty that must be fulfilled by the people with respect to one another . . . The conditions, limits, and nature of this duty will be specified by law. (This is in accordance with the Qur'anic verse: . . . 'The believers, men and women, are guardians of one another . . .' [9:71]).

The foregoing views of commentators and the excerpts from the three instruments examined underline the relative importance in Islam of individual duties compared with rights and their collectivist or communitarian orientation.

Confucianism

Prior to the reception of Western political ideals at the end of the nineteenth century, there was no explicit concept of human rights in East Asian culture.[54] Asian cultures have tended to place a heavy emphasis upon order and societal stability. The official ideologies of Tokugawa Japan and the Korean Yi Dynasty associated inequality with order and equality with chaos.[55] Western notions of rights and democracy were imported into Asia because there was indigenous dissatisfaction with the old order and these ideals helped Asian activists to articulate their principles and goals.[56]

From a historical point of view, the Chinese philosophy of life was emphasised the responsibility of the individual to society and the importance of safeguarding the interests of the community over those of the individual. This collectivist, as opposed to individualist, perception of society is due in no small measure to the influence of Confucianism in East Asia over thousands of years. Confucianism is essentially a system of ethics developed by the Chinese philosopher, Confucius, which emphasised devotion to family, peace, justice and the importance of acting humanely. Confucius identified certain fundamental human or social relationships and prescribed various mutual obligations which were inherent in them. Although some commentators have researched Confucianism with a view to identifying Confucian forerunners or antecedents to contemporary conceptions of human rights, the balance of opinion, particularly amongst Asian scholars themselves, appears to be that the Western idea of human rights has never been recognised or accepted as part of the Chinese philosophy of life because it is rooted in metaphysical concepts which are alien to traditional Chinese culture.[57] According to Wejen Chang, the Confucian classics do not contain a term that is close to 'human rights'.[58] And, as Kwok aptly states, a study of Confucianism 'reveals a preponderant concern with "rites" rather than "rights"'.[59]

From a historical point of view, the Chinese philosophy of life was founded on agriculture. In the earliest records, the ordinary people were regarded as the backbone and working force of the economy and constituted the reason for the political formation. According to the Chinese philosopher Mencius (372-289 B. C.), '[t]he people are the most important element in a nation; the spirits of the

---

54   Chung-sho Lo 'Human Rights in the Chinese Tradition' in U.N.E.S.C.O. (ed.) Human Rights: Comments and Interpretations (1973) p. 187.

55   M. Freeman 'Human Rights: Asia and the West' in J. Tang (ed.) *Human Rights and International Relations in the Asia-Pacific* (1995) pp. 13, 15.

56   I. Neary 'The Hyongpyongsa, the Suiheisha and the Struggle of Human Rights in East Asia' (unpublished, 1993).

57   P. Woo 'A Metaphysical Approach to Human Rights from a Chinese Point of View' in A. Rosenbaum (ed.) *The Philosophy of Human Rights: Contribution in Philosophy No. 15* (1980) p. 113.

58   W. Chang 'Confucian Theory of Norms and Human Rights' in W. Theodore De Bary and Tu Weiming (eds) *Confucianism and Human Rights* (1998) p. 117.

59   D. W. Y. Kwok 'On the Rites and Rights of Being Human' in W. Theodore De Bary and Tu Weiming (eds) *Confucianism and Human Rights* (1998) p. 83.

land and grain are the next; the sovereign is the lightest'.[60] The aim of benefiting the people was regarded as the original purpose of government and the political leaders or rulers were to concern themselves accordingly with the welfare of the ordinary people.[61] In contrast to the Western tradition, the Lockean notion of surrendering one's right of self-government in exchange for protection was irrelevant in Chinese history as an explanation of the rise of sovereign power. In view of this difference between the Western and Chinese conceptions of the rise of governmental authority, the so-called 'rights of man' never occupied a prominent place in Chinese thinking.[62]

As we shall see, Confucianism is fundamentally duty-based and collectivist in its orientation. Confucius claimed that the ideal relationship between human beings is one based on compassion and benevolence. He and his followers sought to develop a set of norms to help humans live a good life. The basic guiding principle for a person to behave as a human being in human society, according to Confucius, is humanity or to be humane (*ren, jen*), from which all social norms are developed.[63] To be humane is to love all human beings (*ai ren*). Confucius considered a person as humane if he or she is able to practise the 'five virtues': respect, tolerance, trustworthiness in word, diligence in action, and kindness.[64] Clearly, the practice of these virtues presupposes the inherent dignity and worth of human beings. Each of these virtues also takes the form of a correlative duty. When the duties attached to the virtues are performed, one is accorded a place of dignity and respectability in society.[65] Acting humanely in one's relationships is the means by which one can pursue ultimate happiness and fulfillment. The five virtues are also designed to fit the individual into society through an internal, individual process of self-cultivation and self-transformation.[66] The five virtues are also community-oriented in the sense that they represent an individual duty to contribute to the common good.[67]

In Confucianism, a person enters from birth into a network of clan and kin relations which are to be guided by a spirit of humanity (*ren*). According to Kwok, there is no occasion for such a person to develop and proclaim self-centred individualism or to assert his or her own rights.[68] The Confucian requirement to 'behave as a human being' (*zuoren*) rather entails the discharge of duties attached to the five Confucian cardinal relationships: parent and child, ruler and minister/subject, husband and wife, elder and younger, and friend and friend.

---

60   'The Works of Mencius, Tsin-sin' *The Four Books* (translated by James Legge) (Oxford, 1892) Pt 2, p. 483.
61   Woo, *op. cit.*, p. 114.
62   Chung-ying Cheng 'Transforming Confucian Virtues into Human Rights: A Study of Human Agency and Potency in Confucian Ethics' in W. Theodore De Bary and Tu Weiming (eds) *Confucianism and Human Rights* (1998) pp. 142, 144.
63   Chang, *op. cit.*, p. 117.
64   *Idem.* p. 118.
65   Cheng, *op. cit.*, pp. 145-6.
66   Cheng, *op. cit.*, p. 145.
67   Cheng, *op. cit.*, p. 148.
68   Kwok, *op. cit.*, p. 85.

Duties are thus prescribed for every level of the social hierarchy. Henry Rosemont Jr describes the relational obligations inherent in the cardinal relationships:

> So finally I come to the conceptual framework of Confucianism, wherein rights-talk was not spoken, and within which I am not a free, autonomous individual. I am a son, husband, father, grandfather, neighbour, colleague, student, teacher, citizen, friend. I have a very large number of relational obligations and responsibilities, which severely constrain what I do. These responsibilities occasionally frustrate or annoy, they more often are satisfying and they are always binding . . . And my individuality . . . will come from the specific actions I take in meeting my relational responsibilities ... [69]

The only way to be a good person (*haoren*) or to attain self-fulfillment is to discharge one's duties efficiently within this network of behavioural rites. So, for instance, friends are to fulfill their Confucian social duty of mutual respect and mutual assistance towards each other. One of the most important behavioural guidelines to emerge from the five cardinal relationships (specifically from the parent-child relationship) in traditional Chinese society was that of filial piety. This concept imposes a duty upon children to respect and obey their parents and to care for them when they are old and infirm. When persons are in their prime, they care for the elderly and will be cared for in turn when their time comes. Its rationale appears to rest on the recognition that one owes one's very existence to one's parents, that their sacrifices in raising a child are considerable and that one should repay the debt out of a sense of gratitude.[70] This notion of filial piety is so deeply entrenched in the Chinese psyche that in contemporary China it has taken the form of a constitutional duty of parental support. Article 46 of the *Constitution of the People's Republic of China* of 4 December 1982 states in part that '[c]hildren have the duty to support their parents'.

Ancient China was also a society steeped in Confucian 'rites'. The most comprehensive Confucian discussion of the rites is to be found in *The Record of Rites* (*Liji*) which asserts that without the rites, no individual behaviour can be performed properly.[71] The rites were developed essentially to promote individual self-discipline on the one hand and social harmony and political order on the other.[72] They defined every person's position, role and duty (*fen*) - his or her share of the responsibilities each has within the life of the group to which he or she belongs. The rites also prescribed how one should interact with others and how to act reasonably (by, for example, avoiding excesses). Confucius emphasised that in adhering to the rights, a person should conduct himself or herself in a respectful manner. For example, in performing the rites of filial piety, a child should not merely provide parents with physical care but should do so with respect and in a

---

69   H. Rosemont Jr 'Human Rights: A Bill of Worries' in W. Theodore De Bary and
      Tu Weiming (eds) *Confucianism and Human Rights* (1998) pp. 54, 63-4.
70   Chang, *op. cit.*, p. 122.
71   *Idem.* p. 128.
72   Cheng, *op. cit.*, p. 142.

cheerful manner.[73] Thus, the rites served as external standards for judging whether the behaviour of a person is in accordance with his or her *fen*.[74] The ultimate objective of the rites, according to *The Analects* and *The Record of Rites*, is to assist human beings in interacting harmoniously with one another.[75] Confucius considered the rites to be an intrinsic part of a person's nature such that a cultivated person would come to realise and appreciate them through intuition and reason. Those who lacked the skill of introspection must have such moral guidelines imposed on them in the form of external rules. Traditionally, the rites were embodied either in customary uncodified law (*Li*) or in the penal code (*Fa*) which was for the ordinary people who were uneducated and motivated to moral behaviour through fear of punishment. From a contemporary moral viewpoint, the practice of the five virtues and adherence to the system of rites represented a community-based ethic of devotion to the common good.[76] Chinese values were thus determined by the rites of moral behaviour and, unlike the West, were not based on any abstract belief in individual rights. But, as Kwok points out, 'it is not that China's civilization of several thousand years did not recognize individuality, but that it did not feel compelled to turn individuality into a belief in individualism'.[77]

Confucianism was complemented by Taoism and Buddhism. Taoism is a system of religion and philosophy which is based on the teachings of Lao-tse, a Chinese philosopher, who advocated a simple, humble, pious and honest life, natural harmony, and non-interference with the course of natural events. Buddhism is an Asian philosophy founded by the Indian philosopher Gautama Buddha in the fifth century B.C. and later imported into China. It essentially teaches universal benevolence, kindness and compassion as well as regard by human beings for all sentient things around them. Buddhism also taught that perfect bliss could be attained through the extinction of individuality (*nirvana*). These three philosophical schools eventually became integrated into the practical aspects of living in Chinese culture and shaped the traditional Chinese view of life.[78] In combination, they generated a feeling of compassion in human beings towards all beings which entailed the discharge of both negative duties of forbearance and positive duties of assistance. Confucianism, Taoism and Buddhism also repudiated any attempt to separate, conceptually and ontologically, the essential being of the human person from the universe as a whole.[79] Self and society were perceived as an indivisible whole. In view of the acceptance of universal unity and harmony by these three schools, the necessity to protect persons from the community or State through the recognition of inalienable human

---

73   Chang, *op. cit.*, p. 128.
74   *Idem.* pp. pp. 128-9.
75   *Idem.* p. 129.
76   Cheng, *op. cit.*, p. 143.
77   Kwok, *op. cit.*, p. 88.
78   Woo, *op. cit.*, p. 115.
79   *Ibid.*

rights was never acknowledged.[80] These philosophies were more conducive to the promotion of virtuous sentiments in rulers than to the desire for rebellion to gain individual rights for the Chinese people, who were never conscious of having such rights.[81]

In contrast to the Western tradition which perceives human beings as free, autonomous and atomistic units involved in a continual competitive struggle for the vindication of his or her rights, the Chinese believe that no person lives independently of other people or of his or her community. There was never any clear consciousness of the meaning of a person independent of his or her family and society.[82] For the Chinese, human beings are not born autonomous and self-supporting but rather achieve this status through society by the performance of their Confucian social duties. This belief in the inherent sociality of human beings, combined with the rejection of individualism inherent in the Buddhist concept of *nirvana* and the feeling of concern for others which has underlain the three Chinese philosophical schools, motivated the Chinese to realise themselves by being naturally and morally harmonious with others. As Professor Peter Woo has observed:

> [T]he goal of self-realization was not the obtaining of personal advantage but a rational and moral concern for the welfare of other members of a family or a community ... This kind of life perspective cannot allow the struggle for personal freedom, at the expense of other people's happiness, to be a genuine goal of morality. In other words, the general view of life, for a Chinese person, is to submerge his [or her] ego, to disappear, and to be absorbed into the universal harmony.[83]

The Chinese conviction that a person exists for others and is dependent on other people translated the Western notion of freedom to do as one pleases into the Chinese version to do what one would prefer not to do when a higher goal is to be obtained by a concern for the welfare of others.[84] Although Confucianism did not recognise the concepts of 'rights' or 'human rights', the dignity and worth of human beings remained central to its teachings. The Confucians maintained that people should treat each other with love and respect and help one another to live a good, human way of life. In the Confucian utopia, everyone is to have a proper share of this world's bounty.[85] In the following passage, Wejen Chang answers the question of how such a share would be possible for a philosophy and society which had never embraced these concepts:

> [T]he Confucians not only did not talk about 'human rights', they did not talk about 'rights' at all. One may wonder how the ancient Chinese . . . could do

---

80   *Ibid.*
81   *Idem.* p. 117.
82   *Idem.* p. 119.
83   *Ibid.*
84   *Idem.* p. 121.
85   Chang, *op. cit.*, p. 133.

without a concept of 'rights'; yet whenever a person claims a certain 'right', his claim can be fruitful only if others concerned are willing to honor it. The West looks at the relationship from the side of the claimant and gives great weight to his claim; the Confucians looked at it from the other side and considered the willingness of other people to accomodate the claims. Thus, it is not that the Confucians did not think a person could claim something as his due. He could, and it was called his entitlement or 'share' (*fen*). But ... a *fen* is strictly a societal product – a person's *fen* is a share of what is created by the joint efforts of many members in a society, which they see fit to let him enjoy. The validity of a *fen* is thus dependent on the goodwill of those concerned; a person is not born with a *fen*, his *fen* is what his society allows or assigns to him.[86]

Confucianism produced a communitarian society in which duty to family and society pre-empted individual interests. In Confucian society, there was no room for the freestanding, autonomous and unassailable individual. The individual was rather perceived as acting in accordance with the rites within an inter-related and interdependent network of social relations in order to contribute to the harmony of the whole. In traditional Chinese society, the individual was inexorably bound to the collectivity. As Cheng explains:

> As the collective experience of society and community has overwhelmed individual experience, the reality of individual life has been dominated by concerns about the preserving of human relationships so as to secure one's place in society and community. This is how rites and virtue arose together in ancient Chinese culture. Consequently, the primary or immediate consciousness of a human person has been one's power or ability to develop family and community order and harmony as a base for developing oneself as an individual. It has not been to assert oneself first against some political authority . . .[87]

In a similar vein, C. K. Yang observes:

> Self-cultivation, the basic theme of Confucian ethics ... did not seek a solution to social conflict in defining, limiting, and guaranteeing the rights and interests of the individual or in the balance of power and interests between individuals. It sought the solution from the self-sacrifice of the individual for the preservation of the group.[88]

A portion of the Confucian communitarian legacy can be found in the statements by representatives of various Asian governments at the 1993 Vienna World Conference on Human Rights. For example, the Head of the Chinese Delegation maintained that '[n]obody shall place his [or her] own rights and interests above those of the state and society, nor should he [or she] be allowed to impair those of

---

86　　*Idem.* p. 132.
87　　Cheng, *op. cit.*, p. 145.
88　　C. K. Yang *Chinese Communist Society: The Family and the Village* (1959) p. 172.

others and the general public'.[89]   The Malaysian Minister of Foreign Affairs complained:

> Another conceptual lacuna in the current debate on human rights is the manifest emphasis on individual rights at the expense of the rights of the community. The rights of the individual are certainly not in splendid isolation from those of the community.[90]

And, in a direct reference to three of the Confucian cardinal relationships, the Myanmar Minister for Foreign Affairs pointed out that '[i]n ... Myanmar culture, there are precepts about the duties and obligations of the wise ruler to his subjects, parents to their offspring, husband to wife, and vice versa'.[91]   In the context of preparations for the 1993 World Conference on Human Rights, ministers and representatives of Asian states met at Bangkok, Thailand from 29 March to 2 April 1993 pursuant to United Nations General Assembly Resolution 46/116 of 17 December 1991.   On 2 April 1993, the *Bangkok Declaration* was adopted, purporting to contain 'the aspirations and commitments of the Asian region' on human rights issues. Principle 8 makes a tangible, albeit indirect, reference to the important influence of Confucianism on Asian thinking on such issues.   While conceding the universal nature of human rights, Principle 8 insists on 'the significance of national and regional particularities and various historical, cultural and religious backgrounds' being borne in mind in the process of international norm-setting. Arguably, this is a veiled reference to the traditional Asian political ethic that individual interests must be balanced against, and restrained by, societal or communal interests.

Further evidence of the significant influence of Confucianism in Asia today may be garnered from the People's Republic of China and Singapore. It may be argued that Chinese communism/socialism is a logical twentieth-century extension of the rich Confucian heritage in view of their similarities: both place emphasis upon individual self-sacrifice in the interests of community harmony and the collective good. This particular view of the relation between the state and the individual is constitutionally mandated in Article 48 of the *Constitution of the People's Republic of China* of 4 December 1982 which states that '[w]hen exercising their freedoms and rights, citizens of the People's Republic of China must not infringe upon the interests of the State, of society and of the collective, or upon the lawful freedoms and rights of other citizens'. At the opposite end of the political spectrum (in theory, at least), the governments of Singapore and Malaysia have consistently and aggressively argued that the cultural matrix with which

---

89   Statement by Liu Huaqui, Head of the Chinese Delegation, Vienna, 17 June 1993 as contained in J. Tang (ed.) *Human Rights and International Relations in the Asia-Pacific* (1995) p. 215.

90   Statement by Datuk Abdullah Haji Ahmad Badawi, Minister of Foreign Affairs, Malaysia, Vienna, 18 June 1993 as contained in J. Tang, *op. cit.*, p. 236.

91   Statement by U Ohn Gyaw, Minister for Foreign Affairs and Chairman of the Delegation of the Union of Myanmar, Vienna, 15 June 1993 as contained in J. Tang, *op. cit.*, p. 223.

relations between the individual and the State are embedded is fundamentally different in Asian traditions from that of the Western liberal democratic tradition. In 1991, the Singaporean government released an official statement entitled *Shared Values* which emphasised the core Asian values including that of placing society above self and resolving conflicts through consensus rather than confrontation. Despite official claims to the contrary, the communitarian ideals contained in *Shared Values* borrowed heavily from Confucian teachings.[92]

An examination of the basic tenets of Confucianism and of the other main values underpinning contemporary Chinese culture provides a rather different perspective from which the West might learn and grow. Although some non-Western societies may not express moral concerns within a framework of human rights, they may nonetheless legitimately address those concerns within some other conceptual framework, be it an ethical or religious system. In the view of one American commentator, the Confucian tradition is not well served by scholars examining Confucianism for precursors of the human rights concept. Much more will be gained, according to Henry Rosemont Jr, by perceiving the Confucian vision as an alternative to that offered by the Western liberal democratic tradition (and one that may be applied *mutatis mutandis* in the West).[93] As Rosemont argues:

> [W]e should study Confucianism as a genuine alternative to modern Western theories of rights, rather than merely as a potentially earlier version of them. When it is remembered that three-quarters of the world's peoples have, and continue to define themselves in terms of, kinship and community rather than as rights-bearers, we may come to entertain seriously the possibility that if the search for universal moral and political principles is a worthwhile endeavor, we might find more of a philosophical grounding for those principles and beliefs in the writings of Confucius ... than those of John Locke ... and [his] successors.[94]

---

92   The Singaporean government's *Shared Values* policy statement will be discussed in greater detail in Chapter 6.

93   Rosemont, *op. cit.*, p. 60.

94   *Idem.* p. 64 (footnote excluded).

Chapter 5

Individual Criminal Responsibility Under International Law

> While rights exalt individual liberty, duties express the dignity of that liberty.[1]

Introduction

This chapter will examine the extent to which international law has come to impose legal obligations or duties directly upon private individuals. As we shall see in the next chapter, numerous international human rights instruments adopted at the international and regional levels since World War II have expressly recognised that individual human beings possess various human rights which should be respected by their governments. It would appear that today international law by corollary imposes certain duties upon individuals not to commit serious breaches of human rights against others. Thus, a separate branch of international law known as international criminal law has emerged to hold individuals criminally responsible for such breaches. Some human rights breaches are regarded as so serious that they are considered crimes against the international community as such (and punishable as international crimes either at the international or national level). These include piracy, slavery, war crimes, crimes against humanity and genocide. Both conventional and customary international law will be examined with a view to illustrating the emerging trend towards the imposition of a greater number and range of duties upon private individuals to refrain from committing gross human rights violations against other human beings.

The Decline of Traditional Positivist Doctrine in International Law

Traditionally, international law has been mainly concerned to regulate the relations between independent sovereign states (and, more recently, between such states and international intergovernmental organisations). According to the traditional positivist doctrine of international law concerning the position of the individual thereunder, since international law is based on the common consent of individual

---

1   Second preambular paragraph of the 1948 *American Declaration of the Rights and Duties of Man*.

states, and not of individual human beings, states are 'subjects' of international law and private individuals are merely its 'objects'. The significance of this distinction meant that only states were incumbents of rights and duties under international law; private individuals, on the other hand, were merely subject to regulation thereunder in terms of their conduct.

According to positivist doctrine, private individuals possessed rights and obligations within their own country and in any foreign country in which they happened to be residing. There they enjoyed civil capacity and could sue and be sued. They might also commit crimes and suffer punishment. But this could only be done pursuant to the provisions of public and private national or domestic law. Subject to some important exceptions to be discussed in the next section, only the actions of states, and not the actions of private individuals, could be prosecuted within the international sphere.[2] The traditional positivist doctrine was described by Oppenheim as follows:

> Since the Law of Nations is based on the consent of the individual State, and not of individual human beings, States solely and exclusively are the subjects of International Law. This means that the Law of Nations is a law for the individual conduct of States, and not of their citizens . . . An individual human being . . . is never directly a subject of International Law.[3]

For the past 150 years or so, international law has been undergoing a gradual, yet significant, shift from the traditional positivist doctrine to focussing more attention upon the private individual as a legitimate subject of international law. Increased communication and intercourse provide more and more cases that require regulation by international law but that can only be subsumed under positivist doctrine with increasing difficulties. It is clear that the positivist doctrine no longer reflects contemporary realities.[4]

This current trend towards the 'individualisation' of international law has now been recognised and accepted by numerous textwriters.[5] Treaty-based and

---

2   H. Triepel 'Les rapports entre le droit interne et le droit international' *Recueil des cours de l'Academie de droit international de La Haye* 1923-I (Paris, Hachette, 1925) pp. 77-118.

3   L. Oppenheim *International Law: A Treatise* Volume I, *Peace*, H. Lauterpacht (ed.) (London, Longmans, Green, 8th ed., 1955) para. 13.

4   Erica-Irene A. Daes *Freedom of the Individual under Law: A Study of the Individual's Duties to the Community and the Limitations on Human Rights and Freedoms under Article 29 of the Universal Declaration of Human Rights* (United Nations, New York, 1990) p. 43.

5   See, for example, I. Brownlie *Principles of Public International Law* (4th ed., 1990) pp. 37, 561; J. G. Starke *Introduction to International Law* (10th ed., 1989) pp. 58-60; T. Buergenthal *International Human Rights* (1988) pp. 52, 128, 177-9; T. Meron *Human Rights in Internal Strife: Their International Protection* (1987) p. 34; P. Sieghart *The International Law of Human Rights* (1983) p. 42. See also J. Paust 'The Other Side of Right: Private Duties Under Human Rights Law' (1992) 5 Harvard Human Rights Journal p. 51.

customary international law does impose duties on private individuals as such, as well as on states, to maintain the peace and respect humanity by refraining from committing international crimes. It is now generally recognised that there are acts or omissions concerning which international law imposes criminal responsibility on private individuals and for which punishment may be imposed, either by international tribunals or national courts and military tribunals.[6] The United States executive branch of government has acknowledged this trend in a memorandum as *Amicus Curiae* in the case of *Filartiga v Pena-Irala* when it stated that international laws can 'directly create rights and duties of private individuals ... [and] an area in which they do create such rights and duties is the sphere of the minimum standard for the protection of human rights.'[7] In a similar vein, the seventh paragraph of Principle VII of the Final Act of the Helsinki Conference on Security and Co-operation in Europe adopted on 1 August 1975 alludes to the possession by individuals of rights and duties in the field of human rights.[8] Also, in those countries where international treaties are self-executing, international law can impose international rights and duties directly upon their citizens. So, for example, Article 25 of the *Basic Law for the Federal Republic of Germany* of 23 May1949 states:

> The general rules of international law shall be an integral part of federal law. They shall override laws and directly establish rights and obligations for the inhabitants of the federal territory.

The Evolution of the Principle of Individual Duty in International Law

Nearly four centuries ago, the Dutch scholar, jurist and diplomat Grotius (1583-1645) published his treatise entitled *De Jure Belli ac Pacis* (The Law of War and Peace) (1625). One of the principal themes discussed therein was the attribution of international rights and duties to individuals considered apart from their states. This Grotian recognition of private individual duties under international law is clearly reflected in the following passage taken from Justice Wilson's charge to the grand jury in an early American case:

> When men have formed themselves into a political society ... they cannot, by this union, discharge themselves from any duties which they previously owed to those

---

6   Brownlie, *op. cit.*, 561. It is significant to note that in the aftermath of World War II, the International Military Tribunal at Nuremberg and numerous national tribunals did not admit pleas by accused individuals charged with war crimes that they had acted in accordance with their national law.

7   630 F. 2d 878 (2d Cir. 1980) (No. 79-6090) at 18-9 (quoting the Constitutional Court of Germany).

8   The Final Act was signed by representatives of thirty-five states, including the United States and the U.S.S.R. Although the Final Act constitutes an important statement of intent to act in conformity with existing human rights obligations, the instrument is not a treaty carrying legally binding obligations.

who form a part of the political association. Under all the obligations due to the universal society of the human race, the citizens of the state still continue ... On states as well as individuals the duties of humanity are strictly incumbent ... [9]

In certain circumstances, the individual was perceived as coming under an international law duty, customary or conventional, to refrain from committing particular heinous acts. The cases of piracy, slavery and violations of the laws and customs of war constituted, in the words of Professor Starke, a 'natural stumbling block'[10] for the traditional positivist doctrine. These cases are often cited as examples in support of the contention that individuals are subjects, and not mere objects, of international law.[11]

Piracy and Slavery

Under customary rules of international law, the offence of piracy *jure gentium* was regarded as a crime against the law of nations. Accordingly, any individual alleged to have committed this international crime on the high seas was liable to be apprehended, tried and punished by any state as an enemy of humanity. In his dissenting opinion in the *Lotus* case, Judge Moore described the offence of piracy *jure gentium* and the principle of universal jurisdiction which attached to it as follows:

> In the case of what is known as piracy by law of nations, there has been conceded a universal jurisdiction under which the person charged with the offence may be tried and punished by any nation into whose jurisdiction he may come ... Piracy by law of nations, in its jurisdictional aspects, is *sui generis*. Though statutes may provide for its punishment, it is an offence against the law of nations; and as the scene of the pirate's operations is the high seas, which it is not the right or duty of any nation to police, he is denied the protection of the flag he may carry, and is treated as an outlaw, as the enemy of all mankind - *hostis humani generis* - whom any nation may in the interest of all capture and punish.[12]

This customary rule conceding a universal jurisdiction on all states to arrest, prosecute and punish pirates (irrespective of their nationality or the place of the commission of the offence) was to ensure that such a serious offence did not go unpunished. This rule has been described by Kelsen as a rule 'imposing a legal duty directly upon individuals and establishing individual responsibility'.[13] The only other well-established case of universal jurisdiction attaching to an international crime is the case of war crimes which will be discussed in the next section.

---

9   *Henfield's Case* 11 F. Cas. 3099, 1107 (C.C.D.Pa. 1793) (No. 6, 360) *per* Wilson J.
10   Starke, *op. cit.*, p. 58.
11   Daes, *op. cit.*, p. 42.
12   P.C.I.J., Ser. A, No. 10 (1927), p. 70.
13   H. Kelsen *Peace Through Law* (1944) p. 76.

As a result of various international treaties, certain rights of protection and duties of forbearance have been respectively bestowed and imposed on slaves and slave-traders. For example, Article 13 of the *Geneva Convention on the High Seas* of 29 April 1958 states:

> Every State shall adopt effective measures to prevent and punish the transport of slaves in ships authorized to fly its flag, and to prevent the unlawful use of its flag for that purpose. Any slave taking refuge on board any ship, whatever its flag, shall, *ipso facto*, be free.

This provision has now been replicated in Article 99 of the United Nations *Convention on the Law of the Sea* of 10 December 1982. In addition, according to Professor Jordan Paust, there is simply no question that the *Slavery Convention* of 25 September 1926 and the *Supplementary Convention on the Abolition of Slavery, the Slave Trade, and Institutions and Practices Similar to Slavery* of 7 September 1956 implicate human rights and also attempt to regulate private actor behaviour.[14] For example, Article 3(1) of the latter instrument states:

> The act of conveying or attempting to convey slaves from one country to another by whatever means of transport, or of being accessory thereto, shall be a criminal offence under the laws of the States Parties to this Convention and persons convicted thereof shall be liable to very severe penalties.

Thus, in the cases of both piracy and slavery, rules of international customary and conventional law have respectively attempted to regulate the conduct of private individuals by imposing a duty upon them to refrain from committing these international crimes.

War Crimes

Private individuals can be punished for committing human rights violations in wartime. War crimes are violations of the laws and customs of armed conflict. Prior to World War II, private individuals had been prosecuted for such crimes which were traditionally tried and punished in the courts of the victim nation and usually by the victorious nation. Many of the war crimes trials held after World War II were conducted by military tribunals or national courts in nations which had been occupied by German forces (such as Poland, France and Holland). Military tribunals were also set up by the governments of the United Kingdom, the United States of America and Australia to hear charges against alleged Nazi and Japanese war criminals. Persons alleged to have committed war crimes have also been tried by courts or military tribunals in their own country.[15]

---

14   Paust, *op. cit.*, pp. 56-7.
15   During World War I, German submarines attacked and sank a number of British hospital ships in the unfounded belief that they were being used to transport troops and ammunition. In one case, defenceless survivors in a lifeboat from one of the ships, the *Llandovery Castle*, were fired upon. After World War I, the German

Although war crimes are crimes against international law,[16] the process for their punishment prior to World War II was one of municipal or military law in national courts or military tribunals. Towards the end of World War II when the Allies were formulating plans to prosecute war criminals, there was some uncertainty as to whether international law could reach out to punish heads of state, ministers and military and administrative functionaries responsible for initiating the war and authorising the perpetration of atrocities.[17] This uncertainty was largely driven by traditional positivist doctrine. In the event, however, this theoretical objection was cast aside pursuant to an agreement which was without precedent in international law and which marked the emergence of the modern international law on individual criminal responsibility as well as an international process for the prosecution of international crimes. On 8 August 1945, the *Agreement for the Prosecution and Punishment of the Major War Criminals of the European Axis*[18] was signed in London. The *Agreement* was signed by the United States of America, the United Kingdom of Great Britain and Northern Ireland, France and the Union of Soviet Socialist Republics. In the *Charter of the International Military Tribunal* annexed to the *Agreement*, the jurisdiction of the Nuremberg Tribunal extended to individual criminal responsibility for crimes against peace, war crimes and crimes against humanity, whether or not violations of the municipal law where the alleged violations took place had occurred. Article 6 of the *Charter* provided:

> The following acts, or any of them, are crimes coming within the jurisdiction of the Tribunal for which there shall be individual responsibility:
>
> (a) Crimes against peace. Namely, planning, preparation, initiation or waging of a war of aggression, or a war in violation of international treaties, agreements or assurances, or participation in a common plan or conspiracy for the accomplishment of any of the foregoing.
>
> (b) War crimes. Namely, violations of the laws or customs of war. Such violations shall include, but not be limited to, ill-treatment or deportation to slave labour or for any other purpose of civilian population of or in occupied territory, murder or ill-treatment of prisoners of war or persons on the seas, killing of

---

government refused to hand over alleged war criminals for trial, instead undertaking to hold its own war crimes trials. Charges laid against the German submarine commanders and others responsible for the sinking of hospital ships and shooting lifeboat survivors were among the few war crimes trials heard by the German Supreme Court in 1921. A more recent example is the trial and conviction by a United States military tribunal in 1971 of Lieutenant William Calley, a member of the armed forces of the United States of America, for atrocities against civilians at My Lai during the Vietnam War.

16   See, for example, The Hague *Convention IV concerning the Laws and Customs of War on Land* of 1907.

17   Starke, *op. cit.*, p. 61.

18   The text can be located at (1945) 39 *American Journal of International Law*, Suppl., pp. 258, 259-60. See also United Nations, *Treaty Series*, Vol. 82, 279.

hostages, plunder of public or private property, wanton destruction of cities, towns or villages, or devastation not justified by military necessity.

(c)   Crimes against humanity.   Namely, murder, extermination, enslavement, deportation, and other inhumane acts committed against any civilian population, before or during the war, or persecutions on political, racial or religious grounds in execution of or in connection with any crime within the jurisdiction of the Tribunal whether or not in violation of the domestic law of the country where perpetrated.

Although war crimes had existed prior to the Nuremberg *Charter*, its significance lay in the detailed exposition of offences which attracted individual criminal responsibility.   The third type of international crime dealt with in the *Charter* - crimes against humanity - was probably the most innovative for its time in 1945. The recognition of this offence was clearly designed to protect civilian populations, whether or not the offence took place in occupied territory.   Crimes against humanity were regarded as the most serious offences which could be perpetrated against the civilian population.   Although there may or may not exist some overlap between crimes against humanity and war crimes,[19] the offence of crimes against humanity under the Nuremberg *Charter* was somewhat limited in scope.   Such an offence would only have been committed if done 'in execution of or in connection with any crime within the jurisdiction of the Tribunal': in other words, the alleged crimes against humanity had to be somehow linked to war crimes or crimes against peace.   Recently, however, in the context of the Yugoslavian and Rwandan conflicts, insistence on such a linkage has been dropped and a more fundamental distinction between war crimes and crimes against humanity has begun to develop. That distinction is based on the requirement that crimes against humanity be perpetrated on a systematic or widespread scale.[20]   Thus, the offence must be driven by a policy which requires that a certain type of unlawful behaviour take place in a given situation, rather than being a random offence committed on a whim.[21]

Another important provision of the Nuremberg *Charter* was Article 7 which provided in part that '[t]he official position of the defendants, whether as Heads of State or responsible officials in Government Departments, shall not be considered as freeing them from [individual criminal] responsibility or mitigating punishment'.   The Nuremberg Tribunal was composed of judges from the four

---

19   For example, while the shooting of an unarmed civilian may constitute a war crime, the shooting of that same person because he or she belongs to a particular ethnic group may simultaneously constitute a crime against humanity if a policy to kill members of that ethnic group exists.

20   See Article 3 of the *Statute of the International Tribunal for Rwanda* of 8 November 1994 which expressly requires crimes against humanity be 'committed as part of a widespread or systematic attack against any civilian population'.

21   S. Kaye and R. Piotrowicz *Human Rights in International and Australian Law* (2000) p. 163.

major Allied Powers - the United States, the United Kingdom, France and the Soviet Union. Twenty-two leading Nazi officials, including Goering, Hess and von Ribbentrop, were arraigned before the Tribunal. After hearing evidence over many months of the atrocities for which it was alleged they were responsible, the Tribunal delivered its judgment on 30 September 1946. Nineteen of the accused Nazis were convicted. Seven were sentenced to imprisonment while the remainder were sentenced to death by hanging. In the following passage, the Nuremberg Tribunal recognised the concept of individual criminal responsibility under international law:

> It was submitted that international law is concerned with the actions of sovereign States, and provides no punishment for individuals; and further, that where the act in question is an act of State, those who carry it out are not personally responsible but are protected by the doctrine of the sovereignty of the State. In the opinion of the Tribunal, both these submissions must be rejected. *That international law imposes duties and liabilities upon individuals as upon States has long been recognized* ... the very essence of the [Nuremberg] Charter is that individuals have international duties which transcend the national obligations of obedience imposed by the individual State. He who violates the laws of war cannot obtain immunity while acting in pursuance of the authority of the State, if the State in authorising action moves outside its competence under international law ... Crimes against international law are committed by men, not by abstract entities, and only by punishing individuals who commit such crimes can the provisions of international law be enforced.[22]

In so holding, the Nuremberg Tribunal adopted a functional approach in so applying the concept of individual criminal responsibility explicitly stipulated by Article 6; to hold otherwise would have clearly frustrated the administration of justice. The foregoing passage shook the foundations of traditional positivist doctrine concerning the question of an individual's capacity to commit crimes against international law.[23] This judicial reasoning marked a significant development in international law with respect to the position of individuals thereunder. Prior to World War II, the concepts of an 'international crime' and individual criminal responsibility were virtually unknown within the international states system. The Nuremberg Tribunal, however, recognised that individuals are clearly capable of being regarded as subjects of international law and, accordingly, being made criminally responsible on an individual basis thereunder before an international forum. Subsequent United Nations practice concerning the setting up of the international criminal tribunals for the former Yugoslavia and Rwanda has effectively endorsed the stance taken by the Nuremberg Tribunal in this regard.

The trial of major Japanese war criminals was conducted in accordance with the same principles. General Douglas MacArthur, the Supreme Commander

22   Judgment delivered on 1 October 1946 by the International Military Tribunal at Nuremberg. Transcript of Proceedings, p. 16,878 (emphasis supplied by author). See also Official Record, Vol. I, *Official Documents*, at p. 223.
23   Daes, *op. cit.*, p. 42.

for the Allied Powers in the Far East, issued a special proclamation on 19 January 1946 establishing the International Military Tribunal for the Far East. The Tribunal was vested with jurisdiction similar to that of the Nuremberg Tribunal to hear charges of international crimes which had allegedly been committed within the Pacific theatre of war. Eleven countries[24] were represented on the Tribunal which sat at Tokyo to hear charges against twenty-eight Japanese accused of crimes against peace, war crimes and crimes against humanity. The judgment of the Tokyo Tribunal was delivered on 12 November 1948 and was largely based on the principles contained in the judgment of the Nuremberg Tribunal. Twenty-five of those accused were convicted. Seven were sentenced to death while the remainder were sentenced to imprisonment.

Apart from their recognition of the individual as a subject of international law to which rights and liabilities could be directly attributed by international law, the Nuremberg and Tokyo Tribunals were the first war crimes tribunals to be set up at the international level and, as such, constituted precursors of the international criminal tribunals for the former Yugoslavia and Rwanda and for the International Criminal Court.[25] Article 6 of the Nuremberg *Charter*, moreover, has come to represent general international law.[26] In Resolution 95(I) adopted unanimously on 11 December 1946, the United Nations General Assembly affirmed 'the principles of international law recognized by the Charter of the Nuremberg Tribunal and the judgment of the Tribunal'.

The concept of individual responsibility under international criminal law confirmed by the Nuremberg and Tokyo Tribunals was reaffirmed and strengthened only a few years later when the International Law Commission formulated in 1950 an instrument entitled *Principles of International Law Recognized in the Charter of the Nuremberg Tribunal and in the Judgment of the Tribunal*.[27] As the title of the instrument suggests, it largely codifies or sets out existing law. The instrument addresses the criminal responsibility of individuals for the commission of certain international crimes: crimes against peace, war crimes and crimes against humanity. Principle I states: 'Any person who commits an act which constitutes a crime under international law is responsible therefore and liable to punishment'. Similar to the previously mentioned Article 7 of the Nuremberg *Charter*, Principle III provides that '[t]he fact that a person who committed an act which constitutes a crime under international law acted as Head of State or responsible government official does not relieve him from responsibility under international law'. Article 7 and Principle III recognise that gross human rights violations are perpetrated not only by those who actually carry them out but also by those who are behind such acts further up in the political and military chain

---

24   The eleven countries were Australia, Canada, China, France, India, Netherlands, New Zealand, Philippines, the United Kingdom of Great Britain and Northern Ireland, the Union of Soviet Socialist Republics and the United States of America.
25   The mandate of these tribunals will be discussed in succeeding sections.
26   Brownlie, *op. cit.*, p. 562.
27   *Report of the International Law Commission to the General Assembly* U.N. G.A.O.R., 5th Sess., Supp. No. 12, at 11, U.N. Doc. A/1316 (1950).

of command. Both provisions effectively negate the previously well established rule that heads of state enjoy immunity from criminal liability for acts or omissions while in office. International law would no longer countenance guilty individuals sheltering behind the veil of state sovereignty.

This international law trend towards attaching direct criminal responsibility to individuals was reaffirmed by the United Nations General Assembly on 9 December 1948 when it adopted the *Convention on the Prevention and Punishment of the Crime of Genocide.*[28] Article II of the Genocide Convention lists various acts (such as murder and the imposition of birth prevention measures) which, when 'committed with intent to destroy, in whole or in part, a national, ethnical, racial or religious group, as such', will be deemed to constitute the international crime of genocide. Pursuant to Article I, '[t]he Contracting Parties confirm that genocide, whether committed in time of peace or in time of war, is a crime under international law which they undertake to prevent and to punish'.[29] In its extension to 'time of peace', Article I thereby constitutes an expansion of the scope of the international crime of genocide over that of Article 6 of the Nuremberg *Charter* which, as we have already noted, requires a linkage between crimes against humanity (which include genocide) and either war crimes or crimes against peace. Consistent with Article 7 of the Nuremberg *Charter* and Principle III of the *Principles of International Law Recognized in the Charter of the Nuremberg Tribunal and in the Judgment of the Tribunal*, Article IV of the *Genocide Convention* states that '[p]ersons committing genocide . . . shall be punished, whether they are constitutionally responsible rulers, public officials *or private individuals*' (emphasis supplied). Thus, Article IV explicitly provides for individual criminal responsibility while making no concession of immunity to heads of state or government officials. Article VI of the *Genocide Convention* requires that persons charged with genocide 'shall be tried by a competent tribunal of the State in the territory of which the act was committed, or by such international penal tribunal as may have jurisdiction with respect to those Contracting Parties which shall have accepted its jurisdiction'.[30]

The proposition that private individuals, as subjects of international law, possess certain duties thereunder not to commit international crimes involves by corollary the further proposition that they can also be the bearers of international rights. In the immediate aftermath of World War II, the direct imposition of duties on individuals and the attribution of international criminal responsibility for breaches thereof went hand in hand with the vesting of human rights in individuals under international law. One of the main purposes of the United Nations identified in Article 1(3) of its *Charter* is 'promoting and encouraging respect for human

---

28   Approved by United Nations General Assembly Resolution 260 A (III) of 9 December 1948 (entry into force 12 January 1951).

29   The use of the word 'confirm' is significant in denoting that Article I is merely purporting to be declaratory of existing international law.

30   Pursuant to Article 6 of the *Rome Statute* which will be discussed later in this chapter, the International Criminal Court is vested with jurisdiction to try persons accused of genocide as defined by the *Genocide Convention*.

rights and for fundamental freedoms for all'. And, one day after the United Nations General Assembly adopted the *Genocide Convention*, it adopted and proclaimed on 10 December 1948 the *Universal Declaration of Human Rights*,[31] many of whose provisions are now widely conceded to have fallen into the *corpus* of international customary law. The effect of these developments was the recognition of individual human beings as independent jural entities within the international legal system. Not only would individuals be internationally criminally responsible for breaches of international duties; they would also enjoy rights independently of the states under whose jurisdiction they resided. As from the end of World War II, international law became applicable *ex proprio vigore* to individuals directly, and not only through the intermediary activity of states.[32]

The Geneva Conventions

Yet another prominent example of the individual bearing individual responsibility under international law is the four *Geneva Conventions* of 1949 which in substance provide for individual responsibility for serious human rights violations or 'grave' breaches of obligations which are laid down therein.[33] The *Geneva Conventions* seek to provide assistance and protection for combatants, prisoners of war and civilians caught up in land and maritime armed conflicts. The primary enforcement method adopted in the *Geneva Conventions* is the imposition of penal sanctions for grave breaches of the *Conventions*. The relevant provisions are:

> *Geneva Convention for the Amelioration of the Condition of the Wounded and Sick in Armed Forces in the Field of August 12, 1949* Articles 49 and 50;

> *Geneva Convention for the Amelioration of the Condition of Wounded, Sick and Shipwrecked Members of Armed Forces at Sea of August 12, 1949* Articles 50 and 51;

> *Geneva Convention Relative to the Treatment of Prisoners of War of August 12, 1949* Articles 129 and 130;

> *Geneva Convention Relative to the Protection of Civilian Persons in Time of War of August 12, 1949* Articles 146 and 147.

'Grave breaches' are defined in the four *Geneva Conventions* to include the following acts when committed against persons or property protected by the *Conventions*:

- wilful killing, torture or inhuman treatment, including biological experiments;

---

31 United Nations General Assembly Resolution 217 A (III) of 10 December 1948.
32 Daes, *op. cit.*, 42 and n. 95.
33 It would appear, however, that many of the obligations contained in the *Geneva Conventions* of 1949 already existed in general international law: see *Nicaragua v United States (Merits), I.C.J. Reports* (1986), 14 at 113-5 (paras. 217-20).

- wilfully causing great suffering or serious injury to body or health;

- extensive destruction and appropriation of property, not justified by military necessity and carried out unlawfully and wantonly;

- compelling a prisoner of war or civilian to serve in the forces of the hostile power;

- wilfully depriving a prisoner of war or civilian of the rights of fair and regular trial;

- taking of civilian hostages;

- unlawful deportation or transfer or unlawful confinement of a civilian.

Although the *Geneva Conventions* of 1949 avoid the term 'war crimes' in relation to 'grave breaches' listed in the above-mentioned provisions, there can be no doubt that grave breaches are tantamount to war crimes (and international crimes) and are concerned with individual responsibility for breaches of the laws of war.[34] The language employed in the British *Manual of Military Law* (Part III: *The Law of War on Land*) leaves no doubt that the individual is regarded as being bound directly by the laws of war.[35] Indeed, Article 85(5) of the *Protocol Additional to the Geneva Conventions of 12 August 1949, and Relating to the Protection of Victims of International Armed Conflicts (Protocol I)* states in part that 'grave breaches of these instruments [that is to say, of the *Geneva Conventions* of 1949 *and Protocol I*] shall be regarded as war crimes'.

    States which are parties to the four *Geneva Conventions* of 1949 'undertake to enact any legislation necessary to provide effective penal sanctions for persons committing, or ordering to be committed, any ... grave breaches ...'[36] They are also under an obligation to search for such persons and to bring them, regardless of their nationality, before their own courts for prosecution. Alternatively, a High Contracting Party 'may also, if it prefers, and in accordance with the provisions of its own legislation, hand such persons over for trial to another High Contracting Party concerned, provided such High Contracting Party has made out a *prima facie* case'. This primary enforcement mechanism common to the four *Geneva Conventions* essentially vests a universal jurisdiction on High Contracting Parties to prosecute war criminals.[37] There is no requirement that the

---

34   Brownlie, *op. cit.*, p. 563.

35   *Ibid.* See also *H.M.S.O.* (1958), para. I.

36   For example, in 1957, Australia ratified the four *Geneva Conventions* and Parliament enacted legislation to fulfill Australia's obligation to prosecute individuals alleged to have committed grave breaches of the Conventions. The *Geneva Conventions Act 1957* provides punishment for those individuals, regardless of their nationality, found guilty of having committed a grave breach of the Conventions, either in Australia or elsewhere.

37   For the application of the principle of universal jurisdiction to piracy, see an earlier section of this Chapter entitled 'Piracy and Slavery'.

accused be tried in the country where the alleged grave breaches were committed. This is to make it more difficult for suspects to escape justice by fleeing to another jurisdiction. This mechanism also adopts the *aut punire aut dedere* principle: that is, the offender is either to be punished by the state on whose territory he or she is found or is to be surrendered (extradited) to a state which is competent and desirous of assuming jurisdiction. Consistently with state practice prior to World War II, alleged offenders are to be prosecuted in national courts.

Apart from the grave breaches enforcement provisions discussed above, it is clear that the four *Geneva Conventions* of 1949 directly confer rights on private individuals as subjects of international (humanitarian) law. This proposition is implicit in those provisions of the *Conventions* which provide that in no circumstances may protected persons (wounded and sick soldiers, shipwrecked persons, chaplains, medical personnel, prisoners of war and civilians) renounce the rights secured to them under the *Conventions*.[38] By corollary, it is not surprising that a number of private individual duties have also been prescribed by the *Conventions*.[39] So, for example, Article 18 of *the Geneva Convention for the Amelioration of the Condition of the Wounded and Sick in Armed Forces in the Field* requires members of the civilian population to respect wounded and sick soldiers and to abstain from offering them violence. Pursuant to Article 53 of the same *Convention*, both public and private individuals are to abstain at all times from using the emblem or designation 'Red Cross'. Under the *Geneva Convention for the Amelioration of the Condition of Wounded, Sick and Shipwrecked Members of Armed Forces at Sea*, Article 46 imposes a duty on the Commanders-in-Chief of the High Contracting Parties to ensure the detailed execution of the operative provisions of that Convention. In terms of the *Geneva Convention Relative to the Treatment of Prisoners of War*, Article 12 alludes to the 'individual responsibilities' of individual soldiers to treat prisoners of war humanely at all times. Pursuant to Article 39, the responsible commissioned officer placed by the detaining power in charge of a prisoner-of-war camp is under a duty to ensure that the provisions of that *Convention* are known to the camp staff and guard and is responsible for its application. On the other hand, under Article 50, prisoners of war may be compelled to do certain types of work listed therein which have no military character or purpose.[40] And, under the *Geneva Convention Relative to the Protection of Civilian Persons in Time of War*, Article 29 alludes to the possibility

---

38   See Article 7 of the First, Second and Third *Conventions* and Article 8 of the Fourth *Convention*.

39   J. Pictet *IV Commentary, Geneva Convention Relative to the Protection of Civilian Persons in Time of War* (1958) 79, 581.

40   Other operative provisions of the *Prisoner of War Convention* which purport to impose individual duties include Article 32 (prisoners of war who, though not attached to the medical service of their armed forces, are physicians, surgeons, dentists, nurses or medical orderlies, may be required by the detaining power to exercise their medical functions in the interests of prisoners of war) and Article 80 (prisoners' representatives are placed under a duty to 'further the physical, spiritual and intellectual well-being of prisoners of war'.).

of 'individual responsibility' which may be incurred by agents of the occupying power for the maltreatment of the civilian population. Article 64 of the same *Convention* indirectly imposes a duty on individual members of the civilian population of occupied territory to obey measures which are deemed essential to enable the occupying power to fulfill its obligations thereunder and to maintain the orderly government of the territory.

All of the foregoing provisions relate to international armed conflicts occurring between two or more High Contracting Parties. Article 3 of each of the four *Geneva Conventions* of 1949 (widely referred to as common Article 3), however, is limited in its scope of application to 'armed conflict not of an international character' (in other words, internal armed conflicts or civil wars) occurring in the territory of one of the High Contracting Parties. Apart from requiring that wounded and sick combatants be collected and cared for, common Article 3 imposes on soldiers of each party to the conflict a duty to treat humanely in all circumstances persons taking no active part in the hostilities, including civilians and soldiers who have surrendered or been placed *hors de combat* through sickness, wounds or detention. Common Article 3 specifically prohibits the following acts:

- violence to life and person, in particular murder of all kinds, mutilation, cruel treatment and torture;

- taking of hostages;

- outrages upon personal dignity, in particular humiliating and degrading treatment;

- the passing of sentences and the carrying out of executions without previous judgment pronounced by a regularly constituted court, affording all the judicial guarantees which are recognized as indispensable by civilized peoples.

Although none of the four *Geneva Conventions* of 1949 include amongst their grave breaches provisions violations of common Article 3, it is nonetheless still open to each High Contracting Party to prosecute alleged war criminals in their own courts and pursuant to national legislation. It is clear that common Article 3, by its terms, attempts to regulate the conduct not only of members of the regular armed forces of each High Contracting Party but also those who are parties to the internal conflict but who lack the status of state actors or those acting under the colour of the State.[41]

The Cold War, the Vietnam War and post-colonial struggles for self-determination prompted a substantial review of the four *Geneva Conventions* of 1949 in the mid-1970s. This review culminated in the strengthening of international humanitarian law in the form of the adoption in 1977 of two protocols additional to these *Conventions*: *Protocol Additional to the Geneva Conventions of 12 August 1949, and Relating to the Protection of Victims of International Armed*

---

41   Paust, *op. cit.*, p. 58.

Conflicts (Protocol I) and *Protocol Additional to the Geneva Conventions of 12 August 1949, and Relating to the Protection of Victims of Non-International Armed Conflicts (Protocol II).* While both *Protocol I* and *Protocol II* are designed to supplement the provisions of the four *Geneva Conventions* of 1949, the former instrument applies only to international armed conflicts while the latter is restricted in its application to internal armed conflicts or civil wars.

In extending the obligations assumed by the High Contracting Parties under the *Geneva Conventions* of 1949 to prosecute and punish war criminals, Article 85 of *Protocol I* adds the following acts as grave breaches thereof which, as noted previously, are to be regarded as war crimes pursuant to Article 85(5):

• the carrying out of physical mutilations or medical or scientific experiments on protected persons which are not indicated by the state of their health and which are not consistent with generally accepted medical standards (see Article 11);

• making the civilian population the object of attack;

• launching an indiscriminate attack affecting the civilian population or civilian objects in the knowledge that such attack will cause excessive loss of life, injury to civilians or damage to civilian objects;

• launching an attack against works or installations containing dangerous forces in the knowledge that such attack will cause excessive loss of life, injury to civilians or damage to civilian objects;

• making non-defended localities and demilitarized zones the object of attack;

• making a person the object of attack in the knowledge that he or she is *hors de combat* ;

• the perfidious use of the distinctive emblem of the red cross;

• the transfer by the occupying power of parts of its own civilian population into the territory it occupies, or the deportation or transfer of the population of the occupied territory within or outside this territory, in violation of Article 49 of the *Geneva Convention Relative to the Protection of Civilian Persons in Time of War of August 12, 1949* (so-called 'ethnic cleansing');

• unjustifiable delay in the repatriation of prisoners of war or civilians;

• practices of *apartheid* and other inhuman and degrading practices involving outrages upon personal dignity, based on racial discrimination;

• making the clearly-recognised historic monuments, works of art or places of worship which constitute the cultural or spiritual heritage of the population the object of attack;

• depriving a protected person of the rights of fair and regular trial.

Another important innovation achieved by *Protocol I* is the imposition of various duties on the military commanders of the High Contracting Parties relating to the prevention and investigations of breaches of the four *Geneva Conventions* of 1949 and of *Additional Protocol I*. The relevant provision is Article 87 which states in part:

> Article 87 - *Duty of Commanders*
>
> 1. The High Contracting Parties ... shall require military commanders, with respect to members of the armed forces under their command ... to prevent and, where necessary, to suppress and report to competent authorities breaches of the Conventions and of this Protocol.
>
> 2. In order to prevent and suppress breaches, High Contracting Parties ... shall require that ... commanders ensure that members of the armed forces under their command are aware of their obligations under the Conventions and this Protocol.
>
> 3. The High Contracting Parties . . . shall require any commander who is aware that subordinates or other persons under his control are going to commit or have committed a breach of the Conventions or of this Protocol, to initiate such steps as are necessary to prevent such violations of the Conventions or this Protocol, and, where appropriate, to initiate disciplinary or penal action against violators thereof.

In terms of the strengthening of international humanitarian law as it applies to civil wars, *Protocol II* represents, by contrast, a more modest result. Although *Protocol II* does extend the range of protections available in internal armed conflicts, like common Article 3 of the *Geneva Conventions* of 1949, it is devoid of 'grave breaches' provisions which impose obligations on High Contracting Parties to prosecute and punish serious breaches of *Protocol II*. Article 4 of *Protocol II* supplements common Article 3 by adding the following acts to those which cannot be taken against protected persons: collective punishments, acts of terrorism, rape, enforced prostitution, slavery and pillage. The commission of such acts will not constitute a grave breach of *Protocol II*, although it is possible, as is the case with common Article 3, for High Contracting Parties to prosecute alleged war criminals in their own courts pursuant to national legislation. Article 7 also imposes a duty on government soldiers and private individuals to respect and protect the wounded and sick, whether or not they have taken part in the armed conflict.

The Eichmann Case

The importance of this case lies in how the Israeli Government and courts were willing and prepared to rely on the principle of universal jurisdiction to bring Adolf Eichmann to justice for having violated his international duties not to commit the international crimes of genocide, war crimes and crimes against humanity.

Adolf Eichmann was a lieutenant-colonel in the *Gestapo* (the Nazi secret police) and Head of the Jewish Office during World War II. He was placed in charge of the 'Final Solution' - the policy which led to the extermination of approximately six million Jews in German and occupied territories. Eichmann escaped from Europe, thereby evading trial with the other major Nazi war criminals at Nuremberg. He was located in Argentina in 1960, abducted by Israeli undercover agents and brought to Israel for trial. He was charged under the Israeli *Nazi and Nazi Collaborators (Punishment) Law* of 1951, before the District Court in Jerusalem, with crimes against the Jewish people (in other words, genocide), crimes against humanity and war crimes.

Eichmann's defence counsel put forward a number of preliminary jurisdictional objections at the trial: that as a German national, Eichmann was not subject to the laws of the Israeli *Knesset* (Parliament), and that as Eichmann's actions occurred in Europe during World War II before the State of Israel was actually founded, the alleged offences were committed against people who were not Israeli citizens. The District Court rejected these objections, however, stating:

> The abhorrent crimes defined in this [1951] Law are not crimes under Israel law alone. These crimes, which struck at the whole of mankind and shocked the conscience of nations, are grave offences against the law of nations itself ... Therefore, so far from international law negating or limiting the jurisdiction of countries with respect to such crimes, international law is, in the absence of an International Court, in need of the judicial and legislative organs of every country to give effect to its criminal interdictions and to bring the criminals to trial. The jurisdiction to try crimes under international law is universal.[42]

The links between Eichmann's actions and the State of Israel were, moreover, obvious enough. Although Israel did not exist as a nation when the crimes took place, as the state of the Jewish people, it had close links to the victims, both living and deceased. As the 'victim country' it had a legal and moral right to try and punish those accused of serious violations of the human rights of the Jewish people and, indeed, had asserted its jurisdictional competence to that effect by enacting the 1951 legislation. The District Court accordingly found Eichmann guilty of the crimes with which he was charged and he was sentenced to death. The Supreme Court of Israel, sitting as an appellate court, relied on and applied the principle of universal jurisdiction in upholding the conviction and sentence.[43] Eichmann was hanged in May 1962.

The International Crimes of Apartheid and Hostage-Taking

Two further developments of the 1970s reaffirmed the notion that individuals owe international duties to humanity and possess a responsibility derived therefrom. These developments took the form of the adoption by the United Nations General Assembly of the *International Convention on the Suppression and Punishment of*

---

42   *Eichmann v Attorney-General of Israel* (1961) 36 *I.L.R.* 5.
43   *Eichmann v Attorney-General of Israel* (1962) 36 *I.L.R.* 277.

the Crime of Apartheid on 30 November 1973[44] and of the *International Convention Against the Taking of Hostages* on 17 December 1979.[45]

Article II of the *Apartheid Convention* defines the crime of *apartheid* by reference to a list of acts 'committed for the purpose of establishing and maintaining domination by one racial group of persons over any other racial group of persons and systematically oppressing them'. Pursuant to Article I, '[t]he States Parties ... declare that *apartheid* is a crime against humanity ...' Individual criminal responsibility shall apply in terms of Article III, irrespective of the motive involved, to individuals, members of organisations and institutions and state representatives whenever they commit, or are otherwise involved in the commission of, the crime of *apartheid*. Persons charged with the crime of *apartheid* 'may be tried by a competent tribunal of any State Party to the Convention which may acquire jurisdiction over the person of the accused or by an international penal tribunal having jurisdiction with respect to those States Parties which shall have accepted its jurisdiction' (Article V). As previously mentioned, Article 85(4)(c) of *Additional Protocol I* declares that practices of *apartheid* constitute grave breaches thereof. It is also worthwhile noting that the crime of *apartheid* is included within the category of 'crimes against humanity' as that category is defined by Article 7(1)(j) of the *Rome Statute* setting up the International Criminal Court. Nevertheless, in contrast to the *Apartheid Convention*, the scope of application of this offence is considerably restricted by Article 7 of the *Rome Statute* which requires that crimes against humanity be committed as part of 'a widespread or systematic attack directed against any civilian population'. There is no such limitation in the *Apartheid Convention*.

Pursuant to Article 5 of the *Hostages Convention*, each State Party is required to take such measures as may be necessary to establish its jurisdiction over the offence of 'hostage-taking' which is defined in Article 1 in the following terms:

> Any person who seizes or detains and threatens to kill, to injure or to continue to detain another person (hereinafter referred to as the 'hostage') in order to compel a third party, namely, a State, an international intergovernmental organization, a natural or juridical person, or a group of persons, to do or abstain from doing any act as an explicit or implicit condition for the release of the hostage commits the offence of taking of hostages ('hostage-taking') within the meaning of the Convention.

The offence of hostage-taking also constitutes a war crime. As we have already seen, hostage-taking constitutes a breach of common Article 3 of the four *Geneva Conventions* of 1949 in the context of civil war as well as a grave breach in international armed conflicts. Hostage-taking is also considered to be a war crime,

---

44   United Nations General Assembly Resolution A/RES/3068 (XXVIII).
45   United Nations General Assembly Resolution 34/146.

in the context of both international and internal armed conflicts, by Article 8 of the *Rome Statute* setting up the International Criminal Court.[46]

What these conventions demonstrate is that certain breaches of human rights are considered so serious that they have been acknowledged to constitute crimes of concern to the international community as such. Both conventions purport to regulate not only the conduct of public officials but that of private individuals as well.

The International Criminal Tribunals for the Former Yugoslavia and Rwanda and the International Criminal Court

In 1991, the federal State of Yugoslavia began to disintegrate when the Republics of Slovenia and Croatia declared their independence therefrom. Soon afterwards, the Republic of Bosnia-Herzegovina followed suit and a ferocious inter-ethnic conflict involving Muslims, Croats and Serbs broke out in 1992. This conflict was notable not so much for the way the combatants fought each other but for the gross maltreatment of civilians and detainees. Crimes of the utmost cruelty, including murder, rape, ethnic cleansing, disappearances and starvation of detainees, were perpetrated on a mass scale. The United Nations Security Council was eventually stung into action when, on 25 May 1993, it decided to act under Chapter VII of the *Charter of the United Nations* (entitled 'Action With Respect to Threats to the Peace, Breaches of the Peace, and Acts of Aggression') which permits the Council to take action to deal with threats to international peace and security. Accordingly, the Security Council adopted *Resolution 827 (1993) on Establishing an International Tribunal for the Prosecution of Persons Responsible for Serious Violations of International Humanitarian Law Committed in the Territory of the Former Yugoslavia.*[47] This resolution establishes the International Tribunal for the Former Yugoslavia (hereinafter referred to as the 'ITY') and sets out its constituent document known as the *Statute of the International Tribunal.*

Like the Nuremberg Tribunal, the ITY does not have general jurisdiction. Under Article 1 of its *Statute*, its competence is limited to the prosecution of 'persons responsible for serious violations of international humanitarian law committed in the territory of the former Yugoslavia since 1991 ...' Four types of crime are made punishable under the *Statute*: grave breaches of the *Geneva Conventions* of 1949, violations of the laws or customs of war, genocide, and crimes against humanity. Article 2 vests the ITY with the power to prosecute persons committing, or ordering to be committed, grave breaches of the *Geneva Conventions* of 1949.[48] Pursuant to Article 3 (which appears under the rubric 'Violations of the laws or customs of war'), the ITY is granted the power to

---

46 See Article 8(2)(a)(viii) (international armed conflicts) and Article 8(2)(c)(iii) (internal armed conflicts).

47 (1993) 32 International Legal Materials 1192 (text of Statute), 1203 (text of Resolution).

48 For the full list of such grave breaches, see the earlier section of this chapter entitled 'Geneva Conventions'.

prosecute persons who are alleged to have committed other war crimes not already addressed by Article 2. These other war crimes include, but, in terms of Article 3, are not limited to the following:

•   employment of poisonous weapons or other weapons calculated to cause unnecessary suffering;

•   wanton destruction of cities, towns or villages, or devastation not justified by military necessity;

•   attack, or bombardment, by whatever means, of undefended towns, villages, dwellings, or buildings;

•   plunder of public or private property.

The meaning of Article 3 was discussed in *Prosecutor v Tadic (Jurisdiction)*[49] where the ITY held (at paragraphs 87 and 89) that Article 3 was merely illustrative of the offences included, and that it includes all violations of international humanitarian law not included in Articles 2, 4 and 5 of the *Statute* of the ITY. The significance of this holding is that Article 3 therefore includes breaches of common Article 3 of the *Geneva Conventions* of 1949, thereby establishing the ITY's jurisdiction over the Yugoslavian conflicts, whether or not they are considered to be internal or international in nature.   Article 4 of the ITY's *Statute* vests jurisdiction in it to prosecute persons alleged to have committed genocide as that crime is defined by Article II of the *Genocide Convention*. Article 5 grants to the ITY the power to prosecute persons alleged to have committed the following crimes against humanity provided they were committed in armed international or internal conflict and directed against any civilian population: murder, extermination, enslavement, deportation, imprisonment, torture, rape, persecutions on political, racial and religious grounds, and other inhumane acts.

As for individual criminal responsibility, Article 6 of the ITY *Statute* vests the ITY with jurisdiction over natural persons.   Article 7(1) states that '[a] person who planned, instigated, ordered, committed or otherwise aided and abetted in the planning, preparation or execution of a crime [which is within the ITY's jurisdiction], shall be individually responsible for the crime'.   Consistently with Article 7 of the Nuremberg *Charter*, Principle III of the *Nuremberg Principles* and Article IV of the *Genocide Convention*, Article 8(2) of the ITY *Statute* provides that '[t]he official position of any accused person, whether as Head of State or Government or as a responsible Government official, shall not relieve such person of criminal responsibility nor mitigate punishment'.   This negation of official immunity recently came into play with the apprehension and prosecution of Slobodan Milosevic, the former President of the Federal Republic of Yugoslavia, before the ITY in The Hague.   The individual criminal responsibility of commanding officers is dealt with in Article 7(3) which reads:

---

49   (1996) 35 *International Legal Materials* p. 32.

> The fact that [any of the crimes over which the ITY has jurisdiction] was committed by a subordinate does not relieve his superior of criminal responsibility if he knew or had reason to know that the subordinate was about to commit such acts or had done so and the superior failed to take the necessary and reasonable measures to prevent such acts or to punish the perpetrators thereof.

It would appear that Article 7(3) exceeds the level of responsibility engaged by Article 86(2) of *Additional Protocol I* which does not go so far as to cover the case of a superior officer who, although not otherwise involved, becomes aware afterwards of the commission of the offence but fails to take any investigatory or punitive action. Article 86(2) of *Additional Protocol I* states in part:

> The fact that a breach of the Conventions or of this Protocol was committed by a subordinate does not absolve his superiors from ... responsibility ... if they knew, or had information which should have enabled them to conclude in the circumstances at the time, that he was committing or was going to commit such a breach and if they did not take all feasible measures within their power to prevent or repress the breach.

The judgment of the International Tribunal for Yugoslavia in the case of *Prosecutor v Tadic (Merits)*[50] is significant for its observations on individual criminal responsibility. After analysing various precedents, the ITY concluded (at para. 669) that customary international law already recognised the notion of individual criminal responsibility as outlined in Article 7 of the ITY *Statute*. The *Tadic* case offers a useful assessment of what level of involvement is required before one is considered to be a participant in the commission of an international crime. Although Tadic was convicted of personally committing a number of such crimes, he was also found guilty of participating indirectly in the commission of others by encouraging others to commit them. The ITY calibrated the requisite level of involvement (at para. 689) as follows:

> ... aiding and abetting includes all acts of assistance by words or acts that lend encouragement or support, as long as the requisite intent is present ... presence alone is not sufficient if it is an ignorant or unwilling presence.

The International Tribunal for Rwanda (hereinafter referred to as the 'ITR') was set up by the United Nations Security Council on 8 November 1994, acting under the same powers it had invoked to establish the ITY. The Council had by that time satisfied itself that the inter-ethnic conflict between the Tutsi and Hutu peoples of Rwanda had developed into a threat to international peace and security. The *Statute of the International Tribunal for Rwanda* is set out in Security Council *Resolution 955 Establishing the International Tribunal for Rwanda*.[51] Pursuant to Article 1 of its *Statute*, the ITR 'shall have the power to prosecute persons

---

50   (1997) 36 *International Legal Materials* p. 908.
51   (1994) 33 *International Legal Materials* p. 1598.

responsible for serious violations of international humanitarian law committed in the territory of Rwanda and Rwandan citizens responsible for such violations committed in the territory of neighbouring States, between 1 January 1994 and 31 December 1994 ...' While the statutes of the ITY and the ITR have much in common, there are some differences concerning crimes for which individual criminal responsibility will arise. The similarities include the provisions concerning personal jurisdiction (Article 5 ITR *Statute*; Article 6 ITY *Statute*), individual criminal responsibility (Article 6 ITR *Statute*; Article 7 ITY *Statute*) and the crime of genocide (Article 2 ITR *Statute*; Article 4 ITY *Statute*). The differences between the two statutes stem from the differences in the nature of the two conflicts. In the former Yugoslavia, the conflict tended to be more of an international armed conflict while the Rwandan situation tended towards an internal struggle characterised more by genocidal acts rather than any crimes committed as part of an armed conflict. Thus, the definition of 'crimes against humanity' in Article 3 of the ITR *Statute*, unlike Article 5 of the ITY *Statute*, does not require such crimes to take place in the context of an armed conflict. Instead, a crime against humanity will be committed 'when committed as part of a widespread or systematic attack against any civilian population on national, political, ethnic, racial or religious grounds'. Furthermore, the internal nature of the Rwandan conflict is reflected in Article 4 of the ITR *Statute* which vests jurisdiction in the ITR to prosecute persons alleged to have committed serious violations of common Article 3 of the four *Geneva Conventions* of 1949 and of *Additional Protocol II*.[52] Significantly, in the Rwandan context, Article 4, unlike the *Geneva Conventions*, effectively elevates the status of such violations to 'grave breaches' to which individual criminal responsibility will attach.

The most significant development to date in the institutionalisation of an international criminal justice system was the adoption of the *Rome Statute of the International Criminal Court* on 17 July 1998.[53] The International Criminal Court (hereinafter referred to as the 'ICC') is intended to be a permanent or standing international court, unlike its *ad hoc* predecessors which, as we have seen, were concerned only with particular conflicts. At the Rome Conference, consensus was achieved around the nucleus of serious offences which tend to occur during international armed conflicts and civil wars. Article 5 of the *Rome Statute* limits the ICC's jurisdiction to 'the most serious crimes of concern to the international community as a whole': genocide, crimes against humanity, war crimes and the crime of aggression.[54] One of the most significant improvements made in the *Rome Statute* to common Article 3 of the *Geneva Conventions* of 1949 and

---

52   As noted earlier, both deal with non-international armed conflict.

53   Pursuant to Article 126(1) of the *Rome Statute*, it will enter into force on the first day of the month after the 60th day following the date of the deposit of the 60th instrument of ratification. The *Rome Statute* entered into force on 1 July 2002. As of 1 July 2002, there were 139 signatories and 77 parties to the *Rome Statute*.

54   Although the crime of aggression was not included in the statutes of the ITY and the ITR, the crime against peace was included in the respective jurisdictional mandates of the Nuremberg and Tokyo Tribunals.

Additional Protocol II of 1977 is to extend the definition of 'war crimes' to include a comprehensive list of acts in Article 8(2)(e) which occur in 'armed conflict not of an international character'. Now, under the *Rome Statute*, serious violations of common Article 3 and *Additional Protocol II* will be regarded as war crimes within the ICC's jurisdiction. As noted previously, such contraventions did not constitute grave breaches under the *Geneva Conventions* or *Additional Protocol II* and High Contracting Parties were accordingly under no legal obligation to prosecute.

Article 25 of the *Rome Statute* is the critical provision which deals with individual criminal responsibility. Pursuant to Article 25 (1) and (2) respectively, the ICC is granted jurisdiction over natural persons and any person who commits a crime within the jurisdiction of the Court 'shall be individually responsible and liable for punishment'. Article 25(3) engages responsibility for a range of conduct including the individual or joint commission of a crime, the ordering, solicitation or inducement of the commission of a crime, and the aiding, abetting or otherwise assisting in its commission. Article 27 adheres to past precedents in declaring that ' ... official capacity as a Head of State or Government, a member of a Government or Parliament, an elected representative or a government official shall in no case exempt a person from criminal responsibility ... '. Article 28 is cast in very similar terms to Article 86 (2) of *Additional Protocol I* in its imposition of a duty on military commanders to exercise control over his or her forces to prevent the commission of crimes within the ICC's jurisdiction. A military commander will be criminally responsible for crimes committed by forces under his or her effective control when the commander had either actual or constructive knowledge that the forces were committing, or about to commit, such crimes but failed to take 'all necessary and reasonable measures within his or her power to prevent or repress their commission'.

Conclusion

This chapter has attempted to illustrate that numerous contemporary treaties do impose duties either directly or indirectly on public and private individuals *qua* individuals and as subjects of international law. A discernible trend towards international instruments purporting to reach private, non-state conduct is evident.[55] The growing panoply of treaties reaffirming the notion of individual criminal responsibility for serious human rights violations confirms that individual duties not to commit international crimes are now well established under both conventional and customary international law. This is as it should be. The outrages upon human dignity inherent in slavery, war crimes, crimes against humanity, genocide, hostage-taking and *apartheid*, when perpetrated at the hands of private individuals or groups, are no more tolerable and can be no less destructive than those imposed under the colour of state authority.[56]

---

55   Paust, *op. cit.*, p. 59.
56   *Id.* p. 62.

Chapter 6

The Position of Individual Duty within the International and Regional Human Rights System

> Everyone has duties to the community in which alone the free and
> full development of his personality is possible.[1]

Introduction

In the preceding chapter, numerous international humanitarian law instruments were examined and a number of private or individual duties identified in the context of the protection of human rights during times of armed conflict. The focus of this chapter will be the identification and discussion of the position of individual duties contained in international and regional human rights instruments in the peacetime context.

It has been said that 'the language of individual duty in the universal human rights system is rare'.[2] One of the main purposes of this chapter will be to test the accuracy of that proposition. The author will attempt to demonstrate that a significant number of human rights instruments adopted at both the international and regional levels since World War II has provided explicit or implied recognition of private or individual duties. These instruments not only impose obligations on governments; they also impose duties on individuals and groups. Human rights instruments demonstrate the existence of individual duties in two basic ways.[3] First, human rights are generally conferred without any express reference to the scope of the correlative duty or those who owe such duty. Nevertheless, it is clear that private individuals do owe a correlative duty to the right-holder. So, for instance, the effective exercise of the right to freedom of expression contained in Article 19 of the *Universal Declaration of Human Rights* of 1948 requires other individuals to respect that right. Secondly, human rights instruments sometimes

---

1   Article 29(1) of the *Universal Declaration of Human Rights* of 1948.
2   H. Steiner and P. Alston *International Human Rights in Context: Law, Politics, Morals* (1996) p. 181.
3   J. Paust 'The Other Side of Right: Private Duties Under Human Rights Law' (1992) 5 *Harvard Human Rights Journal* pp. 51, 52.

explicitly affirm that private individuals do owe duties. It is with this second situation that this chapter is primarily concerned.

The Position of Individual Duties Under International Human Rights Instruments

At the United Nations Conference on International Organization held in San Francisco in 1945, which drafted the *Charter of the United Nations*, a proposal was put forward which contained a declaration on the essential rights of human beings. This proposed declaration was to be appended to the *Charter* and become an integral part of it. One paragraph of the preamble of the declaration concerned the duties of individuals to the community. It read as follows:

> In society complete freedom cannot be attained; the liberties of the one are limited by the liberties of others, and the preservation of freedom requires the fulfilment by individuals of their duties as members of society.[4]

In the event, the Conference did not proceed with this proposal, stating that it required more detailed consideration.[5] The *Charter of the United Nations* was adopted by the San Francisco Conference and brought into force on 24 October 1945. Despite the failure of the Conference to adopt the proposal, Erica-Irene Daes, Special Rapporteur of the United Nations Sub-Commission on Prevention of Discrimination and Protection of Minorities, has argued that it is in the *Charter of the United Nations* that the individual first appears post-World War II as the bearer of fundamental human rights, duties and responsibilities.[6] The relevant preambular provisions of the *Charter* state:

WE THE PEOPLES OF THE UNITED NATIONS DETERMINED

> to save succeeding generations from the scourge of war, which twice in our lifetime has brought untold sorrow to mankind, and

> to reaffirm faith in fundamental human rights . . .

> [implicitly recognised their duty and undertook the responsibility]

> to promote social progress and better standards of life in larger freedom,

AND FOR THESE ENDS

---

4   United Nations Conference on International Organization, Document G/7 (g)(2).
5   Erica-Irene A. Daes *Freedom of the Individual under Law: A Study on the Individual's Duties to the Community and the Limitations on Human Rights and Freedoms under Article 29 of the Universal Declaration of Human Rights* (United Nations, New York, 1990) p. 17.
6   *Idem.* p. 53.

> to practise tolerance and live together in peace with one another as good neighbours, and

> to unite our strength to maintain international peace and security ...

These preambular provisions do not purport to impose on individuals any legally binding obligations to practise tolerance and live peaceably with one's neighbour, although they arguably possess an aspirational or moral charge. Nevertheless, Article 31(2) of the *Vienna Convention on the Law of Treaties* of 23 May 1969[7] does provide that '[t]he context for the purpose of the interpretation of a treaty shall comprise ... its preamble ...' It is therefore possible to interpret the human rights operative provisions[8] of the *Charter* in light of its preambular provisions.

The Universal Declaration of Human Rights

On 10 December 1948, the *Universal Declaration of Human Rights* (hereinafter referred to as the '*UDHR*') was unanimously adopted by the United Nations General Assembly in its Resolution 217A (III).[9] In supplementing and elaborating upon the human rights provisions[10] of the United Nations Charter, the *UDHR* marked the first step towards securing an *International Bill of Rights*.

The *UDHR* is essentially a generally accepted and comprehensive catalogue of the principal human rights and fundamental freedoms that United Nations member states considered in 1948 ought to be recognised as a matter of good policy. Its intended original and limited purpose was that of a 'pioneering' statement of ideals or aspirations. In its five decades of existence, however, the *UDHR* has come to be perceived as 'an authoritative guide ... to the interpretation of the [human rights] provisions in the [U.N.] Charter'.[11] The *UDHR* did not purport to have the status of a legally binding instrument when it was adopted in 1948. The overwhelming majority of U.N. member states did not regard the *UDHR* as creating any legal obligations.[12] Indeed, in a memorandum prepared in 1962 by the Office of Legal Affairs of the United Nations Secretariat, the effect of the use of the term 'declaration' was described as follows:

> In United Nations practice, a 'declaration' is a formal and solemn instrument, suitable for rare occasions when principles of great and lasting importance are being enunciated, such as the Declaration of Human Rights ... A 'declaration' ...

---

7   1155 *U.N.T.S.* p. 331; (1969) 8 *I.L.M.* p. 679 (entry into force 27 January 1980).
8   Article 1(3) of the *Charter* defines the purposes of the United Nations to include 'promoting and encouraging respect for human rights and for fundamental freedoms for all . . .' Article 55(c) states that the United Nations shall promote 'universal respect for, and observance of, human rights and fundamental freedoms for all without distinction . . .'
9   U.N. Doc. A/810 at 71 (1948).
10   See n. 8 *supra*.
11   I. Brownlie *Principles of Public International Law* (4th ed., 1990) pp. 570-571.
12   H. Lauterpacht *International Law and Human Rights* (1950) p. 413.

is adopted by resolution of a United Nations organ. As such it cannot be made binding upon Member States, in the sense that a treaty or convention is binding upon the parties to it, purely by the device of terming it a 'declaration' ... However, in view of the greater solemnity and significance of a 'declaration', it may be considered to impart, on behalf of the organ adopting it, a strong expectation that Members of the international community will abide by it. Consequently, in so far as the expectation is gradually justified by State practice, a declaration may by custom become recognized as laying down rules binding upon States.[13]

Nevertheless, the provisions of the *UDHR* have been enacted in municipal constitutional and ordinary legislation and cited in numerous international conventions.[14] National and international tribunals have also referred to the *UDHR* in their decisions.[15] As an authoritative guide to the interpretation of the human rights provisions of the *United Nations Charter*, the *UDHR* is regarded by the United Nations General Assembly itself and by numerous jurists as the *ius constituendum* of the United Nations Charter with regard to the term 'human rights and fundamental freedoms'.[16] The General Assembly declared in 1970 that the *Charter*-inspired human rights precepts embodied in the *UDHR* 'constitute basic principles of international law'.[17] These factors have contributed to the 'indirect legal effect'[18] of the *UDHR*.

Some commentators even contend that some of the provisions of the *UDHR* have now become part of customary international law.[19] Goler Teal Butcher observes:

---

13   See the report of the Commission on Human Rights on its eighteenth session, (*Official Records of the Economic and Social Council, Thirty-fourth Session, Supplement No. 8* (E/3616/Rev. 1)), para. 105.

14   See, for example, the *Preambles* of the *International Covenant on Civil and Political Rights* and the *International Covenant on Economic, Social and Cultural Rights* (both of which are cited and discussed *infra*). Almost all of the constitutions of the former French territories of Africa, including Benin, Gabon and the Ivory Coast, incorporate the provisions of the *U.D.H.R.* in their preambles by reference.

15   See, for example, *Robinson v Secretary-General of the United Nations* (1952) 19 *Int. L. R.* at 496; *Extradition of Greek Nationals* case (1955) 22 *Int. L. R.* at 524; *Vanderginste v Sulman* (26 April 1956) (Court of First Instance of Courtrai, Belgium) as reported in *Yearbook on Human Rights for 1956* (United Nations publication, Sales No. 58.XIV.2), p. 23 (*U.D.H.R.* used as a guide to the interpretation and application of national laws).

16   A. Pappas 'Introduction to Law and the Status of the Child' (1981-82) p. 13 *Columbia Human Rights Law Review* xxx.

17   G. A. Res. 2625 (XXV) (24 October 1970).

18   Brownlie, *op. cit.*, p. 571.

19   H. Waldock 'Human Rights in Contemporary International Law and the Significance of the European Convention' *International and Comparative Law Quarterly* Supplementary Publication No. 11 (1965) 1, pp. 14-15; R. Lillich 'Invoking International Human Rights Law in Domestic Courts' (1985) p. 54 *University of Cincinnati Law Review* pp. 367, 394-5.

Even though the [Universal] Declaration was intended as a hortatory instrument, to a significant extent it has gained, with respect to some of its provisions on civil and political rights, such universal consensus that its provisions on these rights are acknowledged generally to have become customary international law, that is binding on all states.[20]

Support for this view can be derived from the proceedings of the United Nations International Conference on Human Rights held in Teheran in 1968, with the *Proclamation of Teheran* solemnly proclaiming that 'the Universal Declaration of Human Rights states a common understanding of the peoples of the world concerning the inalienable and inviolable rights of all members of the human family and constitutes an obligation for the members of the international community'.[21]

The idea of combining individual rights and duties in a human rights document was first pioneered in the *UDHR*. Two types of individual duties appear in the *UDHR* - explicit and implicit (or correlative). Most of the provisions of the *UDHR* speak generally of the particular rights and freedoms of everyone without any mention of which person or entity might owe a corresponding duty. The implication of this is that most of the human rights enumerated in the *UDHR* can be claimed not merely against the State but also against groups or individuals.[22] This implication is reinforced by the language used in the preamble of the *UDHR* which '[p]roclaims this universal declaration of human rights as a common standard of achievement for all peoples and all nations, to the end that every individual and every organ of society … shall strive by teaching and education to promote respect for these rights and freedoms …' This suggests an implied duty resting on 'every individual' to adhere to the standards and spirit of the *UDHR*. Article 1 of the *UDHR* declares that all human beings 'should act towards one another in a spirit of brotherhood', implying both positive duties of beneficence and negative duties of forbearance. Article 30 prescribes an important qualification to the exercise of individual rights and freedoms: 'Nothing in this Declaration may be interpreted as implying for any State, group or person any right to engage in any activity or to perform any act aimed at the destruction of any of the rights and freedoms set forth herein'. Article 30 thus closely links the rights and freedoms enumerated in the *UDHR* with private or individual duties.

The most significant provision of the *UDHR* in terms of the explicit recognition of private, non-state duties is Article 29(1) which states: 'Everyone has duties to the community in which alone the free and full development of his [or her] personality is possible'. According to Meron, the drafters of the *UDHR*

---

20   G. Butcher 'The Relationship of Law to the Hunger Problem' (1987) 30 *Harvard Law Journal* pp. 193, 197.

21   U.N. Doc. A/CONF, 32/41, at 4; (1969) 63 *A.J.I.L.* p. 674.

22   Paust, *op. cit.*, p. 53.

regarded the individual as a direct subject of obligations.[23] According to Daes, 'this provision is of a moral nature in the sense that it lays down a general rule for individual behaviour in the community to which the individual belongs'.[24] The final wording of Article 29(1) constitutes a compromise text and is the product of complex and difficult preparatory work. When the terms of reference of the Commission on Human Rights were laid down by the Economic and Social Council in 1946, the first item on its work programme was 'An international bill of rights'. At its second session (6-17 December 1947), the Commission on Human Rights had before it the report of the Drafting Committee, to which were annexed various drafts that contained provisions concerning human duties. In the draft outline of an international bill of rights prepared by the United Nations Secretariat, one of the provisions proposed for inclusion in the preamble stated that ' ... man does not have rights only; he owes duty to the society of which he forms part'.[25] Another suggested provision on human duties read as follows:

> As human beings cannot live and achieve their objects without the help and support of society, each man owes to society fundamental duties which are: obedience to law, exercise of a useful activity, acceptance of the burdens and sacrifices demanded for the common good.

These proposals were ultimately rejected and there were concerns expressed by some delegations involved in the drafting process within the Commission on Human Rights that the draft text of Article 29(1) failed to contain any concrete individual duties whatsoever.[26] During the consideration of the draft international declaration of human rights by the Third Committee of the United Nations General Assembly, it was emphasised that it was not possible to draft a declaration of rights without proclaiming the duties implicit in the concept of freedom.[27] Moreover, it was impossible for the individual to be free of society, given the inherent social nature of human beings. It was therefore important to achieve a proper balance between individual and societal interests and between individual rights and collective rights. Individual liberty must therefore be balanced with the liberty of other individuals and with the reasonable demands of the community in order to further social stability.[28] It was also pointed out in the Third Committee that the purpose of Article 29(1) was to make plain the interdependence of individual rights

---

23   T. Meron *Human Rights in International Strife: Their International Protection* (1987) p. 34.

24   Daes, *op. cit.*, p. 17.

25   *Report of the Drafting Committee of an International Bill of Human Rights to the Commission on Human Rights* (E/CN.4/21), annex H, p. 94.

26   Report of the Commission on Human Rights on its third session (Lake Success, New York, 24 May-18 June 1948) (*Official Records of the Economic and Social Council, Seventh Session, Supplement No. 2* (E/800)), appendix, p. 31, subparagraph (e).

27   Daes, *op. cit.*, p. 19.

28   *Ibid.*

and duties. If an individual possessed natural and inalienable rights, he or she also had duties to society.[29]

The final version of Article 29(1) has been criticised for not affirming in detail the duties of individuals in relation to the community and the State. To be fair to the drafters, however, the main focus of the *UDHR* was the protection of the individual from the State by explicitly recognising individual rights. Nevertheless, given its particular position at the end of the operative provisions of the text of the *UDHR*, it is arguable that in imposing general, unspecified duties to the community on individuals, as opposed to enumerating specific duties, Article 29(1) effectively involves an overriding individual duty of respect for others and consideration of collective interests, to which the exercise of individual specified rights is conditioned. In explicitly mentioning individual duties to the community, Article 29(1) strikes a balance between the due recognition of individual human rights and the acknowledgement of individual duties to the community and the State.

The Refugees, Statelessness and Racial Discrimination Conventions

Between the adoption of the *Universal Declaration of Human Rights* in 1948 and the adoption of the Twin International Covenants[30] by the United Nations General Assembly in 1966, a number of important international conventions explicitly imposed individual duties on private or non-state actors. So, for example, Article 2 of *the Convention relating to the Status of Refugees* [31] of 28 July 1951 states:

> Every refugee has duties to the country in which he finds himself, which require in particular that he conform to its laws and regulations as well as to measures taken for the maintenance of public order.

Article 2 of the *Convention relating to the Status of Stateless Persons* [32] of 28 September 1954 imposes an identical duty on stateless persons.

Although somewhat less direct in its imposition of duties, the *International Convention on the Elimination of All Forms of Racial Discrimination* [33] of 21 December 1965 nonetheless imposes significant obligations on private individuals and groups not to engage in acts of racial discrimination. Article 1(1) of the *Convention* limits its imposed obligations to circumstances or events 'in the political, economic, social, cultural or any other field of public life'. However, as Paust and Meron observe, this 'public life' limitation does not limit obligations to

---

29   *Ibid.*

30   These instruments will be discussed in the next section of this chapter.

31   189 *U.N.T.S.* p. 137 (entry into force 22 April 1954).

32   Adopted on 28 September 1954 by a Conference of Plenipotentiaries convened under Economic and Social Council Resolution 526 A (XVII) of 26 April 1954 (entry into force 6 June 1960).

33   Adopted by the United Nations General Assembly as an annex to its Resolution 2106 (XX) on 21 December 1965. For the text see 660 *U.N.T.S.* p. 195 (entry into force 4 January 1969).

those of the State.[34] Private acts of discrimination are not beyond the purview of the *Convention* as long as they have, in terms of Article 1(1), the 'purpose or effect' of impermissibly affecting the enjoyment of human rights in a 'field of public life'. The potential reach of the *Convention* to private behaviour is illustrated more directly in those provisions of the *Convention* which prescribe measures which States Parties must take. Article 2(1)(d) requires each State Party to 'prohibit and bring to an end, by all appropriate means, including legislation as required by circumstances, racial discrimination by any persons, group or organization'. Article 4(b) also requires that States Parties 'declare illegal and prohibit organizations, and also organized and all other propaganda activities, which promote and incite racial discrimination, and shall recognize participation in such organizations or activities as an offence punishable by law'.

The Twin International Covenants

The adoption of the *Universal Declaration of Human Rights* by the United Nations General Assembly in 1948 marked the completion of the first stage of the United Nations' human rights agenda to achieve an 'International Bill of Rights'. The second stage envisioned the adoption of an international convention which would transform the principles contained in the *Universal Declaration* into legal obligations for those states ratifying or acceding to the convention.

On 16 December 1966, the General Assembly adopted[35] the *International Covenant on Civil and Political Rights* [36] and the *International Covenant on Economic, Social and Cultural Rights*.[37] Together with the *Universal Declaration of Human Rights*, these instruments comprise the 'International Bill of Rights', embracing an impressive panoply of civil, political, economic, social and cultural rights. Both *Covenants* are part of conventional international law and, as such, are legally binding on those states which have ratified or acceded to them. The *Covenants* are general and widely accepted international human rights agreements which have attributed the force of law to a more detailed version of the human rights catalogued by the *Universal Declaration*. Professor Brownlie has observed that 'the nature of the subject-matter is such that even for non-parties the content of the Covenants represents authoritative evidence of the content of the concept of human rights as it appears in the Charter of the United Nations'.[38]

The *International Covenant on Economic, Social and Cultural Rights* (hereinafter referred to as the '*ICESCR* ') prescribes in some detail such 'second

---

34   Paust, *op. cit.*, p. 59. T. Meron 'The Meaning and Reach of the International Convention on the Elimination of All Forms of Racial Discrimination' (1985) 79 *A.J.I.L.* pp. 283, 287, 291-304.

35   G.A. Res. 2200 (XXI), 21 U.N. G.A.O.R., Supp. No. 16 at pp. 49, 52.

36   U.N. Doc. A/6316 (1966) (adopted 16 December 1966; entered into force 23 March 1976).

37   U.N. Doc. A/6316 (1966) (adopted 16 December 1966; entered into force 3 January 1976).

38   I. Brownlie (ed.) *Basic Documents in International Law* (2nd ed., 1972) p. 150.

generation' rights as the right to work (Article 6), the right to society security (Article 9), the right to education (Article 13) and the right to an adequate standard of living (Article 11). The type of legal obligation assumed by States Parties to the *ICESCR* has been described as 'programmatic' in nature, in the sense that a State Party 'undertakes to take steps ... to the maximum of its available resources, with a view to achieving progressively the full realization of the rights recognized [thereunder]'.[39]

A number of the provisions of the *ICESCR* refer explicitly or impliedly to individual duties. Its fifth preambular paragraph recites the realisation of the States Parties 'that the individual, having duties *to other individuals* and to the community to which he [or she] belongs, is under a responsibility to strive for the promotion and observance of the rights recognized in the present Covenant' (emphasis supplied). In terms of the preparatory work concerning the fifth preambular paragraph, the work of the Commission on Human Rights at its fifth session (9 May-20 June 1949), particularly with regard to the preambular provisions of the Twin Covenants, was based upon the report of the Drafting Committee on an International Bill of Rights. This report stated in part:

> The Preamble shall refer to the four freedoms and to the provisions of the Charter relating to human rights and shall enunciate the following principles:
>
> ...
>
> (2) that man does not have rights only; he owes duties to the society of which he forms part;
>
> ...

At the Commission's eighth session, however, the delegations of Australia and Sweden submitted an amendment[40] to the wording of the proposed preambular provision on individual duties which was virtually identical to the present wording of the fifth preambular paragraph. The mover of this amendment stated that although the draft covenant before the Commission was concerned with the obligations of States, as States are the sum of individuals, the latter must co-operate if the covenant was to be implemented. The Australian-Swedish amendment was designed to emphasise this point very clearly.[41]

It is significant that the wording of the fifth preambular paragraph goes beyond that of Article 29(1) of the *Universal Declaration of Human Rights* in also recognising that individuals owe duties not only to their community but to other individuals. Nevertheless, as is the case with the preambular provisions of the *United Nations Charter*, the fifth preambular paragraph of the *ICESCR* does not purport to impose any legally binding duties on individuals. The duties are rather, at best, aspirational and moral in nature. Moreover, as with Article 29(1) of the

---

39   Article 2(1).
40   E/CN.4/L. p. 171.
41   E/CN.4/SR.308, p. 13.

Universal Declaration of Human Rights, the reference to individual duties is vague in neither prescribing the precise nature of the duties or their scope. On the other hand, the individual duties prescribed in the operative provisions of the *ICESCR* are more solemn and capable of legal enforcement against the individual. These individual duties involve obligations not to exercise one's rights in such a manner as to derogate from the collective good or to undermine the exercise by others of their rights. The two relevant *ICESCR* provisions are as follows:

> Article 4
>
> The States Parties . . . recognize that, in the enjoyment of those rights provided by the State in conformity with the present Covenant, the State may subject such rights only to such limitations as are determined by law only in so far as this may be compatible with the nature of these rights and solely for the purpose of promoting the general welfare in a democratic society.
>
> Article 5
>
> 1. Nothing in the present Covenant may be interpreted as implying for any State, group or person any right to engage in any activity or to perform any act aimed at the destruction of any of the rights or freedoms recognized herein, or at their limitation to a greater extent than is provided for in the present Covenant.

Article 4 arguably contains an implied duty such that it is incumbent on the individual not to exercise any of his or her *ICESCR* rights in such a manner as to compromise the general welfare. Article 5(1) is very similar to Article 30 of the *Universal Declaration of Human Rights* in imposing on individuals a duty not to engage in any activity or to perform any act whose purpose is to negate or limit any of the *ICESCR* rights enjoyed by others. It is possible in light of Article 31(2) of the *Vienna Convention on the Law of Treaties* to rely on the fifth preambular paragraph to interpret these operative provisions.[42] Thus, at a minimum, an individual must not deny or violate the *ICESCR* rights of others if he or she is to fulfill the preambular duty in relation 'to other individuals' to 'strive for the promotion and observance of the rights recognized in the [*ICESCR*]'.[43]

---

42   It is a normal function of the preamble of a treaty to give expression to its objectives and to act as an aid to interpretation of its operative provisions. For the purpose of the interpretation of a treaty, the meaning of the term 'context' of a treaty is defined in Article 31(2) of the *Vienna Convention on the Law of Treaties* as including the preamble.

43   Article 8(1)(a) of the *ICESCR* is also worthy of mention in relation to the right to form trade unions and the right to join the trade union of one's choice. Governments are permitted to impose restrictions prescribed by law on the exercise of these rights in the interests of national security or public order or for the protection of the rights of others. This implies that individuals should not exercise these rights in such a manner that would trigger the operation of these restrictions.

The *International Covenant on Civil and Political Rights* (hereinafter referred to as the '*ICCPR*') recognises such classical 'first generation' human rights as life (Article 6), liberty and security of the person (Article 9), equality before the law (Article 14) and the due process of law (Article 14). Like the *ICESCR*, it too explicitly and impliedly recognises private or individual treaties within its preamble and operative provisions; indeed, perhaps to a greater extent. The *ICCPR* also contains a fifth preambular paragraph and an Article 5(1) which are identical in language to their *ICESCR* counterparts and, accordingly, the same considerations previously discussed in relation to the latter provisions apply. The *ICCPR*, however, goes considerably beyond the *ICESCR*. Some of its provisions impliedly and indirectly impose a duty on individuals to respect the life, liberty, bodily integrity and dignity of other persons. So, for example, Article 6(1) of the *ICCPR* states:

> Every human being has the inherent right to life. This right shall be protected by law. No one shall be arbitrarily deprived of his life.

The words 'shall be protected by law' were intended to emphasise not only the obligation of States Parties to protect life but the duty of each individual to respect the international and municipal law concerning the protection of human life.[44] Other provisions of the *ICCPR* which also purport to prescribe an indirect, implied obligation on private individuals include the following:

> Article 7
>
> No one shall be subjected to torture . . .
>
> Article 8
> 1. No one shall be held in slavery; slavery and the slave-trade in all their forms shall be prohibited.
>
> Article 20
>
> 1. Any propaganda for war shall be prohibited by law.
>
> 2. Any advocacy of national, racial or religious hatred that constitutes incitement to discrimination, hostility or violence shall be prohibited by law.

In relation to torture, a State Party to the *ICCPR* must itself refrain from torture and must also use reasonable efforts to enforce that obligation against any private, non-governmental actor who tortures. In this context, the duties which are correlative to individual rights under the *ICCPR* affect private individuals as well as governments.[45] The prohibition of slavery contained in Article 8(1) consolidates previous such prohibitions under international law discussed in the previous

---

44   Daes, *op. cit.*, p. 58.
45   Steiner and Alston, *op. cit.*, pp. 278-9.

chapter and arguably also effectively imposes a duty on individuals to refrain from engaging in slavery or the slave-trade in view of its prohibition under both international and municipal law. As regards Article 20, sub-articles (1) and (2) thereof respectively impose an indirect duty on individuals to refrain from becoming involved with propaganda for war and to refrain from advocacy of national, racial or religious hatred that constitutes incitement to discrimination, hostility or violence.[46]

Apart from these provisions, there are five additional articles of the *ICCPR* which confer on individuals important human rights but which subject their exercise to the operation of so-called 'clawback' clauses. These articles include:

> Article 12
>
> 1. Everyone lawfully within the territory of a State shall, within that territory, have the right to liberty of movement and freedom to choose his residence.

> Article 18
>
> 1. Everyone shall have the right to freedom of thought, conscience and religion . .

> Article 19
>
> 2. Everyone shall have the right to freedom of expression . . .

> Article 21
>
> The right of peaceful assembly shall be recognized . . .

> Article 22
>
> 1. Everyone shall have the right to freedom of association with others, including the right to form and join trade unions for the protection of his interests.

In the case of each of these five articles, the government of each State Party to the *ICCPR* may impose restrictions on the exercise of the various human rights mentioned provided, however, that these restrictions are prescribed by law (for example, in statutes or regulations) and are necessary and imposed only for one or more of the following reasons:

---

46   Daes, *op. cit.*, pp. 53-4. In this context, see also Article 4 of the *International Convention on the Elimination of All Forms of Racial Discrimination* discussed *supra* and Articles II and III of the *International Convention on the Suppression and Punishment of the Crime of Apartheid* discussed in the preceding chapter.

- national security;

- public order (*ordre public*);

- the protection of public health or morals;

- the protection of the fundamental rights and freedoms of other individuals;

- public safety.

Article 19(3) of the *ICCPR* contains a clawback provision which is unique in explicitly mentioning 'special duties and responsibilities' incumbent on individuals. Article 19(3) states:

> The exercise of the rights provided for in paragraph 2 of this Article [relating to the right to freedom of expression] carries with it special duties and responsibilities. It may therefore be subject to certain restrictions, but these shall only be such as are provided by law and are necessary:
>
> (a) For respect of the rights or reputations of others;
>
> (b) For the protection of national security or of public order (*ordre public*), or of public health or morals.

Article 19(3) thereby acknowledges that freedom of expression is not only a precious heritage; it is also a delicate instrumentality given the ever-increasing powerful influence the modern media of expression exert.[47] Thus, the individual exercise of the right to freedom of expression is subject to municipal laws on slander and libel, treason and official secrets.

These clawback provisions of the *ICCPR* are a tacit recognition that the law not only protects individuals against each other and against the power of the State; the law also protects the State and the people against the exercise of excessive individualism. As one United Nations Special Rapporteur has observed:

> The ideal of the free individual does not mean that the individual is completely unrestrained and devoid of any responsibility towards his fellow human beings and the community ... The citizen should be aware that his is not the only will in the world, and he should be concerned, in one way or another, with bringing harmony out of the conflicting wills that exist within his community. The individual ... is essentially circumscribed by his neighbours.[48]

The clawback provisions recognise the practical reality that the exercise of human rights by individuals is not unqualified or absolute. Individuals are asked to reflect on how the exercise of their rights in particular circumstances might adversely

---

47   Daes, *op. cit.*, p. 58.
48   *Idem.* p. 52.

affect other individuals and the community. This duty to exercise human rights sensitively or responsibly is based on the presumption explicitly referred to in Article 29(1) of the *Universal Declaration of Human Rights* that the full development of the individual is only possible when individuals take care about how their conduct would impact on others. By rejecting the egotistical individual whose only concern is fulfilling self, the clawback provisions enhance the level of consideration owed to other individuals and the community.[49]

Examples of Recent International Conventions Recognising Individual Duties

Certain recent international conventions have explicitly recognised individual or private duties within their operative provisions. So, for example, Article 5(b) of the *Convention on the Elimination of All Forms of Discrimination Against Women* of 18 December 1979[50] provides that 'States Parties shall take all appropriate measures to ensure that family education includes a proper understanding of maternity as a social function and *the recognition of the common responsibility of men and women in the upbringing and development of their children ...*' (emphasis supplied by author). Similarly, Article 30 of the *Convention Concerning Indigenous and Tribal Peoples in Independent Countries* of 27 June 1989[51] states that 'governments shall adopt measures appropriate to the traditions and cultures of the peoples concerned, to make known to them their rights and duties, especially in regard to labour, economic opportunities, education and health matters, social welfare and their rights deriving from this Convention'. The individual duties to work and to acquire a basic education, in particular, will be discussed in the next chapter.

The Torture Convention

Although the United Nations *Convention Against Torture and Other Cruel, Inhuman or Degrading Treatment or Punishment* of 10 December 1984[52] purports to regulate only state-sponsored or condoned acts of torture, its scope of operation may well reach private, non-governmental conduct. Article 1(1) of the *Convention* defines the term 'torture' as follows:

---

49   Makau Wa Mutua 'The Banjul Charter and the African Cultural Fingerprint: An Evaluation of the Language of Duties' (1995) 35 *Virginia Journal of International Law* pp. 339, 369.

50   Adopted and opened for signature, ratification and accession by the United Nations General Assembly Resolution 34/180 of 18 December 1979 (entry into force 3 September 1981).

51   *Convention No. 169* adopted by the General Conference of the International Labour Organization at its 76th Session (entry into force 5 September 1991).

52   Adopted and opened for signature, ratification and accession by United Nations General Assembly Resolution 39/46 of 10 December 1984, U.N. G.A.O.R., 39th Sess., Supp. No. 51, at 197, U.N. Doc. A/39/51 (entry into force 26 June 1987).

> For the purpose of this Convention, the term 'torture' means any act by which severe pain or suffering, whether physical or mental, is intentionally inflicted on a person for such purposes as obtaining from him or a third person information or a confession, punishing him for an act he or a third person has committed or is suspected of having committed, or intimidating or coercing him or a third person ... *when such pain or suffering is inflicted by or at the instigation of or with the consent or acquiescence of a public official or other person acting in an official capacity* ... (emphasis supplied).

In so restricting the application of the *Convention* to acts of torture committed 'by or at the instigation of or with the consent or acquiescence of a public official or other person acting in an official capacity', it is clear that the misconduct intended to be addressed is acts of torture committed by the State or in its name rather than purely private acts of torture. Nevertheless, even if the person committing torture 'by or at the instigation of or with the consent or acquiescence of a public official' is not himself a public official or a 'person acting in an official capacity', that person will still be caught under the *Convention*.[53] Admittedly, the main thrust of the *Torture Convention* is to impose on each State Party an obligation to ensure that public officials refrain from committing acts of torture. The obligation assumed does not stop there, however. Each State Party must also use reasonable efforts to prevent any private, non-governmental actor from commiting torture. Private individuals also have a correlative, negative duty not to commit acts of torture by respecting the dignity and bodily integrity of other individuals.[54]

The Convention on the Rights of the Child

Like the United Nations *Torture Convention*, the United Nations *Convention on the Rights of the Child* of 20 November 1989[55] appears to be primarily directed towards imposing obligations on the governments of the States Parties in the public sphere. Nevertheless, the *Convention on the Rights of the Child* contains articles which purport to intrude quite considerably into the private realm. For example, Article 3(1) addresses 'all actions concerning children ... undertaken by ... private social welfare institutions ...' Other provisions of the *Convention* address rights and protections which can reach right into the home environment: Article 9 (separation of the child from his or her parents against their wishes), Article 16(1) (prohibition of interference with the child's 'privacy, family, [or] home ...') and Article 19(1) (protection of the child from all forms of abuse 'while in the care of parent(s), legal guardian(s) or any other person who has the care of the child').
 Beyond that, the *Convention on the Rights of the Child* contains a number of provisions which explicitly recognise not only the rights but the duties of

---

53   Paust, *op. cit.*, p. 61. The same position appears to obtain concerning the regional *Inter-American Convention to Prevent and Punish Torture* of 9 December 1985 which will be discussed later in this chapter.

54   Steiner and Alston, *op. cit.*, pp. 278-9.

55   U.N. G.A.O.R., 44th Session, 61st plenary meeting, Annex, U.N. Doc. A/RES/44/25 (1989).

parents, legal guardians, family members and other individuals legally responsible for the child. These provisions include the following:

Article 3

2. States Parties undertake to ensure the child such protection and care as is necessary for his or her well-being, taking into account the rights and duties of his or her parents, legal guardians, or other individuals legally responsible for him or her ...

Article 5

States Parties shall respect the responsibilities, rights, and duties of parents or, where applicable, the members of the extended family or community as provided for by the local custom, legal guardians or other persons legally responsible for the child, to provide, in a manner consistent with the evolving capacities of the child, appropriate direction and guidance in the exercise by the child of the rights recognized in the present Convention.

Article 14

2. States Parties shall respect the rights and duties of the parents and, when applicable, legal guardians, to provide direction to the child in the exercise of his or her rights in a manner consistent with the evolving capacities of the child.

Article 18

1. States Parties shall use their best efforts to ensure recognition of the principle that both parents have common responsibilities for the upbringing and development of the child. Parents or, as the case may be, legal guardians, have the primary responsibility for the upbringing and development of the child ...

Article 27

2. The parent(s) or others responsible for the child have the primary responsibility to secure, within their abilities and financial capacities, the conditions of living necessary for the child's development.

These provisions make it abundantly clear that the primary responsibility for the care and raising of children lies with the parents rather than with the state. This is designed to protect parents from excessive state intervention in the performance of their child-raising functions as well as to indicate to them that they cannot always expect the state to intervene.[56] Nevertheless, the role of the state in a child's upbringing is supplementary or facilitative in nature. So, for example, Article

---

56   S. Detrick (ed.) *The United Nations Convention on the Rights of the Child: A Guide to the Travaux Preparatoires* (1992) 265, para. 91.

18(2) provides that 'States Parties shall render appropriate assistance to parents and legal guardians in the performance of their child-rearing responsibilities'. Similarly, Article 27(3) requires States Parties to 'take appropriate measures to assist parents and others responsible for the child' to implement the child's right to a standard of living adequate for his or her development. Throughout the drafting process, there was never any controversy over this fundamental distribution of power and responsibility and its weighting as between the parents and the state.[57]

The *Convention on the Rights of the Child* not only imposes duties and responsibilities on parents and others legally responsible for the child; it also purports to impose duties on the children themselves, albeit in an indirect manner. Articles 13, 14 and 15 of the *Convention on the Rights of the Child* confer on children the rights to freedom of expression, freedom of thought, conscience and religion, and the freedoms of association and peaceful assembly. Nevertheless, reminiscent of the clawback provisions of the *International Covenant on Civil and Political Rights* discussed earlier in this chapter, the exercise of each of these rights by children is subject to the same restrictions which must be prescribed by law. Thus, children come under an indirect duty, for example, to respect the fundamental rights and freedoms of others while exercising their own rights. Such duty is reinforced by Article 29(1)(d) of the *Convention on the Rights of the Child* which records the agreement of the States Parties that 'the education of the child shall be directed to the preparation of the child for responsible life in a free society ...'

Some critics of the *Convention on the Rights of the Child* have argued that the *Convention* should have gone further in imposing duties directly on children. This is not without precedent. Article 31(a) of the *African Charter on the Rights and Welfare of the Child* of 1990[58] provides that '[t]he child, subject to his age and ability, ... shall have the duty to work for the cohesion of the family, to respect his parents and elders at all times and to assist them in case of need'. Indeed, a similar provision had been proposed by the representative of Senegal during the drafting of the *Convention*. It read: 'The child has the duty to respect his parents and to give them assistance, in case of need'.[59] Some participants during the drafting deliberations indicated that, although they shared the concerns of the author of the Senegalese proposal, they were still hesitant to support it because the duty to respect parents was, in their view, more of a moral than a legal obligation. Moreover, in practical terms, it would hardly be possible for States Parties to report on their compliance with such a provision.[60] Other delegations, however, voiced their support for the inclusion of the Senegalese proposal into the draft *Convention*, arguing that in quite a number of international instruments rights were

---

57 M. Flekkoy and N. Kaufman *The Participation Rights of the Child: Rights and Responsibilities in Family and Society* (1997) p. 58.

58 Adopted in July 1990 by the African Member States of the Organization of African Unity, O.A.U. Doc. CAB/LEG/TSG/Rev. 1.

59 Detrick, *op. cit.*, p. 156, para. 704.

60 *Idem*. 156, para. 706.

accompanied by corresponding duties.[61] The circuit-breaker to this impasse was provided by the observer for Canada who expressed the view that the Senegalese proposal could more appropriately be considered within the framework of issues to be addressed under what was to become Article 29(1) of the *Convention* dealing with the objectives of the child's education.[62] The final wording of Article 29(1)(c) refers to 'the development of respect for the child's parents' as one of the objectives of the child's education.   This diluted and weakened version disappointed Islamic, African and Asian representatives whose societies consider a child's duties to his or her parents, elders and extended family members to be an important aspect of family life. The *Convention* was therefore perceived somewhat warily, initially at least, as constituting a threat to the existence of the traditional family and its moral values.

Declaration on the Right and Responsibility of Individuals, Groups and Organs of Society to Promote and Protect Universally Recognized Human Rights and Fundamental Freedoms

On 16 March 1984, the United Nations Commission on Human Rights decided[63] to establish an open-ended working group to draft a declaration on the right and responsibility of individuals, groups and organs of society to promote and protect universally recognised human rights and fundamental freedoms.[64] Fourteen years on, the process culminated in the adoption[65] by the United Nations General Assembly on 9 December 1998 of the *Declaration on the Right and Responsibility of Individuals, Groups and Organs of Society to Promote and Protect Universally Recognized Human Rights and Fundamental Freedoms.* As the title of this instrument suggests, the scope of the individual duty prescribed is confined rather narrowly to a duty to promote and protect certain human rights. As a mere declaration, this instrument does not purport to impose any legally binding obligations on individuals.[66] Nevertheless, it frequently happens that 'pathfinding' declarations are eventually transformed into international conventions carrying binding legal obligations.[67]

---

61   *Idem.* 156, para. 707.
62   *Idem.* 157, para. 709.
63   Decision 1984/116 of 16 March 1984.
64   The idea of a draft declaration on the principles governing the responsibilities of the individual, particularly concerning the promotion and observance of human rights and fundamental freedoms, was first proposed in 1980 by Erica-Irene A. Daes, a Special Rapporteur of the United Nations Sub-Commission on Prevention of Discrimination and Protection of Minorities. See Daes, *op. cit.*, p. 65.
65   A/RES/53/144 (9 December 1998).
66   See n. 13 of this chapter and the related text for an explanation of the legal effect of a declaration.
67   As happened in the case of the *Declaration of the Rights of the Child* proclaimed by United Nations General Assembly Resolution 1386 (XIV) of 20 November 1959; *Declaration on the Elimination of All Forms of Racial Discrimination* proclaimed by United Nations General Assembly Resolution 1904 (XVIII) of 20

The *Declaration* is not intended to relieve states of their responsibilities to uphold human rights. This is made clear by its penultimate preambular paragraph which stresses 'that the primary responsibility and duty to promote and protect human rights and fundamental freedoms lie with the State'. Two other provisions of the preamble of the *Declaration* refer specifically to an individual obligation and responsibility to promote respect for human rights. The third and final preambular paragraphs state:

> Stressing that all members of the international community shall fulfil, jointly and separately, their solemn obligation to promote and encourage respect for human rights and fundamental freedoms for all without distinction of any kind ...

> Recognizing the right and responsibility of individuals, groups and associations to promote respect for, and foster knowledge of, human rights and fundamental freedoms at the national and international levels ...

The forerunners of these preambular provisions and the duties they recognise can be traced to the fifth preambular paragraph common to the Twin Covenants discussed earlier, as well as to the proclamation by the United Nations General Assembly in the preamble of the *Universal Declaration of Human Rights* 'that every individual and every organ of society, keeping this Declaration constantly in mind, shall strive by teaching and education to promote respect for these rights and freedoms ...' A further antecedent is Paragraph 1 of the *Proclamation of Teheran* adopted by the First United Nations Conference on Human Rights in 1968: 'It is imperative that the members of the international community fulfil their solemn obligations to promote and encourage respect for human rights and fundamental freedoms for all without distinction of any kind ...'[68]

As for the operative provisions of the *Declaration*, some of them specifically mention individuals and explicitly or impliedly impose duties on them, while others do not. In the latter category is Article 16 which merely acknowledges the importance of individuals in promoting public knowledge of human rights. In the former category are the following provisions:

Article 10

No one shall participate, by act or failure to act where required, in violating human rights and fundamental freedoms ...

November 1963; *Declaration on the Elimination of Discrimination Against Women* proclaimed by United Nations General Assembly Resolution 2263 (XXII) of 7 November 1967.

68   Text of the *Proclamation of Teheran* from Final Act of the International Conference on Human Rights, Teheran, April 22-May 13 1968. U.N. Doc. A/CONF.32/41.

Article 11

... Everyone who, as a result of his or her profession, can affect the human dignity, human rights and fundamental freedoms of others should respect those rights and freedoms and comply with relevant national and international standards of occupational and professional conduct or ethics.

Article 18

1. Everyone has duties towards and within the community in which alone the free and full development of his or her personality is possible.

2. Individuals, groups, institutions and non-governmental organizations have an important role to play and a responsibility in safeguarding democracy, promoting human rights and fundamental freedoms and contributing to the promotion and advancement of democratic societies, institutions and processes.

3. Individuals ... have an important role and a responsibility in contributing, as appropriate, to the promotion of the right of everyone to a social and international order in which the rights and freedoms set forth in the Universal Declaration of Human Rights and other human rights instruments can be fully realized.

The wording of Article 18(1) is wider than that contained in Article 29(1) of the *Universal Declaration of Human Rights* which is confined to 'duties to the community'. The implication of the wider wording of Article 18(1) is that individuals owe duties not only to their communities but to other individuals as well ('duties ... within the community'). Article 18(2) is rather unique in conferring on individuals a specific duty to promote a particular ideology (which can be a value-laden exercise). Article 18(3) is based on Article 28 of the *Universal Declaration of Human Rights.* The individual duty imposed thereunder can only be described as vague, soft and aspirational in nature; indeed, such a provision is quite incapable of being measured in terms of compliance. The other provisions of the *Declaration* worth mentioning are Articles 17 and 19. The former is a standard clawback provision imposing a duty on individuals to exercise their rights and freedoms in a responsible manner. The latter substantially repeats the provisions of Article 30 of the *Universal Declaration of Human Rights* which was discussed earlier in this chapter.

Conclusion

The foregoing discussion has demonstrated that a significant number of important international human rights instruments provide express or implied recognition of private duties of individuals, notwithstanding that their primary emphasis is upon securing for individuals rights against the State.

The Position of Individual Duties Under Regional Human Rights Instruments

Regional human rights conventions and systems have been adopted and implemented in Europe, America and Africa. Although attempts have been made, no conventions or formal systems have so far been adopted and implemented in Asia or the Pacific. Nevertheless, some policy statements on human rights have from time to time emanated from the Asia-Pacific region, and it is therefore proposed to examine in this section of this chapter the position of the individual as the bearer of private duties in all of these regions. Moreover, as a preface to a discussion of the African regional human rights system, a brief cultural relativist critique will be presented.

The American Regional Human Rights System

In May 1948 the ninth Inter-American Conference, convened at Bogota, Colombia, adopted the *Charter of the Organization of American States*,[69] thereby creating the Organization of American States (O.A.S.). The Bogota Conference also adopted the *American Declaration of the Rights and Duties of Man*.[70] The Inter-American system thus had a human rights declaration seven months before the adoption of the *Universal Declaration of Human Rights* by the United Nations on 10 December 1948 and two-and-a-half years before the *European Convention for the Protection of Human Rights and Fundamental Freedoms* was adopted by the Council of Europe in Rome on 4 November 1950.

    Like the *Universal Declaration*, the *American Declaration* was originally intended as a non-legally binding manifesto of universally recognised rights. Because of delays in the drafting and adoption of the *American Convention on Human Rights*, however, the Inter-American Commission on Human Rights was empowered, by resolution of the O.A.S. in November 1965, to apply the provisions of the *American Declaration* in considering the human rights situation in O.A.S. Member States.[71] Thus, the *American Declaration* did attain some legal status.[72] In terms of rights, the *American Declaration* is quite similar in content to the *Universal Declaration*. What distinguishes it therefrom are ten articles contained in Chapter Two specifically setting out the duties of the citizen. The very title of the *American Declaration* indicates that careful attention was paid to formulating

---

69   Entered into force 13 December 1951.
70   Resolution XXX. Final Act, Ninth International Conference of American States, Bogota, Colombia, March 30-May 2 1948 (Pan American Union, 1948), p. 38. Signed 2 May 1948, OEA/Ser.L./V/II.71, at 17 (1988).
71   T. Buergenthal *et al. Protecting Human Rights in the Americas – Selected Problems* (2nd ed., 1986) p. 6.
72   The legal status of the *American Declaration of the Rights and Duties of Man* is also confirmed by its reference in the third preambular paragraph of the *American Convention on Human Rights* of 22 November 1969. Article 29(d) of the latter instrument states that none of its provisions 'shall be interpreted as excluding or limiting the effect that the American Declaration of the Rights and Duties of Man and other international acts of the same nature may have'.

the duties of private or individual actors.   The preamble of the *American Declaration* enumerates the following general individual duties:

> All men are born free and equal, in dignity and in rights, and, being endowed by nature with reason and conscience, they should conduct themselves as brothers one to another.

> The fulfillment of duty by each individual is a prerequisite to the rights of all. Rights and duties are interrelated in every social and political activity of man. While rights exalt individual liberty, duties express the dignity of that liberty.
> Duties of a juridical nature presuppose others of a moral nature which support them in principle and constitute their basis.

> Inasmuch as spiritual development is the supreme end of human existence and the highest expression thereof, it is the duty of man to serve that end with all his strength and resources.

> Since culture is the highest social and historical expression of that spiritual development, it is the duty of man to preserve, practise and foster culture by every means within his power.

> And, since moral conduct constitutes the noblest flowering of culture, it is the duty of every man to hold it in high respect.

The first preambular paragraph of the *American Declaration* cited above is very similar to the wording of Article 1 of the *Universal Declaration of Human Rights*. The call for individuals to act towards one another 'as brothers' implies both positive duties of assistance and negative duties of forbearance.   The second preambular paragraph rightly emphasises the high degree of interdependence of rights and duties. Ten additional duties of a more specific nature are prescribed in Chapter Two (Articles XXIX-XXXVIII) which forms part of the operative provisions of the *American Declaration* :

> Article XXIX
>
> It is the duty of the individual so to conduct himself in relation to others that each and every one may fully form and develop his personality.
>
> Article XXX
>
> It is the duty of every person to aid, support, educate and protect his minor children, and it is the duty of children to honor their parents always and to aid, support and protect them when they need it.
>
> Article XXXI
>
> It is the duty of every person to acquire at least an elementary education.

Article XXXII

It is the duty of every person to vote in the popular elections of the country of which he is a national, when he is legally capable of doing so.

Article XXXIII

It is the duty of every person to obey the law and other legitimate commands of the authorities of his country and those of the country in which he may be.

Article XXXIV

It is the duty of every able-bodied person to render whatever civil and military service his country may require for its defense and preservation, and, in case of public disaster, to render such services as may be in his power.

Article XXXV

It is the duty of every person to co-operate with the state and the community with respect to social security and welfare, in accordance with his ability and with existing circumstances.

Article XXXVI

It is the duty of every person to pay the taxes established by law for the support of public services.

Article XXXVII

It is the duty of every person to work, as far as his capacity and possibilities permit, in order to obtain the means of livelihood or to benefit his community.

Article XXXVIII

It is the duty of every person to refrain from taking part in political activities that, according to law, are reserved exclusively to the citizens of the state in which he is an alien.

The *American Declaration* goes far beyond the *Universal Declaration* and the Twin Covenants. While the latter instruments merely signal that individuals owe duties to other individuals and to the community, the former instrument actually prescribes what these duties are that individuals owe to the family, the community and the State. These duties in themselves are relatively uncontroversial, since a significant number of them would have already been embodied in the domestic laws of the O.A.S. member states at the time of the adoption of the *American Declaration* in 1948. What makes this statement of duties innovative is their appearance for the very first time in an international human rights instrument.

The drafting and adoption of a regional human rights convention in Latin America took a considerably longer period compared with the *American Declaration*. Although the drafting of the *American Convention on Human*

Rights[73] began in 1959, the *Convention* was not adopted by the O.A.S. until 26 November 1969, and did not enter into force for the States Parties until 18 July 1978. The organs of the *Convention* are the Inter-American Commission on Human Rights and the Inter-American Court of Human Rights. Pursuant to Article 44, any individual, group of persons or legally recognised non-governmental entity may lodge petitions with the Commission complaining of a violation of the *Convention* by a State Party. Reminiscent of Article 5(1) common to the Twin Covenants, Article 29(a) of the *American Convention on Human Rights* states that none of its provisions 'shall be interpreted as permitting any ... person to suppress the enjoyment or exercise of the rights and freedoms recognized in this Convention ...' The existence of an individual duty was thereby recognised, albeit indirectly. Unlike the *American Declaration*, however, the *American Convention* contains only one article which explicitly recognises individual duties. Article 32, which is the only article to appear in the section of the *American Convention* headed 'Chapter V- Personal Responsibilities', states:

> Article 32 - Relationship between Duties and Rights
>
> 1. Every person has responsibilities to his family, his community, and mankind.
>
> 2. The rights of each person are limited by the rights of others, by the security of all, and by the just demands of the general welfare, in a democratic society.

Notwithstanding the lack of a detailed enumeration of individual duties, however, it is significant to note that the *American Convention* twice refers to the *American Declaration* - first in its third preambular paragraph and secondly in Article 29(d) which states in part that '[n]o provision of this Convention shall be interpreted as excluding or limiting the effect that the American Declaration of the Rights and Duties of Man ... may have'. It is arguable, then, that those operative provisions of the *American Declaration* which prescribe the duties of citizens may be incorporated by reference into Article 32(1) for interpretative purposes.[74] The standard clawback clause contained in Article 32(2) once again prescribes an indirect individual duty to temper the exercise of one's rights and freedoms in deference to the common good and to other individuals so that they may more fully enjoy their rights.

Beyond the *American Declaration* and *American Convention*, reference may also be made to the *Inter-American Convention to Prevent and Punish Torture*[75] as another example of a regional treaty implicating private or individual duties. The second paragraph of the preamble of the latter instrument reaffirms 'that *all* acts of torture or *any* other cruel, inhuman, or degrading treatment or

---

73   22 November 1969, 36 *O.A.S.T.S.*, reprinted in (1970) 9 *I.L.M.* p. 673.
74   As for the preambular reference to the *American Declaration*, see the discussion *supra* concerning the effect of Article 31(2) of the *Vienna Convention on the Law of Treaties*.
75   9 December 1985, 67 *O.A.S.T.S.*, reprinted in (1986) p. 25 *I.L.M.* 519 (entered into force 28 February 1987).

punishment constitute an offense against human dignity ... and are violations of the fundamental human rights and freedoms proclaimed in the American Declaration ... and the Universal Declaration of Human Rights' (emphasis supplied). It is thus clear that the expansive language employed in the preamble effectively expands the scope of application of the *Inter-American Torture Convention* to include private acts of torture committed with state involvement or acquiescence.

The European Regional Human Rights System

Western European nations established the Council of Europe in 1949 as the social and cultural counterpart to the defence-oriented North Atlantic Treaty Organisation (N.A.T.O.). One of the first tasks undertaken by the Council of Europe was the drafting of a European regional human rights convention for the protection of civil and political rights. The drafters of the *European Convention for the Protection of Human Rights and Fundamental Freedoms*[76] relied to a large extent on drafts of the *International Covenant on Civil and Political Rights* which was then being considered by the United Nations Commission on Human Rights. Unlike the *American Convention*, the *European Convention* was drafted and adopted within a relatively short period of time. The *European Convention* was adopted in Rome on 4 November 1950 and entered into force on 3 September 1953. Since that time, a number of protocols to the *European Convention* have entered into force.

The *European Convention* itself covers only civil and political rights, although its *First Protocol*[77] contains a 'second generation' socio-economic right to education in Article 2. Social, economic and cultural rights in Europe are more systematically protected by the *European Social Charter*[78] adopted by the Council of Europe in Turin, Italy on 18 October 1961. The *European Convention* established a European Commission and Court of Human Rights to examine complaints by one member state against another member state concerning alleged breaches of the *Convention*. Provided, moreover, that the respondent member state has lodged a declaration that it recognises the competence of the Commission to receive petitions, the Commission may investigate petitions received from any person, group of individuals or non-governmental organisation claiming to be a victim of a *Convention* violation.[79] Once the Commission has investigated the complaint, the case may be referred to the European Court by the Commission itself or by a member state concerned.[80] The European regional human rights system is widely considered to be the most advanced and sophisticated regional system. The European Commission and Court have made a substantial

---

76   Adopted by the Council of Europe on 4 November 1950, 213 *U.N.T.S.* p. 221.
77   *Protocol No. 1 to the European Convention for the Protection of Human Rights and Fundamental Freedoms*, adopted 20 March 1952, entered into force 18 May 1954, *E.T.S.* p. 9.
78   529 *U.N.T.S.* 89 (entry into force 26 February 1965).
79   See Articles 24 and 25 of the *European Convention*.
80   See Article 44.

contribution to human rights jurisprudence, with the former having handed down decisions in over 12,000 cases and the latter in excess of 120 cases.

The *European Convention* generally does not directly or explicitly impose duties upon private individuals. Like the *International Covenant on Civil and Political Rights*, however, it does so indirectly. So, for example, Articles 9 and 11 of the *European Convention* respectively confer on individuals the rights to freedom of thought, conscience and religion, and freedom of peaceful assembly and of association. Both articles are subject, however, to the same type of clawback provisions found in the *International Covenant on Civil and Political Rights*. Article 10 recognises everyone's right to freedom of expression but conditions the exercise of such right to a uniquely-worded clawback provision contained in Article 10(2) which states:

> The exercise of [the right to freedom of expression], since it carries with it duties and responsibilities, may be subject to such formalities, conditions, restrictions or penalties as are prescribed by law and are necessary in a democratic society, in the interests of national security, territorial integrity or public safety, for the prevention of disorder or crime, for the protection of health or morals, for the protection of the reputation or rights of others, for preventing the disclosure of information received in confidence, or for maintaining the authority and impartiality of the judiciary.

Article 10(2) is the only clawback provision in the *European Convention* which refers explicitly to individual 'duties and responsibilities' and is similar in this respect to its counterpart provision Article 19(3) of the *International Covenant on Civil and Political Rights*. As is the case with Article 30 of the *Universal Declaration of Human Rights* and Article 5(1) common to the Twin Covenants, Article 17 of the *European Convention* contains a 'State, group or person' implied individual duty clause.

Several protocols to the *European Convention* also recognise individual duties or responsibilities, either directly or indirectly. In the former category is Article 5 of *Protocol No. 7 to the European Convention for the Protection of Human Rights and Fundamental Freedoms*[81] which states that '[s]pouses shall enjoy equality of rights and responsibilities of a private law character between them, and in their relations with their children, as to marriage, during marriage and in the event of its dissolution'.[82] In the latter category is Article 2 of *Protocol No. 4 to the European Convention for the Protection of Human Rights and Fundamental Freedoms*.[83] Article 2(3) thereof subjects the right to liberty of

---

81   Adopted 22 November 1984, entered into force 1 November 1988, *E.T.S.* 117, reprinted in (1985) 24 *I.L.M.* p. 435.
82   This wording ('equality of . . . responsibilities') goes beyond that of Article 5(b) of the *Convention on the Elimination of All Forms of Discrimination Against Women* which merely refers to 'the common responsibility of men and women in the upbringing and development of their children'.
83   Adopted 16 September 1963, entered into force 2 May 1968, *E.T.S.* p. 46.

movement to a standard clawback clause which includes 'the protection of the rights and freedoms of others' as a limiting criterion.

Those European states which have participated in the so-called 'Helsinki Process' have also recognised, albeit in a non-legally binding way, individual duties in the human rights field. The seventh paragraph of Principle VII of the *Final Act of the Helsinki Conference on Security and Co-operation in Europe* records the confirmation of the participating states of 'the right of the individual to know and act upon his rights and duties in [the human rights] field'.[84] Similarly, the Committee of Ministers of the Council of Europe has acknowledged that human rights entail individual responsibilities. Principle IV(iii) of the *Declaration Regarding Intolerance - A Threat to Democracy*[85] of 29 April 1982 refers to the promotion of 'an awareness of the requirements of human rights and the ensuing responsibilities in a democratic society ...'

The Asian-Pacific Region

In April 1985, the Human Rights Committee of the non-governmental organisation, the Law Association for Asia and the Pacific (LAWASIA), convened a conference in Fiji in order to begin to develop a regional human rights body for the Pacific region. This led to the formation of a drafting committee which, in 1986, delivered a report on the issues involved in establishing a regional human rights body. This report included a model human rights treaty which was based on the *African Charter on Human and Peoples' Rights* of 27 June 1981 (which will be discussed in the next section of this chapter). The report of the drafting committee also proposed a human rights body which would both supervise the implementation of the model treaty and assist the governments of states in the Pacific region in meeting their international human rights treaty obligations. It was anticipated that the foundation parties to the model human rights treaty would be the independent states of Australia, New Zealand, Micronesia, Melanesia and Polynesia. A working party was subsequently established to consider the report of the drafting committee. The working party proposed as a first step that a Pacific Human Rights Commission should be established to work in consultation with the governments of these countries with a view to laying the groundwork for the adoption of the *Draft Pacific Charter of Human Rights*.[86] The position at the time of writing is that negotiations between these governments are ongoing.

The *Draft Pacific Charter* identifies the wide-ranging rights that the peoples of the Pacific recognise as relevant for their protection and development, provides for implementation mechanisms and defines the duties of governments and individuals. As for the latter, the final preambular paragraph of the *Charter*

---

84   1 August 1975, (1975) 14 *I.L.M.* pp. 1292, 1295.
85   Adopted by the Committee of Ministers of the Council of Europe on 29 April 1982 at its 70th Session.
86   Meeting under the auspices of LAWASIA in Apia, Western Samoa, 15-17 May 1989, some 20 delegates from Micronesia, Polynesia, Melanesia, Australia and New Zealand produced the latest draft of the *Pacific Charter of Human Rights*.

expresses the concern of the States Parties 'that persons, having duties to their families and communities, and to other persons, are under an obligation to observe the rights and duties recognized in the present Charter'. These individual duties are prescribed in a separate section entitled 'Duties of Individuals' in the operative part of the *Charter* which comprises the following three articles:

Article 27

1. Individuals shall have duties towards their families and society, the Parties and other legally recognized communities and the regional and international community.

2. Individuals shall exercise their rights and freedoms with due regard to the rights of others, collective security, morality and common interest.

Article 28

Individuals shall have the duty to respect and consider their fellow human beings without discrimination, and to develop and maintain relations aimed at promoting, safeguarding and reinforcing mutual respect and tolerance.

Article 29

Individuals shall have the duty:

1. To preserve harmonious development of the family and to work for its cohesion and respect.

2. To work to the best of their abilities and competence, to use their skills and abilities for the betterment of their communities, and to pay taxes imposed by law in accordance with their means in the interests of society.

3. To preserve and strengthen positive Pacific cultural values in their relations with other members of the society, in the spirit of tolerance, dialogue and consultation and, in general, to contribute to the promotion of the well-being of society.

Articles 27 and 28 replicate Articles 27 and 28 of the *African Charter on Human and Peoples' Rights.* Article 29(1) once again duplicates Article 29(1) of the *African Charter* but fails to mention any individual duty of parental respect and maintenance. Sub-Articles (2) and (3) of Article 29 are respectively taken from Sub-Articles (6) and (7) of the *African Charter.* Curiously, however, Article 29 of the *Pacific Charter* neglects to mention a number of important individual duties incorporated within Article 29 of the *African Charter,* such as national community service, defence and a duty not to compromise state security.

As for the Asian region, the concept of an individual or private duty in the human rights field has been recognised in both governmental and non-governmental non-legally binding policy statements. In 1983, the non-governmental organisation, the Regional Council on Human Rights in Asia, adopted the *Declaration of the Basic Duties of ASEAN Peoples and Governments* to address widespread human rights violations in South-east Asia. The opening preambular paragraph of the *ASEAN Declaration* implicitly acknowledges the correlative relationship between human rights and duties in its reference to 'rights that are the duties of other persons'. References to individual duties to be found in the operative provisions of the *ASEAN Declaration* include the following:

Article I. Basic Principles

3. It is the duty of all individuals ... to exercise their rights and freedoms in the spirit of human solidarity, respecting and defending the rights and freedoms of others. It is likewise the duty of all individuals ... to preserve and enhance their culture and identity, to develop and use their native talents, abilities and resources for the betterment of society, to respect and obey the laws which accord with this Declaration, and to denounce and resist persistent violations of their basic rights and freedoms.

4. The specification of a duty in this Declaration does not preclude the existence of other duties.

Article VI. Education

4. It is the duty of the people to avail themselves of the national educational system to the fullest extent possible in order to discover and develop their native talents, to continue educating themselves after formal schooling ends, and to participate in the social, economic, cultural and political life of their communities and of the country, using their skills, talents and critical and creative faculties for the promotion and enhancement of the rights of all and for the welfare of the nation.

Article VII. Mass Communications Media

4. It is the duty of authors, artists, journalists and writers to use their rights and freedoms responsibly, respect the right to privacy of all persons, refrain from injuring reputations unless necessary in the public interest, and abstain from all propaganda for, advocacy of, or incitement to, war or national, racial or religious discrimination, hatred, hostility or violence.

By contrast, efforts at the governmental level have been considerably less specific and prescriptive in this context. Meeting in Kuala Lumpur, Malaysia, 20-23 September 1993, the Second Plenary Session of the 14th General Assembly of the ASEAN Inter-Parliamentary Organisation approved the *Kuala Lumpur*

Declaration on Human Rights[87] whose relevant operative provisions include the following:

Article 1

All human beings, individually and collectively, have a responsibility to participate in their total development, taking into account the need for full respect of their human rights as well as their duties to the community. Freedom, progress and national stability are promoted by balance between the rights of the individual and those of the community.

Article 12

Everyone has the right to freedom of expression which carries inherent duties and responsibilities.

Article 20

It is the task and responsibility of each Member State and every citizen to ensure the promotion, implementation and protection of human rights.

Compared with the American and European regional human rights systems, however, the individual duties alluded to in the *ASEAN Declaration* and the *Kuala Lumpur Declaration* carry no legal weight and are therefore merely, for the time being at least, aspirational and pioneering in nature.

The Influence of Cultural Relativism on the African Regional Human Rights System

Prior to examining the position of individual duties under the *African Charter on Human and Peoples' Rights* of 27 June 1981, it is proposed to briefly canvass the universalist and cultural relativist arguments concerning the applicability of human rights. This is necessary due to the significant influence the latter arguments have had in the formulation of specific individual duties within the *African Charter.*

Universalism

Universalism is the basis upon which the contemporary system of international human rights conventions has been implemented. Universalism presupposes an underlying human unity which entitles all individuals to certain basic, minimum rights, or human rights. These human rights are to be recognised and enjoyed independent of time and place, and irrespective of the individual's ethnicity, religion, ideology, culture or value system. These rights are conceived as individual entitlements which are fundamental, inalienable and universal in

---

87   Its text can be located at F. de Varennes *Asia-Pacific Human Rights Documents and Resources* (1998) Vol. 1, p. 107.

application, in the sense that religious and cultural traditions cannot be invoked to deny or to dilute them.

Those who advocate the universalist position draw on, *inter alia*, certain preambular provisions of the International Bill of Rights to reinforce their arguments. In its preamble, the *Universal Declaration of Human Rights* is described as 'a common standard of achievement for all peoples and all nations'. Its first preambular paragraph further recites that 'recognition of the *inherent* dignity and of the equal and *inalienable* rights of *all* members of the human family is the foundation of freedom, justice and peace in the world' (emphasis supplied). Similarly, the first two preambular paragraphs common to the *International Covenant on Civil and Political Rights* and the *International Covenant on Economic, Social and Cultural Rights* state:

> *Considering* that, in accordance with the principles proclaimed in the Charter of the United Nations, recognition of the inherent dignity and of the equal and inalienable rights of all members of the human family is the foundation of freedom, justice and peace in the world,
>
> *Recognizing* that these rights derive from the inherent dignity of the human person
> ...

Proponents of the universalist position argue that the deliberate use by the drafters of terms such as 'inherent', 'inalienable' and 'all' signifies a clear intent that the human rights contained in the three instruments are to be applied uniformly and without exception. Confirmation of the correctness of this position can be gleaned from the proceedings of the Second United Nations World Conference on Human Rights held in Vienna in June 1993. On 25 June 1993, the Conference adopted the *Vienna Declaration and Programme of Action*, Paragraph 5 of which states:

> All human rights are universal, indivisible and interdependent and interrelated. The international community must treat human rights globally in a fair and equal manner, on the same footing, and with the same emphasis. While the significance of national and regional particularities and various historical, cultural and religious backgrounds must be borne in mind, it is the duty of States, regardless of their political, economic and cultural systems, to promote and protect all human rights and fundamental freedoms.

Cultural Relativism

The historical contingency of human rights is generally conceded today. As one writer has remarked, '[t]he concept of human rights ... is legally international, philosophically universal and historically Western'.[88] The contemporary human rights movement stems principally from the Western liberal democratic tradition and its emphasis on individual rights. The conceptions and content of human

---

88   M. Freeman 'Human Rights: Asia and the West' in J. Tang (ed.) *Human Rights and International Relations in the Asia-Pacific* (1995) pp. 13, 17.

rights, as reflected in the International Bill of Rights, have been significantly influenced by Western philosophy, ideology and social order.[89] This has prompted the condemnation of the universalist position by cultural relativists as 'Eurocentric' and neo-imperialist. The charge is made that, through its export of the human rights movement, the West seeks to impose its own moral conceptions, based on the Judeo-Christian heritage, on a majority of the world's population which does not share this particular moral or cultural frame of reference. A loss of Asian cultural identity is feared.

In the last decade or so, particularly within Asia, the universalisation of Western values and increased Western pressure for an improvement in the Asian human rights record have been perceived by Asian governments as yet another example of Western global hegemony. The Malaysian Prime Minister, Dr Mahatir Mohamad, has maintained that the end of the Cold War has coincided with the imposition of a new world order in which powerful Western nations have claimed the right to impose their own system of government, values and human rights on everyone else.[90] A leading Western human rights academic lawyer has succinctly stated the position thus:

> Western governments, having won their Cold War with communism, have taken their fight for human rights to the Third World. This has brought them into conflict with some Asian governments. Human rights violations in several Asian countries have been targets of Western criticism. However, the economic success of some East Asian societies has given their governments the confidence to resist this initiative on the basis of what they believe to be the proven worth of their cultures. What appears, from the Western perspective, to be a noble campaign for universal human rights, is interpreted, from an Asian perspective, as cultural imperialism ... The renewed assertion of non-Western cultural values has called into question the universalist interpretation of human rights. Some Asian governments accuse the West of trying to impose on them alien values derived from the Western liberal tradition.[91]

A typical Asian response to Western criticisms of Asian human rights violations has been to engage in a moral critique of the West. Asian political leaders have argued that the social achievements of Western societies are such that the West has no moral right to lecture them.[92] Indeed, one American social commentator has castigated his fellow citizens in the following terms:

> ... [H]ow can Americans justify insisting - by diplomatic, military, economic, or other means - that every other society adopt the moral and political vocabulary of

---

89   Z. Motala 'Human Rights in Africa: A Cultural, Ideological, and Legal Examination' (1989) 12 *Hastings International and Comparative Law Review* p. 373.

90   H. P. Lee 'Constitutional Values in Turbulent Asia' (1997) 23 *Monash University Law Review* pp. 375, 377.

91   M. Freeman, *op. cit.*, p. 14.

92   K. Mahbubani 'Live and Let Live: Allow Asians to Choose their Own Course' *Far Eastern Economic Review* 17 June 1993, p. 26.

[universal human] rights? With our own ideological house falling apart, with no agreement on how to shore up its foundations, how can we demand the remodeling of other houses?[93]

While cultural relativists are wary of the universalist school of thought as Eurocentric and neo-imperialist, they maintain that their own position reflects cultural egalitarianism in a multicultural world. The manner in which rights are exercised and duties performed varies across cultures, reflecting different cultural values and traditions.[94] These traditions adhere, quite legitimately, to different views of what a good, human way of life should be. In the words of one African commentator:

> Human rights are not the monopoly or the sole prerogative of any one culture or people ... In one culture, the individual may be venerated as the primary bearer of rights; while, in another, individual rights may be harmonized with the corporate body. Rather than assert the primacy of one over the other, or argue that only one cultural expression and historical experience constitutes human rights, this author views each experience as a contributor to the whole.[95]

Cultural relativist theory essentially posits that universal respect for human rights will be better achieved by promoting conceptions of human rights located in each society's customs and internal norms. It is said that so-called universal human rights norms simply do not conform with the diversity of religious, ethnic and cultural practices found throughout the world. Human values tend to vary a great deal and are a function of different cultural perspectives. What is considered to be a human right in one society (for example, the right of individual proprietorship of land) may be regarded as anti-social in another society (or even by the same society in a different historical period). Cultural characteristics and historical perspectives, therefore, do and should play a role in determining the value or weight each culture attributes to a particular human rights provision, such that it is interpreted and applied in accordance with local customs and traditions. These considerations were forcefully articulated in an impassioned speech delivered on 14 June 1993 by the then Indonesian Minister for Foreign Affairs, Ali Alatas, to the Vienna World Conference on Human Rights:

> ... [W]hile we in the developing world do understand and appreciate the genesis of the thinking and motivation underlying present-day Western policies and views on human rights, we should at least expect similar understanding and appreciation of the historical formation and experiences of non-Western societies and the attendant development of our cultural and social values and traditions. For many developing countries, some endowed with ancient and highly developed cultures, have not gone through the same history and experience as the Western nations in

---

93   H. Rosemont Jr 'Human Rights: A Bill of Worries' in W. Theodore De Bary and Tu Weiming (eds) *Confucianism and Human Rights* (1998) pp. 54, 60.
94   M. Flekkoy and N. Kaufman, *op. cit.*, p. 10.
95   Makau Wa Mutua, *op. cit.*, pp. 345-6.

developing their ideas on human rights and democracy. In fact, they often developed different perceptions based on different experiences regarding the relations between man and society, man and his fellow man and regarding the rights of the community as against the rights of the individual ... [T]herefore this is also a call addressed to all of us to develop a greater sensitivity ... and greater humility and less self-righteousness in addressing human rights issues.[96]

As for Africa, the Projects Director of Harvard Law School's Human Rights Program has expressed similar concerns with the universalist position:

> The transplantation of the narrow formulation of Western liberalism cannot adequately respond to the historical reality and the political and social needs of Africa. The sacralization of the individual and the supremacy of the jurisprudence of individual rights in organized political and social society is not a natural, 'transhistorical,' or universal phenomenon, applicable to all societies, without regard to time and place. The ascendancy of the language of individual rights has a specific historical context in the Western world.[97]

Moderate cultural relativists do concede that there are many values which are shared by different societies (Eastern and Western alike) and which have the potential to form the basis of a broad consensus on crucial aspects of human rights. Certain core values which should be recognised and protected irrespective of historical and cultural contexts include the following: the right to life, liberty and security of the person, freedom from slavery, freedom from torture, the right to equality before the law and freedom from arbitrary arrest, detention and exile (see respectively Articles 3, 4, 5, 7 and 9 of the *Universal Declaration of Human Rights*). To the extent that these cross-culturally held values are enshrined in the *Universal Declaration of Human Rights*, most cultural relativists concede the universalist position. Nevertheless, they point to the content of the *Universal Declaration* and the manner of its adoption as demonstrating that it also represents a conception of human rights peculiar to the West. Although the *Declaration* purports to be universal in intent, it is not universal in derivation. The *Declaration* was drafted at a time when, compared with today, there were few independent African and Asian states which were members of the United Nations.[98] All 18 of the drafts of the *Declaration* submitted to the United Nations emanated from the West.[99] In terms of content, the *Declaration* is particularly strong in the area of civil and political rights which are highly cherished in the Western liberal democratic tradition, but comparatively weak in the area of economic, social and

---

96   As reported in J. Tang (ed.) *Human Rights and International Relations in the Asia-Pacific* (1995) p. 230.
97   Makau Wa Mutua, *op. cit.*, pp. 341-2.
98   At the time of the drafting of the *Universal Declaration of Human Rights*, there were only three independent African states: Ethiopia, Liberia and Egypt.
99   A. Renteln *International Human Rights: Universalism versus Relativism* (1990) p. 24.

cultural rights, as well as group rights, which are regarded as more important in African, Asian and socialist states.

Since the early 1960s and the hastening of the decolonisation process, however, the membership of the United Nations has changed markedly with the admission of many newly independent African and Asian states. This resulted in an evolving conception of human rights which involved cultural orientations and priorities which were different to those held by Western states.[100] The universalist position began to be questioned. The proliferation of independent, non-Western states was accompanied by a growing concern as to the failure of international human rights law to recognise and accomodate global diversity. Non-Western states, comprising African, Indian, Islamic and East Asian perspectives, objected to what they consider to be an undue emphasis in Western liberal democratic thought on the individual and his or her protection from the community and the State. This results, in their view, in a failure to recognise the inherent social nature of human beings, their role within the wider community and the importance of individual duties and their performance.

Over the last two decades or so, there has been a growing recognition that some human rights were either entirely or primarily the products of the West. The right to individual ownership of land is one such example. Article 17(1) of the *Universal Declaration of Human Rights* provides that '[e]veryone has the right to own property alone as well as in association with others'. As such, Article 17(1) is at odds with traditional African conceptions of property ownership which viewed land as community property. In traditional African societies, the individual merely had a right to use the land to produce food for oneself and family.[101] While the *African Charter on Human and Peoples' Rights* does guarantee the right to property, it significantly departs from the wording of the *Universal Declaration*. The first sentence of Article 14 of the *African Charter* merely states that '[t]he right to property shall be guaranteed'. Thus, the *African Charter* does not specifically guarantee the right of individual ownership of property in keeping with African cultural traditions. It is therefore more difficult to argue that the concept of individual land ownership as guaranteed by the *Universal Declaration* should be perceived as a universal human right.

The Acknowledgement of Cultural Relativism Within International Human Rights Instruments

Two of the more notable examples of the explicit recognition of cultural relativism within international and regional human rights conventions are the *African Charter on Human and Peoples' Rights* of 27 June 1981 and the *Convention on the Rights of the Child* of 20 November 1989. The influence of cultural relativist theory is also evident in the Final Declarations of two of the Regional Meetings which met to prepare for the 1993 Vienna World Conference on Human Rights.

---

100   Motala, *op. cit.*, pp. 377-8.
101   *Idem.* pp. 382-3.

In relation to the States Parties, the fifth preambular paragraph of the *African Charter* states:

> *Taking* into consideration the virtues of their historical tradition and the values of African civilization which should inspire and characterize their reflection on the concept of human and peoples' rights;

The explicit emphasis on traditional African values represents a significant departure from previous international human rights documents. While the drafters of the *African Charter* drew heavily upon the *Universal Declaration* and the Twin Covenants, they also sought to incorporate within the *Charter* an African conception of human rights. As we shall see in the next section of this chapter, the *Charter* emphasises peoples' or group rights, various types of individual duties and the importance of the role of the individual within the community. The fifth preambular paragraph of the *African Charter* thus signals an attempt by its drafters to reclaim some of the cultural distinctiveness systematically denied to the African continent by the colonising West. This is arguably one of the rationales of regional human rights protection systems and consistent with one of the fundamental values in the human rights movement, namely the preservation of, and respect for, difference.[102]

Several provisions of the *Convention on the Rights of the Child* also place importance on the cultural traditions of peoples in the children's rights context. The penultimate preambular paragraph recites the need to take due account of 'the importance of the traditions and cultural values of each people for the protection and harmonious development of the child'. Similarly, Article 5 mentions 'local custom' as material in identifying those members of the extended family or community who, in the exercise of their rights and duties, can provide appropriate guidance to the child in the exercise of his or her own rights.[103]

Pursuant to United Nations General Assembly Resolution 45/155 of December 1990, three regional meetings were convened at Bangkok, Thailand, San Jose, Costa Rica, and Tunis, Tunisia in order to prepare for the 1993 Vienna World Conference on Human Rights. These meetings provided an opportunity for governmental representatives to formulate a common position on human rights issues. The final declarations of the African and Asian regional meetings embraced cultural relativist theory, while not denying the global scope of human rights. Paragraph 5 of the final declaration of the African regional meeting, known as the *Tunis Declaration* of 6 November 1992, provided as follows:

> The observance and promotion of human rights are undeniably a global concern and an objective to the realization of which all States, without exception, are called upon to contribute. However, no ready-made model can be prescribed at the

---

102   Steiner and Alston, *op. cit.*, p. 696.
103   See Paragraph 180 of the *travaux preparatoires* of the *Convention on the Rights of the Child* as reported in S. Detrick (ed.) *The United Nations Convention on the Rights of the Child: A Guide to the Travaux Preparatoires* (1992) p. 161.

universal level since the historical and cultural realities of each nation and the traditions, standards and values of each people cannot be disregarded.

Similarly, Paragraph 8 of the final declaration of the Asian regional meeting, known as the *Bangkok Declaration* of 2 April 1993, recognised that:

> ... while human rights are universal in nature, they must be considered in the context of a dynamic and evolving process of international norm-setting, bearing in mind the significance of national and regional particularities and various historical, cultural and religious backgrounds.

Thus, while the African and Asian regional declarations appear to concede the universality of human rights, they nonetheless reserve the right to interpret and apply international human rights norms in the context of regional and national historical, cultural and religious particularities.

This stance taken concerning the qualification of universalism by cultural relativism was reinforced by numerous statements made by representatives of Asian governments at the 1993 Vienna World Conference on Human Rights. Japan was the only Asian nation to unconditionally adhere to the universalist position. Nobuo Matsunaga, Envoy of the Government of Japan, expressed the official Japanese position:

> Human rights are universal values common to all mankind ... Japan firmly believes that the international community must remain committed to the principles set forth in the [Universal] Declaration [of Human Rights] and the [Twin] Covenants. It is the duty of all States, whatever their cultural tradition, no matter what their political or economic system, to protect and promote those values.[104]

Other Asian nations, such as the Republics of Korea and Indonesia, appeared to acknowledge the universalist position while sounding a cultural relativist cautionary note. Han Sung-joo, Minister of Foreign Affairs of the Republic of Korea, stated:

> Human rights are universal, indivisible and interdependent. They cannot be altered according to circumstances. It is neither justifiable nor appropriate to deny some human rights in order to guarantee others. ... It is also true that regional and national circumstances need to be taken into account in the promotion and protection of human rights. Yet, history shows us that special circumstances do not justify abuses of human rights.[105]

Likewise, Ali Alatas, Minister for Foreign Affairs of the Republic of Indonesia, attached a 'clawback' proviso to his endorsement of the universalist position:

---

104   As reported in J. Tang (ed.) *Human Rights and International Relations in the Asia-Pacific* (1995) p. 217.
105   *Idem.* p. 220.

While human rights are indeed universal in character, it is now generally acknowledged that their expression and implementation in the national context should remain the competence and responsibility of each government. This means that the complex variety of problems, of different economic, social and cultural realities, and the unique value systems prevailing in each country should be taken into consideration.[106]

At the opposite end of the spectrum, the most relativistic position expressed by those Asian nations which embraced cultural relativism was that taken by the People's Republic of China. In the words of Liu Huaqiu, Head of the Chinese delegation:

The concept of human rights is a product of historical development. It is closely associated with specific social, political and economic conditions and the specific history, culture and values of a particular country. Different historical development stages have different human rights requirements. Countries at different development stages or with different historical traditions and cultural backgrounds also have different understanding and practice of human rights. Thus, one should not and cannot think of the human rights standard and model of certain countries as the only proper ones and demand all other countries to comply with them.[107]

U Ohn Gyaw, Minister for Foreign Affairs of the Union of Myanmar, added:

[E]ven as we seek universality of human rights, our diversity in historical, cultural and religious backgrounds must never be minimized or forgotten. There is no unique model of human rights implementation that can be superimposed on a given country.[108]

Datuk Abdullah Haji Ahmad Badawi, the Malaysian Minister of Foreign Affairs, noted the ongoing lack of consensus on the universality of all human rights due to a conceptual divide arising from different perceptions and positions.[109] Wong Kan Seng, Minister for Foreign Affairs of the Republic of Singapore, warned that universal recognition of human rights can be harmful if universalism is used to deny or mask the reality of diversity.[110] According to the Singaporean Foreign Minister:

We cannot ignore the differences in history, culture and background of different societies. They have developed separately for thousands of years, in different ways and with different experiences. Their ideals and norms differ.[111]

---

106   *Idem.* p. 232.
107   *Idem.* p. 214.
108   *Idem.* p. 223.
109   *Idem.* p. 235.
110   *Idem.* p. 243.
111   *Idem.* p. 244.

Such statements have been challenged. This is primarily due to a fear held by Western governments and non-governmental human rights organisations that non-Western governments will exploit cultural relativism to deflect criticism of their own internal human rights violations. Naive acceptance of cultural relativism may therefore compromise the ability to condemn repressive human rights practices. Professor Michael Freeman has cautioned that traditions can be manipulated to serve contemporary political purposes such that '[i]f the doctrine of human rights can be used to disguise Western neo-imperialism, the doctrine of cultural relativism can be used to conceal or to justify oppression by Asian elites'.[112]

The Impact of the Universalist-Cultural Relativist Debate on the Principle of Individual Duty

African and Asian support for the cultural relativist perspective has brought into sharper focus several differences in emphasis. Non-Western states generally feel uncomfortable with what they perceive in the West to be an excessive emphasis upon the individual and obsession with his or her protection against the community and State, the failure to sufficiently recognise the social role of each individual within the community, and the preoccupation with human rights at the expense of human duties.

In the African context, the community was considered as more important than the individual in traditional societies. President Kenneth Kaunda of Zambia describes African humanism in practice:

> The tribal community was a *mutual* society. It was organized to satisfy the basic needs of all its members ... individualism was discouraged.[113]

Thus, the individual was not viewed as standing apart from society or in contest with it. The rights and duties of the individual were enjoyed through or within society, of which each individual was only a component part.[114] African commentators have rejected the notion that the individualist rights perspective is superior or preferable to a more community-based conception of rights. As Josiah Cobbah has maintained:

> In the same way that people in other cultures are brought up to assert their independence from their community, the average African's worldview is one that places the individual within his community. [This African worldview] is for all intents and purposes as valid as the European theories of individualism and the social contract.[115]

---

112   M. Freeman, *op. cit.*, p. 15.
113   K. Kaunda *A Humanist in Africa* (1966) pp. 24-5.
114   Motala, *op. cit.*, p. 381.
115   J. Cobbah 'African Values and the Human Rights Debate: An African Perspective' (1987) 9 *Human Rights Quarterly* pp. 309, 323.

Most Asian states similarly tend to place greater emphasis on collectivity over individuality. Several statements made by Asian governmental representatives at the 1993 Vienna World Conference on Human Rights reflect this bias. So, for instance, Liu Huaqiu, Head of the Delegation of the People's Republic of China, adamantly declared that '[n]obody shall place his [or her] own rights and interests above those of the state and society, nor should he [or she] be allowed to impair those of others and the general public'.[116] Ali Alatas, the then Indonesian Foreign Minister, explained in more detail the reasons underlying this Asian concern that wider community interests be fully taken into account:

> [I]mplementation of human rights implies the existence of a balanced relationship between individual human rights and the obligations of individuals toward their community. Without such a balance, the rights of the community as a whole can be denied, which can lead to instability and even anarchy, especially in developing countries. In Indonesia, as in many other developing countries, the rights of the individual are balanced by the rights of the community, in other words, balanced by the obligation equally to respect the rights of others, the rights of the society and the rights of the nation. Indonesian culture as well as its ancient well-developed customary laws have traditionally put high priority on the rights and interests of the society or nation, without however in any way minimizing or ignoring the rights and interests of individuals and groups.[117]

In order to better defend themselves against Western charges of human rights violations, Asian governments have begun to articulate inherent 'Asian values'. In the early 1990s, the Singaporean government launched its 'Shared Values' campaign to facilitate economic development and the nation-building process. This campaign is premised upon the notion that collectivities have rights which transcend those of the individual such that the State is better empowered to pursue goals which benefit society. This emerging discourse attempts to define a national culture based on harmony and consensus by promoting the values of community over self, family as the basic social unit, problem-solving by consensus (rather than the Western adversarial system) and religious tolerance.[118] The 'Shared Values' campaign emerged under the leadership of Lee Kuan Yew and has been perpetuated by the current Prime Minister Goh Chok Tong. These Singaporean leaders hoped to curtail what they considered to be the negative Western influence of excessive individualism and its by-product, moral decay. According to Lee Kuan Yew:

> The expansion of the right of the individual to behave or misbehave as he [or she] pleases has come at the expense of orderly society. In the East the main object is

---

116   Tang, *op. cit.*, p. 215.
117   *Idem.* p. 231.
118   Z. bin Rasheed 'Searching for Singapore's National Values' in Z. bin Rasheed (ed.) *In Search of Singapore's National Values* (1990) p. 92.

to have a well-ordered society so that everybody can have maximum enjoyment of his [or her] freedoms'.[119]

These 'Asian values' or 'Shared Values' of discipline, restraint, family responsibility and obedience to authority are deemed to be an effective antidote to Western problems of drug abuse, crime, promiscuity and family breakdown. The maintenance of social stability through the placing of community over self and obedience to authority, deeply rooted in Confucianism, constitutes the cornerstone of this set of Asian values.

The universalist-cultural relativist debate has also resulted in greater prominence being accorded to the principle of individual duty. Prior to Western colonisation, the quintessence of the formulation of human rights in traditional African societies was the conception of the individual as a moral being endowed with rights but also bounded by duties. The individual proactively united his or her needs with the needs of others within a tightly-knit community.[120] The necessity to preserve a balance between the exercise of individual rights and the performance of individual duties had strong roots in African traditional society which was consumed by the socialisation of the individual through corporate family and community structures.[121] As we shall see in the next section of this chapter, this historical African emphasis on duty has had a pronounced effect upon the content of the *African Charter on Human and Peoples' Rights*.

Recourse to Asian and African values is not intended to deny the validity of the contribution of the Western liberal democratic tradition to the contemporary human rights movement or to undermine the universality of certain core values of norms. As Mutua maintains:

> [T]he current human rights movement must be understood as only a piece of the whole. Its roots in the Western liberal tradition necessarily deny its completeness, though not the universality of many of its ideals and norms. To paraphrase the famous metaphor, the gourd is only partially filled by the Western tradition: it falls on other traditions to fill it.[122]

The African Regional Human Rights System

The African regional human rights system has been described as '[t]he newest, the least developed or effective, the most distinctive and the most controversial of the regional human rights regimes'.[123] The *African Charter on Human and Peoples' Rights,* sometimes referred to as the '*Banjul Charter*', forms the basis of Africa's

---

119   As quoted in F. Zakaria 'Culture is Destiny: A Conversation with Lee Kuan Yew' (1994) 7 *Foreign Affairs* p. 111.
120   Makau Wa Mutua, *op. cit.*, p. 363.
121   *Idem.* p. 344.
122   *Ibid.*
123   Steiner and Alston, *op. cit.*, p. 689.

continental human rights system.[124] On 27 June 1981, the 18th Assembly of Heads of State and Government of the Organization of African Unity adopted the *African Charter* which entered into force on 21 October 1986.

What makes the African regional human rights system the most distinctive of such systems is the emphasis placed in the *African Charter* on individual duties and the importance of community. The detailed attention given to the notions of individual duty and community far outweighs that of the *Universal Declaration of Human Rights* and the Twin Covenants discussed earlier in this chapter. The underlying rationale of the *African Charter* is a belief by its sponsors that a duty-based system, in the African context at least, is the most appropriate means of ensuring individuals' basic needs are met in a manner that promotes social harmony and cohesion.[125] This is not surprising considering that, generally speaking, 'Africans think more of their obligations to their community than any claims against it'.[126] In order to better understand and appreciate these distinctive features of the *African Charter*, and by way of introduction to an analysis of its duty provisions, a brief explanation of pre-colonial African culture and traditional values will first be undertaken.

Pre-colonial African Culture and Traditional Values

Jomo Kenyatta, the first post-colonial president of Kenya, wrote a book entitled *Facing Mount Kenya: The Tribal Life of the Gikuyu* which was published in 1965. The following excerpts, which appear in Chapter 5 entitled 'System of Education', stress elements of duty inculcated in the children of the Gikuyu people. Although the following extract is lengthy, it provides a number of valuable insights into traditional African values and 'worldview', particularly in relation to the importance of performing individual duties within the pervasive social context of the community:

> [The children] are also taught . . . respect [for] their parents and kinsfolk. Under all circumstances they must stay with them and share in their joys and sorrows. It will never do to leave them and go off to see the world whenever they take the notion, especially when their parents are in their old age. They must give them clothes, look after their garden, herd their cattle, sheep and goats, build their grain stores and houses. It thus becomes a part of their outlook on life that their parents

---

124   *African Charter on Human and Peoples' Rights*, 27 June 1981, O.A.U. Doc. CAB/LEG/67/3/Rev. 5 (1981), reprinted in (1982) 21 *I.L.M.* p. 59. The *African Charter* is also known as the *Banjul Charter* because the final draft of the instrument was produced in Banjul, the capital of The Gambia. The sole implementation organ of the *Charter* is the African Commission on Human and Peoples' Rights which was established in 1987.

125   A. Devereux 'Should "Duties" Play a Larger Role in Human Rights? A Critique of Western Liberal and African Human Rights Jurisprudence' (1995) 18 *University of New South Wales Law Journal* pp. 464, 465.

126   O. Ojo 'Understanding Human Rights in Africa' in F. Berting *et al.* (eds) *Human Rights in a Pluralist World: Individuals and Collectives* (1990) pp. 115, 120.

shall not suffer want nor continue to labour strenuously in their old age while their children can lend a hand and do things to give them comfort. ... [T]he community can be mobilised very easily for corporate activity. House-building, cultivation, harvesting, digging trap-pits, putting up fences around cultivated fields, and building bridges, are usually done by the group; hence the Gikuyu saying: '*Kamoinge koyaga ndere,*' which means collective activities make heavier tasks easier. ... [T]he individual boy or girl soon learns to work with and for other people. An old man who has no children of his own is helped by his neighbour's children in almost everything. His hut is built, his garden dug, firewood is cut and water is fetched for him. ... The old man reciprocates by treating the children as though they were his own. Children learn this habit of communal work like others, not by verbal exhortations so much as by joining with older people in such social services. ... All help given in this way is voluntary, and kinsfolk are proud to help one another. There is no payment or expectation of payment. ... The whole thing rests on the principle of reciprocal obligations. It is taken for granted that the neighbour whom you assist in difficulty or whose house you help to build will do the same for you when in similar need. Those who do not reciprocate these sentiments of neighbourliness are not in favour. ... The selfish or self-regarding man has no name or reputation in the Gikuyu community. An individualist is looked upon with suspicion and is given a nickname of *mwebongia*, one who works only for himself. ... He may lack assistance when he needs it. ... In the Gikuyu community there is no really individual affair, for every thing has a moral and social reference. The habit of corporate effort is but the other side of corporate ownership. ... In spite of the foreign elements which work against many of the Gikuyu institutions and the desire to implant the system of wholesale Westernisation, this system of mutual help and the tribal solidarity in social services, political and economic activities are still maintained by the large majority of the Gikuyu people. It is less practised among those Gikuyu who have been Europeanised or detribalised. The rest of the community look upon these people as mischief-makers and breakers of the tribal traditions, and the general disgusted cry is heard: '*Mothongo ne athogonjire borori,*' i.e. the white man had spoiled and disgraced our country.[127]

In a very practical sense, then, Africans living in traditional societies were each other's keeper. Co-operation and working together for the benefit of the tribal community were fundamental values of these societies. Indeed, the community was perceived as more important than the individual members thereof. As Ronald Cohen has observed:

> Many African cultures value the group - one should never die alone, live alone, remain outside social networks unless one is a pariah, insane, or the carrier of a feared contagious disease. Corporate kinship in which individuals are responsible for the behaviour of their group members is a widespread tradition.[128]

---

127 J. Kenyatta *Facing Mount Kenya: The Tribal Life of the Gikuyu* (1965) pp. 113-120.

128 R. Cohen 'Endless Tears: Prolegomena to the Study of Human Rights in Africa' in R. Cohen *et al.* (eds) *Human Rights and Governance in Africa* (1993) p. 14.

Even the enjoyment of wealth and property occurred within a collectivist perspective. Traditional African societies generally distributed their wealth evenly and provided security for all members of society.[129]

Numerous African writers have highlighted the priority of collective loyalties and kinship ties over individual claims. Okere observes that the 'African conception of man is not that of an isolated and abstract individual, but an integral member of a group animated by a spirit of solidarity'.[130] By contrast, Ake disparages Western human rights systems for creating 'a society which is atomized and individualistic, a society of endemic conflict ... [and] of people conscious of their separateness'.[131] Traditional African persons are not similarly 'locked in a constant struggle against society for the redemption of their rights'.[132] The following passage taken from the writings of Asmarom Legesse graphically illustrates the Western individualist/African collectivist dichotomy:

> The critical difference between the African and Western traditions concerns the importance of the human individual. In the liberal democracies of the Western world the ultimate repository of rights is the human person. The individual is held in a virtually sacralized position. There is a perpetual, and in our view obsessive, concern with the dignity of the individual, his worth, personal autonomy, and property. ... If Africans were the sole authors of the Universal Declaration, they might have ranked the rights of communities above those of individuals, and they might have used a cultural idiom fundamentally different from language in which the ideas are now formulated. No aspect of Western civilization makes an African more uncomfortable than the concept of the sacralized individual whose private wars against society are celebrated. If we turn the situation around and view it from an African perspective, the individual who is fighting private wars against his society is no hero. ... The heart of African culture is egalitarian and antiheroic in character. ... Most African cultures, whether they are formally egalitarian or hierarchical, have mechanisms of distributive justice that ensure that individuals do not deviate so far from the norm that they can overwhelm the society. This is the factor that was widespread throughout pre-colonial Africa and served as the cornerstone of African morality.[133]

---

129   F. Awogu *Political Institutions and Thought in Africa: An Introduction* (1975) p. 82.

130   B. Obinna Okere 'The Protection of Human Rights in Africa and the African Charter on Human and Peoples' Rights: A Comparative Analysis with the European and American Systems' (1984) 6 *Human Rights Quarterly* pp. 141, 148.

131   C. Ake 'The African Context of Human Rights' quoted by R. Howard 'Group versus Individual Identity in the Africa Debate on Human Rights' in A. An-Na'im and F. Deng (eds) *Human Rights in Africa: Cross-Cultural Perspectives* (1990) pp. 159, 173.

132   R. Kiwanuka 'The Meaning of "People" in the African Charter on Human and Peoples' Rights' (1988) p. 82 *American Journal of International Law* pp. 80, 82.

133   A. Legesse 'Human Rights in African Political Culture' in K. Thompson (ed.) *The Moral Imperatives of Human Rights* (1980) pp. 123, 124.

Thus, in traditional African societies, the individual's welfare was furthered in harmony, rather than in competition, with the welfare of the community. Individuals were socialised to serve collective interests rather than to consider their own particular interests as distinct from those of the group.

Traditional African societies also exhibited great respect for human dignity. The torture, killing or detention of tribal members was prohibited.[134] The principles and ideals common to the kinship system of various traditional African societies, sometimes aggregated by African commentators under the rubric 'African humanism', comprised the following:

-   **respect** for, and protection of, the individual within the family, whereby each family member recognised the place and rights of other family members;

-   **deference** to age (because a long life is generally wise and knowledgeable);

-   **restraint** (or the balancing of individual rights with the requirements of the community);

-   **responsibility** to family members, other persons and the community (manifested by a commitment to work with and help others);

-   **reciprocity** in labour matters and on occasions of generous acts;

-   **solidarity** with fellow human beings, especially in times of need;

-   **common ownership** of property and the equal distribution of benefits on the basis of individual need;

-   **duty to work** (every family member has the right to food and shelter but also has an obligation to work provided he or she is capable of doing so).[135]

The consciousness of rights and duties was ingrained in community members from birth and formed the basis of the kinship system.[136] Nevertheless, traditional African societies were primarily duty-based systems designed to strengthen community ties and social cohesion and to secure the welfare of each individual within a community setting. Individuals were members of matrilineal kinship lineages which generated duties. The primary duties owed by tribal members were duties concerning the well-being of their kin. A family member in need was considered a matter of shame for the entire family. Traditional African societies constituted 'mutual societies' in which another's welfare was a matter of concern and individual duty. As Nahum remarks: 'To the ancient question, am I my brother's keeper, the answer is an emphatic yes and so is your brother your

---

134   Motala, *op. cit.*, p. 387.
135   Makau Wa Mutua, op. cit., p. 352. Laziness, like other breaches of duty, carried a social stigma and was considered a ground for expulsion from the family and community: see Motala, *op. cit.*, pp. 381-2.
136   *Idem.* p. 362.

keeper!'[137] The Dinka concept of *cieng* required positive assistance to one's fellow human beings, whilst among the Bantu peoples the concept of a person, *mtu* in Kiswahili, referred to a person who lives in peace and is helpful to his or her community.[138] As in Confucianism, a person could enhance his or her social status and prestige by conscientiously discharging duties such as participating in public works or by sustaining a prosperous household.[139] Duties in the pre-colonial African context often went beyond meeting correlative rights and involved considerable sacrifice.[140]

The African Charter on Human and Peoples' Rights

Human rights issues in Africa were not considered to be a high priority on the agenda of the Organization of African Unity (O.A.U.) until relatively recently.[141] African governments devoted greater attention during the 1960s and 1970s to dismantling colonialism and consolidating their newly-acquired independence. Scant attention was paid to domestic human rights practices except for the O.A.U.'s condemnation of the practice of *apartheid* by the South African government. African governments generally regarded human rights abuses as matters falling within the domestic jurisdiction of each African state. O.A.U. member states consistently invoked Article 3(2)[142] of the *Charter of the Organization of African Unity* of 23 May 1963 to prevent other member states from interfering in their internal affairs. In the late 1970s, however, world-wide publicity of gross human rights transgressions committed by, amongst others, President Idi Amin of Uganda and the Tanzanian invasion of Uganda in 1979 prompted the O.A.U. to seriously consider human rights generally at a summit conference in Monrovia, Liberia. This culminated in the drafting of the *African Charter on Human and Peoples' Rights*.

The adoption of the *African Charter* recognised that human rights breaches in any O.A.U. member state are a legitimate matter of concern for all other O.A.U. member states. But beyond that, its drafters attempted to incorporate within the *Charter* a unique African outlook, reflecting African needs, traditional values and legal philosophy. The preamble of the *Charter* provides some useful insights into its operative provisions. Apart from the fifth preambular paragraph which stresses the importance of considering the virtues and values of the African historical tradition and African civilisation, the seventh paragraph acknowledges that 'the enjoyment of rights and freedoms also implies the performance of duties on the part of everyone'. It is inherent in the African community-oriented

---

137   As quoted in Motala, *op. cit.*, p. 388.
138   *Idem.* p. 360.
139   *Idem.* p. 348, n. 26.
140   A. Devereux, *op. cit.*, p. 480.
141   Motala, *op. cit.*, pp. 395-7.
142   Article 3(2) of the *Charter of the Organization of African Unity* provides that O.A.U. member states 'solemnly affirm and declare their adherence to the' [principle of] '[n]on-interference in the internal affairs of States'.

approach towards human rights that rights and duties form a common whole, and this the seventh paragraph recognises.[143]   Prior to the *African Charter*, most international human rights instruments were only concerned with duties owed by the State to its citizens and residents. There were modest exceptions, for example Article 29(1) of the *Universal Declaration of Human Rights* and the fifth preambular paragraph of the Twin Covenants previously discussed in this chapter. For the first time, however, the *African Charter* attempted to systematically articulate the duties owed by individuals to other individuals, his or her family and the State.[144] In this respect, the *Charter* goes well beyond the conventional notion that duties are correlative to rights; it extends to the recognition of imperfect or non-correlative or freestanding duties.[145]   This innovation was not solely attributable to mere tradition, as socialist states such as Ethiopia and Mozambique encountered difficulties reconciling the International Bill of Rights[146] with socialist philosophy. To secure the wider adoption of the *African Charter*, its drafters accepted the proposition that if the individual is to have rights recognised by the State, then he or she must have obligations flowing back to the State.[147]

As for the operative provisions of the *African Charter*, Article 1 provides that the States Parties 'shall recognize the rights, duties and freedoms enshrined in this Charter and shall undertake to adopt legislative or other measures to give effect to them'. Thus, States Parties are legally obliged to implement not only individual rights and freedoms but individual duties as well. Another obligation concerning individual duties is imposed on States Parties by Article 25 which essentially requires them to disseminate an understanding of the rights and freedoms contained in the *Charter* as well as their correlative or 'corresponding obligations and duties'. A duty is indirectly imposed on individuals by Article 5 which states in part that '*[a]ll* forms of exploitation and degradation ... particularly slavery, slave trade, torture, cruel, inhuman or degrading punishment and treatment shall be prohibited' (emphasis supplied). Such expansive language necessarily covers both public and private forms of exploitation and degradation.[148] As in the case of Articles 18 and 21 of the *International Covenant on Civil and*

---

143   W. Benedek 'Peoples' Rights and Individuals' Duties as Special Features of the African Charter on Human and Peoples' Rights' in P. Kunig *et al.* (eds) *Regional Protection of Human Rights by International Law* (1985) pp. 59, 63.

144   It will be recalled that the *American Declaration on the Rights and Duties of Man*, discussed earlier in this chapter, also attempted an enumeration of individual duties. However, unlike the *African Charter*, the *American Declaration* does not impose any legally binding obligations on states.

145   See Chapter 3 for a discussion of the meaning of these terms.

146   Consisting of the *Universal Declaration of Rights*, the *International Covenant on Civil and Political Rights* and the *International Covenant on Economic, Social and Cultural Rights*.

147   R. Gittelman 'The Banjul Charter on Human and Peoples' Rights: A Legal Analysis' in C. Welch and R. Meltzer (eds) *Human Rights and Development in Africa* (1984) pp. 152, 154. Chapter 8 will endeavour to provide an analysis of the principle of individual duty within the context of socialist theory.

148   Paust, *op. cit.*, p. 56.

Political Rights, Articles 8 and 11 of the *African Charter* respectively guarantee the rights to freedom of conscience, religion and assembly but subject to clawback provisions. Accordingly, individuals are once again subject to an indirect duty to exercise these rights responsibly in a manner which respects the rights of others as well as conduces to the collective good.

The centrepiece of the *African Charter* concerning individual duties, however, is Chapter II of Part I entitled 'Duties'. Chapter II consists of three provisions - Articles 27, 28 and 29. Given their importance, it is proposed to set out their text in full:

Article 27

1. Every individual shall have duties towards his family and society, the State and other legally recognized communities and the international community.

2. The rights and freedoms of each individual shall be exercised with due regard to the rights of others, collective security, morality and common interest.

Article 28

Every individual shall have the duty to respect and consider his fellow beings without discrimination, and to maintain relations aimed at promoting, safeguarding and reinforcing mutual respect and tolerance.

Article 29

The individual shall also have the duty:

1. To preserve the harmonious development of the family and to work for the cohesion and respect of the family; to respect his parents at all times, to maintain them in case of need;

2. To serve his national community by placing his physical and intellectual abilities at its service;

3. Not to compromise the security of the State whose national or resident he is;

4. To preserve and strengthen social and national solidarity, particularly when the latter is threatened;

5. To preserve and strengthen the national independence and the territorial integrity of his country and to contribute to its defence in accordance with the law;

6. To work to the best of his abilities and competence, and to pay taxes imposed by law in the interest of the society;

7. To preserve and strengthen positive African cultural values in his relations with other members of the society, in the spirit of tolerance, dialogue and consultation and, in general, to contribute to the promotion of the moral well-being of society;

8. To contribute to the best of his abilities, at all times and at all levels, to the promotion and achievement of African unity.

The explicit duties prescribed by Articles 27, 28 and 29 were intended in part to recreate the bonds of the pre-colonial era among individuals and between individuals and the community.[149] This is particularly evident in the calls to individuals made in Sub-Articles (4) and (7) of Article 29 respectively to 'preserve and strengthen social ... solidarity' and to 'preserve and strengthen positive African cultural values'.[150] These provisions represent a rejection of the individual 'who is utterly free and utterly irresponsible and opposed to society'.[151] Article 27(1) is innovative in identifying the recipients or beneficiaries of the individual duties owed. Only the community and other individuals were so identified by the *Universal Declaration of Human Rights* and the Twin Covenants. Article 27(1) also identifies family members and the State as well as other legally recognised communities[152] and the international community.[153] Article 27(2) requires individuals to exercise their rights and freedoms 'with due regard to the rights of others, collective security, morality and common interest'. This indirect duty imposed on individuals to exercise their rights sensitively is consistent with the way rights and privileges were enjoyed in traditional African societies.[154]

Some of the duties mentioned in Article 29 are already justiciable and enforceable under the domestic law of O.A.U. member states. These are duties owed by the individual to the state. Such duties are not distinctive to African states as many of them are standard obligations that modern states impose on their citizens. Duties in this category would include the duties to pay taxes, of national service and defence and not to compromise state security. Other duties are more programmatic and unenforceable in nature. As Benedek notes, some of the duties enumerated in the *African Charter* 'spell out a general philosophy and principles of behavior [sic] rather than operational legal concepts'.[155] These duties include those mentioned in Article 28 ('to respect and consider his fellow beings without discrimination, and to maintain relations aimed at promoting, safeguarding and reinforcing mutual respect and tolerance'), Article 29(6) ('[t]o work to the best of his abilities and competence'), Article 29(7) ('[t]o preserve and strengthen positive

---

149   Makau Wa Mutua, *op. cit.*, p. 368.
150   See the preceding section of this chapter entitled 'Pre-colonial African Culture and Traditional Values' for a description of these values.
151   Address of President Leopold Sedar Senghor of Senegal to the Meeting of Experts for the Preparation of the Draft African Charter on Human and Peoples' Rights, Dakar, Senegal (28 November - 8 December 1979), O.A.U. Doc. CAB/LEG/67/3/Rev. 1, at 2.
152   Other legally recognised communities would include the Organization of African Unity.
153   An example of an individual duty owed to the international community would be an obligation not to commit the international crime of genocide.
154   Motala, *op. cit.*, p. 403.
155   Benedek, *op. cit.*, p. 63.

African cultural values ... and ... to contribute to the promotion of the moral well-being of society') and Article 29(8)('[t]o contribute to the best of his abilities ... to the promotion and achievement of African unity'). These latter duty provisions lack specificity and it would accordingly be difficult for a State Party to invoke the *African Charter* to establish that an individual is not duly discharging his or her duties. The African Commission on Human and Peoples' Rights, established under Article 30 of the *African Charter*, has not yet taken steps to provide an interpretation or elaboration of Articles 27, 28 and 29 or to indicate by whom or in which forum the duties would be enforced, if at all. It has been suggested that it should be the duty of the African Commission in its jurisprudence to clarify which of the individual duties prescribed by Articles 27, 28 and 29 are legal, as opposed to merely moral, obligations, to delimit their scope of application and to suggest how the duties might be practically implemented.[156] As two commentators have pointed out, some of the duties 'are of such breadth and so ambiguous in their connotations that a regime of serious enforcement without some degree of prior elaboration is difficult to imagine'.[157] The position would appear to be that these 'soft' duties were never intended to be legally binding or justiciable, although the values they encapsulate are consistent with traditional African values.[158] One commentator has questioned the viability of a State-enforced system of individual moral duties on the basis that States do not have a sufficient connection or interest in restraining breaches of individual duty.[159] In this context, the local community might be better placed to implement such duties through customary and religious rules. As suggested by a former chairman of the African Commission, however, State responsibility for the implementation of the individual duties included in the *African Charter* entails a 'minimum obligation to inculcate the underlying principles and ideals in their subjects'.[160]

Article 29(1) is also innovative. It requires individuals to 'preserve the harmonious development of the family' as well as prescribing a duty of parental respect and maintenance. In African traditional society, the extended family was a key constituent of social organisation as recognised by Article 18 of the *African Charter* which recognises the family in its Sub-Article (1) as 'the natural unit and basis of society' and in Sub-Article (2) as 'the custodian of morals and traditional values recognized by the community'. Article 29(1) is similar to Article XXX of the *American Declaration of the Rights and Duties of Man* in imposing a duty of parental respect and maintenance but falls short of Article XXX in failing to

---

156   Makau Wa Mutua, *op. cit.*, p. 375. As part of its mandate, the African Commission on Human and Peoples' Rights is empowered by Article 45(3) of the *African Charter on Human and Peoples' Rights* to interpret the provisions of the *Charter*.
157   Steiner and Alston, *op. cit.*, pp. 694-5.
158   Motala, *op. cit.*, p. 404.
159   Devereux, *op. cit.*, p. 477.
160   U. Oji Umozurike 'The African Charter on Human and Peoples' Rights' (1983) p. 77 *American Journal of International Law* pp. 902, 907. See also Article 25 of the *African Charter on Human and Peoples' Rights*.

explicitly prescribe a parental duty to maintain and educate minor children.[161] These duties incorporated within Article 29(1) reflect basic underlying problems for African states, notably underdeveloped economies and the lack of adequate social security. Such conditions force families to provide their own welfare net to their own members.[162] As Makau Wa Mutua explains:

> The care of the aged and needy falls squarely on family and community members. This requirement - a necessity today - has its roots in the past: it was unthinkable to abandon a parent or relative in need. The family guilty of such an omission would be held in disgrace and contempt pending the intervention of lineage or clan members. Such problems explain why the family is considered sacred and why it would be simply impracticable and suicidal for Africans to adopt wholesale the individualist conception of rights.[163]

The *African Charter on Human and Peoples' Rights* is thus a unique human rights instrument in two main respects: it is the first such legally binding instrument at any level to attempt a comprehensive articulation of duties owed by individuals and the first regional instrument to incorporate cultural relativist theory. The most serious and general criticism levelled against the language of duties expressed in the *African Charter* is the danger that African states might exploit the duty provisions to violate other guaranteed rights.[164] However, this may be a theoretical and overstated danger only as it is difficult to envisage how recourse to cultural relativism could credibly justify serious breaches of fundamental human rights.

Mention should also be made of another recent African regional human rights instrument which contains significant provisions concerning individual duties. The *African Charter on the Rights* and *Welfare of the Child* of 1990 imposes individual duties not only upon parents but upon minor children as well. Three provisions in particular are noteworthy. The penultimate preambular paragraph of this instrument recites the conviction of the States Parties 'that the promotion and protection of the rights and welfare of the child also implies the performance of duties on the part of everyone'. Article 20(1) headed 'Parental Responsibilities' prescribes the following individual duties for parents, legal guardians and extended family or clan members for the upbringing of children:

---

161   By way of a general comparison of the *American Declaration of the Rights and Duties of Man* and the *African Charter on Human and Peoples' Rights*, the former instrument is heavily weighted towards the imposition of civic duties on individuals whereas the latter instrument emphasises to a greater degree duties owed by individual family members and duties to preserve indigenous culture and values.

162   O. Eze *Human Rights in Africa: Some Selected Problems* (1984) p. 215.

163   Makau Wa Mutua, *op. cit.*, pp. 369-70 (footnotes excluded).

164   R. Cohen, *op. cit.*, p. 15.

Article 20: Parental Responsibilities

1. Parents or other persons responsible for the child shall have the primary responsibility for the upbringing and development of the child and shall have the duty:

(a) to ensure that the best interests of the child are their basic concern at all times;

(b) to secure, within their abilities and financial capacities, conditions of living necessary to the child's development; and

(c) to ensure that domestic discipline is administered with humanity and in a manner consistent with the inherent dignity of the child.

Article 31 headed 'Responsibilities of the Child' is a unique provision in the sense that its contents do not find any counterpart in the United Nations *Convention on the Rights of the Child* of 1989. The inclusion of Article 31 in the *African Charter on the Rights and Welfare of the Child* was designed to remedy this lacuna within the African context. The complete text of Article 31 which follows is very similar to the duties prescribed for individuals by Article 29 of the *African Charter on Human and Peoples' Rights:*

Article 31: Responsibilities of the Child

Every child shall have responsibilities towards his family and society, the State and other legally recognised communities and the international community. The child, subject to his [or her] age and ability, and such limitations as may be contained in the present Charter, shall have the duty:

(a) to work for the cohesion of the family, to respect his [or her] parents and elders at all times and to assist them in case of need;

(b) to serve his [or her] national community by placing his [or her] physical and intellectual abilities at its service;

(c) to preserve and strengthen social and national solidarity;

(d) to preserve and strengthen African cultural values in his [or her] relations with other members of the society, in the spirit of tolerance, dialogue and consultation and to contribute to the moral well-being of society;

(e) to preserve and strengthen the independence and the integrity of his [or her] country;

(f) to contribute to the best of his abilities, at all times and at all levels, to the promotion and achievement of African unity.

It is difficult to envisage how a young child, at least, could meaningfully discharge these duties, although Article 31 does tie their performance to age and ability criteria. In any event, these 'soft' individual duties imposed on children are non-justiciable in nature. Nevertheless, it is conceivable that the African Committee of Experts on the Rights and Welfare of the Child, established under Part II of the *African Charter on the Rights and Welfare of the Child*, could make suggestions to the States Parties on how these duties might be practically implemented.

Chapter 7

Particular Individual Duties Explicitly Recognised Under International and Regional Human Rights Law and by National Law

People only respect a society which makes demands on them.[1]

Introduction

Generally speaking, duties have not been as systematically identified, defined and explicated as have rights, particularly at the international and regional levels. Rights theorists have not been as preoccupied with delineating the scope of duties which human beings owe to each other. This may be due in part to the inherent controversy and disagreement which would accompany such a task. One commentator has speculated that the lack of a comprehensive enumeration of human duties is attributable to 'the view of "rights" as all-important and providing for human needs, such that separate consideration of "duties" is unnecessary'.[2] The view has also been ventured that a duty-based social order is inherently less subject to universalisation than a rights-based social order. The argument runs that the content of individual duties is very much the product of the religious, social and political culture in which a person lives, whereas the content of individual rights is less context-specific and therefore more amenable to formulation in the abstract.[3] Be that as it may, this chapter will be devoted to illustrating that there are certain 'core' human duties which are universally recognised at the international, regional and national levels, regardless of culture or context. Indeed, the content of most of

---

1   I. Kristol *Republican Virtue Versus Servile Institutions* (1974) p. 13.

2   A. Devereux 'Should "Duties" Play a Larger Role in Human Rights? A Critique of Western Liberal and African Human Rights Jurisprudence' (1995) 18 *University of New South Wales Law Journal* pp. 464, 468.

3   H. Steiner and P. Alston *International Human Rights in Context: Law, Politics, Morals* (1996) p. 186.

these duties is consistent and uniform. The following individual duties[4] will be examined in this chapter:

- the duty to exercise human rights responsibly and with due consideration for the rights of others;

- the duty to strive for the promotion and observance of human rights;

- the duty not to incite racial hatred and not engage in propaganda;

- the duty to support family members;

- the duty to work;

- the duty to acquire an education;

- the duty of military service;

- the duty of national or public service;

- the duty to obey the constitution and other laws;

- the duty to pay taxes;

- the duty to vote;

- the duty to preserve cultural values;

- the duty to contribute to social welfare;

- the duty to safeguard a particular ideology (particularly democracy).

Other duties recognised at the national level will also be briefly canvassed. These include the duty to render national disaster assistance, the duty to preserve the natural environment, the duty to exercise property rights consistently with the public welfare, the duty of aliens to pay taxes and to obey the law, the duty of physical self-care, the duty to render jury service, the duty to render assistance to public authorities in law enforcement matters, the duty to render assistance to persons in distress, and the duty to assist public health authorities.

The Duty to Exercise Human Rights Responsibly

The Roman jurist Justinian summarised the duties of the individual towards other individuals in three legal maxims or precepts: 'to live honestly, to hurt no one and

---

4   Although this list is meant to be illustrative rather than exhaustive, it does canvass the most widely recognised human duties.

to give to every man his own *(Iuris praecepta sunt haec: honeste vivere, alterum non laedere, suum cuique tribuere)*.[5] In the 'Introduction' to *On Liberty* (1859), John Stuart Mill endorsed this 'harm principle' or duty of respect when he wrote:

> The only liberty which deserves the name, is that of pursuing our own good in our own way, so long as we do not attempt to deprive others of theirs, or impede their efforts to obtain it.

This is a candid acknowledgement of the fact that rights inescapably live at each other's expense, such that 'no right or moral claim can be pushed to its limits without injuring other moral claims or virtues'.[6] The duty to exercise one's human rights responsibly and with due consideration for the rights of others is but 'an expression of the *constraints of membership of the civic order*'.[7] Such duty circumscribes the bounds of individual licence and freedom. In an earlier era, Immanuel Kant had observed:

> All evil in the world springs from freedom ... It is essential, therefore, that man should restrain by rules the free actions which relate to himself. These are the rules of his self-regarding duties.[8]

Kant's antidote to such unbounded freedom was what he described as 'the duty of free respect to others'. He perceived such duty as a negative, rather than positive, one 'of not exalting oneself above others'.[9] Kant's duty of free respect and Mill's harm principle are ethical imperatives and practical necessities for the maintenance of the civic order.[10] They both presuppose the destructive effects upon the civic order of the unrestrained drive to satisfy human needs and desires. Kant and Mill attempted to demarcate an area within which a person was free to do as he or she pleases without external interference. The delimitation line would be crossed where individual action harmed the interests of other identifiable individuals or the wider interests of society as a whole. So, for example, we may all exercise the right to freedom of expression so long as we do not go so far as to defame the good reputation of others or incite sedition against the government.

---

5   As quoted in Erica-Irene A. Daes *Freedom of the Individual under Law: A Study on the Individual's Duties to the Community and the Limitations on Human Rights and Freedoms under Article 29 of the Universal Declaration of Human Rights* (United Nations, New York, 1990) p. 41.

6   E. Kamenka and A. E.-S. Tay 'The Philosophical Bases of Human Rights' *Human Rights for Australia* (Human Rights Commission Monograph Series No. 1, Canberra, Australian Government Publishing Service, 1986) pp. 77, 83.

7   D. Selbourne *The Principle of Duty* (1994) 149 (emphasis in original).

8   I. Kant *Lectures on Ethics* (translated by L. Infield, New York, 1963) p. 123.

9   I. Kant 'The Doctrine of Virtue' in *The Metaphysics of Morals* (translated by M. Gregor, 1964) p. 116.

10   Selbourne, *op. cit.*, p. 234.

One of the earliest instruments to explicitly recognise these considerations was the French *Declaration of the Rights of Man and of the Citizen* of 26 August 1789. The following provisions echo the views of Kant and Mill:

Article 4

Liberty consists in the power of doing whatever does not injure another. Accordingly, the exercise of the natural rights of every man has not other limits than those which are necessary to secure to every other man the free exercise of the same rights; and these limits are determinable only by the law.

Article 5

The law ought to prohibit only actions hurtful to society. What is not prohibited by the law should not be hindered . . .

Article 10

No man is to be interfered with because of his opinions, not even because of religious opinions, provided his avowal of them does not disturb public order as established by law.

Article 11

The unrestrained communication of thoughts or opinions being one of the most precious rights of man, every citizen may speak, write and publish freely, provided he be responsible for the abuse of this liberty, in the cases determined by law.

The duty of individuals to respect the rights of other individuals has been enshrined in Anglo-American and Australasian law for centuries in the form of criminal and tort law. As the late Sir Alfred Lord Denning once remarked, the freedom of the just individual is worth little if he or she can be preyed upon by murderer or thief.[11] The duty to respect other individuals in the exercise of their lawful rights and freedoms has also been recognised in other ethical and cultural systems. Confucius urged his followers to perform the Confucian rites with feelings of respect and reverence.[12] The principle of respect was similarly engrained in the morals and legal norms of traditional African society, which involved respect for oneself and for the place and rights of other family and community members.[13]

---

11   A. Denning *Freedom under the Law* (1949) p. 5.
12   W. Chang 'Confucian Theory of Norms and Human Rights' in W. Theodore De Bary and T. Weiming (eds) *Confucianism and Human Rights* (1998) pp. 117, 128. See also the section in Chapter 4 entitled 'Confucianism'.
13   Z. Motala 'Human Rights in Africa: A Cultural, Ideological, and Legal Examination' (1989) 12 *Hastings International and Comparative Law Review* 373, 381-2; Makau Wa Mutua 'The Banjul Charter and the African Cultural Fingerprint: An Evaluation of the Language of Duties' (1995) p. 35 *Virginia Journal of International Law* pp. 339, 352.

Since the aftermath of World War II, international human rights law has explicitly recognised that the enjoyment of human rights and fundamental freedoms is not absolute and may be suspended or qualified in times of war or public emergency and even in normal circumstances in the interests of certain overriding considerations.[14] The exercise of individual human rights may have to yield to the aggregate common interest in preserving national security, public safety and order, public health and morals and the rights and freedoms of others. Any measures attempting to limit the exercise of individual rights and freedoms must be taken pursuant to law in order to ensure that such derogations are made only by governmental authorities and to avoid arbitrary decision-making.[15]

A typical illustrative example of how international human rights law attempts to balance the protection of the exercise of individual human rights with the safeguarding of the aggregate common interest is provided by the following provisions taken from the *Universal Declaration of Human Rights* of 1948:

Article 2

Everyone is entitled to all the rights and freedoms set forth in this Declaration, without discrimination of any kind ...

Article 29(2)

In the exercise of his [or her] rights and freedoms, everyone shall be subject only to such limitations as are determined by law solely for the purpose of securing due recognition and respect for the rights and freedoms of others and of meeting the just requirements of morality, public order and the general welfare in a democratic society.

Article 30

Nothing in this Declaration may be interpreted as implying for any State, group or person any right to engage in any activity or to perform any act aimed at the destruction of any of the rights and freedoms set forth herein.

While these provisions acknowledge the freedom of each individual to fully develop his or her personality, they also simultaneously restrict this freedom by the duty imposed on each individual to exercise his or her rights in such a manner as to enable everyone else to do the same.[16] These provisions essentially challenge individuals to reflect sensitively on how the exercise of their rights in certain situations might adversely affect other individuals or the community. Such duty is based on the presumption that the full development of the individual is only possible when he or she is concerned about how his or her actions might impact on

---

14   A. Mayer *Islam and Human Rights: Tradition and Politics* (2nd ed., 1995) p. 61.

15   *Idem.* p. 62.

16   Daes, *op. cit.*, p. 41.

others. This duty has venerable roots in the harm principle espoused by Justinian and J. S. Mill.

The Twin Covenants contain similar provisions. Article 5(1) common to both the *International Covenant on Civil and Political Rights* of 1966 and the *International Covenant on Economic, Social and Cultural Rights* of 1966 replicates the above-mentioned Article 30 of the *Universal Declaration of Human Rights*. Moreover, as discussed in the previous chapter, the *ICCPR* contains five articles which confer on individuals important human rights but which subject their exercise to the operation of clawback clauses. These provisions are: Article 12 (right to liberty of movement), Article 18 (right to freedom of thought, conscience and religion), Article 19 (right to freedom of expression), Article 21 (right of peaceful assembly) and Article 22 (right to freedom of association). In the case of each article, a State Party may impose restrictions on the exercise of these rights pursuant to law for reasons of national security, the protection of the fundamental rights and freedoms of other individuals and so forth. Similarly, Articles 13, 14 and 15 of the *Convention on the Rights of the Child* of 1989 respectively confer on children the rights to freedom of expression, freedom of thought, conscience and religion, and freedom of association and peaceful assembly. But, once again, the exercise of these important human rights is conditioned by the same type of clawback clause. Thus, the cumulative effect of these provisions is to impose on individuals a duty to exercise their human rights and fundamental freedoms responsibly in such a manner that gives due consideration to the rights and interests of other individuals, the community and the State.

The regional human rights systems for Europe, Africa, Latin America and the Asia-Pacific also explicitly recognise such duty. The *European Convention for the Protection of Human Rights and Fundamental Freedoms* of 1950 contains in its Article 17 a virtually identical counterpart to Article 5(1) common to the Twin Covenants discussed above. The relevant provisions of the *African Charter on Human and Peoples' Rights* of 1981 are as follows:

Article 27(2)

The rights and freedoms of each individual shall be exercised with due regard to the rights of others, collective security, morality and common interest.

Article 28

Every individual shall have the duty to respect and consider his fellow beings without discrimination, and to maintain relations aimed at promoting, safeguarding and reinforcing mutual respect and tolerance.

In the Pacific region, Articles 27(2) and 28 of the *Draft Pacific Charter of Human Rights* of 1989[17] repeat almost verbatim the above-mentioned provisions of the African Charter. Article I(3)of the *Declaration of the Basic Duties of ASEAN*

---

17   For more information on the *Draft Pacific Charter*, see the sub-section in Chapter 6 entitled 'The Asia-Pacific Region'.

Peoples and Governments of 1983[18] states in part that '[i]t is the duty of all individuals ... to exercise their rights and freedoms in the spirit of human solidarity, respecting and defending the rights and freedoms of others'.

The Latin American regional human rights system also pays heed to the principle of respect. The following two provisions of the *American Declaration of the Rights and Duties of Man* of 1948 are prominent in this regard:

Article XXVIII

The rights of man are limited by the rights of others, by the security of all, and by the just demands of the general welfare and the advancement of democracy.

Article XXIX

It is the duty of the individual so to conduct himself in relation to others that each and every one may fully form and develop his personality.

Article 32(2) of the *American Convention on Human Rights* of 1969 essentially repeats the content of Article XXVIII of the *American Declaration*.[19] The individual duty of respect for others has also been recognised in the Arab world. Article 4(a) of the *Arab Charter on Human Rights* adopted in Cairo on 15 September 1994 by the Council of the League of Arab States states that '[n]o restrictions shall be placed on the rights and freedoms recognized in the present Charter except where such is provided by law and deemed necessary to protect the national security and economy, public order, health or morals or the rights and freedoms of others'.

The duty to exercise one's rights and freedoms responsibly has also been constitutionally entrenched by numerous states with varying political and socio-economic structures. Article 2(1) of the *Basic Law for the Federal Republic of Germany* of 23 May 1949 [20] states that '[e]verybody has the right to self-fulfilment in so far as they do not violate the rights of others or offend against the constitutional order or morality'. In Article V (entitled 'Duties and Obligations of Citizens') of the *Constitution of the Republic of the Philippines* of 17 January 1973, Section 2 proclaims that '[t]he rights of the individual impose upon him [or her] the corresponding duty to exercise them responsibly and with due regard for the rights of others'. Article 40 of the *Constitution of the Islamic Republic of Iran* of 28 July 1989 provides that '[n]o one is entitled to exercise his [or her] rights in a

---

18   Adopted by the Regional Council on Human Rights in Asia. For more information on the *ASEAN Declaration*, see the section in Chapter 6 entitled 'The Asia-Pacific Region'.

19   While the *American Convention on Human Rights* carries binding legal obligations for its States Parties, the *American Declaration* does not. Article 32(2) of the *American Convention* states: 'The rights of each person are limited by the rights of others, by the security of all, and by the just demands of the general welfare, in a democratic society'.

20   As revised and updated January 1994.

way injurious to others or detrimental to public interests'.   In terms of the constitutional recognition of the respect principle in communist states, Article 48 of *the Constitution of the People's Republic of China* of 4 December 1982 states:

> When exercising their freedoms and rights, citizens of the People's Republic of China must not infringe upon the interests of the State, of society and of the collective, or upon the lawful freedoms and rights of other citizens.

The *Constitution (Fundamental Law) of the Union of Soviet Socialist Republics*, adopted by the Supreme Soviet at its Ninth Convocation on 7 October 1977, sets out in Chapter 7 the basic rights, freedoms and duties of citizens of the U.S.S.R. Article 65 states in part that '[a] citizen of the U.S.S.R. is obliged to respect the rights and lawful interests of other persons'.   Article 63 of the *Constitution of the Republic of Cuba of 24 February 1976* similarly provides in part that '[e]veryone has the duty of ... respecting the rights of others'.   It is thus apparent that the individual duty to exercise one's rights and freedoms responsibly is widely recognised at the international, regional and national levels.

The Duty to Strive for the Promotion and Observance of Human Rights

The genesis of the duty to strive for the promotion and observance of human rights is the eighth preambular paragraph of the *Universal Declaration of Human Rights* which provides in part:

> *Now, Therefore,*
>
> THE GENERAL ASSEMBLY
>
> *proclaims*
>
> *This universal declaration of human rights* as a common standard of achievement for all peoples and all nations, to the end that every individual ..., keeping this Declaration constantly in mind, shall strive by teaching and education to promote respect for these rights and freedoms and ... to secure their universal and effective recognition and observance ...

The fifth preambular paragraph common to both the *International Covenant on Civil and Political Rights* and the *International Covenant on Economic, Social and Cultural Rights* reinforces this duty in the following terms:

> *Recognizing* that the individual, having duties to other individuals and to the community to which he [or she] belongs, is under a responsibility to strive for the promotion and observance of the rights recognized in the present Covenant...

Further recognition of an individual duty to strive for the promotion and observance of human rights is to be found in a number of other instruments.

Article 1 of the *Proclamation of Teheran* adopted on 13 May 1968 by the United Nations International Conference on Human Rights maintained that '[i]t is imperative that the members of the international community fulfil their solemn obligations to promote and encourage respect for human rights and fundamental freedoms for all ...' Within Asia, Article 20 of the *Kuala Lumpur Declaration on Human Rights* of 1993[21] proclaims that '[i]t is the task and responsibility of each Member State and every citizen to ensure the promotion, implementation and protection of human rights'. Most recently, Article 18(2) of the United Nations *Declaration on the Right and Responsibility of Individuals, Groups and Organs of Society to Promote and Protect Universally Recognized Human Rights and Fundamental Freedoms* of 1998[22] states in part that '[i]ndividuals ... have an important role to play and a responsibility in ... promoting human rights and fundamental freedoms ...' Nevertheless, none of these provisions purport to impose a legally binding obligation on individuals, either because they are mere preambular (non-operative) provisions of an international instrument (as in the case of the *Universal Declaration* and the Twin Covenants) or they appear in an instrument which was never intended to impose such an obligation (as in the case of the *Proclamation of Teheran,* the *Kuala Lumpur Declaration* and the *Declaration on the Responsibility of Individuals to Promote Human Rights and Fundamental Freedoms).*

The Duty to Support Family Members

The family is a universal phenomenon and one of the most basic social institutions. Indeed, the family is our earliest experience of community.[23] The word 'family' is derived from the Latin word *'familia'* which means household. From ancient times the family has been regarded as the foundation of the civic order itself. Cicero referred to the family as the 'seed-plot of the whole commonwealth'.[24] As Selbourne points out, this metaphor suggests that successful family nurture is vital to the well-being of the civic order.[25]

The family is also one of the oldest objects of practical duty in the human community.[26] This is not surprising, for as Kaplan observes:

---

21   For more information on the *Kuala Lumpur Declaration,* see the sub-section in Chapter 6 entitled 'The Asia-Pacific Region'.

22   Adopted by the United Nations General Assembly pursuant to its Resolution 53/144 of 9 December 1998.

23   D. Hodgson 'The International Legal Recognition and Protection of the Family' (1994) 8 *Australian Journal of Family Law* 219.

24   Cicero *Offices, Essays and Letters* translated by T. Cockman (1690), London, (1909),I, xvii.

25   D. Selbourne, *op. cit.,* p. 227.

26   *Idem.* p. 228.

> That charity begins at home is an ancient doctrine. Blood is thicker than water: in every society kinship entails special rights and obligations. To care for one's own first or to care more, if it be a moral failing at all, is at any rate a universal one.[27]

The legal and moral status of the family unit and its organic societal importance are widely acknowledged in contemporary instruments. Article 22 of the *Charter of the Spanish People* of 16 July 1945[28] accords a higher or natural law status to the family in the following terms:

> The State recognizes and protects the family as a natural and fundamental institution of society with rights and duties prior and superior to all human positive law.

Article 10 of the *Constitution of the Islamic Republic of Iran* of 28 July 1989 describes the family as 'the fundamental unit of Islamic society'.

The extent to which the family unit has been recognised since 1948 by international and regional human rights instruments as a social entity worthy of assistance and protection is impressive.[29] Article 16(1) of the *Universal Declaration of Human Rights* of 1948 acknowledges that '[m]en and women of full age, without any limitation due to race, nationality or religion, have the right to marry and to found a family'. Article 16(3) of the same instrument declares that '[t]he family is the natural and fundamental group unit of society and is entitled to protection by society and the State'.[30] Sub-Articles (1) and (2) of Article 23 of the *International Covenant on Civil and Political Rights* of 1966 repeat in substantially identical terms the content of Sub-Articles (1) and (3) of Article 16 of the *Universal Declaration*. Article 10(1) of the *International Covenant on Economic, Social and Cultural Rights* of 1966 pitches at a high level the importance and protection of the family in the following terms:

---

27   A. Kaplan 'Human Relations and Human Rights in Judaism' in A. Rosenbaum (ed.) *The Philosophy of Human Rights, Contribution in Philosophy No. 15* (1980) pp. 53, 66.

28   *Fuero de los Espanoles* 16 July 1945, amended 15 December 1966.

29   International and regional human rights instruments have not attempted to define the term 'family'. Nevertheless, this may well be a deliberate and prudent omission. The perceived role, form and functions of the family have varied considerably throughout history and may differ from state to state, owing to varying cultural, religious, sociological and legal perspectives and individual preferences. In a document entitled 'General Comments' recently adopted by the Human Rights Committee under Article 40(4) of the *International Covenant on Civil and Political Rights*, the Committee maintained the view that for these reasons 'it is not possible to give the concept [of the family] a standard definition'. See CCPR/C/21/Rev. 1/Add. 2 (19 September 1990) pp. 1-2.

30   See also Article 23(3) ('Everyone who works has the right to just and favourable remuneration ensuring for himself and his family an existence worthy of human dignity …) and Article 25(1) ('Everyone has the right to a standard of living adequate for the health and well-being of himself and of his family …) of the *Universal Declaration of Human Rights*.

> The widest possible protection and assistance should be accorded to the family, which is the natural and fundamental group unit of society, particularly for its establishment and while it is responsible for the care and education of dependent children.[31]

The *Convention on the Rights of the Child* of 1989 acknowledges generally the family's leading role in preparing children for participation in society and the assumption of adult responsibilities. In particular, its fifth preambular paragraph affirms that 'the family, as the fundamental group of society and the natural environment for the growth and well-being of all its members and particularly children, should be afforded the necessary protection and assistance so that it can fully assume its responsibilities within the community'.

Regional human rights instruments also accord pre-eminence to the family concerning its status as a social unit and its entitlement to state and societal protection. Article 16 of the *European Social Charter* of 1961 provides for the following comprehensive protection for the family unit:

> With a view to ensuring the necessary conditions for the full development of the family, which is a fundamental unit of society, the Contracting Parties undertake to promote the economic, legal and social protection of family life by such means as social and family benefits, fiscal arrangements, provision of family housing, benefits for the newly married, and other appropriate means.

In Latin America, Article 17(1) of the *American Convention on Human Rights* of 1969 states that '[t]he family is the natural and fundamental group unit of society and is entitled to protection by society and the state'. Article 15 of the *Additional Protocol to the American Convention on Human* Rights *in the Area of Economic, Social and Cultural Rights* of 17 November 1988[32] requires the States Parties to accord adequate protection to the family which is referred to as 'the natural and fundamental element of society'. In keeping with African tradition, Article 18 of the *African Charter on Human and Peoples' Rights* of 1981 similarly regards the family as 'the natural unit and basis of society' and 'the custodian of morals and traditional values' which it is the duty of the state to assist and protect'. Article 29(1) of the *African Charter* imposes on each individual the duty '[t]o preserve the harmonious development of the family and to work for the cohesion and respect of the family ...'. The Council of the League of Arab States has also endorsed the central importance to society of the family unit in its adoption in Cairo on 15 September 1994 of the *Arab Charter on Human Rights*. Article 38(a) thereof refers to the family as 'the basic unit of society, whose protection it shall enjoy'. In the privacy context, a number of international and regional human rights

---

31   See also Article 11(1) of the *ICESCR* ('The States Parties to the present Covenant recognize the right of everyone to an adequate standard of living for himself and his family ...').

32   Otherwise known as the *'Protocol of San Salvador'*. For the full text of this instrument, see (1989) 28 *I.L.M.* p. 156.

instruments have affirmed the principle that no one shall be subjected to arbitrary or unlawful interference with his or her family.[33]

The family has also been affirmed and received support in a number of declarations. Article VI of the *American Declaration of the Rights and Duties of Man* of 1948 affirms the family as 'the basic element of society'. Principle 6 of the United Nations-sponsored *Declaration of the Rights of the Child* of 20 November 1959 states that the child 'shall, wherever possible, grow up in the care and under the responsibility of his [or her] parents'. Repeated reference to the family by these various instruments reflects the continuing respect and concern of states for this institution. In light of this wide recognition, it is at least arguable that state and societal protection of the family has crystallised into a rule of customary law.

Due to economic and social changes and the drive towards development, however, the family has been undergoing considerable transformation. Families are experiencing increasing stress in having to cope with unemployment, poverty, domestic violence, drug and alcohol addiction, child abuse and neglect, disease and sickness, and displacement due to armed conflicts, environmental degradation and famine. Rising rates of divorce and births out of wedlock and the emergence of single parenting of children have had the effect of transferring traditional family duties and responsibilities from the private to the state sector.[34] In response to these destablising trends, the United Nations proclaimed 1994 'The International Year of the Family'[35] and, in so doing, has placed the family higher on the international agenda. The objectives of the International Year of the Family are, *inter alia*, to increase awareness of the importance of the family and family issues among governments and the private sector, to enhance understanding of the functions and problems of families and, perhaps most critically, to focus attention on the rights and responsibilities of all family members. The importance of family life and the family as a social unit has also been reaffirmed by the United Nations World Conference on Human Rights held in Vienna in June, 1993. Conference delegates proclaimed in the *Vienna Declaration and Programme of Action* that 'the child for the full and harmonious development of his or her personality should grow up in a family environment which accordingly merits broader protection'.[36]

It is readily apparent from the foregoing that the family has been recognised as a social institution worthy of the protection of society and the State at the international, regional and national levels. But state and societal protection alone is no guarantor of its success. Such protection is a necessary, but not sufficient, precondition for its maintenance and development. The recognition and

---

33   Article 12 of the *Universal Declaration of Human Rights*; Article 17(1) of the *International Covenant on Civil and Political Rights*; Article 16 of the *Convention on the Rights of the Child*; 11(2) of the *American Convention on Human Rights*; Article 8(1) of the *European Convention on the Protection of Human Rights and Fundamental Freedoms*.

34   Selbourne, *op. cit.*, p. 228.

35   On 8 December 1989, the United Nations General Assembly proclaimed 1994 as the International Year of the Family (Resolution 44/82).

36   Part I, Paragraph 21.

discharge of individual familial duties towards other family members is also essential. As one commentator has remarked, '[t]o respect the dictates of the "bond of nature" ... remains a particular duty of the citizen ...'[37] Therefore, in the next two sub-sections, an examination will be undertaken under both international and national constitutional law of the nature and extent of the duties owed by parents towards their minor children as well as the duties owed by children towards their parents.

Parental Duties Towards Children

The primary responsibilities of a mother and father towards their children include their nurture, socialisation and education. The English jurist Sir William Blackstone described these evolving common law parental duties thus:

> The duty of parents to provide for the maintenance of their children, is a principle of natural law; an obligation laid on them not only by nature itself, but by their own proper act, in bringing them into the world ... By begetting them ... they have entered into a voluntary obligation to endeavour, as far as in them lies, that the life which they have bestowed shall be supported and preserved. And thus the children will have a perfect right of receiving maintenance from their parents.[38]

Parental duty, however, goes well beyond preserving the life of the child through protective oversight measures and the provision of basic material necessities such as food, clothing and shelter. As John Stuart Mill declared, '[i]t is one of the most sacred duties of parents ... after summoning a human being into the world to give that being an education fitting him to perform his part well in life towards others and towards himself'.[39] It is within the family and home where each new generation acquires its moral anchoring.[40] Immediate family members such as a mother, father, sibling, aunt or uncle provide a basic and informal educational medium through which social and religious values and cultural identity are preserved and transmitted. The character and independent decision-making capacity of children are gradually developed, thereby enabling them to realise their potential and assume useful roles as responsible adults within their community.

Within most contemporary legal systems, the moral or ethical duty to maintain and educate one's minor children has been transformed into an enforceable legal duty (the non-performance of which may be attended by sanctions). Such positive legal duties are the product of the special personal relationship which exists between parent and child. Within the educational sphere, the principle of universal compulsory education is recognised in the legislation of some countries through the imposition of legal duties on parents. So, for example,

---

37   Selbourne, *op. cit.*, p. 228.
38   Sir William Blackstone *Commentaries on the Laws of England* Vol. 1 (1829) p. 446.
39   J. S. Mill *On Liberty* (1859) p. 189.
40   A. Etzioni *The Spirit of Community* (1995) p. 256.

the parental duty to educate minor children is provided for in Section 36 of the English *Education Act 1944* in the following terms:

> It shall be the duty of the parent of every child of compulsory school age to cause him to receive efficient full-time education, suitable to his age, ability and aptitude, either by regular attendance at school or otherwise.[41]

Indeed, the parental duty to maintain and educate minor children is constitutionally entrenched in some countries, signifying its elevated status in the hierarchy of duties. Some constitutional provisions explicitly confine the parental duty to providing a basic education. So, for example, Article 31(2) of the *Constitution of the Republic of Korea of 29 October 1987* states that '[a]ll citizens who have children to support shall be responsible at least for their elementary education and other education as provided by law'. Article 55 of the *Constitution of the Republic of Venezuela* of 23 January 1961 likewise provides:

> Education shall be compulsory within the degree and conditions fixed by law. Parents and representatives are responsible for compliance with this duty ...

Other constitutional provisions concerning parental duty are more general in scope. Article 23 of the *Charter of the Spanish People of 16 July 1945* states in part that '[p]arents are obliged to provide for, educate, and instruct their children'. In Part One of the *Constitution of Italy of 27 December 1947* entitled 'Rights and Duties of Private Citizens', Article 30 provides that '[i]t is the duty and right of parents to support, instruct and educate their children, even those born out of wedlock ...' Some constitutions go so far as to attribute natural law origins to the parental duty to nurture and educate minor children. For instance, Article 6(2) of the *Basic Law for the Federal Republic of Germany of 23 May 1949* states:

> The care and upbringing of children are a natural right of parents and a duty primarily incumbent on them. It is the responsibility of the community to ensure that they perform this duty.

Article 1(10) of the *Constitution of the Republic of Gabon of 21 February 1961* similarly provides that '[t]he care to be given to children and their education shall constitute, for parents, a natural right and a duty which they shall exercise . . . with the assistance of the State ...' And Article 15 of the *Constitution of the Republic of Senegal of 8 March 1963* provides:

> Parents have the natural right and the duty to bring up their children. They shall be supported in that task by the State and by the community.

Communist and socialist states have also constitutionally entrenched such a duty. Article 66 of the *Constitution (Fundamental Law) of the [former] Union of Soviet*

---

41   For further examples, see Chapter 2 of D. Hodgson *The Human Right to Education* (1998).

Socialist Republics of 7 October 1977 stated in part that '[c]itizens ... are obliged to concern themselves with the upbringing of children, to train them for socially useful work, and to raise them as worthy members of socialist society'.

The parental duty to maintain and educate minor children has also been extensively recognised by international and regional human rights instruments. Such recognition tends to be somewhat indirect in the Twin Covenants in the sense that the relevant provisions refer only to the family rather than to the duties of parents or legal guardians. Article 24(1) of the *International Covenant on Civil and Political Rights* states that '[e]very child shall have ... the right to such measures of protection as are required by his [or her] status as a minor, on the part of his family, society and the State'. Article 10(1) of the *International Covenant on Economic, Social and Cultural Rights* records the recognition of the States Parties that '[t]he widest possible protection and assistance should be accorded to the family, which is the natural and fundamental group unit of society, particularly for its establishment and while it is responsible for the care and education of dependent children ...' It is the *Convention on the Rights of the Child,* however, which, as an international convention, most systematically and comprehensively identifies and prescribes the various aspects of the parental duty to maintain and educate minor children. As was discussed in some detail previously, Articles 3(2), 5, 14(2), 18(1) and 27(2) explicitly recognise the common and primary responsibility of each parent for the care and upbringing of his or her minor children.[42]

As far as regional recognition of the parental duty to maintain and educate minor children is concerned, the first regional human rights instrument to recognise such a duty was the *American Declaration of the Rights and Duties of Man* of 1948. Article XXX thereof provides in part that '[i]t is the duty of every person to aid, support, educate and protect his [or her] minor children ...' In the Islamic world, Article 7(a) of *The Cairo Declaration on Human Rights in Islam* of 5 August 1990 states in part that '[a]s of the moment of birth, every child has rights due from the parents, society and the state to be accorded proper nursing, education and material, hygenic and moral care'. The parental duty of care has been most comprehensively recognised on a regional basis within Africa. Article 27(1) of the *African Charter on Human and Peoples' Rights* of 1981 states in part that '[e]very individual shall have duties towards his family ...' Article 29(1) thereof also imposes on the individual the duty '[t]o preserve the harmonious development of the family and to work for the cohesion and respect of the family ...'[43] It is the *African Charter on the Rights and Welfare of the Child* of 1990, however, which explicates in most detail the nature of parental duties in this context. Article 20 entitled 'Parental Responsibilities' reads:

---

42   For the full text of these provisions, see the sub-section in Chapter 6 entitled 'The Convention on the Rights of the Child'.

43   See also Articles 27(1) and 29(1) of the *Draft Pacific Charter of Human Rights* of 1989 which virtually replicates Articles 27(1) and 29(1) of the *African Charter on Human and Peoples' Rights*.

1. Parents or other persons responsible for the child shall have the primary responsibility for the upbringing and development of the child and shall have the duty:

(a) to ensure that the best interests of the child are their basic concern at all times;

(b) to secure, within their abilities and financial capacities, conditions of living necessary to the child's development; and

(c) to ensure that domestic discipline is administered with humanity and in a manner consistent with the inherent dignity of the child.

In the educational context, Article 11(4) refers to 'the rights and duties of parents ... to choose for their children schools ... to ensure the religious and moral education of the child ...' It is thus clear from the foregoing that the parental duty to maintain and educate minor children has received extensive instrumental recognition at the international, regional and national (particularly constitutional) levels.

The Duty of Parental Support

It has been said that '[t]he principle of respect for parents and for old age, a constituent part of the principle of duty, has been largely lost from sight in the corrupted liberal orders ...'[44] Nonetheless, the principle of respect for one's elders and a duty to support one's parents have long been recognised in various religious and cultural traditions and ethical systems.   In Judaism, one of the Ten Commandments exhorted believers to '[h]onour thy father and thy mother'.[45] The Wisdom literature makes a pragmatic argument against discriminatory treatment of the aged: 'Do not dishonour the old; we shall all be numbered among them' (ben Sirach 8:6). In the *Book of Job*, the aged are seen as especially qualified by experience to give counsel in daily living: 'Wisdom is with the aged, and understanding in length of days'.[46] Deference to old age because a long life is generally wise and knowledgeable has also been a central tenet of African humanism.[47] In traditional African societies, parents are owed a duty of respect and maintenance by their children.[48]   Within Asia, one of the most important behavioural guidelines to emerge from the parent-child cardinal relationship in traditional Chinese society was that of filial piety. Children are under a duty to respect and obey their parents and to care for them when they are old and infirm. This notion of filial piety is so deeply entrenched in the Chinese psyche that in

---

44   Selbourne, *op. cit.*, p. 154.
45   *Book of Exodus*, Chapter 20, Verse 12.
46   Chapter 12, Verse 12. See A. Kaplan, *op. cit.*, p. 73.
47   Makau Wa Mutua, *op. cit.*, p. 352.
48   For more detailed information on the duty of parental support in African society, see the section in Chapter 6 entitled 'The African Regional Human Rights System'.

contemporary China it has taken the form of a constitutional duty of parental support. Article 46 of the *Constitution of the People's Republic of China* of 4 December 1982 states in part that '[c]hildren have the duty to support their parents'. Duties of parental support have also been constitutionally entrenched in communist and socialist countries. For instance, Article 66 of *the Constitution (Fundamental Law) of the Union of Soviet Socialist Republics* of 7 October 1977 provides in part that '[c]hildren are obliged to care for their parents and help them'.

At the international level, the duty of parental support has not been explicitly recognised as such by any human rights instrument. The closest analogy may be found in Article 29(1)(c) of the *Convention on the Rights of the Child* of 1989 which records the agreement of the States Parties that 'the education of the child shall be directed to the development of respect for the child's parents ...' Nevertheless, such a provision falls far short of the unsuccessful attempt to include in the *Convention* the following provision 'The child has the duty to respect his [or her] parents and to give them assistance, in case of need'.[49] By contrast, the duty of parental support has been recognised more directly and extensively by regional human rights instruments, particularly in Africa. Article 29(1) of the *African Charter on Human and Peoples' Rights* of 1981 states in part that '[t]he individual shall also have the duty ... to respect his [or her] parents at all times [and] to maintain them in case of need'. Article 31(a) of the *African Charter on the Rights and Welfare of the Child* of 1990 similarly provides:

> Article 31: Responsibilities of the Child
>
> Every child shall have responsibilities towards his family ... The child, subject to his [or her] age and ability ... shall have the duty:
>
> (a) to work for the cohesion of the family, to respect his [or her] parents and elders at all times and to assist them in case of need ...

These African provisions thus significantly exceed the *Convention on the Rights of the Child* in the context of acknowledging a duty of parental support. Within Latin America, the duty of parental support is also explicitly referred to in Article XXX of the *American Declaration of the Rights and Duties of Man* of 1948 which acknowledges 'the duty of children to honor their parents always and to aid, support and protect them when they need it'. The duty of parental support has also been recognised in the Islamic world, although not quite as directly. Article 7(c) of *The Cairo Declaration on Human Rights in Islam* of 1990 states that '[b]oth parents are entitled to certain rights from their children ... in accordance with the tenets of the Shari'ah'. Nevertheless, this correlative duty imposed upon children, subject to their age and capacity, would almost certainly include a duty of parental respect and support in circumstances of hardship.

---

49   S. Detrick (ed.) *The United Nations Convention on the Rights of the Child: A Guide to the Travaux Preparatoires* (1992) pp. 156-7. See also the section in Chapter 6 entitled 'The Convention on the Rights of the Child'.

The Duty to Acquire a Basic Formal Education

As a concept, education can be variously defined.[50] Education occurs in its widest sense in the interaction of the individual with the social and natural environment to which he or she belongs. This process transcends the school setting and includes informal sources of education such as the printed and electronic mass media. Education begins within the home where the child learns a first language and is socialised into the parent-child and sibling relationships. Individual attitudes and behaviour develop as a result of the child's interaction with family members and the wider social environment.

Education may be defined in a broader sense to encompass 'all activities by which a human group transmits to its descendants a body of knowledge and skills and a moral code which enable that group to subsist'.[51] In this sense, then, education is primarily concerned with the transmission to the younger generation of the skills necessary to effectively undertake the tasks of daily living and with the inculcation of the social, cultural, religious and philosophical values held by the particular community. The General Conference of the United Nations Educational, Scientific and Cultural Organization (hereinafter referred to as 'U.N.E.S.C.O.') has itself defined the term 'education' to imply 'the entire process of social life by means of which individuals . . . learn to develop consciously within, and for the benefit of, [various] communities, the whole of their personal capacities, attitudes, aptitudes and knowledge'.[52]

Education can, in turn, be more narrowly confined to refer to formal or professional 'instruction imparted within a national, provincial or local education system, whether public or private'.[53] The European Court of Human Rights has distinguished education in its wide sense from education in its narrow sense in the following terms:

> [education in the wider sense refers to] the whole process whereby, in any society, adults endeavour to transmit their beliefs, culture and other values to the young, whereas teaching or instruction refers in particular to the transmission of knowledge and to intellectual development.[54]

It is generally the case that the term 'education' is used in international human rights instruments to refer to formal institutional instruction. For example, the General Conference of U.N.E.S.C.O. has defined the term 'education' for the

---

50   D. Hodgson *The Human Right to Education* (1998) pp. 3-4.
51   Amadou-Mahtar M'Bow 'Introduction' in G. Mialaret (ed.) *The Child's Right to Education* (1979) pp. 9, 11.
52   Article 1(a) of the *Recommendation Concerning Education for International Understanding, Co-operation and Peace and Education Relating to Human Rights and Fundamental Freedoms 1974.*
53   M'Bow, *op. cit.*, p. 11.
54   *Campbell v Cosans v United Kingdom*, Judgement of 25 February 1982, Series A, no. 48 (1982) 4 *E.H.R.R.* 433 at para. 33.

purposes of its *Convention against Discrimination in Education* of 15 December 1960 to mean 'all types and levels of [formal] education, and includes access to education, the standard and quality of education, and the conditions under which it is given'.[55] For present purposes, 'education' will refer merely to formal institutional teaching or instruction.

Education, like work, may be perceived concurrently as both an individual right and duty. So, for instance, Article 5 of the *Charter of the Spanish People* of 16 July 1945 proclaims that '[a]ll Spaniards have a right to receive education and instruction and the duty of acquiring them either in the family circle or in private or public centers of their own free election ...' Likewise, Article 44 of the *Constitution of the People's Republic of China* of 4 December 1982 states that '[c]itizens of the People's Republic of China have the right and obligation to receive education ...' As we shall see shortly, most international and regional human rights instruments today regard the acquisition of a basic formal education as an individual right. There are some international human rights instruments, however, and numerous national constitutional provisions which regard the acquisition of such an education as an individual duty.

Perceived solely as an individual duty, the discharge of the duty to acquire a basic formal education will enure to the benefit of a number of different individuals and entities. First of all, the duty of educating oneself and of availing oneself of educational opportunities is essentially a duty to oneself (or, in Kantian terminology, a 'self-regarding duty'). For John Stuart Mill, the term 'duty to oneself' meant 'self-respect or self-development'.[56] But the efficent discharge of the individual duty to acquire a basic formal education will also have certain other collateral or derivative beneficial effects. Thus, the acquisition of sufficient knowledge and technical expertise will enhance the individual's employment prospects, thereby assisting in the provision of maintenance to his or her dependants and contributing to the economy. The State may also have its own selfish but understandable reasons for insisting on its citizens receiving a basic education. In his famous treatise *On Liberty*, John Stuart Mill, the father of contemporary liberal democratic theory, asked the question '[i]s it not almost a self-evident axiom that the State should require and compel the education, up to a certain standard, of every human being who is born its citizen?'[57] The well-being of a democratic civic order requires that the rights and duties of suffrage be exercised and discharged responsibly. This in turn requires that the voter be sufficiently knowledgeable to be able to make an informed electoral choice.[58] To borrow from Immanuel Kant, the role of education (both general and civics) in this context is 'the forming of the mind for the civil state'.[59] In his *Democracy in America*, Alexis De Tocqueville stated (perhaps somewhat optimistically) that '[w]hen the right of every citizen to co-operate in the government of society is

---

55   Article 1(2).
56   J. S. Mill *On Liberty* (1859) p. 141.
57   *Idem.* p. 175.
58   Selbourne, *op. cit.*, p. 235.
59   I. Kant *Lectures on Ethics* (translated by L. Infield) (1963) p. 248.

acknowledged, every citizen must be presumed to possess the power of discriminating between the different opinions of his contemporaries ...'[60]

Some national constitutions perceive the acquisition of a basic education solely in terms of an individual duty. For example, Section 69 of the *The Constitution of the Kingdom of Thailand* of 9 December 1991 states that '[e]very person shall have a duty to ... receive education and training ... as provided by law'. Likewise, Article 9 (g) of the *Constitution of the Dominican Republic* of 28 November 1966 declares that '[i]t is the duty of all persons who inhabit the territory of the Dominican Republic to attend the educational institutions of the nation in order to acquire, at least, an elementary education'. Other national constitutions, however, are less direct or explicit in terms of the imposition upon individuals of a duty to acquire a basic education. For instance, Article 55 of the *Constitution of the Republic of Venezuela* of 23 January 1961 merely provides that '[e]ducation shall be compulsory within the degree and conditions fixed by law'. This wording, however, carries the reasonable implication that the parents or legal guardian as well as the child are responsible for ensuring the latter's attendance at an educational institution during the compulsory component of the child's formal education.

At the international and regional levels, the acquisition of a basic formal education is more commonly perceived in human rights instruments as an individual right rather than duty, but certain exceptions which will be noted do exist. Article 26(1) of the *Universal Declaration of Human Rights* of 1948 states in part as follows:

> Everyone has the right to education. Education shall be free, at least in the elementary and fundamental stages. Elementary education shall be compulsory ...

Article 26(1) is somewhat of a hybrid provision in the sense that although it purports to view the acquisition of education as an individual right, there is an element of compulsion produced by the inclusion of the third sentence. In the case of a child, both he or she and his or her parents or legal guardian must ensure that that child receives an elementary education. Such requirement is often codified in domestic legislation at the national level with non-compliance involving sanctions.[61] Both the *International Covenant on Economic, Social and Cultural Rights* of 1966 and the *Convention on the Rights of the Child* of 1989 adopt the same hybrid approach. Article 13(1) of the former instrument recognises 'the right of everyone to education' while Article 13(2)(a) requires that '[p]rimary education shall be compulsory and available free to all'. Article 28(1)(a) of the latter instrument is in substantially the same terms.

At the international level, one human rights instrument which appears to regard the acquisition of a basic formal education as an individual duty as well as right is the *Convention Concerning Indigenous and Tribal Peoples in Independent*

---

60   A. De Tocqueville *Democracy in America* (2nd ed., 1838) p. 163.
61   See the previous sub-section of this chapter entitled 'Parental Duties Towards Children'.

Countries of 27 June 1989.   Article 30(1) thereof provides in part that
'[g]overnments shall adopt measures appropriate to the traditions and cultures of
the peoples concerned, to make known to them their rights and duties, especially in
regard to labour, economic opportunities, education and health matters ...'   Other
international human rights instruments which do not purport to impose on
individuals a duty to acquire a basic education but which encourage the imparting
of knowledge concerning individual duties as part of the educational curriculum
include the *Declaration on the Promotion Among Youth of the Ideals of Peace,
Mutual Respect and Understanding Between Peoples* of 7 December 1965[62] and
U.N.E.S.C.O.'s *Recommendation Concerning Education for International
Understanding, Co-operation and Peace and Education Relating to Human Rights
and Fundamental Freedoms 1974.*[63]

At the regional level, the acquisition of a basic formal education has once
again generally been developed as an individual human right.[64]   The right to
education is most comprehensively dealt with by the Latin American regional
human rights system. The 'right to education' features prominently in the *Charter
of the Organization of American States* of 1948 as amended by the *Protocol of
Buenos Aires* of 1967.[65] The acquisition of education, however, is considered both
an individual right and duty by the *American Declaration of the Rights and Duties
of Man* of 1948. Pursuant to Article XII, which appears in Chapter One entitled
'Rights', '[e]very person has the right to an education . . .' But in Chapter Two
entitled 'Duties', Article XXXI states that '[i]t is the duty of every person to
acquire at least an elementary education'.   Most recently, Article 13 of the
*Additional Protocol to the American Convention on Human Rights in the Area of
Economic, Social and Cultural Rights* of 1988 recognises the right of everyone to
education and guarantees to the child the right to free compulsory elementary
education. As for Europe, although the original text of the *European Convention
for the Protection of Human Rights and Fundamental Freedoms* of 1950 contained
no provision concerning the right to education, Article 2 of the *First Protocol*[66] to
the *European Convention* adopted by the Council of Europe on 20 March 1952

---

62   Proclaimed by United Nations General assembly Resolution 2037 (XX) of 7
       December 1965. Principle VI declares that '[y]oung people must become
       conscious of their responsibilities in the world they will be called upon to manage
       ...'

63   Paragraph III(4)(e) recommends that an 'awareness not only of the rights but also
       of the duties incumbent upon individuals' should constitute a major guiding
       principle of educational policy.

64   For greater detail, see D. Hodgson *The Human Right to Education* (1998) pp. 56-
       62.

65   *Charter of the Organization of American States* signed at Bogota, Colombia on 30
       April 1948; entry into force 13 December 1951, No. 1609, (1952) 119 *U.N.T.S.* 3,
       as amended by the *Protocol of Amendment to the Charter of the Organization of
       American States* ('*Protocol of Buenos Aires*') signed 27 February 1967; entry into
       force 27 February 1970, No. 1609, (1970) p. 721 *U.N.T.S.* 324. See Articles 31(h)
       and p. 47.

66   Entry into force 18 May 1954.

states that '[n]o person shall be denied the right to education'. In the African context, Article 17(1) of the *African Charter on Human and Peoples' Rights* of 1981 provides simply that '[e]very individual shall have the right to education'. The most comprehensive formulation of the right to education in a regional African human rights instrument is to be found in the *African Charter on the Rights and Welfare of the Child* of 1990. Like Article 28(1)(a) of the *Convention on the Rights of the Child*, Articles 11(1) and 11(3)(a) of the *African Charter on the Rights and Welfare of the Child* guarantee every child the right to education but make basic education compulsory.

The most detailed formulation of the duty to acquire a basic formal education is to be found in Article VI(4) of the *Declaration of the Basic Duties of ASEAN Peoples and Governments* of 1983 which reads as follows:

> It is the duty of the people to avail themselves of the national educational system to the fullest extent possible in order to discover and develop their native talents, to continue educating themselves after formal schooling ends, and to participate in the social, economic, cultural and political life of their communities and of the country, using their skills, talents and critical and creative faculties for the promotion and enhancement of the rights of all and for the welfare of the nation.

On balance, at the international level at least, the acquisition of a basic formal education is perceived more as an individual right than duty. Nevertheless, even at this level, an indirect individual duty is impliedly recognised by the insistence of compulsory basic education. At the regional level, education is perceived more often than not as a right but is recognised more often as a duty than at the international level. At the national (constitutional) level, the acquisition of education tends to be equated more often as an individual duty than right.

The Duty to Work

Like the individual duty to acquire a basic formal education, engagement in work or labour has been perceived both as an individual right and as a duty. This is particularly so at the regional and national (constitutional) levels. Perhaps this should come as no surprise for, as Article 51(2) of the *Constitution of the Portuguese Republic* of 2 April 1976 states, '[t]he duty to work is inseparable from the right to work, except for those persons whose capacities have been diminished by age, sickness or disability'. As Kenneth Minogue has observed in the context of the guarantee of the right to work provided by international human rights law:

> To have the right to be provided with an actual job . . . has an obverse side. It is the right - which may also become a duty - to do a socially necessary job.[67]

---

67   K. Minogue 'The History of the Idea of Human Rights' in W. Laqueur and B. Rubin (eds) *The Human Rights Reader* (1979) pp. 14-15.

The duty to work has ancient roots particularly in the Judaic-Christian tradition. The injunction 'Six days shall you labour and do all your work, but the seventh day is the sabbath of the Lord, your God'[68] is as much a commandment to work as it is to rest on the seventh day.[69] John Locke declared in his *Two Treatises of Civil Government* that 'God when He gave the world in common to mankind, commanded man also to labour'.[70] As in the case of the duty to acquire a basic education, there is a clearly discernible utilitarian basis for the individual duty to work. Such basis is very well captured by Article 9(f) of the *Constitution of the Dominican Republic* of 28 November 1966:

> Every person has the obligation to engage in work of his own choice in order to provide fittingly for the maintenance of himself and his family, to achieve the broadest possible improvement of his personality, and to contribute to the well-being and progress of society.

Like education, work transcends the status of a self-regarding duty in which the bearer attains a greater degree of self-fulfillment and personal financial independence. Efficient discharge of the individual duty to engage in work enures to the benefit of one's immediate dependants and also contributes to the economy and the well-being of the civic order.[71] The latter utilitarian source of the duty to work has indeed been explicitly mentioned in various constitutional instruments. So, for instance, Article 24 of the *Charter of the Spanish People* of 16 July 1945 provides that '[a]ll Spaniards have a right to work and the duty to occupy themselves in some socially useful activity'. In a similar vein, Article 56 of the *Constitution of the Republic of Costa Rica* of 7 November 1949 states in part that '[l]abor is a right of the individual and obligation to society ...'

At the national level, it is generally the case that the constitutions of socialist and communist states regard the engagement in work as a duty rather than a right of the citizen.[72] This is consistent with the basic tenets upon which these societies have been founded.[73] As Article 12 of the *Constitution (Fundamental Law) of the Union of Soviet Socialist Republics* of 5 December 1936 states:

> Work in the U.S.S.R. is a duty and a matter of honor for every able-bodied citizen, in accordance with the principle: 'He who does not work, neither shall he eat.'

> The principle applied in the U.S.S.R. is that of socialism: 'From each according to his ability, to each according to his work.'

---

68   *Book of Exodus*, Chapter 20, Verses 9-10.
69   Kaplan, *op. cit.*, p. 76.
70   Book II, para. 32.
71   Selbourne, *op. cit.*, p. 152.
72   An exception is Article 44 of the *Constitution of Cuba* of 24 February 1976 which states in part that '[w]ork in a socialist society is a *right* and duty ... for every citizen' (emphasis supplied by author).
73   A more detailed discussion will be presented in Chapter 8.

A more recent version of the Soviet constitutional duty to work is to be found in Article 60 of the *Constitution (Fundamental Law) of the Union of Soviet Socialist Republics* of 7 October 1977:

> It is the duty of, and a matter of honour for, every able-bodied citizen of the U.S.S.R. to work conscientiously in his chosen useful occupation ... Evasion of socially useful work is incompatible with the principles of socialist society.

Work is described in Article 41 of the *Constitution of the People's Republic of China* of 4 December 1982 as 'a glorious duty of every able-bodied citizen'. Articles 83 and 82 of the *Socialist Constitution of the Democratic People's Republic of Korea* of 9 April 1992 respectively state that '[w]ork is the noble duty and honour of a citizen' and that '[c]itizens shall . . . work devotedly for the good of society and the people'.

The perception of work exclusively as an individual duty, however, is not confined to socialist and communist states. The constitutions of a number of western liberal democracies couch the constitutional duty to work in the language of personal duty. For instance, Section 3 of Article V (entitled 'Duties and Obligations of Citizens') of the *Constitution of the Republic of the Philippines* of 17 January 1973 states that '[i]t shall be the duty of every citizen to engage in gainful work to assure himself and his family a life worthy of human dignity'. Likewise, Article 54 of the *Constitution of the Republic of Venezuela* of 23 January 1961 provides that '[l]abour is a duty of every person fit to perform it'. However, the constitutions of other western and Asian liberal democracies employ the language of both right and duty in the context of work. So, for example, Article 13 of the *Constitution of the Arab Republic of Egypt* of 11 September 1971 describes work as 'a right, a duty and an honor guaranteed by the State ...' And Article 32 of the *Constitution of the Republic of Korea* of 29 October 1987 provides in part:

> Article 32
>
> (1) All citizens shall have the right to work . . .
>
> (2) All citizens shall have the duty to work. The State shall prescribe by law the extent and conditions of the duty to work ...

It would appear, however, that the right to work and the duty to work are not necessarily coterminous in the sense that age, sickness and disability may be relevant factors in relieving persons from any constitutional duty to engage in gainful employment.

At the international level, the engagement in work or labour is generally considered to be an individual right rather than duty. Article 23(1) of the *Universal Declaration of Human Rights* of 1948 states that '[e]veryone has the right to work, to free choice of employment, to just and favourable conditions of work and to protection against unemployment'. Article 6(1) of the *International Covenant on Economic, Social and Cultural Rights* of 1966 similarly recognises 'the right to work, which includes the right of everyone to the opportunity to gain his [or her] living by work which he [or she] freely chooses or accepts ...' Any element of legal or moral compulsion is thus absent in these provisions. However, that is not to say that such compulsion can never be recognised as legitimate under international law. The Geneva-based International Labour Organization (hereinafter referred to as the 'I.L.O.'), a specialised agency of the United Nations, has from time to time had occasion to consider this issue as part of its overall mandate to assist in the task of improving the conditions of labour among the nations of the world. To this end, the I.L.O. has since its inception developed international labour standards which are to be found in international conventions and recommendations.[74] I.L.O. conventions are designed to be ratified as international treaties requiring ratifying nations to discharge legal obligations as a matter of international law. The I.L.O. has developed procedures for regular supervision of the discharge of these obligations. The major monitoring body is the Committee of Experts on the Application of Conventions and Recommendations. In general, I.L.O. conventions are not directly concerned with individual duties. Certain provisions, however, can be considered as recognising such duties. Attention may be drawn in particular to the *Convention Concerning Forced or Compulsory Labour (I.L.O. No. 29)* of 28 June 1930.[75] Article 2 thereof states in part:

> (2)   Nevertheless, for the purposes of this Convention, the term 'forced or compulsory labour' shall not include:

> (a)   any work or service exacted in virtue of compulsory military service laws for work of a purely military character;

> (b)   any work or service which forms part of the normal civil obligations of the citizens ...;

> ...

> (d)   any work or service exacted in cases of emergency, that is to say, in the event of war or of a calamity or threatened calamity, such as fire, flood, famine, earthquake, violent epidemic ... and in general any circumstance that would endanger the existence or the well-being of the ... population.

> (e)   minor communal services of a kind which, being performed by the members of the community in the direct interest of the said community, can therefore be considered as normal civic obligations incumbent upon the members of the community ...

74   See generally E. Osieke *Constitutional Law and Practice in the International Labour Organisation* (1985).

75   Entry into force 1 May 1932. For the full text, see 39 *U.N.T.S.* 55. See also the *Convention Concerning the Abolition of Forced Labour (I.L.O. No. 105)* adopted on 25 June 1957, entered into force 17 January 1959. For the full text, see 320 *U.N.T.S.* p. 291.

Some national constitutions have incorporated these provisions. For example, Section 6(2) of the *Constitution of Botswana* of 30 September 1966 prohibits forced labour. However, Section 6(3) thereof excludes from the definition of 'forced labour' 'any labour required of a member of a disciplined force in pursuance of his duties as such' and 'any labour reasonably required as part of reasonable and normal communal or other civic obligations'. Examples of work which the I.L.O. Committee of Experts on the Application of Conventions and Recommendations has considered as forming part of normal civic obligations, and thus excluded from the term 'forced or compulsory labour', include ' . . . compulsory jury service, the duty to assist a person in danger or to assist in the enforcement of law and order'.[76]

In various surveys on forced labour, the Committee of Experts has examined the question of the existence of a duty to work under international law. The Committee is of the view that where the duty to work exists merely as a moral obligation and does not take the form of a legal obligation enforced by sanctions, it does not breach the various I.L.O. conventions on forced labour. On the other hand, national legislation which actually creates a legal obligation to engage in work, failing which those concerned are liable to compulsory direction to specified work or to penal sanctions, is incompatible with the relevant conventions.[77] The fact that Article 2(2) of the *Convention Concerning Forced or Compulsory Labour (I.L.O. No. 29)* provides for a limited number of exceptions to the ban on forced labour would not in itself provide a sufficient basis for considering that under international law there exists a general and legally enforceable duty to work. The limited exceptions concerning normal civic obligations, military service, emergency work and minor communal services cannot be invoked to justify a general recourse to forms of compulsory work or service.[78]

By contrast, the regional human rights instruments are readier to consider engagement in work as an individual duty. The leading example is the *African Charter on Human and Peoples' Rights* of 1981. While Article 15 thereof recognises the right to work of every individual, Article 29(6) imposes on the individual 'the duty to work to the best of his [or her] abilities and competence ...' Article 29(6) better captures the traditional African outlook on engagement in work. The concept of ujamaa, the Kiswahili concept for kinship, was based on three prongs, one of which was the obligation to work. Somewhat reminiscent of socialist principles, while every family member had the right to eat and receive shelter, he or she also had a duty to work.[79] Work constituted a duty inherent in

---

76 *Report of the Committee of Experts* (1968), Part Three, para. 37.
77 Daes, *op. cit.*, p. 62. See also *Report III (Part 4B), General Survey of the Reports relating to the Forced Labour Convention, 1930 (No. 29), and the Abolition of Forced Labour Convention, 1957 (No. 105)*, International Labour Conference, 65th Session, 1979 (Geneva, 1979) para. 45.
78 Daes, *op. cit.*, p. 62.
79 Makau Wa Mutua, *op. cit.*, p. 352, n. 40.

being a community member, such that laziness was considered a sufficiently serious breach of duty to warrant expulsion from the family and community.[80]

In Latin America, the hybrid nature of engagement in work is once again evident in the *American Declaration of the Rights and Duties of Man* of 1948. While Article XIV recognises the right of every person 'to work, under proper conditions, and to follow his vocation freely', Article XXXVII acknowledges that '[i]t is the duty of every person to work, as far as his capacity and possibilities permit, in order to obtain the means of livelihood or to benefit his community'. More recently, however, engagement in work has tended to be regarded exclusively as an individual right. Article 6(1) of the *Additional Protocol to the American Convention on Human Rights in the Area of Economic, Social and Cultural Rights* of 1988 provides that '[e]veryone has the right to work, which includes the opportunity to secure the means for living a dignified and decent existence by performing a freely elected or accepted lawful activity'. As for Europe, the right to work is most comprehensively prescribed by Parts I and II of the *European Social Charter* signed at Turin, Italy on 18 October 1961 by the members of the Council of Europe.[81] But the focus is on individual right and opportunity with no mention, express or implied, of individual duty, perhaps reflecting underlying cultural norms at variance with Africa and Latin America.

The Duty to Obey the Law

The individual has a fundamental duty to abide faithfully by the constitution and to obey the laws and regulations made for the benefit and welfare of society and legitimate commands of the public authorities of his or her country as well as those of the country in which he or she is residing. Such duty is of ancient origin. Plato's *Crito* illustrated the kind of respect Plato believed the secular laws merited, even if he considered them unjust. For Plato, it was the individual's duty to execute the orders of the civil authorities unless the State could be induced by legitimate means to alter its decision. A person who enjoyed civic rights was free to renounce them and leave the country, but those who remained entered wittingly into a contract to obey the laws.[82] In the Christian religious tradition, the exhortation by Jesus Christ to 'render unto Caesar what be Caesar's, and to render into God what be God's'[83] is an injunction to obey secular law as well as divine law. For Thomas Aquinas, the influential Catholic theologian and philosopher, the morally committed citizen has a fundamental duty to obey the laws of the community, even unjust laws, where the alternatives of 'scandal or riot' are even worse. In other cases, however, Aquinas foreshadowed passive forms of civil disobedience in saying that 'a man is not obliged to obey, if without scandal or

---

80   Devereux, *op. cit.*, p. 475.
81   529 *U.N.T.S.* 89.
82   G. Glotz *The Greek City and its Institutions* (1969) p. 140.
83   *The Gospel According to Matthew*, Chapter 22, Verse 21.

greater damage he can resist'.[84]   For Jean-Jacques Rousseau, freedom is 'obedience to the law one has prescribed for oneself'.[85]

Individuals are bound to obey just laws enacted for the benefit and welfare of society. But what if the laws are unjust or arbitrary in their content or operation? Selbourne addresses these issues and introduces several provisos in the following passage:

> The duty of the citizen to respect and observe the law ... [is] a duty owed by each citizen to live peaceably and sociably in the interests of the well-being of all. In a democratic civic order, such duty is expressed in an obligation to observe laws which are democratically made, impartially administered and enforced, and which are capable of being changed or replaced by democratic means. But in any civic order whatever, it is *prima facie* the citizen's obligation to observe and sustain the law, provided that the making, content and administration of such law are not governed by cruel, inhuman, and wicked intent which causes harm to the well-being of some or all of the citizens themselves.[86]

The so-called Diceyan 'rule of law' doctrine thus is a double-edged sword. Individuals are bound, legally and morally, to obey just laws but may have a right, or indeed a moral or ethical duty, to challenge a law which is unjust or arbitrary in its intent, content or effect.   In parliamentary democracies, individuals currently possess the right to object to, and seek to change, objectionable laws through the electoral process (including voting, public debate, lobbying and so forth) and the judicial process (including the review of the constitutionality of such laws and the legality of governmental decision-making).

The individual duty to obey the law, unlike the various other individual duties previously discussed in this chapter, is primarily a concern of national law (enforceable through both constitutional enactments and ordinary legislation). The instances of international and regional human rights law recognising such a duty are random and diffuse. So, for example, Article 2 of the *Convention relating to the Status of Refugees* of 1951 imposes upon aliens a duty to obey the law of the host state by providing that '[e]very refugee has duties to the country in which he finds himself, which require in particular that he conform to its laws and regulations as well as to measures taken for the maintenance of public order'. Article XXXIII of the *American Declaration of the Rights and Duties of Man* of 1948 imposes a duty of obedience to the law upon citizens and aliens alike:

> It is the duty of every person to obey the law and other legitimate commands of the authorities of his country and those of the country in which he may be.

---

84   As quoted in T. O'Hagan 'Aristotle and Aquinas on Community and Natural Law' in R. Bellamy and A. Ross (eds) *A Factual Introduction to Social and Political Theory* (1996) pp. 35, 44.

85   J.-J. Rousseau *The Social Contract* (1762), Book I, Chapter VIII 'On the Civil State'.

86   Selbourne, *op. cit.*, p. 228.

It is at the national level, however, that the individual duty to obey the law is most widely and comprehensively prescribed, particularly by constitutional instruments. An illustrative and representative sampling of such provisions follows. Article 2 of the *Charter of the Spanish People* of 16 July 1945 proclaims that 'Spaniards owe faithful service to their country, loyalty to the Head of State and obedience to its laws'. Article 54 of the *Constitution of Italy* of 27 December 1947 states that '[a]ll citizens have the duty of fealty to the Republic and shall respect the Constitution and the laws'. Section 1 of Article V (entitled 'Duties and Obligations of Citizens') of the *Constitution of the Republic of the Philippines* of 17 January 1973 provides in part that '[i]t shall be the duty of the citizens . . . to uphold the Constitution and obey the laws ...' Section 67 of *The Constitution of the Kingdom of Thailand* of 9 December 1991 stipulates that '[e]very person shall have a duty to comply with the law'. Some constitutional provisions go somewhat further in requiring obedience not only to the constitution and other laws but also to public authorities and their decisions. For example, Article 52 of the *Constitution of the Republic of Venezuela* of 23 January 1961 declares that '[b]oth Venezuelans and aliens shall comply with and obey the Constitution and the laws, and the decrees, resolutions and orders issued by legitimate agencies of the Public Power in the exercise of their functions'. Pursuant to Article 9(a) of the *Constitution of the Dominican Republic* of 28 November 1966, it is the duty of every individual '[t]o respect and comply with the Constitution and the laws; to respect and obey the authorities established by them'.

The constitutional provisions of communist and socialist states also commonly recognise an individual duty to uphold the constitution and obey the laws of the State. For example, Article 59 of the *Constitution (Fundamental Law) of the Union of Soviet Socialist Republics* of 7 October 1977 states in part that '[c]itizens of the U.S.S.R. are obliged to observe the Constitution of the U.S.S.R. and Soviet laws ...' The *Constitution of the People's Republic of China* of 4 December 1982 perceives the individual duty of obedience to the law as a duty correlative to the rights enjoyed by every citizen under the Constitution and other laws. Article 32 thereof proclaims in part that '[e]very citizen enjoys the rights prescribed by the Constitution and the law and at the same time has the duty to abide by the Constitution and the law'.[87] The formal and solemn nature of the obligation to obey the law is highlighted by Article 65 of the *Constitution of the Republic of Cuba* of 24 February 1976: 'Strict fulfillment of the Constitution and the laws is the bounden duty of all'. Indeed, it is often the case in constitutional instruments generally that a duty to obey the constitution and the laws is placed at the head of a list containing other individual duties, signifying its overarching significance.

---

87   See also Article 50 which states in part that '[c]itizens of the People's Republic of China must observe public order ...'

The Duties to Defend One's Country, to Undertake Military Service and to Maintain Internal Security

Thomas More once said that '[i]t is wisdom that thou look to thine own wealth and to do the same for the commonwealth is no less than thy duty, if thou bearest any reverent love or any natural zeal and affection to thy native country'.[88] For Niccolo Machiavelli, a contemporary of More, liberty is a collective good and the best way for a republic to remain independent of neighbouring states is to have a citizen militia which involves a collective effort by citizens in the defence of their freedom.[89] Echoing Machiavelli's beliefs, Article XIII of the *Virginia Declaration of Rights* of 12 June 1776 proclaimed '[t]hat a well-regulated militia, composed of the body of the people, trained to arms, is the proper, natural and safe defence of a free State ...'. This prompted the inclusion of the citizen's right to bear arms in the *Constitution of the United States of America* of 17 September 1787.[90] For John Stuart Mill, the bearing of a 'fair share in the common defence' is one of 'many positive acts for the benefit of others which [an individual] may rightfully be compelled to perform'.[91]

As will become apparent shortly, the individual's civic duties to defend his or her country and to undertake military service have now become well entrenched as legal obligations under national law (both under constitutional and ordinary enactments). No such individual duties are recognised, however, under international law. As we have already seen in the section entitled 'The Duty to Work', Article 2(2)(a) of the International Labour Organization's *Convention Concerning Forced or Compulsory Labour (I.L.O. No. 29)* of 28 June 1930 provides that the term 'forced or compulsory labour' for the purposes of the Convention does not include 'any work or service exacted in virtue of compulsory military service laws for work of a purely military character'. Therefore, there does not appear to be any legal impediment under international law to the recognition under national law of an individual legal duty to undertake national military service.

The recognition of such a duty at the regional level is somewhat more direct, albeit relatively infrequent. Article XXXIV of the *American Declaration of the Rights and Duties of Man* of 1948 states in part that '[i]t is the duty of every able-bodied person to render whatever civil and military service his [or her] country may require for its defense and preservation'. The requirement that each person be 'able-bodied' constitutes an exception to, or limitation upon, the

---

88   T. More *Utopia*, Book II, Chapter 6 (1516), translated R. Robinson, London, n.d.
89   M. Hollis 'Machiavelli, Milton and Hobbes on Liberty' in R. Bellamy and A. Ross, *op. cit.*, pp. 63, 64.
90   The *Preamble* refers to 'the common defence' as one of the reasons for establishing the *Constitution of the United States of America*. The Second Amendment (Article [II.]) thereto states: 'A well regulated Militia, being necessary for the security of a free State, the right of the people to keep and bear Arms, shall not be infringed'.
91   J. S. Mill *On Liberty* (1859) p. 24.

individual duty to defend the civic order, based on health and safety requirements. Another exception based on conscientious objection has been recognised in the constitutions of a number of countries. For example, Article 276(3) and (4) of the *Constitution of the Portuguese Republic* of 2 April 1976 states:

> (3)   Persons considered unfit for armed military service and conscientious objectors shall perform unarmed military service or civic service suited to their situations.

> (4)   Civic service may be established as a substitute for or as a complement to military service and may be made compulsory by law for citizens not subject to military service.[92]

The other example of regional recognition of a duty to defend one's country may be found in Article 29(5) of the *African Charter on Human and Peoples' Rights* of 1981 which declares that the individual shall have the duty '[t]o preserve ... the territorial integrity of his [or her] country and to contribute to its defence in accordance with the law'. The inclusion of such a duty within the *African Charter* is not surprising. The duty to defend the community and its territory attached by virtue of birth and group membership in traditional African society.[93]

In terms of the constitutions of socialist and communist states, an elevated status is attributed to the duty to defend one's country and to undertake military service. A classic example is provided by Article 52 of the *Constitution of the People's Republic of China* of 4 December 1982:

> It is the sacred duty of every citizen of the People's Republic of China to defend the motherland and resist aggression.

> It is the honorable obligation of citizens of the People's Republic of China to perform military service and to join the militia according to law.

National defence is described by Article 86 of the *Socialist Constitution of the Democratic People's Republic of Korea* of 9 April 1992 as 'the supreme duty and honour of citizens'. Pursuant to that same provision, citizens 'shall defend the country and serve in the army as required by law'. Likewise, Article 78 of the *Constitution of the Polish People's Republic* of 19 December 1963 refers to defence of the country as 'the most sacred duty of every citizen' and military service as 'an honorable patriotic duty of citizens'. Article 64 of the *Constitution of the Republic of Cuba* of 24 February 1976 proclaims that '[d]efense of the

---

92   See also Article 30(2) of the *Constitution of Spain* of 31 October 1978 which states that '[t]he law shall determine the military obligations of Spaniards and shall regulate, with all due guarantees, conscientious objection as well as other causes for exemption from compulsory military service, and it may, when appropriate, impose a substitute social service'.

93   Makau Wa Mutua, *op. cit.*, p. 361.

socialist homeland is the greatest honor and the supreme duty of every Cuban citizen'.[94]

The individual duty to defend one's country and to undertake military service is also widely recognised in Asia and the West and in Islamic countries. In terms of a hierarchy of duties, it perhaps receives somewhat less prominence or fanfare in the constitutions of these countries compared with the socialist and communist constitutions. For example, Section 69 of The *Constitution of the Kingdom of Thailand* of 9 December 1991 merely provides that '[e]very person shall have a duty to defend the country [and] serve in armed forces ...' Likewise, Article 39(1) of the *Constitution of the Republic of Korea* of 29 October 1987 simply states that '[a]ll citizens shall have the duty of national defense as prescribed by law'.

In the European context, Article 30(1) of the *Constitution of Spain* of 31 October 1978 is unique in perceiving national defence both as a right and duty: 'Citizens have the right and duty to defend Spain'.[95] The *Constitution of the Portuguese Republic* of 2 April 1976 attributes added weight to the individual duty of national defence. Article 276(1) and (2) thereof respectively provide that Portugal's defence 'is a *fundamental* duty of every Portuguese' and that '[m]ilitary service shall be compulsory, for a period and on conditions to be laid down by law' (emphasis supplied by author). National defence is declared to be a 'moral duty' as well as being made a legal duty by Article 52 of the *Constitution of Italy* of 27 December 1947:

> The defence of the country is a moral duty of every citizen. Military service is compulsory, within the limits and in the manner laid down by law ...

In the Islamic world, Article 16 of the *Constitution of the Kingdom of Morocco* of 10 March 1972 briefly states that '[a]ll citizens shall contribute to the defence of the nation' while Article 9 of the *Constitution of the Islamic Republic of Iran* of 28 July 1989, with somewhat more flourish, declares that 'the freedom, independence, unity, and territorial integrity of the [Islamic Republic of Iran] are inseparable from one another, and their preservation is the duty of ... all individual citizens'. The *Constitution of the Arab Republic of Egypt* of 11 September 1971, however, does attribute a higher status to the individual duty of defence of one's country. Article 58 thereof states that '[t]he defence of the country and its territory is a *sacred* duty and military service is obligatory in accordance with the law' (emphasis supplied). Pursuant to Article 60 of the *Constitution of the Turkish Republic* of 9 July 1961, the duties to take part in the defence of Turkey and to serve in the Turkish armed forces is to be regulated by law.

---

94   See also Article 36 of the *Constitution of Albania* of 14 March 1946 which states in part that '[p]rotection of the Fatherland is the supreme duty and the highest honour of every citizen ... Military service is compulsory for all citizens'.

95   Article 60 of the *Constitution of the Turkish Republic* of 9 July 1961 also explicitly mentions national defence as 'the right and duty of every Turk'.

Such duties have also been recognised in the constitutions of Latin American countries. Article 51 of the *Constitution of the Republic of Venezuela* of 23 January 1961 proclaims that '[it] shall be the duty of Venezuelans to honour and defend their country, and to safeguard and protect the interests of the nation'. Article 9(b) of the *Constitution of the Dominican Republic* of 28 November 1966 recites that '[e]very able-bodied Dominican has the duty to perform the civilian and military services his [or her] country may require for its defence and preservation'. And military service is declared to be one of the obligatory public services by Article 5 of the *Constitution of Mexico* of 31 January 1917.

Not only do citizens have a duty to safeguard the external security of their country; they are also often obliged under national law to refrain from committing acts (such as high treason) which could jeopardise the internal security of their country. The only international or regional human rights declaration to recognise such a duty is the *African Charter on Human and Peoples' Rights* of 1981. Article 29(3) thereof imposes an individual duty on citizens and residents alike '[n]ot to compromise the security of the State whose national or resident he [or she] is'. At the national level, the individual duty not to jeopardise state security tends to be recognised more often in the constitutions of socialist and communist countries. A leading example is provided by Articles 50 and 51 of the *Constitution of the People's Republic of China* of 4 December 1982:

Article 50

Citizens of the People's Republic of China must safeguard State secrets ...

Article 51

Citizens of the People's Republic of China are duty-bound to safeguard the security, honor and interests of the motherland; acts damaging to the security, honor and interests of the motherland are prohibited.

In somewhat more stirring language, Article 85 of the *Constitution of the Democratic People's Republic of Korea* of 9 April 1992 proclaims that '[c]itizens shall constantly increase their revolutionary vigilance and devotedly fight for the security of the State'. Likewise, Article 79(1) of the *Constitution of the Polish People's Republic* of 19 December 1963 solemnly warns that '[v]igilance against the enemies of the nation and the diligent guarding of State secrets is the duty of every citizen of the Polish People's Republic'. But a duty to safeguard the internal security of one's country is not confined to socialist and communist constitutions. Such a duty appears occasionally in the constitutions of liberal democracies. For example, Article 9(c) of the *Constitution of the Dominican Republic* of 28 November 1966 requires citizens and residents of the Dominican Republic to 'refrain from any act prejudicial to its stability, independence, or sovereignty ...'

From this brief and representative survey of various national constitutions, it is apparent that the duties of citizens to contribute to the defence of their country, not to endanger its internal security and to undertake military service are widely recognised at the national level. These duties are rather generally prescribed within constitutional enactments, leaving it to ordinary legislation to prescribe the terms and conditions for their discharge. At all events, these particular civic duties are generally regarded as so fundamental and overriding in importance that their due performance is a matter of legal obligation enforceable through the administrative and judicial systems of each country.

The Duty to Pay Taxes

A tax is essentially a pecuniary contribution made by a taxpayer (individual, business or corporate) for the maintenance of government.[96] The citizen's duty to maintain the civic order through the payment of national and local taxes is universally recognised and long-established at the national level. In his famous book entitled *An Inquiry into the Nature and Causes of the Wealth of Nations* (1776), the economist Adam Smith declared that '[t]he subjects of every state ought to contribute towards the support of the government as nearly as possible in proportion to their respective abilities'.[97] In taking up Smith's call, Article 13 of the French *Declaration of the Rights of Man and of the Citizen* of 26 August 1789 foreshadowed the implementation of the modern progressive taxation system in the following terms:

> A common contribution being necessary for the support of the public force, and for defraying the other expenses of government, it should be divided equally among the members of the community, according to their abilities.

In order to help fund the Union effort during the American Civil War, President Abraham Lincoln introduced through legislation the first system of income tax for citizens of the United States. Since that time, the number, variety and levels of taxes have increased significantly to help defray the increasing and considerable governmental expenditures required for the functioning of government or demanded by the electorate. But as one commentator has wryly remarked in highlighting a contemporary irony, '[o]ne of the most telling ills of our time is the expectation of many Americans that they are entitled to ever more public services without paying for them (as reflected in public opinion polls that show demands to slash government and taxes but also to expand practically every conceivable government function)'.[98]

The individual duty to pay national and local taxes as a means of contributing to public expenditure on projects beneficial to the community has not been directly recognised as such under international human rights law. It could be argued, however, that provisions such as Article 29(1) of the *Universal Declaration of Human Rights* of 1948 impose an indirect duty upon individuals in

---

96   *Black's Law Dictionary* (Revised Fourth Edition, 1968) p. 1628.
97   Book V, Chapter 2, Part II (I) (1910).
98   A. Etzioni *The Spirit of Community* (1995) p. 261.

this context.   Article 29(1) provides in part that '[e]veryone has duties to the community'.   Although Article 29 does not attempt to explicitly mention any such duties, it is at least arguable that one such implied duty would be the duty to pay taxes, given its virtual universal recognition today at the national level.   By contrast, the duty to pay taxes has been explicitly recognised at the regional level. Article XXXVI of the *American Declaration of the Rights and Duties of Man* of 1948 proclaims that '[i]t is the duty of every person to pay the taxes established by law for the support of public services'.   Similarly, Article 29(6) of the *African Charter on Human and Peoples' Rights* of 1981 imposes on individuals the duty 'to pay taxes imposed by law in the interest of the society'.   Article 29(2) of the *Draft Pacific Charter of Human Rights* of 17 May 1989 also imposes a duty on individuals 'to pay taxes imposed by law in accordance with their means in the interests of society'.

At the national level, the individual duty to pay taxes is a legally enforceable duty prescribed both by constitutional enactments and ordinary legislation. Typically, the constitutional provision will identify the general liability of individuals to pay taxes which must be imposed by law; it is then left to general legislation to prescribe in more detail who are the taxpayers, the incidence and levels of tax liability, legal enforcement measures for non-payment of tax and so forth.[99]   Constitutional provisions do vary, however.   Some only recognise the liability of citizens to pay taxes while others impose such duty on citizens and alien residents alike.   Some constitutions effectively endorse a progressive taxation system while others do not.   A representative and illustrative sampling of such provisions follows.

The duty to pay taxes is concisely stated in some constitutional provisions. Article 53 of the *Constitution of the People's Republic of China* of 4 December 1982 states simply that '[c]itizens of the People's Republic of China are duty-bound to pay taxes according to law'.   Likewise, Article 56 of the *Constitution of the Republic of Venezuela* of 23 January 1961 provides that '[e]very person shall be bound to contribute to the public expenditures'.   Section 69 of *The Constitution of the Kingdom of Thailand* of 9 December 1991 proclaims merely that '[e]very person shall have a duty to … pay taxes and duties …'   Article 61 of the *Constitution of the Arab Republic of Egypt* of 11 September 1971 states that '[p]ayment of taxes and public charges is a duty in accordance with the law'. In more elaborate terms, Article 31(1) of the *Constitution of Spain* of 31 October 1978 provides:

> All shall contribute to the sustenance of public expenditures according to their economic capacity through a just tax system based on the principles of equality and progressiveness, which in no case shall be of a confiscatory scope.

Such a provision not only acknowledges the individual duty to pay taxes; it goes on to identify the rationale for such a duty and the principles upon which the taxation system is to be based. The use of the inclusive word '[a]ll' signifies a legislative

---

99   For example, the Australian *Income Tax Assessment Act 1922* (Cth).

intention on the part of the Spanish *Cortes* to impose the relevant duty upon Spanish citizens and resident aliens alike.[100]

Progressive taxation systems are constitutionally entrenched in some countries. Article 17 of the *Constitution of the Kingdom of Morocco* of 10 March 1972 states that '[e]veryone shall contribute, *according to his [or her] capacity*, to public expenses, which can be established and allocated only by law ...' (emphasis supplied). Article 61 of the *Constitution of the Turkish Republic* of 9 July 1961 provides that '[t]o meet public expenditures every individual is under obligation to pay taxes in proportion to his [or her] financial capacity ...' To the same effect is Article 53 of the *Constitution of Italy* of 27 December 1947: 'Everyone shall contribute to public expenditure in proportion to his [or her] resources ...'

The lack of explicit recognition under international (as opposed to regional) human rights law of an individual duty to pay taxes to maintain governmental services and benefit the community is attributable to three factors. First, such instruments are primarily devoted to a cataloguing of individual human rights and individual duties appear to be mentioned therein somewhat incidentally and haphazardly. Secondly, taxation is a matter essentially within the domestic jurisdiction of states, although 'double taxation' agreements are often entered into between states to avoid double taxation of their citizens. Any attempt internationally to prescribe in detail an individual duty to pay taxes might be perceived by some states as overly intrusive in respect of their internal affairs. And, thirdly, the legally enforceable individual duty to pay taxes is already so widely and deeply entrenched in national (constitutional and ordinary) legislation that it would seem superfluous to acknowledge such duty under international law.

The Duty to Vote

As with acquiring a formal education and engaging in work, the casting of a vote in an election may be dually perceived both as an individual right and duty. Indeed, some instruments which we shall consider shortly consider voting as a concurrent right and duty. In this context, voting may be taken to refer to the expression of the will, preference or choice of a legally qualified elector at a genuine, free and periodic election for the purpose of choosing a representative in a legislative body. Voting has been described as 'one tool for keeping the polity reflective of its constituent communities'.[101] On any measure, the exercise of the franchise is fundamental to the success of the electoral process and the efficacy of democratic responsible government.

---

100 Compare with Article 9 of the *Charter of the Spanish People* of 16 July 1945 which states as follows: '*Spaniards* will contribute to meeting public expenditure according to their economic capacity. Nobody will be obliged to pay tributes that have not been established by laws voted by the Cortes' (emphasis supplied by author).

101 Etzioni, *op. cit.*, p. 261.

At the international level, suffrage has traditionally been regarded as the exercise of an individual right. So, for example, Article 25(b) of the *International Covenant on Civil and Political Rights* of 1966 provides that '[e]very citizen shall have the right and the opportunity ... [t]o vote ... at genuine periodic elections ...'.[102] The exercise of the franchise has also been described as a right in the *Convention on the Political Rights of Women* adopted by the United Nations General Assembly on 20 December 1952.[103] In the preamble thereof, references are made to 'the right [of everyone] to take part in the government of his [or her] country directly or indirectly through freely chosen representatives' and the desire 'to equalize the status of men and women in the enjoyment and exercise of political rights'. Article 1 of the *Convention* states that '[w]omen shall be entitled to vote in all elections on equal terms with men, without any discrimination'. Although Article 1 does not use the word 'right', the choice of the verb 'entitled' implies a right or opportunity rather than compulsion or duty. At the regional level, voting is also generally considered to be the exercise of an individual right.[104] An exception is Article XXXII of the *American Declaration of the Rights and Duties of Man* of 1948 which states that '[i]t is the duty of every person to vote in the popular elections of the country of which he [or she] is a national, when he [or she] is legally capable of doing so'.

At the national level, voting is more often considered as an individual duty in comparison with the international and regional levels. Both constitutional enactments and ordinary legislation prescribe an individual duty to vote. An example of the latter is Section 245(1) of the Australian *Commonwealth Electoral Act 1918* (Cth) which states that '[i]t shall be the duty of every elector to vote at each election'. Section 245 then goes on to establish a penalty for electors who fail to vote in federal elections.[105] In terms of the constitutional entrenchment of the citizen's duty to vote, some constitutional provisions either explicitly or implicitly affirm that voting is both an individual right and duty. An example of the former is Article 97 of the *Fundamental Law of Cuba* of 7 February 1959 which states:

> Universal, equal, and secret suffrage is established for all Cuban citizens as a right, duty, and function.

> This function shall be compulsory and everyone who fails to vote at an election or referendum, except for an impediment admitted by law, shall be subject to the penalties imposed ... by law ...

---

102   See also Article 21 of the *Universal Declaration of Human Rights* of 1948.

103   Opened for signature and ratification by United Nations General Assembly Resolution 640 (VII) of 20 December 1952; entry into force 7 July 1954.

104   Article 13(1) of the *African Charter on Human and Peoples' Rights* of 1981 ('Every citizen shall have the right to participate freely in the government of his [or her] country, either directly or through freely chosen representatives in accordance with the provisions of the law'); Article 23(1)(b) of the *American Convention on Human Rights* of 1969 ('Every citizen shall enjoy the following rights and opportunities ... to vote ... in genuine periodic elections ...').

105   G. Williams *Human Rights Under the Australian Constitution* (1999) p. 159.

An example of the latter is Article 110 of the *Constitution of the Republic of Venezuela* of 23 January 1961 which provides:

> Voting is a right and a public function. Its exercise shall be compulsory, within the limits and conditions established by law.

Other constitutional provisions regard voting exclusively as an individual duty, leaving it to ordinary legislation to prescribe penalties for its non-performance. For example, Article 9(d) of the *Constitution of the Dominican Republic* of 28 November 1966 stipulates that '[e]very Dominican citizen has the duty to vote, provided he [or she] has the legal capacity to do so'. And Article 48 of the *Constitution of Italy* of 27 December 1947 describes voting as 'a civic duty'.[106]

It is arguable that the duty to vote also includes (or should, by implication at least, include) the moral or ethical civic duty to keep oneself adequately informed about public affairs. In other words, a better informed voter is likely to make a sounder judgement at the ballot box. This theme has recently been taken up by the Committee of Ministers of the Council of Europe. On 7 May 1999, the Committee of Ministers adopted the *Declaration and Programme on Education for Democratic Citizenship*. Article 14 of the *Declaration* calls on member states to 'make education for democratic citizenship . . . an essential component of all education, training, cultural and youth policies . . .' Article 3 of the *Programme* states that education for democratic citizenship includes, *inter alia*, the combating of civic apathy, the development of active citizenship, learning about democracy and participation in civil society.

The Duties to Perform Public Services and to Strengthen National Solidarity

Jean-Jacques Rousseau once declared that '[a]s soon as men cease to consider public service as the principal duty of citizens ... we may pronounce the State to be on the very verge of ruin'.[107] The citizen's duty to perform public services for the benefit of the national or local community is not directly recognised as such at the international level. However, such duty may be reasonably implied as falling within the broad language of Article 29(1) of the *Universal Declaration of Human Rights* of 1948 which states in part that '[e]veryone has duties to the

---

106   See also, for example, Section 4 of the *Constitution of the Republic of the Philippines* of 17 January 1973 and Article 36(III) of the *Constitution of Mexico* of 31 January 1917 which regard voting as the 'obligation' of every citizen. Section 68 of *The Constitution of the Kingdom of Thailand* of 9 December 1991 states: 'Every person shall have a duty to exercise his or her right to vote at an election. The person who fails to vote without notifying the appropriate cause of the inability to attend the election shall lose his or her right to vote as provided by law ...'

107   J.-J. Rousseau *The Social Contract* (1762), Book III, Chapter XV.

community ...' The individual duty to perform public services has been more readily acknowledged at the regional level. Article XXXIV of the *American Declaration of the Rights and Duties of Man* proclaims that '[i]t is the duty of every able-bodied person to render whatever civil . . . service his [or her] country may require for its . . . preservation, and, in the case of public disaster, to render such services as may be in his [or her] power'.[108] Pursuant to Article 29 (2) of the *African Charter on Human and Peoples' Rights* of 1981, the individual has the duty '[t]o serve his [or her] national community by placing his [or her] physical and intellectual abilities at its service'.

Duties of public service are most frequently imposed on individuals at the national level by constituent documents and ordinary legislation, particularly in the context of emergencies and public disasters. Section 69 of *The Constitution of the Kingdom of Thailand* of 9 December 1991 provides in part that '[e]very person shall have a duty to ... render assistance to the official service ...' Under Article 8 of the Charter of the Spanish People of 16 July 1945, '[s]uch personal services as are necessary for the national interest or the public need may be made obligatory by laws of a general character'. In the later *Constitution of Spain* of 31 October 1978, Article 30(4) thereof provides that '[t]he duties of citizens in cases of serious risk, catastrophe or public calamity may be regulated by law'. Article 9(c) of the *Constitution of the Dominican Republic* of 28 November 1966 imposes on citizens and residents of the Dominican Republic 'the duty of rendering any services of which they are capable' in the event of a public disaster. Sometimes, duties of public service are prescribed for individuals in ordinary enactments or subordinate legislation. In Ghana, for instance, Section 64 of the *Labour Decree 1967 (N.L.C.D. 157)* provides that the individual is obliged to render service in cases of emergency or calamity or in any circumstances likely to endanger the existence or well-being of the whole or part of the population. The individual may also be called upon to render minor communal services of a kind which are to be performed by the members of a community in the direct interest of the community.[109]

As we have already seen previously in this chapter in the section entitled 'The Duties to Defend One's Country, to Undertake Military Service and to Maintain Internal Security', under the respective constitutions of Spain and Portugal, civic service may be made compulsory by law as a substitute for, or complement to, military service for those citizens exempted therefrom (for reasons of disability or conscientious objection). Article 38(3) of the *Constitution of Spain* of 31 October 1978 goes on to provide that '[a] civilian service may be established for the accomplishment of objectives of general interest'. National constitutions sometimes prescribe individual duties of public service in contexts other than

---

108   Article XXXIV also stipulates that it is also the duty of every able-bodied person 'to hold any public office to which he [or she] may be elected by popular vote in the state of which he [or she] is a national'.

109   Any individual who refuses without reasonable cause to render such service is guilty of an offence and shall be liable to a fine on summary conviction. See Daes, *op. cit.*, p. 24.

emergencies or public disasters. For example, in the context of the electoral process, Article 62 of the *Constitution of the Arab Republic of Egypt* of 11 September 1971 states in part that '[p]articipation in public life is a national duty'.

Although Article 1 of the *Universal Declaration of Human Rights* of 1948 calls on human beings to 'act towards one another in a spirit of brotherhood', a duty to strengthen national solidarity is not directly imposed as such on individuals by any international human rights instrument. At the regional level, however, such a duty has been recognised. Article 29(4) of the *African Charter on Human and Peoples' Rights* of 1981 recognises an individual duty '[t]o preserve and strengthen social and national solidarity, particularly when the latter is threatened'. Such a duty is also recognised at the national constitutional level, mainly for the purposes of national and internal security. A typical example is Article 49 of the *Constitution of the People's Republic of China* of 4 December 1982 which declares that '[c]itizens of the People's Republic of China are duty-bound to safeguard the unity of the country and the unity of all its nationalities'.

The Duty to Safeguard and Promote Democracy or Other Particular Ideologies or Value Systems

The term 'democracy' has been defined as '[t]hat form of government in which the sovereign power resides in and is exercised by the whole body of free citizens, as distinguished from a monarchy, aristocracy, or oligarchy.[110] Democratic rights to participate in the conduct of public affairs are recognised by Article 21 of the *Universal Declaration of Human Rights* of 1948 and Article 25 of the *International Covenant on Civil and Political Rights* of 1966. Such participation is, in terms, either direct or through freely chosen representatives. These political rights have their corresponding duties, such that every citizen has the duty to respect and protect the democratic processes of government of his or her State.[111] This duty has been recently acknowledged by the *Declaration on the Right and Responsibility of Individuals, Groups and Organs of Society to Promote and Protect Universally Recognized Human Rights and Fundamental Freedoms.*[112] Article 18(2) thereof states in part that '[i]ndividuals ... have an important role to play and a responsibility in safeguarding democracy ... and contributing to the promotion and advancement of democratic societies, institutions and processes'. At the regional level, as we have seen previously in this chapter under 'The Duty to Vote', the Committee of Ministers of the Council of Europe has recently recognised the importance of learning about democracy and the requirements of democratic citizenship in its *Declaration and Programme of Education for Democratic Citizenship* of 1999. An example of a national constitution imposing a duty on individuals to safeguard democracy is Section 66 of *The Constitution of the*

---

110   *Black's Law Dictionary* (Revised Fourth Edition, 1968) p. 518.
111   Daes, *op. cit.*, p. 60.
112   For more detail on this instrument, see the section in Chapter 6 entitled 'The Position of Individual Duties Under International Human Rights Instruments'.

Kingdom of Thailand of 9 December 1991 which provides in part that '[e]very person shall have the duty to uphold ... the democratic regime of government ... under this Constitution'.

Other regional instruments and national constitutions have sought to impose similar duties on individuals but in respect of particular strategic objectives and other systems of government. An example of the former is Article 29 (8) of the *African Charter on Human and Peoples' Rights* of 1981 which imposes a duty on every individual '[t]o contribute to the best of his [or her] abilities, at all times and at all levels, to the promotion and achievement of African unity'.[113]   An example of the latter is Article 56 of the *Constitution of the People's Republic of China* of 5 March 1978 which states in part that '[c]itizens must support the leadership of the Communist Party of China [and] support the socialist system ...'[114]

The Duties to Preserve Cultural Values and to Promote Moral Well-being

International human rights instruments do not impose on individuals duties to preserve cultural values and to promote moral well-being. That is not to say that cultural life is not mentioned in these instruments. Article 27(1) of the *Universal Declaration of Human Rights* of 1948 and Article 27 of the *International Covenant on Civil and Political Rights* of 1966 both recognise the enjoyment of one's culture as an individual right. The former provision states that '[e]veryone has the right freely to participate in the cultural life of the community ...' while the latter provision provides that '[i]n those States in which ethnic, religious or linguistic minorities exist, persons belonging to such minorities shall not be denied the right, in community with the other members of their group, to enjoy their own culture ...'

This situation is in stark contrast to regional human rights instruments which explicitly recognise such duties. Although the operative provisions of the *American Declaration of the Rights and Duties of Man* of 1948 do not mention them, the penultimate and final preambular paragraphs read:

> Since culture is the highest social and historical expression of that spiritual development, it is the duty of man to preserve, practise and foster culture by every means within his power.

---

113   It will be recalled that one of the purposes for the creation of the Organization of African Unity was the promotion of 'the unity and solidarity of the African States'. See Article 2(1)(a) of the *Charter of the Organization of African Unity* adopted by a Conference of Heads of State and Government in Addis Ababa, Ethiopia on 25 May 1963. See also Article 31(f) of the *African Charter on the Rights and Welfare of the Child* of 1990 which imposes the same duty on children.

114   Consider also Article 80 of the *Socialist Constitution of the Democratic People's Republic of Korea* of 9 April 1992 which states that '[c]itizens shall firmly safeguard the political and ideological unity and solidarity of the people'.

> And, since moral conduct constitutes the noblest flowering of culture, it is the duty
> of every man always to hold it in high respect.

The duties to preserve cultural values and to promote moral well-being have also
been recognised in Africa and the Asia-Pacific region. Article 29(7) of the *African
Charter on Human and Peoples' Rights* of 1981 imposes on each individual 'the
duty [t]o preserve and strengthen positive African cultural values in his [or her]
relations with other members of the society ... and, in general, to contribute to the
promotion of the moral well-being of society'. In virtually identical language,
Article 31(d) of the *African Charter on the Rights and Welfare of the Child* of 1990
imposes the same obligation on those children who are residing within the
jurisdiction of the States Parties. As for the Asia-Pacific region, Article 29(3) of
the *Draft Pacific Charter of Human Rights* of 1989 repeats *mutatis mutandis* the
wording of Article 29(7) of the *African Charter on Human and Peoples' Rights*.
And Article I(3) of the *Declaration of the Basic Duties of ASEAN Peoples and
Governments* of 1983 states in part that '[i]t is ... the duty of all individuals ... to
preserve and enhance their culture and identity ...'

The individual duty to preserve cultural values has also been recognised in
various national constitutions. So, for instance, Section 69 of *The Constitution of
the Kingdom of Thailand* of 9 December 1991 states in part that '[e]very person
shall have a duty to ... conserve the national arts and culture ...' Article 68 of the
Constitution (Fundamental Law) of the Union of Soviet Socialist Republics of 7
October 1977 declares that '[c]oncern for the preservation of historical monuments
and other cultural values is a duty and obligation of citizens of the U.S.S.R.'. In
somewhat less explicit language, Article 50 of the *Constitution of the People's
Republic of China* of 4 December 1982 requires citizens of the People's Republic
of China to 'respect social ethics and beneficial customs ...'

The Duty to Contribute to Social Welfare

To bear a 'fair share' in 'joint work necessary to the interest of the society of which
he enjoys the protection' was considered by John Stuart Mill to be a 'positive act'
to which the citizen 'may rightfully be compelled'.[115] At the philosophical and
ethical level, the duty of each individual to live responsibly as a member of a
community entails positive as well as negative obligations. As Selbourne has
stated:

> The duty to live peaceably and sociably with one's fellows . . . is more than a
> negative obligation laid upon the citizen to act without violence in the civic order
> to which he belongs. It implies a duty to add to, rather than merely not to subtract
> from, the well-being of the civic order; not simply to maintain, but to help
> construct, such well-being.[116]

---

115   J. S. Mill *On Liberty* (1859) p. 24.
116   Selbourne, *op. cit.*, p. 229.

The individual duty to contribute to social welfare is not recognised as such in any of the mainstream international human rights instruments but its ethical and philosophical underpinnings have.[117] The fourth preambular recital of the *Charter of the United Nations* of 1945 alludes to the determination of the peoples of the United Nations 'to promote social progress and better standards of life'. The importance of social solidarity is underlined by the call in Article 1 of the *Universal Declaration of Human Rights* of 1948 to human beings to 'act towards one another in a spirit of brotherhood'.

The duty to co-operate with the State with respect to social security and welfare has been explicitly and impliedly recognised in a number of regional human rights instruments. The most comprehensive formulation of this duty is to be found in Article XXXV of the *American Declaration of the Rights and Duties of Man* of 1948 which proclaims that '[i]t is the duty of every person to co-operate with the state and the community with respect to social security and welfare, in accordance with his [or her] ability and with existing circumstances'. Article 29(4) of the *African Charter on Human and Peoples' Rights* of 1981 is less explicit, but it is arguable that this provision does impose on individuals an implied duty to make a contribution to social welfare. Article 29(4) imposes on individuals the duty '[t]o preserve and strengthen social ... solidarity ...' The duty to contribute to social welfare is also recognised in the Asia-Pacific region. Article 29(2) of the *Draft Pacific Charter of Human Rights* of 1983 imposes on individuals the duty '... to use their skills and abilities for the betterment of their communities ...' To similar effect is Article I(3) of the *Declaration of the Basic Duties of ASEAN Peoples and Governments* of 1983 which provides in part that '[i]t is the duty of all individuals ... to develop and use their native talents, abilities and resources for the betterment of society ...'

At the national level, constitutional provisions do sometimes impose on individuals a duty to contribute to social welfare. A leading example is Article 9(h) of the *Constitution of the Dominican Republic* of 28 November 1966 which states that '[e]very person has the duty to co-operate with the state in respect of social assistance and social security, in accordance with his [or her] possibilities'. Not as explicit is Section 1 of the *Constitution of the Republic of the Philippines* of 17 January 1973 which provides in part that '[it] shall be the duty of the citizens ... to defend the State and contribute to its development and welfare ... and to co-operate with the duly constituted authorities in the attainment and preservation of a just and orderly society'. Nevertheless, the references in Section 1 to a 'just ... society' and 'State ... welfare' arguably constitute an implied individual duty to contribute to social welfare and the betterment of society.

---

117   But see Article 30(1) of the International Labour Organization's *Convention Concerning Indigenous and Tribal Peoples in Independent Countries* of 1989 which states in part that '[g]overnments shall adopt measures appropriate to the traditions and cultures of the peoples concerned, to make known to them their rights and duties, especially in regard to ... social welfare ...'

The Duty to Exercise Property Rights Consistently With the Public Welfare

We have already seen in the early part of this chapter[118] that individuals have a duty to exercise their human rights responsibly under international human rights law. That is to say, each individual must exercise his or her human rights in such a manner that such exercise does not interfere unduly either with the human rights of other individuals or the interests of the wider community and State. Article 17(1) of the *Universal Declaration of Human Rights* of 1948 recognises that '[e]veryone has the right to own property alone as well as in association with others'. This right presumably includes, by implication, the right to the lawful use and enjoyment of one's property. The exercise of such human right, like others, however, is not absolute or unfettered. For centuries, the common law of such countries as England, the United States of America, Canada, Australia and New Zealand has recognised and developed the law of public and private nuisance in order to restrain landowners or occupiers from continuing to use their property in such a manner that harmful consequences are entailed for adjacent property owners. Such harmful consequences typically include excessive noise, noxious smells, smoke, dust, pollution and vibrations.[119]

Several regional human rights instruments not only recognise the individual's right to enjoy his or her own property but also impliedly recognise the individual's duty to exercise that right responsibly. Article 21(1) of the *American Convention on Human Rights* of 1969 states:

> Everyone has the right to the use and enjoyment of his [or her] property. The law may subordinate such use and enjoyment to the interest of society.

Article 14 of the *African Charter on Human and Peoples' Rights* of 1981 likewise provides:

> The right to property shall be guaranteed. It may only be encroached upon in the interest of the public need or in the general interest of the community and in accordance with the provisions of appropriate laws.

In the case of each provision, the second sentence effectively authorises a limitation to be placed upon the enjoyment of property rights provided such limitation is regulated by law and based upon a wider public interest.

At the national level, the duty to exercise property rights responsibly has received constitutional recognition in those states which do not possess a common law tradition. For instance, Article 23(1) and (2) of the *Constitution of the Republic of Korea* of 29 October 1987 states:

> (1) The right of property of all citizens shall be guaranteed. The contents and limitations thereof shall be determined by law.

---

118   See the section entitled 'The Duty to Exercise Human Rights Responsibly'.
119   See Chapter 21 entitled 'Nuisance' in J. Fleming *The Law of Torts* (9th ed., 1998).

(2) The exercise of property rights shall conform to the public welfare.

A remarkably similar provision appears in the *Basic Law for the Federal Republic of Germany* of 23 May 1949. Article 14(1) and (2) thereof provides:

(1) Property and the right of inheritance shall be guaranteed. Their substance and limits shall be determined by law.

(2) Property entails obligations. Its use should also serve the public interest.

Thus, international and regional human rights law and national law (both constitutional and common law) are at one in recognising an individual duty to exercise property rights with due consideration for the rights of others and the interests of society.

The Duties of Resident Aliens

An alien or non-national living in a state, whether permanently or temporarily, is under a duty to obey the laws of that state in exactly the same way as are its own nationals.[120]   With the exception of those entitled to diplomatic immunity, a resident alien cannot claim exemption from the exercise of territorial jurisdiction. Aliens are often required to register their names with public authorities for internal security purposes and may be compelled to perform civic duties for the protection of the community in which he or she lives under the same conditions as nationals.[121]   Most states also place resident aliens under various restrictions such as the denial of voting rights, the right to practise certain professions and the right to own real estate.[122]

Resident aliens owe a temporary allegiance to the state of residence. However, it has been generally accepted under international law that resident aliens cannot be compelled to serve in the armed forces of the state in which they live, unless the state of which they are a national consents to waive this exemption.[123] Also, resident aliens are not exempt from ordinary civil taxes or customs dues unless they possess diplomatic immunity.   Anglo-American case law has also affirmed the right of states under international law to tax real property physically within their jurisdiction belonging to non-resident aliens.[124]   Under conventional international law, refugees and stateless persons have also been subjected to certain individual duties.   Pursuant to both Article 2 of the *Convention relating to the Status of Refugees* of 1951 and Article 2 of the *Convention relating to the Status of*

---

120   For more detail on the duty of citizens to obey the law, see the earlier section in this chapter entitled 'The Duty to Obey the Law'.

121   Daes, *op. cit.*, p. 63.

122   J. Starke *Introduction to International Law* (10th ed., 1989) p. 349.

123   *Idem.* pp. 349-50.

124   *Winans v Attorney-General* [1910] A.C. 27; *Burnet v Brooks* 288 U.S. 378 (1933).

Stateless Persons of 1954, refugees and stateless persons are respectively placed under a duty to obey the laws of the country of refuge/residence and adhere to measures taken for the maintenance of public order.[125]

Although the mainstream international human rights instruments do not recognise any duties incumbent upon resident aliens, certain regional human rights instruments do. The leading example is the *American Declaration of the Rights and Duties of Man* of 1948. Article XXXIII thereof states in part that '[i]t is the duty of every person to obey the law and other legitimate commands of the authorities of ... the country in which he [or she] may be'. Also, Article XXXVIII provides that '[i]t is the duty of every person to refrain from taking part in political activities that, according to law, are reserved exclusively to the citizens of the state in which he [or she] is an alien'. And Article 29(3) of the *African Charter on Human and Peoples' Rights* of 1981 imposes on each individual the duty '[n]ot to compromise the security of the State whose ... resident he [or she] is'.

The duties of resident aliens have also been explicitly mentioned from time to time in national constitutions. For instance, Article 52 of the *Constitution of the Republic of Venezuela* of 23 January 1961 states:

> Both Venezuelans and aliens shall comply with and obey the Constitution and the laws, and the decrees, resolutions and orders issued by legitimate agencies of the Public Power in the exercise of their functions.

The following provisions of the *Constitution of the Republic of Afghanistan* of June 1990 reflect the position of resident aliens under international law discussed previously:

> Article 37
>
> The Republic of Afghanistan guarantees, according to the law, the rights and freedoms of foreign citizens and individuals residing in Afghanistan without citizenship. They are bound to obey the Constitution and other laws of the Republic of Afghanistan.
>
> Article 62
>
> Citizens of the Republic of Afghanistan and foreigners are bound to pay taxes and duties to the state in accordance with the provisions of the law.

In other national constitutions, the duties of resident aliens are not explicitly mentioned but arise as a matter of constitutional interpretation and reasonable implication from the wording used. A typical example is Article 4 of the *Constitution of the Kingdom of Morocco* of 10 March 1972 which states in part that '[e]veryone must obey the law'. Accordingly, the obligation to abide by the law extends to everyone who is residing in the territory of the Kingdom of Morocco,

---

125   For more detail, see the section in Chapter 6 entitled 'The Position of Individual Duties Under International Human Rights Instruments'.

whether or not he or she is a citizen thereof or merely a permanent resident or transient alien.[126]

The Duty of Spiritual Development

In his *Moral Discourses*, Epictetus set out a hierarchy of individual duties to others (presumably in descending order) in referring to 'my duty to God, to my parents, to my relations, to my community and to strangers'.[127] Particularly in the context of contemporary secularised Western society, it may seem somewhat quaint to speak of an individual duty to pursue spiritual development or a duty to obey the will of God. Today, as with the exercise of many other human rights, the emphasis in this context is on 'right' and 'freedom' rather than on 'duty'. So, for instance, Article 18(1) of the *International Covenant on Civil and Political Rights* of 1966 proclaims:

> Everyone shall have the right to freedom of thought, conscience and religion. This right shall include freedom to have or to adopt a religion or belief of his [or her] choice, and freedom, either individually or in community with others and in public or private, to manifest his [or her] religion or belief in worship, observance, practice and teaching.[128]

Today's right to the free practice of religion has been perceived in former times as an individual duty, not only in the non-Western world but in the Western tradition as well. An entire provision in the *Virginia Declaration of Rights* of 12 June 1776 was devoted to the guarantee of 'the free exercise of religion' but which also included explicit reference to individual duty. Article XVI thereof declared:

> That religion, or the duty which we owe to our Creator, and the manner of discharging it, can be directed only by reason and conviction, not by force or violence; and therefore all men are equally entitled to the free exercise of religion, according to the dictates of conscience; and that it is the duty of all to practise Christian forbearance, love and charity towards each other.

Invocations of Christian morality from the bench of the United States Supreme Court were more common in the nineteenth century and are relatively rare in the recent past. In *United States v Macintosh*,[129] however, Justice Sutherland, speaking for the majority of that leading American bastion of individual freedom and liberty, declared:

---

126   Daes, *op. cit.*, p. 27.
127   Epictetus *Moral Discourses* (translated by E. Carter) (1910) II, xvii, 2.
128   To the same effect is Article 18 of the *Universal Declaration of Human Rights.*
129   283 U.S. 605 (1931).

> We are a Christian people ... according to one another the equal right of religious freedom, and acknowledging with reverence the duty of obedience to the will of God.[130]

The practice of religion, belief or spirituality today is primarily perceived in the West as a fundamental right or freedom.[131] But in other parts of the world, the pursuit of religious belief or spiritual development is still acknowledged to be an individual duty. For example, the fourth preambular recital of the *American Declaration of the Rights and Duties of Man* of 1948 states:

> Inasmuch as spiritual development is the supreme end of human existence and the highest expression thereof, it is the duty of man to serve that end with all his strength and resources.

One of the foundation premises of *The Cairo Declaration on Human Rights in Islam* of 5 August 1990 is the importance of the submission of each individual to the will of God (or Allah). Article 1(a) thereof begins by proclaiming that '[a]ll human beings form one family whose members are united by submission to God ...' At the national level, in Chapter IV (entitled 'Duties of the Thai People') of *The Constitution of the Kingdom of Thailand* of 9 December 1991, Section 66 states in part that '[e]very person shall have the duty to uphold ... religions ...' As a justification for its dual perception as both a duty and right, it could be argued that the pursuit of God (however the deity is perceived by the individual) or other system of belief or spirituality is, to borrow from the wording of Article 29(1) of the *Universal Declaration of Human Rights* of 1948, desirable in helping each individual to further 'the free and full development of [their] personality'.

The Duties to Refrain from Propaganda for War and Advocacy of National, Racial or Religious Hatred or Discrimination

These duties arise for individuals pursuant to a concatenation of various provisions contained in mainstream international human rights instruments. The primary source of these individual duties is to be found in Article 20 of the *International Covenant on Civil and Political Rights* of 1966 which reads as follows:

(1) Any propaganda for war shall be prohibited by law.

(2) Any advocacy of national, racial or religious hatred that constitutes incitement to discrimination, hostility or violence shall be prohibited by law.

---

130   283 U.S. 605, 625 (1931).

131   Indeed, the right to freedom of religion guaranteed by Article 18 of the *International Covenant on Civil and Political Rights* of 1966 is considered so fundamental that it has been made a non-derogable right pursuant to Article 4(2) of the same instrument.

Article 20 is mainly concerned with imposing upon States Parties a legally binding obligation to include in their relevant legislation an explicit provision prohibiting the conduct sought to be proscribed by Article 20. Nevertheless, Article 20 also effectively imposes on individuals an indirect duty to refrain from engaging in any of these outlawed activities.[132] Such duty admittedly is only a moral or ethical duty for the individual at the international level but will be converted into an enforceable legal obligation at the national level once the State Party has faithfully implemented its treaty obligation by including the prohibition as part of its domestic law.

The *International Convention on the Elimination of All Forms of Racial Discrimination* of 1965 is also relevant in this context. Article 4(a) thereof provides in part that:

> States Parties condemn all propaganda and all organizations which are based on ideas or theories of superiority of one race or group of persons of one colour or ethnic origin, or which attempt to justify or promote racial hatred and discrimination in any form, and undertake to adopt immediate and positive measures designed to eradicate all incitement to, or acts of, such discrimination and, to this end, ... [s]hall declare an offence punishable by law all dissemination of ideas based on racial superiority or hatred, incitement to racial discrimination, as well as all acts of violence or incitement to such acts against any race or group of persons of another colour or ethnic origin ...

Thus, in the context of racial hatred and racial discrimination, the same observations which were identified in relation to Article 20 of the *International Covenant on Civil and Political Rights* apply *mutatis mutandis*. As was discussed in an earlier chapter,[133] acts of discrimination by individuals in the private sector are not beyond the purview of the *Racial Discrimination Convention*. It is also worth noting Article 2(1) of the *Declaration on the Elimination of All Forms of Racial Discrimination* adopted by the United Nations on 20 November 1963.[134] This provision declares that '[n]o ... individual shall make any discrimination whatsoever in matters of human rights and fundamental freedoms in the treatment of persons, groups of persons or institutions on the ground of race, colour or ethnic origin'. Although this instrument does not purport to confer binding legal obligations on either states or individuals, it is an explicit acknowledgement that individuals have an ethical or moral duty not to engage in arbitrary acts of discrimination.[135]

---

132   Daes, *op. cit.*, pp. 53-4.

133   For more detail, see the section in Chapter 6 entitled 'The Position of Individual Duties Under International Human Rights Instruments'.

134   Proclaimed by United Nations General Assembly Resolution 1904 (XVIII) of 20 November 1963.

135   See also Articles 2 and 3 of the *International Convention on the Suppression and Punishment of the Crime of Apartheid* of 30 November 1973 which engages the international criminal responsibility of individuals committing the crime of *apartheid*.

The Duty to Protect the Natural Environment

Two centuries ago, the philosopher Immanuel Kant foreshadowed the assumption by each individual of obligations of protection and custodianship of the natural environment when he declared that a 'propensity to wanton destruction of what is beautiful in inanimate nature (*spiritus destructionis*) is opposed to man's duty to himself'.[136] Today, we each possess a moral or ethical duty to protect the natural environment not only for our own sake and the good of the community but to ensure as well that future generations inherit from us a liveable natural environment.[137] This may be deemed to be an 'inter-generational' duty. One commentator has formulated this duty in the following terms:

> [T]o safeguard the future well-being of the civic order, the individual citizen is under an ethical and practical obligation, dictated by the principle of duty and subject to sanction, to minimise such avoidable harm to the physical or material environment as may be caused by his [or her] own actions ... [138]

Traditionally, the primary duty-holder in this context has been the State. The historic United Nations Conference on the Human Environment which met in Stockholm in June 1972 represented the first major effort to solve the global problem of protecting the quality of the human environment by international agreement. One of the principal achievements of the Stockholm Conference included the adoption of the *Declaration on the Human Environment,* Principles 21 and 22 of which recognised the responsibility of states for ensuring that activities within their jurisdiction or control do not cause damage to the environment of other states, or of areas beyond the limits of national jurisdiction. Generally speaking, general international law and international human rights law have not so far directly or explicitly recognised an individual duty to protect the natural environment. An exception, however, may be found in the law of international armed conflict, specifically in the text of the *Protocol Additional to the Geneva Conventions of 12 August 1949, and Relating to the Protection of Victims of International Armed Conflicts (Protocol I)* adopted by the Diplomatic Conference on the Reaffirmation and Development of International Humanitarian Law Applicable in Armed Conflicts on 8 June 1977. Article 55 thereof states:

> Article 55 - Protection of the natural environment
> 1. Care shall be taken in warfare to protect the natural environment against widespread, long-term and severe damage. This protection includes a prohibition of the use of methods or means of warfare which are intended or may be expected to cause such damage to the natural environment and thereby to prejudice the health or survival of the population.

---

136   I. Kant *The Metaphysics of Morals* (including *The Doctrine of Virtue*), translated by M. Gregor, Cambridge (1991) p. 237.
137   A. Etzioni *The Spirit of Community* (1995) pp. 10-11.
138   Selbourne, *op. cit.*, p. 243.

2. Attacks against the natural environment by way of reprisals are prohibited.[139]

Thus, military commanders and soldiers on the ground are placed under an indirect duty to avoid methods of warfare which may cause serious damage to the natural environment.

An individual duty to protect the natural environment is more commonly recognised in national constitutional law. For instance, Section 69 of *The Constitution of the Kingdom of Thailand* of 9 December 1991 states in part that '[e]very person shall have a duty to ... conserve natural resources and the environment ...' Article 67 of the *Constitution (Fundamental Law) of the Union of Soviet Socialist Republics* of 7 October 1977 states that 'Citizens of the U.S.S.R. are obliged to protect nature and conserve its riches'. The dual nature of environmental issues has sometimes been acknowledged. Some constitutional provisions in this context contain both the language of individual 'right' and 'duty'. For example, Article 66 of the *Constitution of the Portuguese Republic* of 2 April 1976 and Article 45 of the *Constitution of Spain* of 31 October 1978 respectively provide as follows:

> Article 66 (Environment and quality of life)
>
> 1. Everyone shall have the right to a healthy and ecologically balanced human environment and the duty to defend it.

> Article 45
>
> 1. Everyone has the right to enjoy an environment suitable for the development of the person as well as the duty to preserve it.

Japan has also promulgated comparatively detailed constitutional provisions on duties of the individual to the community concerning environmental pollution and the conservation of nature. Pursuant to Article 6 of the *Basic Law for Environmental Pollution Control (responsibility of citizens),* '[c]itizens shall endeavour to contribute to the prevention of environmental pollution in all appropriate ways, such as co-operating with the State and with local government bodies in the implementation of control measures'. And Article 1 of the *Nature Conservation Law (obligation of the people)* states that '[t]he people shall endeavour properly to conserve the natural environment and to co-operate with the State and local public bodies in their implementation of the plans for conservation of the natural environment'.[140] Generally, it is left to ordinary legislation in these countries to formulate more precisely the obligations of individuals in this context and to prescribe sanctions for non-compliance.

---

139   See also Article 35(3) of *Additional Protocol I* which states: 'It is prohibited to employ methods or means of warfare which are intended, or may be expected, to cause widespread, long-term and severe damage to the natural environment'.

140   Daes, *op. cit.*, p. 26.

Other Miscellaneous Individual Duties Recognised Primarily Under National Law

It remains to discuss various other duties which have been prescribed for individuals in national legislation. The following brief list is not intended to be exhaustive but merely illustrative of the different types of duties which are so recognised. Generally speaking, these duties have not been recognised by international and regional human rights instruments.

The Duty of Self-care

In Kantian terms, the duty of each individual to take care of himself or herself is a 'self-regarding duty' or one which is owed to oneself.[141] In a distant era, Cicero declared:

> We should ... have respect ... to the preservation of our health and strength, in our victuals, clothes and other conveniences belonging to the body. How base and unworthy a thing to dissolve in luxury and not to keep within the bounds of reason and moderation.[142]

The individual duty of self-care has been formulated as 'the assumption by the individual ... of responsibility for himself [or herself] in the first instance and as a first resort, rather than the transfer - in the first instance and as a first resort - of such responsibility to others, in particular to officials and servants of the civic order'.[143]

In today's terms, however, the enjoyment of good health is perceived rather as an individual right under international human rights law. Article 12(1) of the *International Covenant on Economic, Social and Cultural Rights* of 1966 provides that '[t]he States Parties ... recognize the right of everyone to the enjoyment of the highest attainable standard of physical and mental health'.[144] To be sure, such an acknowledgement is indeed salutary. Few would argue with the proposition that one of the primary responsibilities of the State is to provide its citizens with the basic conditions of a healthy existence through publicly-funded hospitals and medicare systems. But one is reminded of that homely adage: 'An

---

141   I. Kant *Lectures on Ethics* (including *Universal Practical Philosophy and Ethics*), translated by L. Infield, New York (1963) p. 123.

142   Cicero *Offices, Essays and Letters* translated by T. Cockman (1690), London, (1909), I, XXX.

143   Selbourne, *op. cit.*, p. 239.

144   An example of health matters being perceived as both a right and duty may be found in Article 30(1) of the International Labour Organization's *Convention Concerning Indigenous and Tribal Peoples in Independent Countries* of 1989 which states in part that '[g]overnments shall adopt measures appropriate to the traditions and cultures of the peoples concerned, to make known to them their rights and duties, especially in regard to ... health matters ...'

ounce of prevention is worth a pound of cure'. In the context of the increasing burden and cost of pain and sickness from excess and lack of self-care and their transfer to society as a whole through taxpayer cross-subsidisation, would it not, then, also be prudent to acknowledge in a more prominent manner the moral and ethical duty of each individual to take greater responsibility for their own health and well-being. Indeed, some countries appear to have adopted this approach in their legislation. Article 64(1) of the *Constitution of the Portuguese Republic* of 2 April 1976 provides that '[e]veryone shall have the right to protection of his [or her] health and the duty to defend and foster it'. Other pieces of national legislation, however, are not only intended in their intent and effect to protect the health of the duty-bearer but also to protect the health of those with whom he or she may come into contact. The World Health Organization, a specialised agency of the United Nations, has identified various provisions of national legislation concerning obligations of individuals, including the requirements to submit to health examinations or vaccinations for the prevention of communicable diseases, to notify the health authorities when suffering from communicable diseases and to undergo examination, treatment, isolation or hospitalisation.[145] For example, Article 76 of the *Constitution of the Republic of Venezuela* of 23 January 1961 states that '[e]very person shall be bound to submit to the health measures established by law, within limits imposed by respect for the human person'.

The Duty to Assist in Public Law Enforcement

In order to help maintain the integrity and well-being of the civic order, some countries have incorporated within their constitutional or ordinary legislation an individual duty to notify public authorities of the commission of serious crimes. The following provisions of the *Constitution (Fundamental Law) of the Union of Soviet Socialist Republics* of 7 October 1977 offer a good example:

Article 61

Citizens of the U.S.S.R. are obliged to preserve and protect socialist property. It is the duty of a citizen of the U.S.S.R. to combat misappropriation and squandering of state and socially-owned property . . .

Article 65

A citizen of the U.S.S.R. is obliged to . . . help maintain public order.

An example of an ordinary enactment containing such a duty may be found in Article 138 of the *Penal Code* of the Federal Republic of Germany which obliges persons to notify the public authorities of serious crimes.[146]

---

145   Daes, *op. cit.*, p. 32.
146   *Idem.* p. 23.

The Duty to Serve on a Jury

To be a free and responsible citizen in ancient Athens involved, *inter alia*, participation in the administration of justice. All citizens were available to serve on vast juries, whose members were picked by lot and paid an attendance fee. These juries handed down verdicts in both civil and criminal cases. Through such jury service, the people (*demos*) were in direct control of the legal system.[147] The joint civic responsibility of each citizen for the administration of justice in modern times has been transformed into an enforceable legal duty in the law of many of those countries which confer on their citizens the right to a trial by jury. Generally speaking, the duty of jury service is regulated by ordinary legislation which prescribes the terms and conditions of such service and recognised grounds for exemption therefrom. Occasionally, the duty of jury service is accorded constitutional recognition. For instance, Article 5 of the *Constitution of Mexico* of 31 January 1917 lists 'jury service' as one of the enumerated 'public services [which] shall be obligatory, subject to the conditions set forth in the respective laws'. Further, Article 36(V) provides in part that ' [t]he obligations of the citizens of the Republic are . . . to fulfil electoral and jury functions'.

The Duty to Render Assistance

In some of those countries which adhere to a civil code legal system rather than the common law system, an enforceable legal duty is prescribed in legislation (usually in a penal code) to furnish assistance to another person or persons in cases of accidents, danger or distress. A good example of the law enforcing such a 'Good Samaritan' duty is Article 63(2) of the French *Penal Code* which provides in part that '[w]hoever abstains voluntarily from giving such aid to a person in peril that he would have been able to give him without risk to himself or to third persons by his personal action or by calling for help ...' is liable to imprisonment and/or a fine.[148]

---

147   T. O'Hagan 'Aristotle and Aquinas on Community and Natural Law' in R. Bellamy and A. Ross (eds) *A Factual Introduction to Social and Political Theory* (1996) pp. 35, 37-8.

148   M. McInnes 'The Question of a Duty to Rescue in Canadian Tort Law: An Answer From France' (1990) 12 *Dalhousie Law Journal* p. 85. See also Article 330c of the *Penal Code* of the Federal Republic of Germany (as cited in Daes, *op. cit.*, p. 23).

Chapter 8

Socialism and Individual Duty

Collectivism is the basis of life of socialist society.[1]

Introduction

The term 'socialism' has been defined in a leading law dictionary as follows:

> Any theory or system of social organization which would abolish, entirely or in great part, the individual effort and competition on which modern society rests, and substitute for it co-operative action, would introduce a more perfect and equal distribution of the products of labor, and would make land and capital, as the instruments and means of production, the joint possession of the members of the community.[2]

In the previous chapter, numerous references were made to the provisions of a cross-section of socialist constitutions. These provisions dealt with matters which are commonly regulated by the constitutions of socialist and liberal democratic states alike. In this chapter, however, it is proposed to examine a number of individual duties enshrined in socialist constitutions which are either unique to, or at least more prevalent in, socialist systems of government. The differences in perception of human rights between the West and the communist bloc will also be briefly and incidentally canvassed.

Historical Overview

According to the writings of Karl Marx (1818-1883), the development of individualistic notions of natural rights liberated people from the bonds of feudalism, giving rise to the emergence of the *bourgeoisie* (capitalist ruling class). But such rights were perceived by Marx, however, as a bourgeois illusion, designed to assist in achieving capitalist ends. For Marx, rights could not be discussed in abstraction from the realities of class rule. As Rees has observed, '[a]s long as class society exists all [such] moral slogans employed by the ruling class will be deceptions designed to secure its interests, to legitimize its power and

---

1   Article 82 of the *Socialist Constitution of the Democratic People's Republic of Korea* of 9 April 1992.

2   *Black's Law Dictionary* (Revised Fourth Edition, 1968) pp. 1561-2.

maintain its ideological hegemony over society'.[3] A further social revolution was required in which private property rights and private control of the means of production would be abolished, thereby enabling a 'truly human community of communism' to emerge and eventually flourish. In such a community, each would give according to their capacity and receive according to their need.[4] A Soviet gloss on this socialist principle is to be found in Article 12 of the *Constitution (Fundamental Law) of the Union of Soviet Socialist Republics* of 5 December 1936 which states in part that '[t]he principle applied in the U.S.S.R. is that of socialism: 'From each according to his ability, to each according to his work'.

Orthodox Marxism regards the concept of human rights as a historical phenomenon and perceives the rights themselves as conditional. In Marxist-Leninist theory, human rights do not inhere in individuals by virtue of their common humanity. They are rather attributes of a 'social being' which can emerge only after the capitalist relations of production have been replaced by socialist relations of production. The enjoyment of human rights is thus also contingent upon the development of a 'socialist personality' acquired through socialist education.[5] Such enjoyment, moreover, is dependent on the individual's human rights not being exercised in such a manner as to harm the socialist cause or undermine collective interests. The full flowering of the human personality in a social context, and not the pre-eminence of individual rights, is seen as the ultimate goal and basic moral criterion of Marxist socialism.[6] The socialist ideal is that of a society in which individuals are fulfilled primarily through co-operative efforts rather than through individual pursuit of self-fulfillment. A further condition precedent to the enjoyment of human rights by socialist citizens is the discharge of their individual duties owed to the socialist community. As we have seen in the preceding chapter and as we shall see shortly, it is not unusual for socialist constitutions to explicitly enumerate not only human rights but also a variety of individual duties. Such inclusion addresses the perceived problem of 'manifestations of individualism and self-seeking interests stemming from allegedly absolute and unlimited freedom of the individual'.[7]

Marxism-Leninism thus accords priority to the development of the socialist order as a condition for the extension of human rights. Priority is accorded to the collective rights of the proletariat class and subsequently to the socialist community itself above the rights of the individual.[8] Unlike the priority accorded to civil and political rights in western liberal democracies which is

---

3   A. Rees 'The Soviet Union' in R. Vincent (ed.) *Foreign Policy and Human Rights Issues and Responses* (1986) pp. 61, 62.

4   A. E.-S. Tay 'Marxism, Socialism and Human Rights' in E. Kamenka and A. E.-S. Tay (eds) Human Rights (1978) pp. 104, 105.

5   Rees, *op. cit.*, p. 62.

6   Tay, *op. cit.*, pp. 104-12.

7   N. Vitruk 'The Constitution of the U.S.S.R. and the Development of the Soviet Legislation on the Rights of the Individual' in *Human Rights Yearbook* (Moscow, 1983) p. 97.

8   Rees, *op. cit.*, p. 62.

intended to secure to the individual an area of freedom and inviolability against state encroachment, emphasis is placed on economic, social and cultural rights in socialist systems. These 'second generation' rights, as they are often referred to, entail a correlative positive duty on states to provide at least the basic necessities of life such as food, clothing, shelter, work and education for their citizens. Socialist rights are more accurately described as enablements rather than claims in the sense that '[t]hey signify the proper ends and capacities of organised co-operative activity rather than the ultimate recourse of aggrieved individuals'.[9] Rather than keeping the State out of the private sphere and free enterprise, the State is required to intervene and proactively assume responsibility for fundamental aspects of social life.

One of the principal tenets of socialist organisation is the equal satisfaction of need at the highest level of fulfillment. In an illuminating passage which follows, Tom Campbell analyses the concept of socialist rights:

> Interpreting the need principle as having primarily to do with the allocation of pre-existing resources for the satisfaction of human needs, the characteristic type of right that it justifies is one which places obligations on those in a position to provide the wherewithal for the satisfaction of the needs of others. Such rights will be positive or affirmative rights in that they correlate with obligations that others take positive steps to meet the needs of right-holders. This assumes the rejection of the liberal assumption that, while there is a general moral requirement not to harm others, there is no equivalent requirement to assist them, even when in need ...

> Consequently, the relationships between right-holders and obligation-bearers is not the simple one-to-one correlation which holds in the case of such typical liberal rights as the right to freedom from bodily injury which are primarily rights which all members of a society have against all other members. The fact that meeting needs requires the co-operative effort of many individuals, involving public or collective procedures, means that the fulfilment of typically socialist duties must be mediated through social procedures. In this sense the individual's rights in a socialist society are rights against society and the correlative obligations can also be seen as obligations to society ...[10]

Thus, the socialist emphasis upon second generation rights results in socialist rights and duties being primarily society-based or collectivist in orientation.

---

9   T. Campbell *The Left and Rights: A Conceptual Analysis of the Idea of Socialist Rights* (1993) p. 142.

10   *Ibid.*

The Socialist Doctrine of the Organic Unity of Individual Rights and Duties

In the following passage, David Selbourne explains the central position the principle of individual duty to the community occupied in the thinking of the early socialists:

> ... historically, 'social-ism' ... was perceived by early nineteenth-century 'social-ists' to be the ethical antithesis to 'individual-ism'. It was an antithesis which rested upon the assertion by 'social-ists' of the ethical and practical importance of the 'social question' of the day, the moral condition of the 'lower orders', in contrast to the casual unconcern shown for their fellows by many privileged members of the civic order. Old socialism was in origin the politics of the 'social question', finding an 'answer' to which was seen by 'social-ists' - but not by 'individual-ists' - as a civic obligation, or expression of the principle of duty to the civic order in practical form.[11]

The foundations of the socialist theory of citizens' rights and duties and their inseparable unity are contained in the works of Marx and Engels. In setting the objectives for the fight waged by the working class or the proletariat, Marx and Engels envisioned a society and State in which, among other things, the unity of rights and duties would be achieved. When subjecting the *Erfurt Draft Programme* of 1891 to constructive criticism, Engels objected to it for the very reason that it contained statements on equal rights but remained silent on individual socialist duties. His reflections were: 'Instead of "everyone shall have equal rights" we would suggest "everyone shall have equal rights and duties"'.[12] The socialist concept of the unity of rights and duties is also expressed in the *Statutes of Organisation of the International Federation of Labour* which were drawn up by Marx and adopted by the Federation's London Conference in 1871. The following statement was included in the Federation's *Statutes*: 'The Federation recognizes that there shall be no rights without duties and no duties without rights'.[13]

The socialist doctrine of the organic unity of rights and duties has been entrenched in some contemporary socialist constitutions. A leading example is provided by Article 59 of the *Constitution (Fundamental Law) of the Union of Soviet Socialist Republics* of 7 October 1977 which states that '[c]itizens' exercise of their rights and freedoms is inseparable from the performance of their duties and obligations'. The first post-revolutionary socialist constitution of the Cuban Republic provides another such example. Article 8 of the *Fundamental Law of Cuba* of 7 February 1959 provides that '[c]itizenship involves duties and rights, the adequate exercise of which shall be regulated by law'. And Article 32 of the *Constitution of the People's Republic of China* of 4 December 1982 states in part

---

11   D. Selbourne *The Principle of Duty* (1994) pp. 38-9.
12   Erica-Irene A. Daes *Freedom of the Individual under Law: A Study on the Individual's Duties to the Community and the Limitations on Human Rights and Freedoms under Article 29 of the Universal Declaration of Human Rights* (United Nations, New York, 1990) p. 40.
13   *Ibid.*

that '[t]he rights of citizens are inseparable from their duties'. The most detailed reference to the doctrine to be found in a socialist constitution is Article 54 of the *Constitution of the Socialist Republic of Vietnam* of 18 December 1980 which provides:

> The rights and obligations of citizens reflect the ... harmonious combination of the requirements of social life and legitimate individual freedoms, and a guarantee of the identity of interests between the state, the collective and the individual, on the principle: each for all, all for each.
>
> The rights of citizens are inseparable from their obligations.
>
> The state guarantees the rights of citizens; and citizens must fulfill their obligations towards the state and society.

Governmental representatives of some socialist states which incorporate the doctrine within their constitutions have made explanatory statements regarding the doctrine. For example, the government of the German Democratic Republic has commented on the unity doctrine and the harmony between individual interests and societal needs in the following terms:

> The coupling of citizens' basic rights and basic duties, as embodied in the Constitution of the German Democratic Republic, stems from an awareness that the enjoyment of the former and the discharge of the latter constitute an organic whole. When citizens exercise their basic rights and discharge their basic duties, they stimulate the successful development of socialist society.[14]

The government of the former Union of Soviet Socialist Republics outlined the Soviet view of the unity doctrine in the following extracts:

> Relations between a socialist State and the citizen are formed on the basis of unity and co-operation between the individual and society ... The proclamation of the rights and duties of citizens in the Fundamental Law of the U.S.S.R. means that the Soviet State, acting on behalf of society, undertakes to ensure by all the means at its disposal, on the one hand, the enjoyment of those rights and, on the other hand, the fulfilment by all citizens of their duties ... The distinction of principle between socialist and bourgeois law is that under socialism the citizen's duties to the community are inseparable from his rights and are regarded as being indissolubly linked with them ... The institution of constitutional rights and duties of citizens of the U.S.S.R. is of equally vital importance to the individual and to society. The exercise of citizens' rights and liberties not only corresponds to their needs and interests but is also an essential condition for the normal functioning of society as a whole. At the same time, the fulfilment by citizens of their constitutional duties is a most important precondition for the untrammelled enjoyment of their rights and for guaranteeing the conditions necessary for such enjoyment ... Constitutional

---

14   *Idem.* p. 23. See generally Articles 19-40 (which are contained in Chapter 1 of Part II entitled 'Fundamental Rights and Fundamental Duties of Citizens') of the *Constitution of the German Democratic Republic* of 7 October 1974.

duties presuppose the State's right, established by law, to demand their fulfilment from the citizens. This is an essential precondition of the maintenance of public order, the normal functioning of the entire mechanism of socialist society, and the further development of socialist democracy.[15]

Individual Socialist Duties

This section will endeavour to examine briefly six individual duties which are either unique to, or at least more prevalent in, socialist constitutions. In many cases, the relevant constitutional provision is framed in abstract or 'in principle' terms, leaving it to ordinary enactments, subordinate legislation and judicial interpretation to elaborate upon the content and scope of the individual duty concerned. In each case, the constitutional provisions cited do not purport to be an exhaustive collection but merely illustrative of typical examples.

The Individual Socialist Duty Not to Undermine Collective Interests in the Exercise of Human Rights

Admittedly, this duty has its counterpart in the constitutions of the Western liberal democracies in the form of 'clawback' clauses which were discussed in Chapter 6. However, as will be seen in the following constitutional provisions, such a duty is articulated in typically socialist terminology:

> None of the freedoms which are recognized for citizens can be exercised contrary to ... the existence and objectives of the socialist state, or contrary to the decision of the Cuban people to build socialism and communism. Violations of this principle can be punished by law. (Article 61 of the *Constitution of the Republic of Cuba* of 24 February 1976.)

> When exercising their freedoms and rights, citizens of the People's Republic of China must not infringe upon the interests of the State, of society and of the collective ... (Article 48 of the *Constitution of the People's Republic of China* of 4 December 1982.)

The Individual Socialist Duty to Promote Social Welfare and Solidarity

The individual socialist duty to promote social welfare and solidarity sits rather uncomfortably with Western liberal individualism.[16] Nevertheless, one is reminded of the call in Article 1 of the *Universal Declaration of Human Rights* of 1948 to human beings to 'act towards one another in a spirit of brotherhood'. This duty of mutual help and solidarity in the socialist context, however, is implicitly but

---

15   *Idem.* pp. 30-31.
16   E. Kamenka and A. E.-S. Tay 'The Philosophical Bases of Human Rights' in *Human Rights for Australia* (Human Rights Commission Monograph Series No. 1, Canberra, Australian Government Publishing Service, 1986) pp. 77, 78.

squarely aimed at the working class or proletariat. Its intended beneficiary is the collective at first instance and ultimately socialist society. Relevant illustrative constitutional provisions follow:

> Citizens shall firmly safeguard the ... solidarity of the people. (Article 80 of the *Socialist Constitution of the Democratic People's Republic of Korea* of 9 April 1992.)

> Citizens of the People's Republic of China are duty-bound to safeguard the unity of the country ... (Article 49 of the *Constitution of the People's Republic of China* of 4 December 1982.)

> Citizens shall cherish their organization and collective and work devotedly for the good of society and the people. (Article 82 of the *Socialist Constitution of the Democratic People's Republic of Korea* of 9 April 1992.)

> Citizens are bound to . . . help promote the . . . welfare of the people. (Article 93 of the *Constitution of Bulgaria* of 4 December 1947.)

The Individual Socialist Duty to Protect Socialist Property

As we saw in the definition of 'socialism' which introduced this chapter, the ownership of land and capital, the primary instruments and means of production, resides jointly with the members of the socialist community. An indication of just what constitutes socialist property is provided in Article 10(1) of *the Constitution of the German Democratic Republic* of 7 October 1974:

> Socialist property consists of the following: societally owned property, joint cooperative property of collectives of working people, and the property of societal organizations of citizens.

Socialist constitutional provisions vary as to the degree of specificity in which the duty to protect socialist property is framed. A few of the more detailed and expansive expositions follow:

> (1) It is the duty of every citizen of the Polish People's Republic to safeguard and strengthen social property, which is the unshakable foundation of the development of the State, the source of the wealth and might of the country.

> (2) Persons who commit sabotage, subversion, inflict damage or who otherwise injure social property, are punishable with all the severity of law. (Article 77 of the *Constitution of the Polish People's Republic* of 19 December 1963.)

> It is the duty of every citizen of the U.S.S.R. to safeguard and fortify public, socialist property as the sacred and inviolable foundation of the Soviet system, as the source of the wealth and might of the country, as the source of the prosperity and culture of all the working people.

Persons committing crimes in respect of public, socialist property are enemies of the people. (Article 131 of the *Constitution (Fundamental Law) of the Union of Soviet Socialist Republics* of 5 December 1936.)

Citizens of the U.S.S.R. are obliged to preserve and protect socialist property. It is the duty of a citizen of the U.S.S.R. to combat misappropriation and squandering of state and socially owned property and to make thrifty use of the people's wealth

Persons encroaching in any way on socialist property shall be punished according to law. (Article 61 of the *Constitution (Fundamental Law) of the Union of Soviet Socialist Republics* of 7 October 1977.)

Citizens shall take good care of State and communal property, combat all forms of misappropriation and waste and manage the nation's economy diligently as the masters.

The property of the State and the social, cooperative organization is inviolable. (Article 84 of the *Socialist Constitution of the Democratic People's Republic of Korea* of 9 April 1992.)

Every citizen is duty-bound to safeguard and consolidate social property (state and co-operative property), the sacred and inviolable basis of the people's democracy, the source of power of the motherland, of the welfare and culture of all the working people.

Those who lay hands on social property are enemies of the people. (Article 35 of the *Constitution of Albania* of 14 March 1946.)

Other socialist constitutional provisions are more concise and indirect in recognising an individual duty to protect socialist property. Those in the former category include the following:

Socialist property is sacred and inviolable. Citizens are obliged to respect and protect it. (Article 79 of the *Constitution of the Socialist Republic of Vietnam* of 18 December 1980.)

It is the duty of the socialist state and its citizens to protect and increase socialist property. (Article 10(2) of the *Constitution of the German Democratic Republic* of 7 October 1974.)

Every citizen of the Socialist Republic of Romania is bound to . . . defend socialist property . . . (Article 39 of *the Constitution of the Socialist Republic of Romania* of 1965.)

Everyone has the duty of caring for public and social property . . . (Article 63 of the *Constitution of the Republic of Cuba* of 24 February 1976.)

Examples of socialist constitutional provisions which impliedly recognise an individual duty to protect socialist property include the following:

Citizens must take care of and protect public property ... (Article 57 of the *Constitution of the People's Republic of China* of 5 March 1978.)

Citizens of the People's Republic of China must ... take care of public property ... (Article 50 of the *Constitution of the People's Republic of China* of 4 December 1982.)

Citizens are bound to protect national property ... (Article 93 of the *Constitution of Bulgaria* of 4 December 1947.)

The Individual Socialist Duty to Observe Socialist Standards of Conduct

While the individual duty to observe socialist standards of conduct is frequently included in socialist constitutions, its content and scope are rarely defined therein. Nevertheless, statements made by representatives of socialist governments from time to time shed some light upon the essence of such duty. First, it involves the necessity of assuming personal responsibility for one's actions and their consequences.[17] This involves the discharge by each individual of socialist moral responsibility and the reaction of public opinion if this responsibility is not acknowledged and upheld.[18] Secondly, social responsibility is regarded as one of the main requirements of the socialist way of life. A true 'socialist' has been described as 'an individual with a developed sense of the collective, an understanding of the importance of his [or her] social functions and an awareness of belonging to the people - the greatest social force ...'[19]

The duty to observe socialist standards of conduct has been most explicitly and directly recognised in the constitutions of the Union of Soviet Socialist Republics, Cuba and North Korea. The relevant provisions follow:

It is the duty of every citizen of the U.S.S.R. to ... perform public duties, and to respect the rules of socialist society. (Article 130 of the *Constitution (Fundamental Law) of the Union of Soviet Socialist Republics* of 5 December 1936.)

. . . Citizens of the U.S.S.R. are obliged to observe the Constitution of the U.S.S.R. and Soviet laws, comply with the standards of socialist conduct, and uphold the honour and dignity of Soviet citizenship. (Article 59 of the *Constitution (Fundamental Law) of the Union of Soviet Socialist Republics* of 7 October 1977.)

---

17   Statement made by representatives of the government of the Byelorussian Soviet Socialist Republic, as cited in Daes, *op. cit.*, p. 22.
18   *Ibid.*
19   Statement made by representatives of the government of the Union of Soviet Socialist Republics, as cited in Daes, *op. cit.*, p. 30.

> Everyone has the duty of . . . observing standards of socialist living and fulfilling civic and social duties. (Article 63 of the *Constitution of the Republic of Cuba* of 24 February 1976.)

> Citizens shall strictly observe the laws of the State and the socialist standards of life . . . (Article 81 of the *Socialist Constitution of the Democratic People's Republic of Korea* of 9 April 1992.)

Some socialist constitutions do not refer to an individual duty to observe socialist standards of conduct as such but utilise language which could reasonably be construed to refer thereto. A leading example may be found in successive versions of the socialist constitutions of the People's Republic of China:

> Citizens must support the . . . socialist system . . . and abide by the constitution and the law.

> Citizens must . . . respect social ethics . . . (Articles 56 and 57 of the *Constitution of the People's Republic of China* of 5 March 1978.)

> Citizens of the People's Republic of China must . . . observe public order and respect social ethics and beneficial customs and habits. (Article 50 of the *Constitution of the People's Republic of China* of 4 December 1982.)

Other examples of socialist constitutional provisions indirectly recognising an individual duty to observe socialist standards of conduct include the following:

> Citizens are obliged to . . . respect the regulations of the socialist society. (Article 78 of the *Constitution of the Socialist Republic of Vietnam* of 18 December 1980.)

> It is the duty of every citizen of the Polish People's Republic to . . . respect the rules of social intercourse and to discharge conscientiously their duties towards the State. (Article 76 of the *Constitution of the Polish People's Republic* of 19 December 1963.)

> Every citizen of the Socialist Republic of Romania is bound to . . . contribute to the strengthening and development of the socialist system. (Article 39 of the *Constitution of the Socialist Republic of Romania* of 1965.)

The Individual Socialist Duty to Engage in Work or Other Socially Useful Activity

As was demonstrated in the section of Chapter 7 entitled 'The Duty to Work', engagement in work or labour has been perceived both as an individual right and as a duty at the national constitutional level. We saw that the constitutions of Western liberal democratic states tended to regard engagement in work as an individual right, although there were some notable exceptions. In the constitutions of socialist states, however, engagement in work or labour is much more often perceived as an individual socialist duty rather than right, although, once again, there exist exceptions whereby it is regarded both as an individual right and duty. For instance, Article 24(2) of the *Constitution of the German Democratic Republic* of 7 October 1974 acknowledges the double-sided nature of engagement in work by individuals in stating in part that '[t]he right to work and the duty to work form a unity'. For socialist states, the citizen's right to work is matched by his or her duty to work, the latter being derived from the constitutional principle that labour, as one of the instruments and means of production, is a duty and a matter of honour for every able-bodied citizen.[20] Evasion of work is deemed to be incompatible with the principles of socialist society.

Engagement in work has always been regarded exclusively as the discharge of an individual socialist duty in the Union of Soviet Socialist Republics, as the following provisions of successive constitutions attest to:

> Work in the U.S.S.R. is a duty and a matter of honour for every able-bodied citizen, in accordance with the principle: 'He who does not work, neither shall he eat.' (Article 12 of the *Constitution (Fundamental Law) of the Union of Soviet Socialist Republics* of 5 December 1936.)

> It is the duty of, and a matter of honour for, every able-bodied citizen of the U.S.S.R. to work conscientiously in his [or her] chosen, socially useful occupation . . . Evasion of socially useful work is incompatible with the principles of socialist society. (Article 60 of the *Constitution (Fundamental Law) of the Union of Soviet Socialist Republics* of 7 October 1977.)

Other socialist constitutions which regard engagement in work solely as an individual duty include those of North Korea[21] and the People's Republic of China.[22]

Other socialist constitutions perceive in the engagement in work by persons its dual and concurrent nature as both individual right and duty. This could be attributable to contemporary human rights developments at the international level and the tacit acknowledgement that a universal or general legally enforceable individual duty to work may fall foul of various forced labour conventions promulgated by the International Labour Organization.[23] Socialist constitutions which apply to engagement in work the socialist doctrine of the organic unity of

---

20   Statement made by representatives of the government of the Ukrainian Soviet Socialist Republic, as cited in Daes, *op. cit.*, p. 30.

21   Article 83 of the *Socialist Constitution of the Democratic People's Republic of Korea* of 9 April 1992 provides in part that '[w]ork is the noble duty and honour of a citizen'.

22   Article 41 of the *Constitution of the People's Republic of China* of 4 December 1982 states in part: 'Work is a glorious duty of every able-bodied citizen. Workers in the State enterprises and in units of the collective economy, urban or rural, should perform their tasks with the attitude of masters of the country. The State promotes socialist labor emulation [and] commends model and advanced workers . . .'

23   For a more detailed discussion of both of these propositions, see the section in Chapter 7 entitled 'The Duty to Work'.

individual rights and duties include those of Vietnam, the former East Germany, Cuba and Bulgaria:

> Work is the primary right, obligation and privilege of citizens. (Article 58 of the *Constitution of the Socialist Republic of Vietnam* of 18 December 1980.)

> Societally useful activity is an honorable duty of every citizen capable of work. The right to work and the duty to work form a unity. (Article 24(2) of the *Constitution of the German Democratic Republic* of 7 October 1974.)

> Work in a socialist society is a right and duty and a source of pride for every citizen ...

> Every worker has the duty to faithfully carry out [his or her work] tasks ... (Article 44 of the *Constitution of the Republic of Cuba* of 24 February 1976.)

> Citizens have the right to work.

> Work is a duty and a matter of honor for every able-bodied citizen. It is the duty of every citizen to engage in socially useful labor and work according to his [or her] powers and ability.

> Citizens' labor service obligations are determined by a special law. (Article 73 of the *Constitution of Bulgaria* of 4 December 1947.)

While these socialist constitutions prescribe a general obligation to engage in work, it is left to ordinary legislation and subordinate legislation to regulate in more detail the requirements of such duty and to provide for any sanctions and compulsory direction to specified work which may be triggered in the event of its non-performance.

There would appear to be no recognised socialist duty to perform unpaid, voluntary labour for the benefit of the socialist community, although such altruism is encouraged in socialist constitutions. The following provisions are typical:

> ... Nonpaid, voluntary work carried out for the benefit of all society in industrial, agricultural, technical, artistic and service activities is recognized as playing an important role in the formation of our people's communist awareness. (Article 44 of the *Constitution of the Republic of Cuba* of 24 February 1976.)

> ... The State encourages citizens to take part in voluntary labor ... (Article 41 of the *Constitution of the People's Republic of China* of 4 December 1982.)

The Individual Socialist Duty to Maintain Socialist Work Discipline

One of the most consistently acknowledged individual duties to be recognised in socialist constitutions is that of maintaining socialist work discipline. Admittedly, such duty is closely associated with the individual socialist duty to engage in work or other socially useful activity examined in the previous section. Although the relevant constitutional provisions rarely explicate the scope of such duty, it would appear to implicate such matters as the conscientious fulfillment of work tasks, obedience to directives issued by superiors, adherence to the rules of the factory or collective, provision of a full day's work for a full day's pay, the avoidance of strikes, work stoppages and industrial disputes, punctual attendance at work and the avoidance of absenteeism without sufficient cause.

A representative sampling of socialist constitutional provisions concerning such duty follows:

> ... Citizens shall willingly and conscientiously participate in work and strictly observe labour discipline and the working hours. (Article 83 of the *Socialist Constitution of the Democratic People's Republic of Korea* of 9 April 1992.)

> It is the duty of every citizen of the Polish People's Republic to . . . maintain socialist work discipline ... (Article 76 of *the Constitution of the Polish People's Republic* of 19 December 1963.)

> Everyone has the duty of ... accepting work discipline ... (Article 63 of the *Constitution of the Republic of Cuba* of 24 February 1976.)

> Citizens are obliged to abide by ... labour discipline ... (Article 78 of the *Constitution of the Socialist Republic of Vietnam* of 18 December 1980.)

> Citizens of the People's Republic of China must ... observe labor discipline ... (Article 50 of the *Constitution of the People's Republic of China* of 4 December 1982.)

> It is the duty of, and a matter of honour for, every able-bodied citizen of the U.S.S.R. to work conscientiously in his [or her] chosen, socially useful occupation, and strictly to observe labour discipline ... (Article 60 of the *Constitution (Fundamental Law) of the Union of Soviet Socialist Republics* of 7 October 1977.)

The Historical Facilitation of the Emergence of Individual Socialist Duties

In certain parts of the world, particularly in Africa and Asia, the groundwork had already been laid so as to more readily enable the transposition of individual socialist duties. This explains, in part at least, why African states such as Ethiopia and Mozambique and Asian states such as the People's Republic of China and the Socialist Republic of Vietnam have embraced socialism and succeeded in imposing through their constitutions a considerable number and variety of individual duties upon their citizens.

As we have seen in an earlier chapter,[24] individual duties were commonly owed in the pre-colonial African era to the family - nuclear and extended - and to the community. It was but a modest step to extend such duties to include those owed to the post-colonial African nation or state. It is not surprising that Chapter

---

24   See the section in Chapter 6 entitled 'Pre-colonial African Culture and Traditional Values'.

II (entitled 'Duties') of the *African Charter on Human and Peoples' Rights* of 1981 contains individual duties which are owed not only to family members and the community but to the State as well.[25] The more noteworthy duties with a socialist inclination falling into the latter category are the individual duties to serve one's national community and to 'preserve and strengthen social and national solidarity' contained respectively in Article 29(2) and Article 29(4) of the *African Charter on Human and Peoples' Rights*. The inclusion of Chapter II in the *African Charter*, however, is not solely attributable to the historical traditions and values of African civilisation. Certain African socialist states had difficulty reconciling traditional human rights instruments with socialist philosophy. As a result, the drafters of the *African Charter* expanded the scope of individual duties recognised therein to include those owed to the State in order to secure its wider adoption.[26]

As for Asia, we have already seen[27] the significant influence of Confucianism in developing a system of mutual obligations attached to various social relationships. It may be recalled that one of the five Confucian cardinal relationships is that of ruler and subject. Confucian philosophy places family and community obligations over individual interests.[28] Chinese socialism may be perceived as a logical continuation of Confucianism in the sense that they both place a similar and important emphasis upon the harmony of the collective/community and obedience to governmental authority. Thus, obedience and duty to the Emperor have been superseded by loyalty and duty to the socialist State and the leadership of the Communist Party of China. Provisions of successive constitutions of the People's Republic of China have entrenched these neo-Confucian values. For example, Article 56 of the *Constitution of the People's Republic of China* of 5 March 1978 declared that '[c]itizens must support the leadership of the Communist Party of China [and] support the socialist system...' And Article 48 of the *Constitution of the People's Republic of China* of 4 December 1982 cautions that '[w]hen exercising their freedoms and rights, citizens of the People's Republic of China must not infringe upon the interests of the State, of society and of the collective ...'

---

25   For a detailed discussion of these duties, see the section in Chapter 6 entitled 'The African Charter on Human and Peoples' Rights'.

26   R. Gittelman 'The Banjul Charter on Human and Peoples' Rights: A Legal Analysis' in C. Welch and R. Meltzer (eds) *Human Rights and Development in Africa* (1984) pp. 152, 154.

27   See the section in Chapter 4 entitled 'Confucianism'.

28   R. Vincent *Human Rights and International Relations* (1986) p. 41.

Chapter 9

Impoverished 'Rights Talk', the Sociology of Duty and the Re-emergence of Communitarianism

> And so, my fellow Americans: ask not what your country can do for you - ask what you can do for your country. (President John F. Kennedy's Inaugural Address of 20 January 1961.)[1]

Introduction

The morality which President Kennedy's words encourage is one which asks persons to reflect first upon their duties and only then to consider their claims or entitlements. Although from a liberal point of view, the late President's stirring words may indeed be controversial, some would argue that his appeal contains a sound theory of what civic virtue requires.[2] Over half a century ago, Max Radin, a Professor of Law of the University of California, extolled the principle of duty in an article which appeared in *The Yale Law Journal* as ' . . . a finer and nobler thing than right'.[3] Perhaps Professor Radin had in mind Jean-Jacques Rousseau's warning concerning the ill-effects of the non-performance of civic duties upon the body politic. The French philosopher had considered as 'an injustice whose spread would cause the ruin of the body politic' the full enjoyment by citizens of their rights without wanting to fulfill their civic duties.[4] Be that as it may, a respected British political and social philosopher lamented that the principle of duty had by the mid-1990s been relegated to 'a mere slogan of reaction'.[5]

---

1   *The Oxford Dictionary of 20th Century Quotations* (1998) p. 169.
2   P. Selznick 'The Idea of a Communitarian Morality' (1987) 75 *California Law Review* pp. 445, 455.
3   M. Radin 'Natural Law and Natural Rights' (1950) 59 *The Yale Law Journal* pp. 214, 217.
4   J.-J. Rousseau *The Social Contract* Book I, Chapter VII ('On the Sovereign').
5   D. Selbourne *The Principle of Duty* (1994) p. 179.

Contemporary philosophers and rights theorists[6] have concentrated their minds upon promoting 'rights' as a sufficient means of ensuring human dignity in the waning years of the twentieth century.[7] Selbourne has complained that:

> It is . . . routine to find that, lip-service to duty once paid, generally at the outset of discussion, it is rights which are the dominating subject of discourse. Duties, never or rarely particularised, are soon forgotten, or alluded to in token or passing fashion as if their content and implications were taken for granted.[8]

This marginalisation of the role of civic duty in the body politic and the lack of an adequate acknowledgement of the social nature of human existence have sparked a renewed attack on the premises of liberalism over the past two decades or so. As Philip Selznick, Professor Emeritus of Law and Sociology of the University of California, has pointed out, there is nothing new about such criticism. A long and impressive list of writers - including Hegel, Marx, the American pragmatist John Dewey, and English liberals John Hobson and L. T. Hobhouse - have recoiled from what they perceived to be an impoverished morality and an inadequate understanding of the social nature of human existence.[9] There must be a limit in any civic order to the indulgence of individual desires and wills. A balance must be sought between the recognition and exercise of individual rights and the acknowledgement and performance of individual duties. These new critics of the liberal premises are called 'communitarians'.

Selznick identifies the crux of the concerns felt by communitarians as follows:

> Liberalism is much preoccupied with rights, understandably so, because it is a philosophy of liberation, not of belonging. This preoccupation has merit, but it too easily separates liberty from association and therefore from discipline and duty. In the process rights become abstract, unsituated and absolute.[10]

One of the failures of the contemporary Western liberal democratic civic order, underpinned by its emphasis upon individual freedom, is the increasingly marginal role allocated to the principle of duty.[11] It is difficult to discern, even in early liberal doctrine, any positive civic ethic. Liberty is envisioned in negative, rather than positive, terms. So, for John Stuart Mill, '[t]he only liberty which deserves the name, is that of pursuing our own good in our own way, so long as we do not

---

6   See, for example, the writings in legal, moral and social philosophy of John Rawls, Ronald Dworkin and Robert Nozick which reaffirm the liberal faith in personal moral autonomy.

7   A. Devereux 'Should "Duties" Play a Larger Role in Human Rights? A Critique of Western Liberal and African Human Rights Jurisprudence' (1995) 18 *University of New South Wales Law Journal* pp. 464, 466.

8   Selbourne, *op. cit.*, p. 2.

9   Selznick, *op. cit.*, p. 445.

10   *Idem* p. 455.

11   Selbourne, *op. cit.*, p. 26.

attempt to deprive others of theirs or impede their efforts to obtain it'.[12] To similar effect is Article 4 of the French *Declaration of the Rights of Man and of the Citizen* of 26 August 1789 which declares that since '[l]iberty consists in the power of doing whatever does not injure another', the exercise of individual rights is constrained only by the necessity to secure to every other rights-holder the free exercise of his or her rights. Thus, the citizen's duty is a negative one of restraint or non-interference into the affairs of others; any positive duty is little more than to do what he or she will be penalised for not doing under the law.

The remainder of this chapter will be devoted to examining the alleged ill-effects and excesses attributable to the perceived current imbalance between rights and duties and the proposed solutions advocated by the communitarian movement. Also, the basis of the so-called 'atomistic' theory of the nature of human existence will be challenged in light of what appears to be a preponderance of social scientific evidence concerning the social nature of human existence and the associated importance of the principle of individual duty therein.

Impoverished 'Rights Talk'

Dworkin's 'Trump Card'

Western legal traditions accord a special position to what are called 'personal' rights (*droits subjectifs*). By recognising certain rights, we give individuals the power to set limits on the actions of society. As a right-holder or subject of law, the individual has the power under law to assert or enforce his or her rights. In some legal jurisdictions, particularly those with a constitutionally entrenched bill of rights, certain public administrative decisions and pieces of legislation can actually be declared null and void by a supervising judiciary.[13]

The American legal philosopher, Ronald Dworkin, has borrowed a metaphor from the game of bridge to explain this process.[14] It is as though the individual is given a 'trump card' which enables him or her to invalidate the results of the normal social decision-making process whenever his or her protected sphere is encroached upon. To use a popular American example, if any attempt is made to abridge my freedom of speech, I can play my so-called 'trump card' and have the decision revoked in a court of law.[15] The metaphorical trump card expresses the concern that personal rights are not meaningful if they are susceptible to being overriden by every collective goal or interest.[16] As Dworkin says, 'It follows from

---

12   J. S. Mill *On Liberty* (1859) ('Introduction').
13   C. Taylor *Human Rights: The Legal Culture* (1986) (U.N.E.S.C.O.) p. 49.
14   The expression 'rights as trumps' was apparently first coined by Ronald Dworkin in 1977. See R. Dworkin *Taking Rights Seriously* (1977) xi.
15   *Ibid.*
16   Selznick, *op. cit.*, p. 455.

the definition of a right that it cannot be outweighed by all social goals . . . but only by a goal of special urgency'.[17]

Dworkin's trump card metaphor has been subjected to scrutiny and criticism in terms of the harmful consequences for society that it may entail. One commentator has decried that ' . . . the free and equal individual calculator of his own interests, who is presumed to know where his own interests lie, asserts the right to act without much reference, and sometimes without reference at all, to the interests of the civic order as a whole'.[18] We have seen in Chapter 2[19] how the early liberal ethic postulated that our liberties are limited by those of others and that we can do what we want provided we do not harm others or society. An undue preoccupation with, and assertion of, individual rights and adulation of the trump card metaphor, however, can lead to the disregard of concern for one another and for society. As Amitai Etzioni observes, 'Soon "I can do what I want as long as I do not hurt others" becomes "I can do what I want, because I have a right to do it"'.[20] Rights-based arguments should not be treated as trump cards which automatically neutralise all other arguments. The individual right which is invoked should be weighed against the rights of other individuals (including society as a whole) who are harmed by its exercise. The mere assertion of personal right should not truncate all debate.[21]

In the United States of America, radical individualists, such as libertarians and the American Civil Liberties Union, have effectively blocked numerous attempts to increase public safety and health. Typically, the individual rights to privacy and bodily integrity are asserted. Among the measures they have systematically opposed are sobriety checkpoints (designed to reduce the carnage on the roads) and all drug testing (even of those, such as pilots and bus drivers, who have the lives of others directly in their control).[22] Another example is the opposition to seat belts and motorcycle helmets. The following lengthy extract from Amitai Etzioni's *The Spirit of Community* highlights the problems with such opposition:

> Libertarians have long argued adamantly that the government should not require people to use these safety devices. They blocked the introduction of seat belt and motorcycle helmet laws in many jurisdictions and ensured the repeal of such regulations in several localities where they had been in place. The main libertarian argument is that people have a right to do with their lives what they wish, including endangering them. People are said to be the best judges of what is good for them, because they will have to live with the consequences of their acts. Therefore we should treat people as adults and not as children, without paternalism
> . . .

---

17   Dworkin, *op. cit.*, p. 92.
18   Selbourne, *op. cit.*, p. 32.
19   See the section on 'John Stuart Mill'.
20   A. Etzioni *The Spirit of Community* (1995) p. 8.
21   *Idem* p. 7.
22   *Idem* p. 11.

Reckless individuals, however, do not absorb many of the consequences of their acts. Drivers without seat belts . . . are also more likely to die and leave their children for society to attend to and pick up the pieces. And, of course, they draw on our community resources, from ambulance services to hospitals, when they are involved in accidents, for which they pay at best a fraction of the cost. To insist that people drive safely and responsibly is hence a concern for the needs of others and the community; there is no individual right that automatically trumps these considerations.[23]

Individual rights as 'trumps' should not automatically be considered more important than most societal or collective interests. The social costs or harm to others resulting from, or anticipated by, the exercise of personal rights must always be factored into the equation.

Dworkin's trump card has been called into question on another front. It is feared that the playing of such card insulates a right-holder from moral scrutiny in the sense that the mere existence of a right signals the non-existence of responsibilities and sensitivity to others constraining its exercise. In turn, that leads to the perception that having a legal right to do something is a sufficient reason to do it or even that legal rights equal moral rightness.[24] Having a legal right to do something, however, does not necessarily mean that it is the right thing to do. Rights *per se* do not provide one with a sufficient reason to exercise them. One would not be hard-pressed to come up with examples in the area of free speech where its exercise has been constitutionally protected and upheld by the United States Supreme Court despite significant hurt or resentment being caused to some groups (including minority groups) within the community. Etzioni has remarked that '[t]here is a gap between rights and rightness that cannot be closed without a richer moral vocabulary - one that invokes principles of decency, duty, responsibility, and the common good, among others'.[25] And to that list might this author respectfully add sensitivity to the needs and feelings of others.

Disquiet Over Excessive Individualism (at the Expense of Society)

A Special Rapporteur of the United Nations Sub-Commission on Prevention of Discrimination and Protection of Minorities has observed that '[t]he law, which protects individuals one against the other, also defends the rights of the individual against the power of the State, and the State against the exercise of individualism'.[26] As we saw in Chapter 6, the law (including human rights law) protects the State against the exercise of excessive individualism through the

---

23   *Idem* p. 8.
24   L. McClain 'Rights and Irresponsibility' (1994) 43 *Duke Law Journal* pp. 989, 993.
25   Etzioni *The Spirit of Community* (1995) p. 263.
26   Erica-Irene A. Daes *Freedom of the Individual under Law: A Study on the Individual's Duties to the Community and the Limitations on Human Rights and Freedoms under Article 29 of the Universal Declaration of Human Rights* (United Nations, New York, 1990) iv.

operation of the so-called 'clawback clause' which incorporates such considerations as national security, public order, and the protection of public health, morals and safety. In this way, a reasonable balance between the exercise of individual right and the protection of societal or community interests is maintained.

Growing anxiety over 'egotistical individualism'[27] (or 'hyperindividualism' in American parlance) and the perceived irresponsible and insensitive exercise of personal rights (and the associated deleterious effects upon society) has been expressed in the West by conservatives and communitarians. However, this anxiety is by no means confined thereto. It is rather ubiquitous. Writing from an Islamic perspective, Ahmad Yamani has asserted that ' . . . the West is [so] over-zealous in its defense of the individual's freedom, rights and dignity, that it overlooks the act of some individuals in exercising such rights in a way that jeopardizes the community'.[28] Social critiques of the West by Asian political leaders (particularly those of Singapore and Malaysia) have become increasingly commonplace over the past twenty years or so. Such critiques have attributed the moral decline of the West to such factors as the breakdown of the family unit, drug abuse, increasing levels of crime, juvenile delinquency and promiscuity, and the promotion or tolerance of excessive individualism. The latter factor is particularly troubling to Asians in view of the ancient Chinese Confucian acknowledgement that no person lives independently of other people or the community, and the notion that self-realisation is not attained through the pursuit of personal advantage but through concern for family and community members.[29] The 1993 United Nations World Conference on Human Rights held in Vienna provided an opportunity for the representatives of many Asian governments to raise such concerns. The following statements delivered at the Conference by Asian governmental representatives are typical:

> Another conceptual lacuna in the current debate on human rights is the manifest emphasis on individual rights at the expense of the rights of the community. The rights of the individual are certainly not in splendid isolation from those of the community. Excessive individual freedom leads to a decay in moral values and weakens the whole social fabric of nations. In the name of individual rights and freedom, racial prejudices and animosities are resurfacing to the extent that we are witnessing the rise of new forms of racism and xenophobia, increasingly manifested in violence.[30]

---

27   Selbourne, *op. cit.*, p. 26.
28   A. Yamani *Islamic Law and Contemporary Issues* (1968) p. 15.
29   P. Woo 'A Metaphysical Approach to Human Rights from a Chinese Point of View' in A. Rosenbaum (ed.) *The Philosophy of Human Rights: Contribution in Philosophy No. 15* (1980) pp. 113, 119.
30   Statement by Datuk Abdullah Haji Ahmad Badawi, Minister of Foreign Affairs, Malaysia, 18 June 1993 as reported in J. Tang (ed.) *Human Rights and International Relations in the Asia-Pacific* (1995) p. 236.

Singapore's political and social arrangements have irked some foreign critics because they are not in accordance with their theories of how societies should properly organize themselves. We have intervened to change individual social behaviour in ways other countries consider intrusive. We maintain and have deployed laws that others may find harsh. For example, the police, narcotics or immigration officers are empowered by the Misuse of Drugs Act to test the urine for drugs of any person who behaves in a suspicious manner. If the result is positive, rehabilitation treatment is compulsory. Such a law will be considered unconstitutional in some countries and such urine tests will lead to suits for damages for battery and assault and an invasion of privacy. As a result, the community's interests are sacrificed because of the human rights of drug consumers and traffickers. So drug-related crimes flourish.[31]

African writers have also expressed concern at what they perceive to be an excessive degree of individualism in the West. Ake, for instance, disparages Western human rights systems as involving ' . . . a society which is atomized and individualistic, a society of endemic conflict . . . [and] people conscious of their separateness'.[32] Asmarom Legesse adds:

> In the liberal democracies of the Western world . . . [t]he individual is held in a virtually sacralized position. There is a perpetual, and in our view obsessive, concern with the dignity of the individual, his worth, personal autonomy, and property . . . No aspect of Western civilization makes an African more uncomfortable than the concept of the sacralized individual whose private wars against society are celebrated. If we turn the situation around and view it from an African perspective, the individual who is fighting private wars against his society is no hero . . . Most African cultures . . . ensure that individuals do not deviate so far from the norm that they can overwhelm the society.[33]

A Western social commentator has lamented that in contemporary liberal civic orders the right of individual self-assertion has come to possess a higher ethical status than the fulfillment of individual duty.[34] The same writer has also expressed reservations at the growing tendency to falsely consider the concepts of 'self-realisation'[35] and 'freedom of choice' as co-terminous with 'individual freedom' as such.[36]

---

31   Statement by Wong Kan Seng, Minister for Foreign Affairs of the Republic of Singapore, 16 June 1993 as reported in J. Tang, *op. cit.*, p. 246.

32   C. Ake 'The African Context of Human Rights' quoted by R. Howard 'Group versus Individual Identity in the Africa Debate on Human Rights' in A. An-Na'im and F. Deng (eds) *Human Rights in Africa: Cross-Cultural Perspectives* (1990) pp. 159, 173.

33   A. Legesse 'Human Rights in African Political Culture' in K. Thompson (ed.) *The Moral Imperatives of Human Rights* (1980) pp. 123, 124.

34   Selbourne, *op. cit.*, p. 156.

35   A historical antecedent to this notion may be found in Thomas Jefferson's famous *Preamble* to the *American Declaration of Independence* of 1776 which includes in its list of 'inalienable rights' 'the Pursuit of Happiness'. For a contemporary example of the constitutional recognition of the notion of individual 'self-

Alleged Symptoms of the Malaise Concerning an Overemphasis Upon Individual Rights

The 'Politics of Dutiless Rights'[37]

Eugene Kamenka has observed that most philosophers agree that the failure to emphasise that most rights involve duties by others is politically conditioned.[38] David Selbourne describes this 'politics of rights' in the following passage:

> [I]n corrupted liberal orders dominated by claims to dutiless right, demand-satisfaction and self-realisation through unimpeded freedom of action, a politics of rights amounts, in conditions of civic disaggregation and disorder, to little more than a politics of individual claims *against* the civic order and of duties owed by the latter *to* the individual. Missing consistently is a third term: the duties of the individual to himself and to fellow-members of the civic order to which he belongs.[39]

Such a politics has resulted in the marginalisation of the principle of individual duty such that it now plays a rather insignificant role in modern political theory. Contemporary liberal ethics are too preoccupied with the ideal of individual self-realisation through freedom of action under state protection to articulate a general theory of individual duty.[40] Associated with the politics of dutiless rights are the transfer of personal responsibility and blame for individual misfortune to others, society and/or the State[41] as well as what Selbourne describes as the phenomenon of 'civic disaggregation'. This has been defined to include '. . . the gradual waning of knowledge of, and respect for, the civic bond and the principle of duty; the gradual transformation of the citizen-members of the civic order into a randomly associated mass of individuals or citizens-turned-strangers; the gradual dissolution, or disassociation, of a civic public possessed of civic consciousness, or civic sense, that is of a sense of co-responsibility for the well-being of the civic order . . .'[42]

---

realisation', see Article 2(1) (entitled 'Personal Freedom') of the *Basic Law for the Federal Republic of Germany* of 23 May 1949 which provides in part that '[e]verybody has the right to self-fulfilment . . .'

36   Selbourne, *op. cit.*, p. 179.
37   This expression is used in David Selbourne's *The Principle of Duty* (1994) *passim.*
38   E. Kamenka and A. E.-S. Tay 'The Philosophical Bases of Human Rights' *Human Rights for Australia* (Human Rights Commission Monograph Series No. 1, Canberra, Australian Government Publishing Service, 1986) p. 82.
39   Selbourne, *op. cit.*, p. 5 (emphasis supplied by author).
40   *Idem* p. 7.
41   *Idem* p. 26.
42   *Idem* pp. 17-18.

Rights Inflation

It has been claimed that the United States of America suffers in recent times from what has been referred to as an explosion of frivolous assertions of personal rights.[43] Indeed, it is probably unfair to single out only the U.S.A. in this respect. Some philosophers and social commentators have begun to express concern at the extent to which the term 'rights' generally and the term 'human rights' in particular are being stretched to cover any urgently felt moral claim.[44] As Robert Cover has observed:

> Social movements in the United States organize around rights. When there is some urgently felt need to change the law or keep it in one way or another a 'Rights' movement is started.[45]

Amitai Etzioni has commented that '[t]he incessant issuance of new rights, like the wholesale printing of currency, causes a massive inflation of rights that devalues their moral claims'.[46] The American social commentator Henry Rosemont Jr provides the following example:

> [T]here is growing worldwide concern about the loss of our woodlands and rain forests. One ingenious response to this concern has been to claim that while trees are not sentient creatures, corporations aren't either; and if the latter have rights, and hence legal standing, so too might trees. Now I applaud any effort to rein in the rapacious lumber industry, but isn't there a hint of desperation in having to claim that trees have rights?[47]

Professor Etzioni sounds the following cautionary note:

> Once, rights were very solemn moral/legal claims, ensconced in the [U.S.] Constitution and treated with much reverence. We all lose if the publicity department of every special interest can claim that someone's rights are violated every time they don't get all they want . . . Unless we want to generate a universal backlash against rights, we need to curb rights inflation and protect the currency of rights from being further devalued.[48]

---

43   McClain, *op. cit.*, p. 989.
44   Kamenka and Tay, *op. cit.*, p. 80.
45   R. Cover 'Obligation: A Jewish Jurisprudence of the Social Order' (1987) 5 *Journal of Law and Religion* p. 65.
46   A. Etzioni *The Spirit of Community* (1995) p. 5.
47   H. Rosemont Jr 'Human Rights: A Bill of Worries' in W. Theodore De Bary and Tu Weiming (eds) *Confucianism and Human Rights* (1998) pp. 54, 58-9. The footnote excluded from the quoted passage refers to C. Stone *Should Trees Have Standing? Toward Legal Rights for Natural Objects* (1974). A Los Angeles lawyer specialising in environmental matters has proposed that sand have legal rights: see A. Etzioni *The Spirit of Community* (1995) p. 9.
48   A. Etzioni *The Spirit of Community* (1995) p. 6.

Strong Sense of Entitlement; Weak Sense of Obligation

The human rights movement is being increasingly subjected to scrutiny and criticism because it appears to place more emphasis upon the rights of individuals than their obligations. The community cannot survive and thrive without its constituents having an adequate sense of civic duty. Undue emphasis on rights, it is said, conduces to libertarian action and an attitude of licence which is at odds with harmonious community relations.[49] In an article entitled 'Social Decline in the Making' which appeared in *The San Francisco Chronicle*,[50] A. Lawrence Chickering, Director of the Institute For Contemporary Studies and newspaper columnist, had this to say:

> One of the greatest challenges facing modern societies is how to balance individual rights against obligations to others. When I was growing up in the 1950s, there was a lot of agreement about how to do this. The sense of obligation was instilled in people. This sense sustained all the associations and relationships that added up to 'society' . . . Today we have lost the sense and even the language of obligation.

A 1989 study[51] has revealed that young Americans expect to be tried before a jury of their peers but are rather reluctant to serve on one. This paradox highlights a major attribute of contemporary Western civic culture: a strong sense of entitlement manifested in a demand that the community and government provide more services and uphold individual rights coupled with a comparatively weak sense of obligation to the local and national communities.[52] The same study noted:

> *Young people have learned only half of America's story.* Consistent with the priority they place on personal happiness, young people reveal notions of America's unique character that emphasize freedom and license almost to the complete exclusion of service or participation. Although they clearly appreciate the democratic freedom that, in their view, makes theirs the 'best democracy in the world to live in', they fail to perceive a need to reciprocate by exercising the duties and responsibilities of good citizenship.[53]

Such imbalance between the insistence on personal rights and the turning away from individual duties is one of the main concerns of contemporary communitarianism which will be addressed later in this chapter.

---

49   P. Bailey *Human Rights: Australia in an International Context* (1990) p. 25.
50   17 March 1994, Page A25.
51   As reported in A. Etzioni *The Spirit of Community* (1995) p. 3.
52   *Ibid.*
53   *Ibid.*

Exacerbated Social Conflict

It has been claimed by numerous commentators that zealous insistence on, and enforcement of, personal rights leads to worsening social conflict. Herbert Fingarette has said:

> [T]he doctrine of individual rights . . . is not so purely beneficent a doctrine as we tend to assume today. Along with its major benefits, it has profound potential as a socially disruptive and anti-human force. It is against the background of a Confucian vision of life that this corrosive effect of a rights-based morality comes clearly into focus.[54]

Charles Taylor has observed that the conflict between different kinds of rights is often related to a worsening social conflict. For him, '[t]he language of rights lends itself easily to extravagance and intransigence'.[55] Etzioni has asserted that '[a] society that is studded with groups of true believers and special-interest groups, each brimming with rights, inevitably turns into a society overburdened with conflicts'.[56] Henry Rosemont Jr adds that he is increasingly struck by two unique features of contemporary American society which, to his mind, are hardly coincidental. First, 'rights talk' more thoroughly permeates American moral and political discourse than in any other country and, secondly, that the United States of America is 'the world's most morally conflicted society'.[57] It is perhaps not surprising that the increase in litigation and litigiousness in modern Western societies has occasioned a trend towards the adoption of alternative dispute resolution mechanisms drawn from less individualistic societies.[58]

In this context, it is worth recalling the reasons for the inclusion of a reference to individual duties to the community in Article 29(1) of the *Universal Declaration of Human Rights*. During the drafting debates, it was emphasised that it was not possible to formulate a universal declaration of human rights without simultaneously proclaiming the duties implicit in the concept of freedom which made it possible to set up a peaceful and democratic society. Without such a reference, freedom based solely upon a rights-based morality might lead to anarchy and tyranny.[59]

---

54   M. Bockover (ed.) *Rules, Rituals, and Responsibility: Essays Dedicated to Herbert Fingarette* (1991) p. 191.
55   C. Taylor, *op. cit.*, p. 49.
56   A. Etzioni *The Spirit of Community* (1995) p. 6.
57   Rosemont, *op. cit.*, p. 56.
58   D. Kwok 'On the Rites and Rights of Being Human' in W. Theodore De Bary and Tu Weiming (eds) *Confucianism and Human Rights* (1998) pp. 83, 90.
59   Daes, *op. cit.*, p. 19.

Unacceptable Social Costs

It has been argued in some quarters that the social costs of an overemphasis upon rights at the expense of individual duties have now become unacceptably high. The social costs which are typically cited include family breakdown, drug abuse, swelling crime rates, urban violence, juvenile delinquency, the deterioration of private and public morality,[60] excessive consumption and environmental degradation.[61] Rosemont has reflected on ' . . . the reality that the United States is the wealthiest society in the world, yet after over two hundred years of human rights talk, many of its human citizens have no shelter, a fifth of them have no access to health care, a fourth of its children are growing up in poverty, and the richest two percent of its peoples own and control over fifty percent of its wealth'.[62] One might also consider that the constitutional right to bear arms of each American citizen[63] has resulted in the highest incidence of death and injury among the young of poor racial minorities.

The Sociology of Duty (or the Atomistic Nature of Human Existence Debunked)

The English poet John Donne once declared that ' . . . to be no part of any body is to be nothing'.[64] Such a view of the nature of human existence, however, has even more venerable roots. For three thousand years or so, Jewish scriptural wisdom has recognised that human beings need one another:

> Two are better than one . . . For if they fall, one will lift up his fellow; but woe to him who is alone when he falls, and has not another to help him up. Again, if two lie together, then they have warmth; but how can one be warm alone?[65]

The ancient Greeks understood well that a person who is completely private is lost to civic or public life. Aristotle had declared, *a priori*, that '[i]t is not right . . . that any of the citizens should think that he belongs just to himself'.[66] Aristotle maintained that human beings are by nature gregarious and sociable, rather than solitary, creatures who are better suited to live together in social groups. Central to

---

60   Recent examples of a breakdown of responsibility in corporate America include the Enron and Worldcom accounting scandals.
61   See, for example, D. Selbourne *The Principle of Duty* (1994) p. 4; A. Etzioni *The Spirit of Community* (1995) p. 2.
62   Rosemont, *op. cit.*, 60 quoting N. Chomsky *World Orders Old and New* (1994) Chapter 2.
63   More detail on this particular right is provided in the section in Chapter 6 entitled 'The Duties to Defend One's Country, to Undertake Military Service and to Maintain Internal Security'.
64   As quoted in D. Selbourne, *op. cit.*, p. 187.
65   *Book of Ecclesiastes*, Chapter 4, Verses 9-11.
66   Aristotle *Politics* translated T. Sinclair, Harmondsworth, 1962, VIII, i, 1337a.

Aristotle's thinking was the phenomenon of *koinonia* or community (that which is shared or held in common as opposed to the private). Families and households were considered forms of *koinonia* which together made up the highest form of community, the *polis* (or city-state).[67] The Catholic theologian and philosopher, Thomas Aquinas, also adhered to this Aristotelian view of the social nature of human existence:

> The fact that man is by nature a social animal - being compelled to live in society because of the many needs he cannot satisfy out of his own resources - has as a consequence the fact that man is destined by nature to form part of a community which makes a full and complete life possible for him.[68]

In more recent times, Professor Michael Freeman has pointed out that '[t]here is ... a strong tradition in Western political theory that objects to the concept of individual rights precisely on the ground that it mistakenly regards the human individual as non-social and consequently grounds a political theory that is incompatible with an orderly and flourishing society'.[69] Thus, criticism of liberal individualism is not merely confined to non-Western thought; it is just as Western as is the basis of its support.[70] Some Western philosophers argued that it is only within a community, with its matrix of human relationships, that individual rights could properly be contextualised. Hegel, for example, believed that '[t]he reality and significance of the human individual are subordinated to the greater reality and significance of human society'.[71] In Ferdinand Tonnies' *Gemeinschaft* human beings are described as being part of 'a social organism, a structured community based on common religious tradition, a hierarchy of power, a network of mutual obligations that made and shaped men rather than served them'.[72]

Today, scholars, sociologists, philosophers and social commentators also acknowledge the importance of the social aspects of human existence. As Professor Louis Sohn has observed:

> One of the main characteristics of humanity is that human beings are social creatures. Consequently, most individuals belong to various units, groups, and communities; they are simultaneously members of such units as a family, religious

---

67   T. O'Hagan 'Aristotle and Aquinas on Community and Natural Law' in R. Bellamy and A. Ross (eds) *A Factual Introduction to Social and Political Theory* (1996) pp. 35, 36, 38.

68   T. Aquinas *Summa Theologiae* as extracted in T. O'Hagan, *op. cit.*, p. 55.

69   M. Freeman 'Human Rights: Asia and the West' in J. Tang (ed.) *Human Rights and International Relations in the Asia-Pacific* (1995) 13, 18, citing J. Waldron (ed.) *Nonsense upon Stilts: Bentham, Burke and Marx on the Rights of Man* (1987).

70   *Ibid.*

71   J. Burns 'The Rights of Man Since the Reformation: An Historical Survey' in F. Vallat (ed.) *Human Rights* (1971) pp. 16, 27.

72   E. Kamenka 'Thinking and Teaching about Human Rights' in A. E.-S. Tay *et al.* (eds) *Teaching Human Rights* (1978) pp. 77, 79.

community, social club, trade union, professional association, racial group, people, nation, and state.[73]

Eighteenth and nineteenth century liberal theories of personal rights fail to adequately recognise these sociological premises. As Richard Bellamy has stated:

> Human beings are not born autonomous and self-supporting; they achieve this status through society. Our social duties are best seen as an acknowledgement of this fact.[74]

Philip Selznick, Professor Emeritus of Law and Sociology of the University of California, Berkeley, points out that the basic postulates of modern sociology undermine the liberal foundations of rights theories. As Professor Selznick states:

> Sociologists have long rejected the atomistic view of man put forward in the seventeenth and eighteenth centuries. Society is not made up of preformed, wholly competent individuals endowed by nature with reason and self-consciousness. In the beginning is society, not the individual. To say that humans are social animals is to say that they depend on others for psychological sustenance, including the formation of their personalities.[75]

Human beings, then, are more accurately regarded as group-orientated natural phenomena rather than the creation of political philosophers.[76] To similar effect are the views of Professor Amitai Etzioni, Professor of Sociology of George Washington University:

> The libertarian perspective, put succinctly, begins with the assumption that individual agents are fully formed and their value preferences are in place prior to and outside of any society. It ignores robust social scientific evidence about the ill effects of isolation, the deep-seated human need for communal attachments, the social anchoring of reasoning itself, and the consistent interactive influence of society members on one another. . . There are no well-formed individuals bereft of social bonds or culture.[77]

Having studied classical Confucianism, Henry Rosemont Jr arrives at the same conclusion:

> My own skepticism is directed not toward any particular moral or political theory in which rights play a role, but toward the more foundational view of human

---

73   L. Sohn 'The New International Law: Protection of the Rights of Individuals Rather Than States' (1982) 32 *American University Law Review* 1, p. 48.
74   R. Bellamy 'Socrates and Locke on Political Obligation' in R. Bellamy and A. Ross (eds) *A Factual Introduction to Social and Political Theory* (1996) pp. 1, 13.
75   Selznick, *op. cit.*, p. 447.
76   Radin, *op. cit.*, p. 217.
77   A. Etzioni 'The Responsive Community: A Communitarian Perspective' (1995 Presidential Address) (1996) 61 *American Sociological Review* 1, pp. 3-4.

beings as free, autonomous individuals on which all such theories more or less rest. The study of classical Confucianism has suggested to me that rights-oriented moral and political theories based on this view are flawed, and that a different vocabulary for moral and political discourse is needed. The concept of human rights and related concepts clustered around it, like liberty, the individual, property, autonomy, freedom, reason, choice, and so on, do not capture what it is we believe to be the inherent sociality of human beings . . . [78]

David Selbourne concurs and also acknowledges the importance of a network of human relationships for the development of each individual:

> The individual human being, whether or not he wishes it, is part of a web of moral relations. These moral relations help to form, and express themselves within, (*inter alia*) the *family*, the *community*, and the *civic order*, of the last of which the principal types are the nation and the city. I take it as axiomatic that the self-realisation and well-being of each individual are dependent in great part upon the existence of such moral relations . . . [79]

Malfrid Grude Flekkoy, a Norwegian clinical child psychologist and the world's first Ombudsman for Children, has stated that ' . . . human rights must always be in relation to other human beings and cannot . . . be stated as rights for an individual living entirely alone'.[80] Erica-Irene A. Daes, United Nations Special Rapporteur of the Sub-Commission on Prevention of Discrimination and Protection of Minorities, has also acknowledged that human existence is inevitably circumscribed by human relationships:

> The ideal of the free individual does not mean that the individual is completely unrestrained and devoid of any responsibility towards his fellow human beings and the community . . . The citizen should be aware that his is not the only will in the world, and he should be concerned, in one way or another, with bringing harmony out of the conflicting wills that exist within his community. The individual . . . is essentially circumscribed by his neighbours.[81]

The German Federal Constitutional Court has described the vision of the individual under the *Basic Law for the Federal Republic of Germany* of 23 May 1949 in the following terms:

---

78 Rosemont, *op. cit.*, p. 55.
79 Selbourne, *op. cit.*, 16 (emphasis supplied by author).
80 M. Flekkoy and N. Kaufman *The Participation Rights of the Child: Rights and Responsibilities in Family and Society* (1997) p. 10.
81 Daes, *op. cit.*, p. 52.

. . . [the Basic Law's] image of the human being is not that of the autocratic individual, but that of a personality rooted in and multiply linked to the community.[82]

This impressive array of opinion from a cross-section of disciplines concerning the social nature of human existence is not, however, confined merely to the West. Rejection of the atomistic theory of human existence is prevalent in African and Asian cultures as well as in indigenous cultures. In the African context, Okere writes that the 'African conception of man is not that of an isolated and abstract individual, but an integral member of a group animated by a spirit of solidarity'.[83] Similarly, Nahum states:

[African humanism] does not alienate the individual by seeing him [or her] as an entity all by himself [or herself], having an existence more or less independent of society. The individual does not stand in contradistinction to society but as part of it'.[84]

The Chinese mentality, informed by centuries of Confucianism, reflects the view that a person exists for others and is dependent, in turn, on other people. The Western liberal notion of the independent and free individual engaged in a competition or struggle for survival and prosperity against others and the State is quite foreign to that mentality.[85] In an address to the United Nations World Conference on Human Rights held in Vienna in June 1993, Ali Alatas, Minister for Foreign Affairs of the Republic of Indonesia, had this to say:

[W]e in Indonesia, and perhaps throughout the developing world as well, do not and cannot maintain a purely individualistic approach toward human rights for we cannot disregard the interests of our societies and nations. We hold that, flowing from the innate quality of the human being as an individual person and at the same time as a member of the community, his or her existence, rights and duties, can only become meaningful within the social context of the community and where, in the words of Article 29 of the [Universal] Declaration of Human Rights, the free and full development of his or her personality becomes possible.[86]

Indigenous populations also place far more emphasis upon community than the individualistic aspects of human existence. This is generally common to the experiences of indigenous peoples in Canada, Australia and New Zealand where,

---

82   BverfGE 8, 45, at 51 (citation for reports of the German Federal Constitutional Court) as cited in M. Herdegen 'Natural Law, Constitutional Values and Human Rights' (1998) 19 *Human Rights Law Journal* pp. 37, 40.

83   B. Obinna Okere 'The Protection of Human Rights in Africa and the African Charter on Human and Peoples' Rights: A Comparative Analysis with the European and American Systems' (1984) 6 *Human Rights Quarterly* pp. 141, 148.

84   As quoted in R. Howard, *op. cit.*, p. 160.

85   Woo, *op. cit.*, p. 121.

86   Statement of 14 June 1993 as reported in J. Tang, *op. cit.*, pp. 231-2.

as in Africa, one cannot perceive an individual as separate from the community to which he or she belongs.[87] As Schwab and Pollis point out:

> ... [I]ndividuals still perceive themselves in terms of their group identity ... The concept of an autonomous individual possessed of inherent, inalienable rights has been meaningless ... Regardless of the particular traditional cultural patterns and the specific social relations, the individual has been perceived as an integral part of a group within which he or she has a defined role or status ... and if the concept of rights has any relevance, it is derived from relations with others.[88]

At the international level, the United Nations has effectively acknowledged in several instruments it has promulgated that the giving of oneself to others is the process by which the individual becomes more fulfilled as a person. Both Article 29(1) of the *Universal Declaration of Human Rights* of 1948 and Article 18(1) of the *Declaration on the Right and Responsibility of Individuals, Groups and Organs of Society to Promote and Protect Universally Recognized Human Rights and Fundamental Freedoms* of 1998 explicitly state that everyone has duties towards and within the community in which alone the free and full development of his or her personality is possible.[89] Indeed, an earlier version of Article 29(1) of the *Universal Declaration of Human Rights* recognised the impossibility for a person to be free of society in view of the fact that we are all at essence social beings. That earlier version provided in part that '[a]s human beings cannot live and achieve their objects without the help and support of society, each man [and woman] owes to society fundamental duties ...'[90] The frequent use of 'clawback clauses' in United Nations instruments[91] also rejects the egotistical individual whose only concern is fulfilling self. These clawback clauses invite individuals to reflect on how the exercise of their personal rights in certain circumstances might adversely affect other individuals or the community. This 'duty of introspection' is once again based on the presumption that the full development of the individual personality is only possible when individuals are sensitive to how their conduct might impact upon others.[92]

---

87   Ross Gordon Green *Justice in Aboriginal Communities* (1998) p. 37.

88   A. Pollis and P. Schwab (eds) *Human Rights Cultural and Ideological Perspectives* (1979) p. 16.

89   For further information on these two instruments, see the section in Chapter 6 entitled 'The Position of Individual Duties Under International Human Rights Instruments'.

90   *Report of the Drafting Committee of an International Bill of Rights to the Commission on Human Rights* (E/CN.4/21), annex D, p. 51.

91   For further information on these clauses, see the section in Chapter 6 entitled 'The Position of Individual Duties Under International Human Rights Instruments'.

92   Makau Wa Mutua 'The Banjul Charter and the African Cultural Fingerprint: An Evaluation of the Language of Duties' (1995) 35 *Virginia Journal of International Law* pp. 339, 369.

What adverse consequences, then, are entailed in the failure to sufficiently recognise the social or relational dimension of human existence? The preamble of *The Responsive Communitarian Platform: Rights and Responsibilities* issued on 18 November 1991 offered this answer:

> Neither human existence nor individual liberty can be sustained for long outside the interdependent and overlapping communities to which all of us belong. Nor can any community long survive unless its members dedicate some of their attention, energy, and resources to shared projects. The exclusive pursuit of private interest erodes the network of social environments on which we all depend and is destructive to our shared experiment in democratic self-government.[93]

The Re-emergence of Communitarianism

In the developing world, there has always been a consistent and articulate discourse denying that either individualism or the concept of abstract individual or personal rights is well suited to Third World traditions and contemporary realities. And in more developed nations, there exists a growing tension between the liberal-individualist historical foundation of human rights theory and the belief that today's emphasis should be on wider social interests, social groups and communities.[94] Perhaps this is not surprising when it has been estimated (the author concedes that such an undertaking defies precise quantification) that three-quarters of the world's peoples continue to define themselves in terms of kinship and community rather than as rights-bearers.[95]

The Concept of 'Community'

Over twenty-three hundred years ago, Aristotle preoccupied himself with the concept and importance of community. For Aristotle, the two primary types of community were the extended household or clan (*oikos*) and the city-state (*polis*). The latter comprised a community of households situated in a particular place and organised for the common advantage and the good life. Citizens of a *polis* rationally choose of their own free will to live together (*syzen*), motivated by a shared conception of a flourishing life (*eudaimonia*) as well as by religious-ideological links.[96] Aristotle believed that the impulse to form such communities is present in all human beings by nature.[97]

---

93   A. Etzioni *The Spirit of Community* (1995) p. 253.
94   E. Kamenka and A. E.-S. Tay 'The Philosophical Bases of Human Rights' *Human Rights for Australia* (Human Rights Commission Monograph Series No. 1, Canberra, Australian Government Publishing Service, 1986) p. 78.
95   Rosemont, *op. cit.*, p. 64.
96   T. O'Hagan 'Aristotle and Aquinas on Community and Natural Law' in R. Bellamy and A. Ross (eds) *A Factual Introduction to Social and Political Theory* (1996) pp. 35, 37.
97   Aristotle *Politics* Book I, p. 1253.

Although Article 29(1) of the *Universal Declaration of Human Rights* of 1948 explicitly recognises that '[e]veryone has duties to the community', no definition of 'community' is provided.[98] It has been complained that the concept of 'community' 'remains vague and elusive'.[99] However that may be, there would appear to be no shortage of attempts to define or illustrate the concept. Indeed, the concept of community has been a cornerstone of sociological thinking in the works, for example, of Durkheim, Tonnies and Marx for nearly two centuries.[100] Two useful attempts at defining the concept of 'community' follow:

> . . . [A] voluntary association of human beings, most commonly settled and maintaining itself in a given place, and held together . . . by virtue of some or all of such habitual social ties as those of extended familial relationships, combined interest and purpose, and shared or related memory, language, belief, values, custom, and knowledge. There may be several, or even many, such communities within a determinate area . . . [101]

> Neighborhood; vicinity, synonymous with locality . . . A society or body of people living in the same place, under the same laws and regulations, who have common rights, privileges, or interests . . . It connotes a congeries of common interests arising from associations - social, business, religious, governmental, scholastic, recreational.[102]

Other features or attributes of 'community' include a minimum level of integration and shared symbolic experience,[103] mutuality (that is to say, doing together what we as human beings cannot, or choose not to, do separately)[104] and a commitment to a set of shared values, a shared history and a shared cultural identity.[105] Communities, moreover, are not merely aggregates of individuals acting as free

---

98   Another example of the term 'community' appearing in an international human rights instrument is Article 5 of the *Convention on the Rights of the Child* of 1989 which states: 'States Parties shall respect the responsibilities, rights, and duties of parents or, where applicable, the members of the extended family or *community* as provided for by local custom, legal guardians or other persons legally responsible for the child, to provide, in a manner consistent with the evolving capacities of the child, appropriate direction and guidance in the exercise by the child of the rights recognized in the present Convention' (emphasis supplied by author).

99   Selznick, *op. cit.*, p. 449.

100   A. Etzioni 'The Responsive Community: A Communitarian Perspective' (1995 Presidential Address) (1996) 61 *American Sociological Review* 1, p. 4.

101   Selbourne, *op. cit.*, p. 16.

102   *Black's Law Dictionary* (Revised Fourth Edition, 1968) p. 350.

103   Selznick, *op. cit.*, p. 449.

104   A. Kaplan 'Human Relations and Human Rights in Judaism' in A. Rosenbaum (ed.) *The Philosophy of Human Rights, Contribution in Philosophy No. 15* (1980) pp. 53, 61.

105   A. Etzioni 'The Responsive Community: A Communitarian Perspective' (1995 Presidential Address) (1996) 61 *American Sociological Review* 1, p. 5.

agents. They are also collectives which have identities and purposes of their own and can act as a unit.[106]

If we were to apply these definitions to contemporary living, the following entities, for example, would be classified as a type of community:

-   an extended family or clan;

-   neighbourhood;

-   village, town or city;

-   the body politic (including the nation and its components such as states or provinces and local government);

-   social, religious and ethnic organisations;

-   trade unions and professional associations;

-   a group of nations closely or loosely associated because of common traditions or for mutual benefit in the political, socio-economic and cultural fields (for example, the European Economic Community or the Organization of African Unity);

-   universal organisations purporting to represent the interests of the international community (such as the United Nations or the former League of Nations).[107]

It is evident that a person may be simultaneously a member of numerous communities within a specific geographical location. However the concept of community is defined and whatever form it takes, sociologists have established its pivotal role as an antidote to alienation and as a key component of a flourishing society.[108] Other social sciences, including political and social philosophy, are now beginning to acknowledge the importance of community to the health of the body politic.[109]

The Ubiquitous Incidence of Community

A dominant theme of Chapters 4, 6 and 8 of this book involves the proposition that many religious, tribal and political organisations of human beings are predominantly community-based and duty-orientated. The discharge of individual duties is at once the consequence of one's membership of a community and the prerequisite to one's possessing membership of society. Some polities are more community-based than others, in theory at least. We saw in Chapter 8 that communist states generally organise socialist life on the basis of the collectivist

---

106   *Ibid.*
107   Daes, *op. cit.,* 39.
108   A. Etzioni 'The Responsive Community: A Communitarian Perspective' (1995 Presidential Address) (1996) 61 *American Sociological Review* 1, 4.
109   *Ibid.*

principle 'One for all and all for one.'[110] We also saw in Chapter 4 that religions and ethical systems such as Judaism, Christianity, Islam and Confucianism are at one in declaring as a fundamental doctrine that all human beings are potential members of a community constituted by those who share specific ideas about the world, humanity and destiny.[111] A. K. Brohi, a former Pakistani Minister of Law and Religious Affairs, has defended the traditional communitarian values upon which the Islamic faith is based in the following terms:

> The individual if necessary has to be sacrificed in order that the life of the organism be saved. Collectivity has a special sanctity attached to it in Islam.[112]

Similarly, in Judaism, the production and sustenance of a sense of community is a fundamental aim of the *Torah*.[113] In Judaic practice, the *kehilla* (the congregation or community) takes priority over the individual.[114] We have also examined in Chapter 4 the Chinese/Confucian view of the individual person as inseparable from the general scheme of the whole (*sub specie universismi*) whereby no person lives independently of other people or of their community.[115] And as discussed in Chapter 6, in the African tribal duty-based system, an individual's welfare is intimately connected with the tribal community, such that he or she does not exist outside the group. Rather, the individual's primary interest is identifying with the community and serving collective interests.[116] Once again, as with Islam, the group and collective interests are perceived as more important than the individual.

Neo-Communitarianism

Communitarianism is not a new philosophy or perspective. As we have seen, Aristotle was very much preoccupied with the concept of 'community' and the vital role two types of community - the household and the city-state - played in maintaining a healthy body politic. The Florentine author and statesman, Niccolo Machiavelli, once declared that ' . . . it is not the well-being of individuals that

---

110   See, for example, Articles 63 and 82 of the *Socialist Constitution of the Democratic People's Republic of Korea* of 9 April 1992 which respectively state: 'In the Democratic People's Republic of Korea the rights and duties of citizens are based on the collectivist principle, 'One for all and all for one.'(Article 63.) 'Collectivism is the basis of life of socialist society. Citizens shall cherish their organization and collective and work devotedly for the good of society and the people'. (Article 82.)

111   Radin, *op. cit.*, pp. 214-5.

112   A. Brohi 'The Nature of Islamic Law and the Concept of Human Rights' in International Commission of Jurists, Kuwait University, and Union of Arab Lawyers, *Human Rights in Islam: Report of a Seminar Held in Kuwait, December 1980* (International Commission of Jurists, 1982) pp. 43, 48.

113   Kaplan, *op. cit.*, p. 61.

114   *Idem* p. 59.

115   Woo, *op. cit.*, p. 119.

116   Devereux, *op. cit.*, p. 476.

makes cities great, but the well-being of the community ...'[117]   In our time, in
response to concerns outlined in an earlier portion of this chapter, a new wave of
communitarian sentiment has emerged, echoing similar views expressed in the late
nineteenth and early twentieth centuries by English liberals such as John A.
Hobson and L. T. Hobhouse and the American pragmatist John Dewey.[118]   Indeed,
some American presidents have recently expressed their support for the
communitarian philosophy. In his inaugural address to the nation on 20 January
1961, John F. Kennedy implored his fellow Americans not to ask what their
country could do for them but rather to ask what they could do for their country.
These sentiments faithfully reflect a critical component of communitarian thinking
- the priority of individual duty over claims or entitlements. As controversial to
liberal individualism as this may be, President Kennedy's words reflect his frank
assessment of what he considered civic virtue requires. As a presidential
candidate, Bill Clinton ran on a 'new covenant' of greater individual
responsibility[119] and as President called for a 'new ethic of personal and family and
community responsibility'.[120] In his 1994 'Message on the State of the Union',
President Clinton traced the roots of contemporary American social problems to
the breakdown of social values, family and community.[121]

As from about the mid-1980s, a marked discontent with a perceived
preoccupation with individual rights and 'rights talk' emerged in the United States
of America, accompanied by calls for a return to greater personal responsibility and
community service. The crux of the problem was considered to be 'too many
rights' and 'too few responsibilities'.[122] Politicians, academics and representatives
of the popular media claimed that an overemphasis upon rights and inattention to
responsibilities was inexorably leading to social decline.[123] In terms of academic
writing, the primary sources of the irresponsibility critique and neo-communitarian
thinking are to be found in the works of Mary Ann Glendon, a Harvard law
professor, and Amitai Etzioni, a sociology professor and Director of the Center for
Communitarian Policy Studies of George Washington University.[124] William
Galston, a political philosopher and former University of Maryland professor and
domestic policy advisor to President Clinton, has also been closely associated with
the Responsive Communitarian movement.

---

117   N. Machiavelli *The Discourses* II, p. 2.
118   Selznick, *op. cit.*, p. 445.
119   'Excerpts from the Platform: A New Covenant With Americans', *New York Times*,
       15 July 1992, at A10.
120   D. Anderson 'Political World Too Secular, President Says', *Washington Post*, 4
       September 1993, at D6.
121   See 'State of the Union: Renewing Values, Revising Welfare' Transcript of
       President Clinton's Message on the State of the Union, *New York Times*, 26
       January 1994, at A16-A17.
122   A. Etzioni *The Spirit of Community: Rights, Responsibilities, and the
       Communitarian Agenda* (1993) p. 161.
123   McClain, *op. cit.*, p. 989.
124   Mary Ann Glendon *Rights Talk: The Impoverishment of Political Discourse*
       (1991); A. Etzioni *The Spirit of Community* (1995).

Striking a Healthy Balance Between Centripetal and Centrifugal Societal Forces

Communities are subject to both centripetal (tending towards centre) and centrifugal (tending from centre) forces.[125] How to simultaneously maintain social stability and respect individual autonomy in a particular society is an age-old political and social dilemma which has long preoccupied the thinking of political and social philosophers and sociologists.[126] The crux of the problem is how to strike a healthy balance between individual rights and interests and collective rights and interests; between the realisation of individual rights and the discharge of individual duties or responsibilities. It is a problem which has persisted, with full vigour, to our time.

A Special Rapporteur of the United Nations Sub-Commission on Prevention of Discrimination and Protection of Minorities has remarked that the most important task in promoting human progress is:

> . . . to find the proper balance between the interests of the individual and the interests of society and between individual and collective rights. Individual liberty [has] therefore to be balanced with the liberty of other individuals and with the reasonable demands of the community.[127]

These considerations have been alluded to in the *Kuala Lumpur Declaration on Human Rights* adopted on 23 September 1993 by the General Assembly of the A.S.E.A.N. Inter-Parliamentary Organization in Kuala Lumpur, Malaysia. After referring to the need for respect of human rights and discharge of individual duties to the community, Article 1 thereof acknowledges that '[f]reedom, progress and national stability are promoted by balance between the rights of the individual and those of the community'. The attainment of a reasonable balance, however, is largely determined by history and social context, varying in accordance with circumstances of time and place.[128] This point was emphatically made by Wong Kan Seng, Minister for Foreign Affairs of the Republic of Singapore, in an address made on 16 June 1993 to the United Nations World Conference on Human Rights held in Vienna:

> Development and good government require a balance between the rights of the individual and those of the community to which every individual must belong, and through which individuals must realize their rights. Where this balance will be

---

125   A. Etzioni 'The Responsive Community: A Communitarian Perspective' (1995 Presidential Address) (1996) 61 *American Sociological Review* 1, p. 6.

126   *Idem* p. 1.

127   Daes, *op. cit.*, p. 19.

128   Professor Etzioni argues, for example, that if we were in the People's Republic of China today, we would argue vigorously for more individual rights (greater centrifugal forces) whereas we would emphasise individual social responsibilities (greater centripetal forces) in contemporary America. See A. Etzioni *The Spirit of Community* (1995) p. 255.

struck will vary for different countries at different points of their history. Every country must find its own way.[129]

Community members have individual needs that cannot always be satisfied by merely being a part of their community. Within the realm of individual autonomy are included the needs for creativity and self-expression, privacy and individualism. Attempts to unduly extend this realm (through an ever-increasing emphasis on individual rights) generate centrifugal forces, producing higher levels of differentiation which, if left unchecked, will eventually undermine communal relationships.[130] On the other hand, centripetal societal forces are generated by an emphasis upon the discharge of individual duties and responsibilities. These forces tend to draw individual duty-bearers into the society by connecting them with other individuals and the community. The separate identity of the individual from society becomes blurred, leading to a more communal and collective lifestyle. Centripetal forces oppose excessive withdrawal and self-centredness but encourage individual efforts which might be compatible with, or contribute to, the common good. These forces involve higher levels of regulation and mobilisation and make demands upon community members' time, resources and energy for what the community endorses as its notion of the common good.[131] These demands commonly take the form, for example, of an individual duty to pay tax, to obey the law and to perform national and community service.

In a communitarian analysis, the extreme bipolar opposites of anarchy (caused by centrifugal forces leading to excessive individualism) and collectivism (caused by centripetal forces leading to the imposition of excessive social duties) are to be avoided.[132] Neither centripetal nor centrifugal forces must be allowed to gain ascendancy, at least not for long. Professor Etzioni has used the analogy of a person riding a bicycle to illustrate the community's attempts to finely balance the interplay of centripetal and centrifugal forces. According to Professor Etzioni, '... the community must respond like a person riding a bicycle; it must continually correct tendencies to lean too far in one direction or the other, as it moves forward over a changing terrain'.[133] With its emphasis upon social responsibilities, the communitarian movement is attempting to counterbalance a period of unduly high centrifugal forces. But, as Professor Etzioni adds:

> When Communitarians argue that the pendulum has swung too far toward the radical individualistic pole . . . we do not seek to push it to the opposite extreme, of encouraging a community that suppresses individuality. We aim for a judicious mix of self-interest, self-expression, and commitment to the commons - of rights and responsibilities, of I and we . . . Balancing the me-istic [centrifugal] forces

---

129   Statement by Wong Kan Seng, Minister for Foreign Affairs of the Republic of Singapore, 16 June 1993 as reported in J. Tang, *op. cit.*, p. 246.

130   A. Etzioni 'The Responsive Community: A Communitarian Perspective' (1995 Presidential Address) (1996) 61 *American Sociological Review* 1, p. 6.

131   *Idem* pp. 5-6.

132   *Idem* p. 9.

133   *Ibid.*

with a fair measure of resumed we-ness [centripetal forces] will bring our [American] society closer to a balanced position, without a significant tilt toward either side, a society able to steer a stable course.[134]

Communities are constantly subjected to centrifugal societal forces which strain efforts to maintain social order and to centripetal forces which undermine individual freedom. When centripetal forces pull too much towards order, an emphasis must be placed upon individual autonomy. Likewise, when centrifugal forces pull too much towards autonomy, order must be attributed greater weight. Thus, communities must be vigilant in monitoring any excessive imbalances in these forces and make the necessary adjustments.

A few basic examples of an appropriate balance being struck between individual rights and the public's right to health and safety may be cited. The *Fourth Amendment* of the *Constitution of the United States* outlaws unreasonable searches and seizures but allows reasonable ones.[135] A reasonable search or seizure is one that has been undertaken pursuant to warrant obtained on oath or affirmation after probable cause has been made out and the place to be searched or the person or thing to be seized has been sufficiently particularised. Another example is the resort to sobriety checkpoints on roadways, airport security screening gates and the drug and alcohol testing of persons who directly affect public safety in the course of their employment (such as pilots, bus drivers and train engineers). Although the individual rights to privacy and bodily integrity may be implicated, the public's right to be protected in their health and safety may be deemed overriding in view of the minimal intrusion involved and the importance of the interests at stake.[136]

The Communitarian Platform (or How to Return to a Healthier Balance Between Centripetal and Centrifugal Societal Forces)

This section is not intended to provide an in-depth analysis of the content of the communitarian philosophy but merely to provide a concise overview of the thrust of the communitarian platform. Unlike liberalism, communitarianism is not a philosophy of personal liberation. The essence of communitarianism is not freedom or independence but belonging. The claim is made that individual dignity is best served in and through social participation.[137] The identity of individuals is to a large extent constituted by their membership in communities where they tend to flourish better.[138] Nevertheless, communitarianism does not reject the basic

---

134   A. Etzioni *The Spirit of Community: Rights, Responsibilities, and the Communitarian Agenda* (1993) pp. 26-7.

135   *Amendment IV* states: 'The right of the people to be secured in their persons, houses, papers, and effects, against unreasonable searches and seizures, shall not be violated, and no Warrants shall issue, but upon probable cause, supported by Oath or affirmation, and particularly describing the place to be searched, and the persons or things to be seized'.

136   A. Etzioni *The Spirit of Community* (1995) pp. 264-5.

137   Selznick, *op. cit.*, p. 454.

138   Freeman, *op. cit.*, p. 20.

postulates of liberalism - personal rights and the human needs of dignity, integrity and some degree of autonomy, individualism and privacy. Unfortunately, from time to time, libertarians have misinterpreted communitarian spokespersons who argue that individual rights have been overemphasised at the expense of individual duties, interpreting these arguments as if they were calling for a curtailment or suspension of personal rights.[139] As Professor Etzioni emphasises in his book *The Spirit of Community*, the communitarian call for increased social responsibilities is not a plea for the curbing of individual rights. On the contrary, strong personal rights presume strong personal responsibilities.[140]

Communitarianism re-emerged in the United States of America during the 1980s to address the types of concerns that were examined earlier in this chapter. Simply put, the communitarian thesis is that an increased and incessant demand for personal rights associated with a neglect or ignorance of individual social responsibilities have resulted in a dearth of civic virtue. Communitarian discontent is also aimed at what is perceived to be an undue subordination of collective rights and interests to the upholding of personal rights. It is also claimed that the social costs of the rights-based American system - increased litigiousness, moral conflict, family breakdown, and so forth - have become unacceptably high. Another consequence of the imbalance between personal rights and duties and between collective and individual rights is the decline of the foundational institutions of the body politic - families and associations. These 'seedbeds of civic virtue', as Cicero referred to them, are necessary, according to the communitarian view, to inculcate the character traits which are required to preserve strong personal rights.[141] A communitarian perspective recognises that the preservation of individual liberty depends on the active maintenance of the institutions of civil society where citizens learn to respect and serve others and acquire a knowledge of personal duties and civic responsibilities.[142]

The Responsive Communitarian Platform: Rights and Responsibilities maintains that 'a communitarian perspective must be brought to bear on the great moral, legal, and social issues of our time' and proposes an array of individual duties to achieve a better balance between individual rights and duties.[143] Such duties include the duty to vote, the duty to pay one's assessed taxes, the duty to serve on a jury when called to do so, the duty to work (thereby contributing to the 'commonwealth') and the duty of self-care and the care of one's dependants. An additional duty proposed by communitarians is that of voluntary community service. As Professor Etzioni maintains, '[s]ome measure of caring, sharing, and

---

139   A.Etzioni 'The Responsive Community: A Communitarian Perspective' (1995 Presidential Address) (1996) 61 *American Sociological Review* 1, p. 8.

140   A. Etzioni *The Spirit of Community* (1995) p. 1.

141   Mary Ann Glendon *Rights Talk: The Impoverishment of Political Discourse* (1991) 109-20.

142   The third paragraph of the *Preamble* of *The Responsive Communitarian Platform: Rights and Responsibilities* as contained in A. Etzioni *The Spirit of Community* (1995) pp. 253-4.

143   (1991-2) 2 *Responsive Community* pp. 4-5.

being our brother's and sister's keeper, is essential if we are not all to fall back on an ever more expansive government, bureaucratized welfare agencies, and swollen regulations, police, courts, and jails'.[144] David Selbourne agrees, adding that '[a] further precondition of the gradual restoration of the civic order from disaggregation is that many of the practical duties which have to do with its guardianship and well-being - and which are at present carried out by paid public servants on its behalf . . . - should be increasingly shared by the citizens themselves'.[145]

The new communitarians seek '[t]o rebuild America's moral foundations [and] to bring our regard for individuals and their rights into a better relationship with our sense of personal and collective responsibility'.[146] It is claimed that the bolstering of personal, family and community responsibility will mitigate the social problems which resulted in the re-emergence of communitarianism. A return to the language of social responsibilities will reduce contentiousness and enhance social co-operation.[147] A moratorium on the minting of new rights will prevent the further devaluation of existing ones. Citizens must also be reminded that some duties do not entail rights. As we saw in Chapter 3, the ancient freestanding duties of charity and rescue do not correlate to any identifiable right, but they nonetheless enjoy universal ethical acclaim.

It is, of course, impossible to empirically and objectively test these communitarian hypotheses. Nevertheless, any social philosophy which pays due heed to the social dimension of human existence and strives to balance competing human and societal tensions cannot be accused of being intellectually blinkered or dogmatic. In this author's view, to borrow a homely turn of phrase from the radio personality and social commentator Alistair Cook, these communitarian propositions are a matter of 'old-fashioned common sense'. Perhaps that is why they enjoy such a wide appeal across the political spectrum, embracing conservatives, liberals and socialists alike.[148]

---

144   A. Etzioni *The Spirit of Community* (1995) 260 (emphasis in original).
145   Selbourne, *op. cit.*, p. 232. Selbourne lists as examples the protection of the environment, nursery care for children, social care for the elderly and auxiliary medical and educational services.
146   *Idem* p. 7.
147   A. Etzioni *The Spirit of Community* (1995) p. 7.
148   P. Selznick, *op. cit.*, p. 445; A. Etzioni *The Spirit of Community* (1995) p. 251; McClain, *op. cit.*, p. 990.

Chapter 10

The Enforcement of Individual Duties

> ... [W]hen a community reaches the point at which these [basic individual] responsibilities are largely enforced by the powers of the state, it is in deep moral crisis.[1]

Introduction

In Plato's ideal republic,[2] the citizen was to have been so well trained and educated as a citizen and so imbued with the principle of duty in general that no enforcement[3] or system of sanction[4] would be required concerning the discharge of particular duties.[5] In the non-Platonic or real world, however, no such expectation can be realistically entertained. Without some type of enforcement (of some individual duties at least) - legal or otherwise - the body politic could not be sustained and maintained.[6]

This chapter will examine legal and non-legal methods used to enforce the performance of individual duties, both at the national and international levels. Particular problems with the efficacious legal enforcement of individual duties will be identified with a view to ascertaining whether some of these problems may be addressed and overcome. A proposal for the flexible legal enforcement of certain positive, non-correlative duties[7] will also be tendered.

By way of prefatory comment (and to take up the point made in the quotation which heads this chapter), it is this author's personal view that voluntary compliance with the performance of individual duties is, generally speaking, preferable to their enforced compliance. Human beings are more prone to discharge duties competently when they willingly and cheerfully take them on

---

1   A. Etzioni *The Spirit of Community* (1995) p. 266.
2   Plato *The Republic* (translated by P. Shorey, 2 volumes, London, 1946).
3   The term 'enforce' has been defined in *Black's Law Dictionary* (Revised Fourth Edition, 1968) 621 as 'To put into execution; to cause to take effect; to make effective . . . to compel obedience to . . .'
4   The term 'sanction' has been defined in part in *Black's Law Dictionary, op. cit.*, 1507 as: 'In the original sense of the word, a penalty or punishment provided as a means of enforcing obedience to a law'.
5   D. Selbourne *The Principle of Duty* (1994) p. 223.
6   *Idem* pp. 223-4.
7   See Chapter 3 entitled 'The Taxonomy of Duties' for an explanation of these terms.

rather than being forced to do so. That individual duties should be complied with for positive, rather than negative, reasons has been acknowledged by sociologists. As Professor Etzioni maintains, '[i]f communities are to function well, most members most of the time must discharge their responsibilities because they are committed to do so, not because they fear lawsuits, penalties or jails'.[8] David Selbourne includes among the principal unchanging necessities of the civic order 'the assumption of responsibility - preferably spontaneous or voluntary rather than induced or coerced by sanction - by its individual members for the condition of the civic order from which they derive their citizen rights and the hopes of the "good life"'.[9] Nevertheless, as we shall see later in this chapter, there are numerous warranted occasions when the State must reserve, at its discretion and as a matter of necessity, the right to enforce certain individual duties by sanction.

Non-Legal Enforcement Methods in Traditional Societies

The enforcement of morality, normative values, customs and individual duties has often been secured in tribal societies through the application of community-based sanctions. Broadly speaking, these sanctions take the form of community sentiment - approval/disapproval and acceptance/non-acceptance of the conduct of the offending actor.[10] Most sociologists recognise community censure as a major instrument for communities to uphold members' commitments to shared values, community service and the maintenance of community order. In the context of the emergence of the modern nation-state, community censure also reduces reliance on the apparatus of the State itself as a source of order through the administration of state-enforced legal sanctions.[11] Society or the community has been described as 'one of the main potential enforcers of general [individual] duties'.[12] In the following passage, Devereux describes the process by which individual duties are enforced in traditional African tribal societies:

> Rather than seeing duties as a subject for the conscience only, duties are regarded as enforceable - primarily by the community, rather than any would-be recipient of the duty. Such enforcement is certainly not regarded as a weak form of ensuring human needs but is regarded as consonant with the general 'community ethos' and emphasis on community well-being. 'Duties' are regarded as part of the 'law' of the community and are enforced in a similar manner as other laws - primarily through custom and religion . . . When duties are promoted, compliance is regarded as necessary and in one's own (society's) interests. An individual in need

---

8   A. Etzioni *The Spirit of Community* (1995) p. 266.
9   Selbourne, *op. cit.*, p. 27.
10   P. Bailey *Human Rights: Australia in an International Context* (1990) p. 27.
11   A. Etzioni 'The Responsive Community: A Communitarian Perspective' (1995 Presidential Address) (1996) 61 *American Sociological Review* pp. 1, 5.
12   A. Devereux 'Should "Duties" Play a Larger Role in Human Rights? A Critique of Western Liberal and African Human Rights Jurisprudence' (1995) 18 *University of New South Wales Law Journal* pp. 464, 471.

can complain to the elders and have the 'justice' of the situation ruled upon and enforced. Enforcement of duties is not simply seen as a private matter but a public one - all have an interest in each other's behaviour and their fulfillment of obligations . . . Such a system of enforcement is not regarded merely as the exercise of rights. What is emphasised is the failure of individuals, an emphasis which in turn is seen to encourage future compliance because of the dissemination of personal knowledge and respect for one's duties.[13]

Individual duties in traditional tribal societies are essentially value-judgments derived from a communal moral standard.[14] When this standard is violated, a number of sanctions may be triggered in order to express communal resentment, ranging from a reduction in status or personhood to social ostracism and a withdrawal of the protection of the social unit.[15] The former sanction is based on the notion that the due discharge of individual duties enhances one's personhood, much like in Confucianism.[16] Conversely, if one fails to contribute to society, his or her personhood is diminished.[17] The latter sanction may range from the total expulsion of the offender from the social group to the withdrawal of association with him or her.[18] Work, for example, constituted an important social obligation inherent in being a community member, such that idleness or laziness carried a social stigma[19] and was a ground for expulsion from the family and the community.[20] In his book entitled *Facing Mount Kenya: The Tribal Life of the Gikuyu*, Jomo Kenyatta describes in the following passage the powerful influence the age-group (*riika*) has in securing conformity with tribal usage:

> The selfish or reckless youth is taught by the opinion of his gang that it does not pay to incur displeasure. He will not be called to eat with the others when food is going. He may be put out of their dances, fined, or even ostracised for a time. If he does not change his ways he will find his old companions have deserted him.[21]

---

13   *Idem* pp. 476-7.
14   M. Radin 'Natural Law and Natural Rights' (1950) 59 *The Yale Law Journal* pp. 214, 222.
15   Z. Motala 'Human Rights in Africa: A Cultural, Ideological, and Legal Examination' (1989) 12 *Hastings International and Comparative Law Review* pp. 373, 381.
16   P. Woo 'A Metaphysical Approach to Human Rights from a Chinese Point of View' in A. Rosenbaum (ed.) *The Philosophy of Human Rights, Contribution in Philosophy No. 15* (1980) pp. 113, 119.
17   Makau Wa Mutua 'The Banjul Charter and the African Cultural Fingerprint: An Evaluation of the Language of Duties' (1995) 35 *Virginia Journal of International Law* pp. 339, 348.
18   *Ibid.*
19   Z. Motala, *op. cit.*, p. 382.
20   Devereux, *op. cit.*, p. 475.
21   J. Kenyatta *Facing Mount Kenya: The Tribal Life of the Gikuyu* (1965) p. 115.

Similarly, a family guilty of abandoning a parent or relative in need would be held in disgrace and contempt, pending the intervention of lineage or clan members.[22] Mutual support and assistance were also withdrawn by the Gikuyu community from the selfish or self-regarding individualist.[23] These sanctions were applied to those members of the community who failed to conform to societal norms, including the requirement to perform individual duties.

Problems With the Legal Enforcement of Individual Duties

From time to time, various problems have been identified and discussed in relation to the meaningful legal enforcement of individual duties. This section will attempt to briefly examine some of the more notable problems in this context.

Lack of Specificity

It has been claimed that individual duties are too wide or ambiguous for effective enforcement.[24] This observation certainly rings true at the international level where individual duties, rarely explicitly alluded to, are even more rarely stipulated in detail. The following two provisions taken from United Nations human rights instruments are good examples in this respect:

> Everyone has duties to the community in which alone the free and full development of his [or her] personality is possible. (Article 29(1) of the *Universal Declaration of Human Rights* of 1948.)

> Individuals . . . have an important role and a responsibility in contributing, as appropriate, to the promotion of the right of everyone to a social and international order in which the rights and freedoms set forth in the Universal Declaration of Human Rights and other human rights instruments can be fully realized. (Article 18(3) of the *Declaration on the Right and Responsibility of Individuals, Groups and Organs of Society to Promote and Protect Universally Recognized Human Rights and Fundamental Freedoms* of 1998.)

Such duty provisions, without more, are incapable of meaningful legal enforcement. The first provision fails to spell out the precise duties which are contemplated as well as by whom the duties are to be enforced, if at all. The second provision is incapable of being measured in terms of compliance because it is linked to an equally ambiguous or unclear individual right. Nevertheless, it must be borne in mind that some internationally-recognised individual human rights (particularly those of a programmatic nature) are also couched in rather open-ended language, making meaningful or effective legal enforcement problematical. Examples include 'the right of everyone to an adequate standard of living' and 'the

---

22   Makau Wa Mutua, *op. cit.*, pp. 369-70.
23   Kenyatta, *op. cit.*, p. 119.
24   Devereux, *op. cit.*, p. 467.

right of everyone to the enjoyment of the highest attainable standard of physical and mental health' contained respectively in Articles 11(1) and 12(1) of the *International Covenant on Economic, Social and Cultural Rights* of 1966.

The Non-Relational Aspect of Some Individual Duties

As we have seen in Chapter 3, there are some non-correlative or freestanding individual duties the objects or beneficiaries of which it is difficult to identify. This has led, in common law jurisdictions at least, to a lack of legal power to enforce such duties. Two leading examples include the duties of charity and rescue. These duties are therefore said to be non-relational. It is argued that given the seemingly greater need to identify the beneficiary of the exercise of one's individual duty if one is to carry it out effectively than the need to identify the other person when one is exercising an individual right, the absence of a relational approach to duties limits their enforceability.[25] Nevertheless, as we shall see in a later section of this chapter ('The Flexible Legal Enforcement of Positive, Non-Correlative Duties'), it is possible to apply a multi-factored formula to make it easier to identify who should be the beneficiaries of the exercise of such freestanding individual duties. Indeed, in many civil law/code jurisdictions, the non-relational aspect of these freestanding duties has not prevented the recognition and enforcement of positive duties of assistance against particular individuals.[26]

Philosophical Objections to the Legal Enforcement of Positive Duties

In his book entitled *The Lockean Theory of Rights*, A. John Simmons has identified two sources of philosophical resistance to the legal enforcement of positive duties of assistance: 'minimalism' and 'liberalism'.[27] According to the minimalist argument, civil society (including its legal system) is in the best interests of every individual. However, some individual liberty must be sacrificed to live in society. Each of us must refrain from doing those acts which make the orderly functioning of society impossible. This sacrifice of our freedom, however, should be kept as low as possible; otherwise, people will rightfully feel oppressed. Since directly harming one another by acts of murder, theft, battery and so forth makes peaceful

---

25 *Idem* pp. 468-9.

26 For example, Article 330c of the *German Penal Code* of 1871 (as amended to May 1950) enforces duties to furnish assistance in cases of accidents and general danger or distress. The text of this provision reads as follows:

> Failure of Duty to Aid in an Accident or Public Emergency or to Assist when Called upon to do so by the Police

Whoever in cases of accident or common danger or emergency does not render aid, although such were his duty in the view of responsible public opinion, especially whosoever does not comply with a police call for assistance, although he could respond to such call without serious risk to himself or without breach of another important duty, shall be punished with imprisonment not exceeding two years or by fine.

27 A. John Simmons *The Lockean Theory of Rights* (1992) pp. 341-2.

pursuit of our interests impossible, the law may legitimately proscribe them. But being charitable and rescuing one another from perilous situations, it is argued, are not similarly necessary for an orderly society. The burden of participating in a scheme of mutual assistance should not be forced on anyone through legal sanction. If at all assumed, this should be done voluntarily.

One aspect of liberalism offers a related ground for opposing the legal enforcement of positive duties. This aspect demands neutrality: the secular law must remain scrupulously neutral among competing moral, religious, ethical or other personal or sectarian conceptions of the good life.[28] The legal system should therefore allow each person the greatest possible freedom to pursue a personal conception of the good life, consistent with allowing everyone else this same freedom. The law's primary focus should therefore be on preventing those exercises of individual liberty which have the potential to directly and seriously harm other persons or to interfere with the legitimate pursuit of their own interests. According to Simmons:

> From the theoretical perspective, our duties not to directly harm others may seem the most defensible, the most nearly objective duties. From the practical viewpoint, the duties not to directly harm others will be the 'lowest common denominator' of competing ethical and religious views; they will be the duties in which people of diverse persuasions can all voluntarily acquiesce. By contrast, the duties to give charity or to rescue those in peril appear, on the one hand, to be theoretically controversial, and on the other hand, to be duties that form a part of only some, not all, ethical views. To allow the law to enforce such duties would be to take precisely the kind of stand on difficult theoretical and practical problems that the liberal is committed to avoiding.[29]

Thus, under the minimalist and liberal views, the negative individual duties to refrain from directly harming others respectively appear to be more imperative (for ordered civil society) and less controversial than positive individual duties of assistance. Both views concur in terms of the undesirability of making the latter type of duties legally enforceable.[30]

Nevertheless, it must be remembered that John Stuart Mill, the philosopher of modern English liberalism, declared that there are not only 'many positive acts for the benefit of others' which 'anyone may rightfully be compelled to perform' but also 'certain acts of individual beneficence, such as saving a fellow-creature's life' which 'whenever it is obviously a man's duty to do, he may

---

28　　　*Ibid.*

29　　　*Idem* p. 342.

30　　　From time to time, eminent English judges have expressed disquiet over the common law enforcing positive individual duties of assistance on the grounds of impracticability, impaired efficiency of the legal system and an undue burden on individual liberty. See, for example, the speech of Lord Atkin in *Donoghue v Stevenson* [1932] A.C. 562, 580 and that of Lord Reid in *Dorset Yacht Company v Home Office* [1970] A.C. 1004, 1027.

rightfully be made responsible to society for not doing'.[31] An individual duty to render positive assistance also received the endorsement of the utilitarian philosopher Jeremy Bentham who believed that such a duty would also promote the greatest happiness for the greatest number:

> Every man is bound to assist those who have need of assistance, if he can do it without exposing himself to sensible inconvenience. This obligation is stronger, in proportion as the danger is greater for the one, and the trouble of preserving him the less for the other.[32]

Common Law Reluctance to Legally Enforce Positive Duties

There are few distinctions more fundamental and deeply rooted in the common law than that between misfeasance and nonfeasance. The former concept involves active misconduct resulting in positive injury to others while the latter term concerns passive inaction or a failure to take steps to benefit others or to protect them from imminent harm not created by any wrongful act of the would-be rescuer.[33] In maintaining this traditional distinction, the common law effectively upholds a Kantian view of the law, aiming to protect the rights and freedoms of persons who are free to do as they please, so long as their actions do not injure others.[34] Although the common law proscribes misfeasance by enforcing a duty 'not to harm our neighbours . . . who might reasonably be expected to be damaged by our harmful acts'[35], it excuses nonfeasance in not recognising a duty of care to take positive action to protect another person from a reasonably foreseeable risk of injury not created by him or her.[36] Such a distinction results in the situation where there is no duty to rescue or render assistance, even where the means of so doing may be well within the would-be Samaritan's capabilities. So, for example, a good swimmer on the beach is free to ignore the call for help from someone in danger of drowning.[37] Thus, the common law does not require altruistic action from each of us in going to the rescue of other persons or their property although, once undertaken, it is prepared to support the attempt. In order to encourage rescuers (or, at least, not to discourage them), common law courts have extended the scope of the tort of negligence to enable some rescuers to recover damages if they should

---

31   J. S. Mill *On Liberty* (1859) p. 24.
32   J. Bentham 'Specimen of a Penal Code' in J. Bowning (ed.) *Works* (Edinburgh, 1843) Volume 1, p. 164.
33   F. Bohlen 'The Moral Duty to Aid Others as a Basis of Tort Liability' (1908) 56 *University of Pennsylvania Law Review* pp. 217, 219.
34   E. Weinrib 'Law as a Kantian Idea of Reason' (1987) 87 *Columbia Law Review* pp. 472, 489.
35   *Donoghue v Stevenson* [1932] A.C. 562, 580 (*per* Lord Atkin).
36   As Windeyer J. observed in *Hargrave v Goldman* (1963) 110 C.L.R. 40, 66, '[t]he law casts no duty upon a man to go to the aid of another who is in peril or distress, not caused by him'.
37   *Gautret v Egerton* (1867) L.R. 2 C.P. 371, 375; *Quinn v Hill* [1957] V.R. 439, p. 446; *Dorset Yacht Company v Home Office.* [1970] A.C. 1004, 1027.

be injured through another's negligence in the course of fulfilling their moral duty as a Good Samaritan.[38]

It has been pointed out that '[t]his manifestation [by the common law] of perhaps excessive individualism is apt to evoke invidious comparison with affirmative duties of good neighbourliness in most countries outside the common law orbit'.[39] Many civil jurisdictions require a person to render assistance to another where he or she 'can give this assistance without risk for himself [or herself] or for other persons, either by his [or her] personal action or by prompting the rescue'.[40] Civil and/or criminal proceedings may be instituted against those refusing to take action without sufficient excuse. France has given significant inducement to the Good Samaritan in the form of Article 63(2) of its *Penal Code* which provides that '[w]hoever abstains voluntarily from giving such aid to a person that he would have been able to give him without risk to himself or third persons by his personal action or by calling help ...' is liable to imprisonment and/or a fine.[41] Unlike the common law, then, French civil law does not excuse nonfeasance in the context of an 'easy rescue'. Moreover, examples of work which the Committee of Experts of the International Labour Organization has considered as forming part of normal civic obligations and thus excluded from the term 'forced or compulsory labour' include the duty to assist a person in danger.[42]

In the following illuminating passage, the late Professor John Fleming observes that the traditional and unflinching common law attitude not to enforce positive duties of assistance by granting a remedy for nonfeasance is being eroded by contemporary developments:

> The early common law furnished redress only for injury wrought directly by affirmative misconduct, because its capacity for effective intervention was fully taxed by the Hobbesian commitment to suppress violations of the peace. Inaction was too remote a focus for imposing legal responsibility . . . The reluctance to extend the reach of legal obligation beyond this point drew sustenance from the later fashionable philosophy of individualism, which was content to condone the indifference of the Priest and the Levite and to dismiss the solicitude of the Samaritan as an aspiration merely of private morality. The laissez-faire approach of the common law restrained men from committing affirmative acts of injury, but shrank from converting the law into an agency for forcing them to help each other. Obviously, it involves a more serious restraint on individual liberty to require a person to act than it is to place limits on his freedom to act. Besides, the plaintiff's loss is unequal in the two situations. In the case of commission, the defendant has positively made his position worse: he has *created* a risk; in the case of inaction,

---

38   *Chapman v Hearse* (1961) 106 C.L.R. 112 (High Court of Australia); J. Ratcliffe (ed.) *The Good Samaritan and the Law* (1966).
39   J. Fleming *The Law of Torts* (9th ed., 1998) p. 164.
40   L. Holland 'The Good Samaritan Laws: A Reappraisal' (1967) 16 *Journal of Public Law* p. 128.
41   [1947] *Dalloz Legislation* 130. See also M. McInnes 'The Question of a Duty to Rescue in Canadian Tort Law: An Answer From France' (1990) 12 *Dalhousie Law Journal* p. 85.
42   *Report of the Committee of Experts* (1968) (I.L.O.) Part 3, para. 37.

he has merely failed to benefit him by not interfering in his affairs. Yet today, though far from defunct, the strength of these sentiments is steadily being sapped by an increasing sense of heightened social obligation and other communitarian tendencies in our midst. Accordingly, the legal doctrine which they once sustained is itself under retreat.[43]

Some would argue that the Christian ideal of the Good Samaritan[44] should also be enshrined in the common law. Some duties of charity and assistance may be as basic and strong as negative duties of forbearance.[45] The Christian parable of the Rich Man and Lazarus, for example, reminds us that a failure to provide aid in some cases does harm others and can prejudice even their most basic and precious of rights.[46] In certain (and perhaps rare and exceptional) circumstances to be canvassed in the next section, taking positive action to assist another may take precedence over an individual's freedom not to act or get involved. Such an infringement upon personal freedom would not be an intolerable burden, but would merely be the opportunity cost of enjoying the security, comfort and well-being of living in a civilised society.[47] From a psychological-sociological standpoint, Sally Kift argues that the time for the imposition of a positive duty of assistance has arrived. Contemporary Western society has become more withdrawn and private and less community-orientated. People are also less inclined to become involved in other peoples' affairs.[48] In the context of rendering assistance to persons in peril, these developments are a source of concern, especially considering the poor reflection on society as a whole when some of the more extreme cases of failure to rescue occur. As Simmons rhetorically queries:

> Are we really confident that Kitty Genovese's neighbours (in Kew Gardens [New York] in 1964) did not wrong her by failing even to call the police when they heard her screams (leaving aside the further fact that none tried to interfere themselves with her prolonged and brutal murder)? Is the duty they had to render at least this minimal aid really controversial, weak, or insignificant?[49]

The Flexible Legal Enforcement of Positive, Non-Correlative Duties

In Chapter 3, we examined the distinction between perfect (or correlative) duties and imperfect (or non-correlative or freestanding) duties. As we saw, imperfect duties - of which the duties of rescue and charity are leading examples - are, by their nature, broader and more indeterminate than perfect duties. These attributes

---

43   Fleming, *op. cit.*, p. 163 (footnotes omitted; emphasis in original).

44   *The Gospel According to Luke*, Chapter 10, Verses 25-37.

45   Simmons, *op. cit.*, p. 345.

46   *The Gospel According to Luke*, Chapter 16, Verses 19-31.

47   McInnes, *op. cit.*, p. 114.

48   S. Kift 'Criminal Liability and the Bad Samaritan: Failure to Rescue Provisions in the Criminal Law, Part 1' (1997) 1 *Macarthur Law Review* p. 218.

49   Simmons, *op. cit.*, p. 347.

have hindered their wider legal enforcement, at least in Western common law legal systems. It was therefore proposed that these systems adopt and apply a multi-factored formula in order to determine whether an imperfect duty should be owed and enforced in a particular set of circumstances. Such a 'calculus of duty' formula would provide the judiciary with a flexible framework to determine the often controversial question whether a particular person is obliged to render positive assistance in a given situation. Such an approach would not be new. Indeed, the United States Supreme Court[50] and the High Court of Australia[51] have long and successfully applied the so-called 'calculus of negligence' factors[52] in civil suits to determine the standard of care required in the particular circumstances of a case.

The factors comprising the 'calculus of duty' formula (which have already been discussed in detail and illustrated in Chapter 3) are:

- special placement (in terms of geographical propinquity or the possession of a special skill by the potential duty-holder);

- cost to the duty-holder (acceptability of the risks, costs or inconvenience entailed in discharging the relevant duty);

- proximity of relationship (closeness of relationship between the duty-holder and the beneficiary);

- need (the degree of the victim's need in the particular case).

These factors would be balanced against each other to determine whether a duty of positive assistance should be recognised and legally enforced in the particular case. No one factor would be conclusive and the judicial decision whether or not to enforce a duty would be made by weighing the four factors in the scales of justice, so to speak. Special placement in a geographical sense is really based on the addage 'charity begins at home' in that our duty to render assistance is stronger in relation to those we personally come into contact with. The more removed we are from a particilar peril or injustice, the less reasonable it would be for the law to enforce a legal duty of action upon us. In terms of the second factor (cost), some rescues are very easy to accomplish. As Simmons remarks, '[i]t is no great moral burden on a person to have to call the police, shout a warning [or] throw a rope to a

---

50   *United States v Carroll Towing Co.* (1947) 159 F. 2d 169, 173; *Conway v O'Brien* (1940) 111 F. 2d 611, p. 612.

51   *Ryan v Fisher* (1976) 51 A.L.J.R. pp. 125, 126; *Wyong Shire Council v Shirt* (1980) 146 C.L.R. pp. 40, 47.

52   These factors are comprised of the likelihood or probability of an accident ensuing, the seriousness or gravity of injury which may be entailed, the burden of precautions placed on the shoulders of the defendant in seeking to avoid the accident and the utility or justifiability of the defendant not taking such precautionary measures.

drowning man ...'[53] Nor is it difficult for most of us to give a modest donation to the poor. These actions do not materially interfere with the autonomous pursuit of our own interests.[54] If the cost of rendering assistance would be minimal to the potential duty-holder, such factor would favour his or her intervention (depending, of course, on the consideration of the other three factors). As for the third factor (proximity of relationship), it seems fair and logical to impose a duty of positive action upon those in a special status relationship and those who are under a contractual duty to so do. Indeed, Anglo-American law already does so in enforcing child maintenance obligations against parents as well as obligations to render assistance against such workers as nurses and lifeguards. Concerning the fourth factor (the beneficiary's need), Jeremy Bentham considered that the strength of a person's duty to assist another was proportionate 'as the danger is greater for the one, and the trouble of preserving him the less for the other'.[55]

Some positive duties of assistance - such as rescuing those in peril or making a charitable donation to a destitute person - can be as fundamental and basic (in terms of the dire consequences of non-discharge) as negative duties to refrain from actively harming others. In the case of both positive and negative duties, moreover, it is arguable that they share the same source - the inherent dignity of the human person. Although the common law has never recognised a right to be rescued or a right to charity, nevertheless it cannot be said that non-correlative duties of positive assistance are not affiliated with any rights of the beneficiary. The rights to life, bodily integrity and health, for example, are all implicated in the situations of those in need of rescue or the basic necessities of life. The adoption by common law systems of a more flexible approach to duties of positive assistance would assist in bringing the common law into line with the more humanitarian position taken in civil law systems. Such a change in policy would pay heed to the recent 'communitarian tendencies' which call for a more social and community-orientated approach to the law. Such a development would not open the 'floodgates' as common law judges could enforce positive duties only in the clearest and least controversial of cases, drawing upon the conditions of liability carefully considered by the civil code drafters for guidance.

National Legal Enforcement of Individual Duties

As we have already seen in Chapter 7, a wide array of individual duties have been legally recognised and enforced for a long time by the legal systems of many countries, the primary rationale being the sustenance and maintenance of the body politic. Some of these individual duties are positive and moral in nature (such as the duty to support and educate family members) while others are positive and civic in nature (such as the duties to perform military service, to pay taxes and to vote). Other individual duties are negative in character, such that individuals are

---

53   Simmons, *op. cit.*, p. 348.
54   Ibid.
55   Bentham, *op. cit.*, p. 164.

required to abide by the constitution and the laws of the country in which they are residing. These duties which have been recognised by the law are enforced by state, rather than by community, sanctions. If people fail to properly discharge their legally-recognised individual duties, they may face prosecution and the imposition of a fine or imprisonment rather than mere ostracism or other community-based sanction. Indeed, it may be the case that the foregoing individual duties are even more enforceable than some human rights, such as the programmatic rights to health, education and an adequate standard of living recognised respectively in Articles 12, 13 and 11 of the *International Covenant on Economic, Social and Cultural Rights* of 1966.

As we have also seen in Chapter 7, most of the individual duties mentioned in the preceding paragraph are regarded as so fundamentally important to the well-being of the national community that they are actually accorded constitutional recognition.[56] It is ordinarily left to enabling legislation to provide greater detail concerning the content and scope of the duty, on whom the duties are imposed and the conditions of their fulfillment. Some individual duties do not enjoy constitutional status but are nonetheless prescribed in ordinary enactments. Examples include the duties to serve on a jury, to give evidence in legal proceedings, to assist the police in law enforcement matters, to assist the civil authorities in the event of emergencies or natural disasters, to register the birth of a child and to ensure that the child receives required vaccinations. The normal mechanism used to enforce individual duties is the judiciary, although in some countries such enforcement may be left to the executive branch of government (that is to say, the government itself or the public service in the form of administrative or military tribunals or departmental public servants).

Despite the reluctance of some liberal philosophers and jurists to permit the secular law to have free reign to reflect or uphold particular moral values (arguing that the law should remain scrupulously neutral in this regard), the law does recognise and enforce some important moral duties, arguably with good reason. Some moral duties relating to the family, community and State are regarded as so inextricably linked to the orderly functioning of society that they have been recognised by the law and subjected to its enforcement. So, for example, in most countries an individual's duties to maintain his or her dependants, to not harm other persons or damage their property and to support (or, at least, not harm) the State itself have been incorporated respectively into systems or codes of family law, tort law and criminal law. Perhaps the most basic and critical of these duties is the joint parental duty of care for the child's physical and emotional well-being and for his or her moral and secular education. Such duties are correlative in the sense that the child has a right to their performance (although they tend to be dealt with in the duty context). The imposition of state-based sanctions for neglect of such duties may well be appropriate in the interests of maintaining the well-

---

56   The practical effect of an individual duty receiving constitutional status is that any ordinary legislation, administrative act or judicial pronouncement which purports to derogate from the true meaning and effect of the constitutional provision enshrining the duty will be null and void to the extent of any inconsistency.

being of the State itself. Indeed, it has been advocated that ' . . . in conditions of accelerating civic disaggregation, the principle of duty dictates that, within the limits of reason and practicality, the moral and legal responsibility of the natural parents of a minor child for the welfare and the actions of such child should be both increased and enforced ...' [57]

International and Regional Legal Enforcement of Individual Duties

Regional Enforcement

As we have seen in Chapter 7, of all of the regional human rights systems in the world today, it is the African regional human rights system which is most advanced in promulgating a system of individual duties. Many of the duty provisions contained in Articles 27 to 29 of the *African Charter on Human and Peoples' Rights* reflect traditional African tribal values. Although the *African Charter* has been hailed as innovative and controversial in this respect, commentators have cast doubt on the extent to which the individual duties recognised by the *Charter* are justiciable or legally enforceable.

It is clear, however, that some of the individual duties contained in the *African Charter* are legally enforceable. These duties are the negative duty not to compromise state security and the positive duties to pay taxes and contribute to the defence of the nation.[58] Other individual duties appear less susceptible to meaningful legal enforcement because of the rather imprecise or open-ended manner in which they are referred to in the *African Charter*. So, for example, the individual shall have the duties '[t]o preserve and strengthen social and national solidarity'[59] and '[t]o work to the best of his [or her] abilities and competence'.[60] Likewise, the following provisions suffer from the same defects:

Article 29

The individual shall also have the duty:

(7) To preserve and strengthen positive African cultural values in his [or her] relations with other members of the society, in the spirit of tolerance, dialogue and consultation and, in general, to contribute to the promotion of the moral well-being of society;

(8) To contribute to the best of his [or her] abilities, at all times and at all levels, to the promotion and achievement of African unity.

---

57   Selbourne, *op. cit.*, pp. 242-3.
58   See Article 29(3)(5) and (6) of the *African Charter on Human and Peoples' Rights*.
59   Article 29(4).
60   Article 29(6).

Mention might also be made of Article 28 of the *African Charter* which imposes a duty upon individuals not to discriminate against their fellow beings without making any reference to forbidden grounds of discrimination. This has prompted the observation that '[t]he duties are of such breadth and so ambiguous in their connotations that a regime of serious enforcement without some degree of prior elaboration is difficult to imagine'.[61] Wolfgang Benedek has also concluded:

> [T]he duties in the African Charter appear to be more of a programmatic character. Some spell out a general philosophy and principles of behaviour rather than operational legal concepts.[62]

Ziyad Motala adds:

> The duty provisions . . . [of the *African Charter*] lack specificity. For example, it is difficult for the state to invoke the African Charter and successfully establish that an individual is not performing his [or her] duties to the best of his [or her] abilities and competence. Likewise it would be difficult for the state to prove whether the individual is acting to preserve and strengthen positive African cultural values. It is therefore questionable whether the above provisions intend to impose specific [enforceable] duties on the individual because they are not justiciable, although the values they try to promote are consistent with traditional practices.[63]

The African Commission on Human and Peoples' Rights[64] has not taken any steps towards interpreting or elaborating upon the duty provisions of the *African Charter*. However, pursuant to Article 45(1)(b) and (3) of the *African Charter*, the Commission may respectively formulate principles and rules relating to human rights and interpret the principles of the *Charter*. Makau Wa Mutua has argued that the African Commission should take the lead in clarifying in its jurisprudence which of these individual duties are moral or legal obligations and what the scope of their intended application ought to be:

> The Commission could lead the way in suggesting how some of the [individual] duties . . . might be implemented. The concept of national service, for example, could utilize traditional notions in addressing famine, public works, and community self-help projects. The care of parents and the needy could be formalized in family/state burden-sharing. The Commission should also indicate how, and in what forum, the state would respond to the breach of individual duties.

61		H. Steiner and P. Alston *International Human Rights in Context: Law, Politics, Morals* (1996) pp. 694-5.
62		W. Benedek 'Peoples' Rights and Individuals' Duties as Special Features of the African Charter on Human and Peoples' Rights' in P. Kunig *et al. Regional Protection of Human Rights by International Law* (1985) pp. 59, 63.
63		Motala, *op. cit.*, 404 (footnotes omitted).
64		Pursuant to Article 30 of the *African Charter on Human and Peoples' Rights*, an African Commission on Human and Peoples' Rights has been established 'to promote human and peoples' rights and ensure their protection in Africa'.

It might suggest the establishment of community arbitration centers to work out certain types of disputes.[65]

International Enforcement

In terms of the international legal enforcement of individual duties, there is a marked difference between the two branches of international law known as international humanitarian law (or the laws of armed conflict) and international human rights law. In order to better understand and appreciate the differences in the possibilities of enforcement as between these two branches, it is first proposed to briefly examine state practice concerning the operation of international law within national legal systems.

State Practice Concerning the Operation of International Law Within National Legal Systems[66]

State practice varies in relation to the application of international norms by national courts. Some rules of international law are automatically binding in national law while other such rules require a specific national incorporation measure to achieve such status. A distinction between customary and treaty rules of international law is often relevant in this respect. British and American practice will be primarily canvassed.

British practice draws a distinction between customary rules of international law and treaty rules of international law. Customary rules of international law are deemed to be part of the law of the land and will be applied as such by British courts subject to two important qualifications. The first qualification is that the customary rule is not inconsistent with any British statute, whether the statute be earlier or later in date than the particular rule sought to be applied.[67] The second qualification is that once the scope of a particular customary rule has been determined by a British court of final authority, all British courts are thereafter bound by that determination even though a divergent customary rule later develops.[68] As Lord Atkin declared in *Chung Chi Cheung v R*:

> The Courts acknowledge the existence of a body of rules which nations accept among themselves. On any judicial issue they seek to ascertain what the relevant rule is, and, having found it, they will treat it as incorporated into the domestic [national] law, so far as it is not inconsistent with rules enacted by Statutes or finally declared by their tribunals.[69]

---

65   Makau Wa Mutua, *op. cit.*, p. 375 (footnotes omitted).
66   For a more detailed discussion, see J. Starke *Introduction to International Law* (10th ed., 1989) pp. 77-88.
67   *Polites v The Commonwealth* (1945) 70 C.L.R. 60 (High Court of Australia).
68   This second qualification has been criticised in terms of its stultifying effect on the ability of the common law to keep pace with the latest developments in international law.
69   [1939] A.C. 160, p. 168.

The effect of these two qualifications is that only a customary rule which is not inconsistent with a British statute (either earlier or later in time) and prior judicial decisions of final authority will be automatically applied by British judges as part of British law.

The position with treaty rules of international law in British practice is different. This difference is explicable primarily by the constitutional principles governing the relations between the executive and parliamentary branches of government.[70] The negotiation, signature and ratification of treaties are undertaken pursuant to Crown (executive) prerogative powers. If, however, the provisions of a treaty concluded by the British government were to automatically become binding British law, this would effectively hand the Crown the power to alter British law without first consulting Parliament and obtaining its approval (thereby eroding the 'separation of powers' doctrine). In order to avoid this, it has become established that treaties which affect the private rights of British subjects or involve any modification of the law (both statute and common) must receive parliamentary assent through an enabling statute and, if necessary, any legislation to effect the requisite changes in the law must be passed.[71]

The American practice is similar to the British practice concerning customary rules of international law. Such rules are administered by American courts as part of the law of the land,[72] and Acts of the United States Congress are construed so as not to conflict therewith,[73] although a later clear statute will prevail over earlier customary international law.[74] In terms of treaty rules of international law, however, there is a significant difference from the British practice. Unlike the latter, the American practice does not depend upon any reconciliation of Crown prerogative powers with the legislative domain. Rather, it depends on the *United States Constitution*[75] which stipulates that 'all Treaties made, or which shall be made under the Authority of the United States . . . [shall be] the supreme Law of the Land' and on a distinction drawn by American courts between 'self-executing' and 'non-self-executing' treaties.[76] A self-executing treaty is one which does not, in the view of American courts, expressly or by its nature require specific legislation to make it operative and binding in municipal law. That question is largely to be determined having regard to the intention of the parties to the treaty and the surrounding circumstances.[77] If a treaty is considered to be self-executing by the American courts, then it is deemed to be operative under the *United States Constitution* as part of the law of the United States. On the other hand, treaties

---

70   Starke, *op. cit.*, p. 81.
71   See, for example, *Walker v Baird* [1892] A.C. 491, 497 and *The Parlement Belge* (1879) 4 P.D. p. 129.
72   *The Paquete Habana* 175 U.S. 677 (1900) at 700.
73   *The Charming Betsy* (1804) 2 Cranch 64, p. 118.
74   *The Over the Top* (1925) 5 F. 2d 838, 842.
75   Article VI, para. 2.
76   *Foster v Neilson* (1829) 2 Peters pp. 253, 314.
77   *Sei Fujii v The State of California* 38 Cal. (2d) 718 (1952) (Cal. Sup. Ct).

which are not self-executing are not binding upon American courts until the necessary legislation has been enacted.

According to an examination undertaken by Professor Starke, the practice of states other than the United Kingdom and the United States of America reveals wide variations.[78]   There appears to be no uniform practice concerning the application of treaties in national law.   While the courts of some countries (for example, the Federal Republic of Germany) will give effect, like American courts, to self-executing treaties, the courts of other countries (such as Belgium) will not apply treaties as part of national law until they have received legislative approval (particularly where the treaty provisions affect the rights of private citizens).   The practice in relation to customary rules of international law is somewhat more uniform.   In a large number of states, such rules are applied by the courts as part of national law without the necessity for any specific act of incorporation, provided that there is no conflict with existing national law.

In terms of the foregoing description of state practice concerning the application of international law by national courts in the municipal legal sphere, a sharp divide emerges between those individual duties which are imposed by international humanitarian law (both treaty and custom) and those which are recognised by international human rights law.   As a general rule, the former branch of international law has a much more developed and sophisticated system of duty enforcement than the latter.   As we saw in Chapter 5 ('Individual Criminal Responsibility under International Law'), a number of mechanisms have been established to deal with the prosecution and punishment of international crimes, including war crimes.   It is not proposed to repeat in this chapter the detailed contents of Chapter 5, but suffice it to say that international humanitarian law has developed the following duty-enforcement methods: *ad hoc* international criminal courts such as the Nuremberg and Tokyo war crimes tribunals and the international criminal tribunals for the former Yugoslavia and Rwanda, the concept of a 'universal jurisdiction' to enable the national prosecution and punishment of persons who have committed certain international crimes, the grave breaches provisions of the *Geneva Conventions* of 1949 (which require the High Contracting Parties to implement these provisions as part of their municipal law) and the creation of a standing International Criminal Court in The Hague.   These duty-enforcement mechanisms are either treaty-based or founded upon long-established customary rules of international law.   The large majority of countries are now party to the *Geneva Convention* system and a substantial number of these have implemented into their own domestic law the enforcement provisions contained therein.   Consequently, the legal enforcement of individual duties by national courts in most countries in the world today presents little problem, in theory at least (leaving aside the practicalities and politics involved in a decision to prosecute).

The situation is markedly different for international human rights law. Although this branch of international law has developed various rights-implementation systems contained in such important international human rights

---

78   Starke, *op. cit.*, pp. 85-6.

instruments as the *International Covenant on Civil and Political Rights*[79] and the *Convention on the Rights of the Child*,[80] the enforcement of individual duties has largely been left to the discretion of States Parties under their own national laws. United Nations human rights monitoring committees have largely confined their attention to human rights as opposed to duties. Their mandate is to ensure that States Parties are making progress in implementing their treaty obligations in good faith.[81] That is not to say that they could never turn their attention to interpreting and elaborating upon provisions of United Nations human rights instruments which refer to individual duties. It is just that they would not have much material to work with. This is due to the sporadic and haphazard manner in which the United Nations has approached the principle of individual duty over the past fifty years or so. Individual duties are referred to only in a minority of United Nations instruments. Their treatment is best described as *ad hoc* rather than systematic. When they are mentioned, the term 'duties' is used generically with no attempt either to provide concrete examples of individual duties or to attribute a specific normative content to them.[82] In other cases, individual duties are left to implication[83] or are relegated to a mere preambular position in the human rights instrument concerned.[84] Sometimes individual duties appear in international instruments which themselves do not possess any legally binding status.[85] Unlike the position of individual duties under international humanitarian law, such duties as are recognised by international human rights law cannot be said to have attained the status of customary law.[86]

---

79   Part IV thereof establishes a Human Rights Committee to monitor the performance of States Parties in implementing into their own law the human rights recognised and guaranteed by the *Covenant*.

80   Part II thereof establishes a Committee on the Rights of the Child to examine the progress made by States Parties in implementing the obligations undertaken in the *Convention*.

81   A main feature of United Nations human rights instruments is to ensure that States Parties respect the human rights recognised therein in relation to their own citizens. On the other hand, it can probably be safely assumed by the United Nations that States Parties will have sufficient incentive and self-interest (without the necessity of United Nations prodding) to enforce individual duties against their own citizens.

82   See, for example, Article 29(1) of the *Universal Declaration of Human Rights*.

83   See, for example, Article 4 of the *International Covenant on Economic, Social and Cultural Rights*.

84   See, for example, the fifth preambular paragraph common to the *International Covenant on Civil and Political Rights* and the *International Covenant on Economic, Social and Cultural Rights*.

85   See, for example, the *Declaration on the Right and Responsibility of Individuals, Groups and Organs of Society to Promote and Protect Universally Recognized Human Rights and Fundamental Freedoms* of 1998.

86   Article 38(1)(b) of the *Statute of the International Court of Justice* defines international custom as 'evidence of a general practice accepted [by states] as law'.

Some of these impediments to the international legal enforcement (or, at least, monitoring) of individual duties under international human rights law could, of course, be overcome. We have already seen in Chapter 6 that the American regional human rights system long ago adopted the *American Declaration of the Rights and Duties of Man* of 1948. This instrument at least catalogues numerous important individual duties, even if their detailed content is somewhat lacking. There is nothing to stop the United Nations from promulgating a *Universal Declaration of Human Duties* to inform United Nations member states in the formulation of their policies and laws. Admittedly, however, given the diversity of culture, traditions and values throughout the world, such an undertaking at the universal level would be more difficult than at the regional level. Indeed, this could result in a truncated and diluted enumeration of individual duties in light of the 'give and take' ethos of the drafting debates. Pending such a United Nations initiative, individual duties recognised by international human rights law (as opposed to international humanitarian law) are probably best left to be administered and enforced at the national level.

Chapter 11

Conclusion

> ... [each individual] might wish to enjoy the rights of the citizen without wanting to fulfill the duties of a subject, an injustice whose spread would cause the ruin of the body politic.[1]

Long ago, in 1819 to be precise, Benjamin Constant delivered a speech on 'The Liberty of the Ancients Compared with that of the Moderns' in which he contrasted the perception of liberty held by the ancients with that of contemporary individuals. According to Constant, liberty for the ancients was the sharing of social power among the citizens. For them, the liberty to participate in the affairs of state was highly cherished; the liberty to engage in a private life was, by contrast, viewed with circumspection. The ancient republican tradition linked freedom with self-government and assigned to citizens a solemn duty to participate in public affairs. Only after they had discharged their public or civic duties were citizens able to indulge in a private life. Liberty for the moderns, on the other hand, is comprised of the enjoyment of security in private pleasures accompanied by the guarantees accorded by governmental and non-governmental institutions to those pleasures.[2] Having warned that the liberty of the ancients could deprive citizens of any meaningful private life, Constant also cautioned that the liberty of the moderns threatens the public life of society. Accordingly, Constant urged his audience to combine the liberties of the ancients and moderns together and maintain a wholesome equilibrium between the two. Society requires institutions which both respect the individual rights of citizens and ensure and facilitate their civic education and participation in public life.[3]

In 2003, debate still turns on attempts to reconcile these bipolar opposites. How best to balance public and private commitments without letting either absorb or completely overwhelm the other. Whether this balance can be struck and in what precise form is still being worked out, perhaps requiring the patience of Job and the wisdom of Solomon. Be that as it may, it has not been the author's purpose to answer those questions but to demonstrate rather that today the pendulum has swung too far towards the liberty of the moderns. In order to obtain

---

1   J.-J. Rousseau *The Social Contract* Book I, Chapter VII ('On the Sovereign').
2   As quoted in M. Hollis 'Machiavelli, Milton and Hobbes on Liberty' in R. Bellamy and A. Ross (eds) *A Factual Introduction to Social and Political Theory* (1996) pp. 63, 70.
3   *Ibid.*

a healthier (if not optimum) balance between community-orientated and civic-minded conceptions of liberty on the one hand and individualistic and private conceptions of liberty on the other, a shift in focus is required from the dominant Western 'rights' discourse to a more inclusive and universal human rights discourse which includes a due emphasis upon individual duties.

If the human rights movement is to enjoy a more universal appeal in both theory and practice, it must attribute more weight to the role of individual duty in meeting basic human needs and upholding human dignity. In the course of the preceding chapters, it has been sought to demonstrate that the current Western emphasis upon rights (and concomitant inattention to duties) sits uncomfortably with a number of important historical developments and contemporary realities. As we saw in Chapter 2, the principle of duty has traditionally occupied a pre-eminent position in political and social philosophy since its embodiment in the Greco-Roman republican ethic and the Aristotelian tradition of virtue ethics. An examination of the role of individual duty in Judaism, Christianity, Islam, Hinduism and Confucianism was undertaken in Chapter 4. This examination revealed the central position that the principle of individual duty occupies in the realm of mainstream religion and ethics. Chapter 5 discussed the impressive extent to which international law, particularly international humanitarian law and international criminal law, now imposes legally enforceable duties upon individuals not to engage in gross human rights violations. The author attempted to demonstrate in Chapter 6 that a significant number of human rights instruments adopted at both the international and regional levels since World War II has provided explicit or implied recognition of private or individual duties. Regional human rights systems, particularly those in Africa and Latin America, explicitly catalogue individual duties in their constituent documents. A cultural relativist perspective was also adopted in Chapter 6 to illustrate that some cultures (principally those of Africa and the Asia-Pacific) place considerably more emphasis upon the acknowledgement and fulfillment of individual duties than upon rights. Chapters 7 and 10 documented, by way of a representative sampling, specific basic individual duties which are commonly enforced by national legal systems with at least the same vigour as individual rights. Chapters 8 and 9 pointed out that in contrast to the dominant Western rights discourse, certain socio-political philosophies such as socialism and communitarianism consciously and systematically address the importance and discharge of individual duties. Chapter 9 also noted the growing disquiet concerning the perception that rights are overemphasised at the expense of duties and the potential deleterious consequences of such a disequilibrium. Certain conventional sociological postulates concerning the social and group-dependent nature of human existence were also invoked to discredit the atomistic basis of human existence in social contract theory and to support a more duty-based human rights movement perspective.

This author respectfully agrees with those who argue that the present human rights system is not an exclusive and comprehensive means of ensuring respect for human dignity and fulfilling human needs.[4] That is not to advocate its complete overhaul or to denigrate its accomplishments and noble objectives. What is suggested is that promoting a greater emphasis upon individual duties and a spirit of community-mindedness is another complementary means by which the existing human rights system could seek to realise its lofty objectives. While cultural relativist debate has focussed on the question of the extent to which the rest of the world should be receptive to the largely Western-inspired current human rights prototype, an equally important and legitimate question is whether it is desirable for the dominant Western rights discourse to pay greater heed to individual duties.[5] It is proposed that it is possible to successfully integrate duty-based philosophies of the nature of human existence with rights-orientated Western liberal philosophies. These philosophies can inform and counterbalance each other in a mutually enhancing symbiotic relationship. After all, they share a common rationale - human beings possess human rights and individual duties because of their shared humanity. They share a common, interactive and dependent existence with and upon other human beings, all of whom possess dignity and basic needs. Whereas a rights-based system seems better suited to protect individual freedoms such as those recognised in the United Nations *International Covenant on Civil and Political Rights* of 1966, a duty-based system seems better adapted to promote individual participation in public affairs and provide some of the material social welfare requirements guaranteed by the *International Covenant on Economic, Social and Cultural Rights* of 1966.

For too long the principle of duty has been given shortshrift in the human rights context. When it is addressed, discussion is confined to the duty of governments to make adequate provision for their citizens' rights. The time has come to expand the scope of that discussion to include individual duties. What advantages might we anticipate therefrom? Duty-based systems intrinsically exert an inward, centripetal force, drawing individual duty-bearers into society and linking them with other individuals and the community in which they live. Alienated citizens or 'citizens-turned-strangers'[6] are drawn out of their private sphere to partake more of the public sphere. A duty-based system also emphasises the role of the individual in assisting those who are part of one's community. There may well be some advantages, particularly in the provision of social welfare, in promoting individual duties as a means of ensuring that basic needs are met.[7] The drift towards conveniently transferring or delegating individual moral and practical responsibility to others or to the State itself must be checked. If it is true to say that the well-being of the civic order is a precondition for individual well-

---

4   A. Devereux 'Should "Duties" Play a Larger Role in Human Rights? A Critique of Western Liberal and African Human Rights Jurisprudence' (1995) 18 *University of New South Wales Law Journal* pp. 464, 482.

5   *Idem.* p. 478.

6   This expression is referred to *passim* in David Selbourne's work *The Principle of Duty* (1994).

7   Devereux, *op. cit.*, p. 478.

being,[8] citizens must begin to reclaim from big government many practical duties in order to restore civic well-being. Some of these duties are currently discharged by paid public servants who can be geographically and emotionally distant from the problem. These duties should be increasingly shared by citizens themselves in the context, for example, of caring for the elderly, the homeless and children at risk, and protecting the neighbourhood and the natural environment and so forth. Citizens must assume a greater measure of being their brother's or sister's keeper if we are to avoid imposing an undue burden on the executive and judicial branches of government in the form of an ever more bloated government, overregulation, bureaucratised welfare agencies and swollen court lists.[9]   Whereas an undue emphasis on rights can lead to competitive, confrontational, antagonistic and litigious attitudes, a greater emphasis upon individual duties implies more co-operative and corporate endeavour for the collective good.[10]

Incorporating a system of individual duties within the dominant Western rights discourse will no doubt attract its share of critics and face a number of challenges.[11]   Consensus must be achieved on what individual duties are owed, their content, their intended objects or beneficiaries and their means of fulfillment. Yet, as we have seen in Chapter 7, the groundwork for this consensus has already been laid, particularly at the regional and national levels. Such consensus would also have to be based upon a stronger community ethic than exists at present. In Western society today, individual liberty or freedom is synonymous with individual self-realisation and self-fulfillment and attaining one's full potential. A duty-based system in the non-Western sense transcends mere correlative duties.[12] Such a system entails greater individual sacrifice and sense of selflessness. In imposing upon individuals duties of positive action which must be undertaken for the benefit of family members, the community or the State, the liberal ethic that one may act in any way one pleases provided the rights and freedoms of others are not undermined must be tempered. The increasing realisation of the many people - the homeless, the unemployed and underemployed and the elderly who form a growing economic underclass - who remain uncared for in the individualistic structure of the West, driven by consumerism and the vagaries of the free market economy, has prompted the re-emergence of communitarianism discussed in Chapter 9.

There has always existed in democratic societies a stable mutuality between individual rights and individual social duties. In the recent past, however, we have come to lose that mutuality. In our zeal to identify and elaborate upon human rights norms and standards since the end of World War II, we have sadly neglected the Aristotelian tradition of virtue ethics, public and community service and a sense of duty-consciousness which shaped Western philosophies for so long. The West must reclaim that tradition if we are serious about shoring up the ailing

---

8   D. Selbourne *The Principle of Duty* (1994) pp. 176, 191.
9   A. Etzioni *The Spirit of Community* (1995) p. 260.
10   See the section in Chapter 9 entitled 'Impoverished "Rights Talk"'.
11   Devereux, *op. cit.*, p. 480.
12   See Chapter 3.

health of the body politic. Of course, we must continue to cherish and jealously safeguard our rights but we must also own up to our responsibilities and discharge our duties diligently. The common good and our individuality must both be protected by deeming us social but not fully social; all of us are part of, and identify with, various communities which command our loyalties but we must never be required to be absorbed within them to such an extent that we lose our individual identities. Different paths to human dignity and meeting basic human needs have been explored in the preceding chapters. The human rights movement is one such important path which can and should now be supplemented and complemented to a greater degree by another more well-trodden parallel path, that of individual duty.

Bibliography

The following bibliography is comprised of the main books, reference works and law journal articles relied on in researching this book.

Alfredsson, G. and Melander, G. (eds) (1997), *The Raoul Wallenberg Compilation of Human Rights Instruments*, Martinus Nijhoff, The Hague.

Bailey, P. (1990), *Human Rights: Australia in an International Context*, Butterworths, Sydney.

Bellamy, R. (1996), 'Socrates and Locke on Political Obligation', in R. Bellamy and A. Ross (eds), *A Factual Introduction to Social and Political Theory*, Manchester University Press, Manchester, pp. 1-34.

Black, H. (Revised Fourth Edition, 1968), *Black's Law Dictionary*, West Publishing Co., St Paul, Minnesota.

Bohlen, F. (1908), 'The Moral Duty to Aid Others as a Basis of Tort Liability', *University of Pennsylvania Law Review*, vol. 56, pp. 217-?

Brownlie, I. (ed.) (Second Edition, 1972), *Basic Documents in International Law*, Clarendon Press, Oxford.

Brownlie, I. (ed.) (1981), *Basic Documents on Human Rights*, Oxford University Press, Oxford.

Brownlie, I. (Fourth Edition, 1990), *Principles of Public International Law*, Clarendon Press, Oxford.

Chang, W. (1998), 'Confucian Theory of Norms and Human Rights', in W. Theodore De Bary and T. Weiming (eds), *Confucianism and Human Rights*, Columbia University Press, New York, pp. 117-41.

Cheng, C. (1998), 'Transforming Confucian Virtues into Human Rights: A Study of Human Agency and Potency in Confucian Ethics', in W. Theodore De Bary and T. Weiming (eds), *Confucianism and Human Rights*, Columbia University Press, New York, pp. 142-54.

Collins Shorter Dictionary & Thesaurus, (Second Edition, 1995), Harper Collins Publishers, Glasgow.

Daes, Erica-Irene A. (1990), *Freedom of the Individual under Law: A Study on the Individual's Duties to the Community and the Limitations on Human Rights and Freedoms under Article 29 of the Universal Declaration of Human Rights*, United Nations, New York, United Nations Publication Sales No. E.89.XIV.5.

Detrick, S. (ed.) (1992), *The United Nations Convention on the Rights of the Child: A Guide to the Travaux Preparatoires*, Dordrecht, The Netherlands.

de Varennes, F. (1998), *Asia-Pacific Human Rights Documents and Resources* (Volume 1), Kluwer Law International, The Hague.

Devereux, A. (1995), 'Should "Duties" Play a Larger Role in Human Rights? A Critique of Western Liberal and African Human Rights Jurisprudence', *University of New South Wales Law Journal*, vol. 18, pp. 464-82.

Donnelly, J. (1989), *Universal Human Rights in Theory and Practice*, Cornell University Press, Ithaca, New York.

Donnelly, J. (1990), 'Traditional Values and Universal Human Rights: Caste in India', in V. Leary and C. Welch, Jr (eds), *Asian Perspectives on Human Rights*, Westview Press, Boulder, Colorado, pp. 55-91.

Etzioni, A. (1995), *The Spirit of Community*, Fontana Press, London.

Etzioni, A. (1996), 'The Responsive Community: A Communitarian Perspective (1995 Presidential Address)', *American Sociological Review*, vol. 61, pp. 1-11.

Flanz, G. (ed.) (various editions and volumes), *Constitutions of the Countries of the World*, Oceana Publications, New York.

Flekkoy, M. G. and Kaufman, N. H. (1997), *The Participation Rights of the Child: Rights and Responsibilities in Family and Society*, Jessica Kingsley Publishers, London.

Fleming, J. G. (Ninth Edition, 1998), *The Law of Torts*, The Law Book Company Limited, Sydney.

Freeman, M. (1995), 'Human Rights: Asia and the West', in J. Tang (ed.), *Human Rights and International Relations in the Asia-Pacific*, Pinter Publishers, London, pp. 13-24.

Garcia, E. (ed.) (1990), *Human Rights Reader: Towards a Just and Humane Society*, National Book Store, Inc., Manila, Philippines.

Hambly D. and Luntz, H. (eds) (Fourth Edition, 1995), *Torts: Cases and Commentary*, Butterworths, Sydney.

Handley, R. and O'Neill, N. (1994), *Retreat from Injustice: Human Rights in Australian Law*, The Federation Press, Sydney.

Herdegen, M. (1998), 'Natural Law, Constitutional Values and Human Rights', *Human Rights Law Journal*, vol. 19, pp. 37-43.

Hodgson, D. (1992), 'The Historical Development and "Internationalisation" of the Children's Rights Movement', *Australian Journal of Family Law*, vol. 6, 252-79.

Hodgson, D. (1998), *The Human Right to Education*, Ashgate Dartmouth, Aldershot, United Kingdom.

Hollis, M. (1996), 'Machiavelli, Milton and Hobbes on Liberty', in R. Bellamy and A. Ross (eds), *A Factual Introduction to Social and Political Theory*, Manchester University Press, Manchester, pp. 63-91.

Kamenka, E. and Tay, A. E.-S. (1986), 'The Philosophical Bases of Human Rights', in Human Rights Commission, *Human Rights for Australia*, Monograph Series No. 1, Australian Government Publishing Service, Canberra, Australia, pp. 77-85.

Kaplan, A. (1980), 'Human Relations and Human Rights in Judaism', in A. Rosenbaum (ed.), *The Philosophy of Human Rights, Contribution in Philosophy No. 15*, Greenwood Press, Westport, Connecticut, pp. 53-77.

Kaye, S. and Piotrowicz, R. (2000), *Human Rights in International and Australian Law*, Butterworths, Sydney.

Kenyatta, J. (1965), *Facing Mount Kenya: The Tribal Life of the Gikuyu*, Secker and Warburg, London.

Kewley, G. (1984), *Humanitarian Law in Armed Conflicts*, V.C.T.A. Publishing, Melbourne.

Kwok, D. (1998), 'On the Rites and Rights of Being Human', in W. Theodore De Bary and T. Weiming (eds), *Confucianism and Human Rights*, Columbia University Press, New York, pp. 83-94.

McClain, L. (1994), 'Rights and Irresponsibility', *Duke Law Journal*, vol. 43, pp. 989-1088.

McInnes, M. (1990), 'The Question of a Duty to Rescue in Canadian Tort Law: An Answer From France', *Dalhousie Law Journal*, vol. 12, pp. 85-122.

Mayer, A. (Second Edition, 1995), *Islam and Human Rights: Tradition and Politics*, Westview Press, Boulder, Colorado.

Melden, A. I. (1970), *Human Rights*, Wadsworth Publishing Co., California.

Mill, J. S. (1859), *On Liberty*, London.

Mitra, K. (1982), 'Human Rights in Hinduism', *Journal of Ecumenical Studies*, vol. 19, pp. 77-84.

Motala, Z. (1989), 'Human Rights in Africa: A Cultural, Ideological, and Legal Examination', *Hastings International and Comparative Law Review*, vol. 12, pp. 373-410.

Mutua, Makau Wa (1995), 'The Banjul Charter and the African Cultural Fingerprint: An Evaluation of the Language of Duties', *Virginia Journal of International Law*, vol. 35, pp. 339-80.

Nasr, S. H. (1980), 'The Concept and Reality of Freedom in Islam and Islamic Civilization', in A. Rosenbaum (ed.), *The Philosophy of Human Rights, Contribution in Philosophy No. 15*, Greenwood Press, Westport, Connecticut, pp. 95-103.

O'Hagan, T. (1996), 'Aristotle and Aquinas on Community and Natural Law', in R. Bellamy and A. Ross (eds), *A Factual Introduction to Social and Political Theory*, Manchester University Press, Manchester, pp. 35-62.

Paust, J. (1992), 'The Other Side of Right: Private Duties Under Human Rights Law', *Harvard Human Rights Journal*, vol. 5, pp. 51-63.

Peaslee, D. (ed.) (various editions and volumes), *Constitutions of Nations*, Martinus Nijhoff, The Hague.

Protocols Additional to the Geneva Conventions of 12 August 1949, (1977), International Committee of the Red Cross, Geneva.

Radin, M. (1950), 'Natural Law and Natural Rights', *The Yale Law Journal*, vol. 59, pp. 214-36.

Rees, A. (1986), 'The Soviet Union', in R. Vincent (ed.), *Foreign Policy and Human Rights: Issues and Responses*, Cambridge University Press, Cambridge, pp. 61-85.

Rosemont Jr, H. (1998), 'Human Rights: A Bill of Worries', in W. Theodore De Bary and T. Weiming (eds), *Confucianism and Human Rights*, Columbia University Press, New York, pp. 54-67.

Selbourne, D. (1994), *The Principle of Duty: An Essay on the Foundations of the Civic Order*, Sinclair-Stevenson, London.

Selznick, P. (1987), 'The Idea of a Communitarian Morality', *California Law Review*, vol. 75, pp. 445-63.

Simmons, A. J. (1992), *The Lockean Theory of Rights*, Princeton University Press, Princeton, New Jersey.

Starke, J. G. (Tenth Edition, 1989), *Introduction to International Law*, Butterworths, London.

Steiner, H. J. and Alston P. (eds) (1996), *International Human Rights in Context: Law, Politics, Morals*, Clarendon Press, Oxford.

Stoljar, S. (1984), *An Analysis of Rights*, Macmillan, United Kingdom.

Street, J. (1996), 'Rousseau and James Mill on Democracy', in R. Bellamy and A. Ross (eds), *A Factual Introduction to Social and Political Theory*, Manchester University Press, Manchester, pp. 205-29.

Tang, J. (ed.) (1995), *Human Rights and International Relations in the Asia-Pacific*, Pinter Publishers, London.

Thapar, R. (1966), 'The Hindu and Buddhist Traditions', *International Social Science Journal*, vol. 18, pp. 31-40.

The Geneva Conventions of 12 August 1949, (July 1970 Reprint), International Committee of the Red Cross, Geneva.

The New American Bible, (Saint Joseph Edition, 1970), Catholic Book Publishing Co., New York.

The Oxford Dictionary of Twentieth Century Quotations, (1998), Oxford University Press, Oxford.

Van Der Wolf, W.J.F.M. (ed.) (1994), *Human Rights Selected Documents*, Global Law Association, Boxtel, The Netherlands.

Waldron, J. (ed.) (1987), *Nonsense Upon Stilts: Bentham, Burke and Marx on the Rights of Man*, Methuen, London.

Williams, G. (1999), *Human Rights under the Australian Constitution*, Oxford University Press, Melbourne.

Woo, P. (1980), 'A Metaphysical Approach to Human Rights from a Chinese Point of View', in A. Rosenbaum (ed.), *The Philosophy of Human Rights, Contribution in Philosophy No. 15*, Greenwood Press, Westport, Connecticut, pp. 113-25.

Index

Tables

CASES

HISTORICAL INSTRUMENTS

NATIONAL CONSTITUTIONS

ORDINARY LEGISLATION

INTERNATIONAL INSTRUMENTS

REGIONAL INSTRUMENTS